D1543125

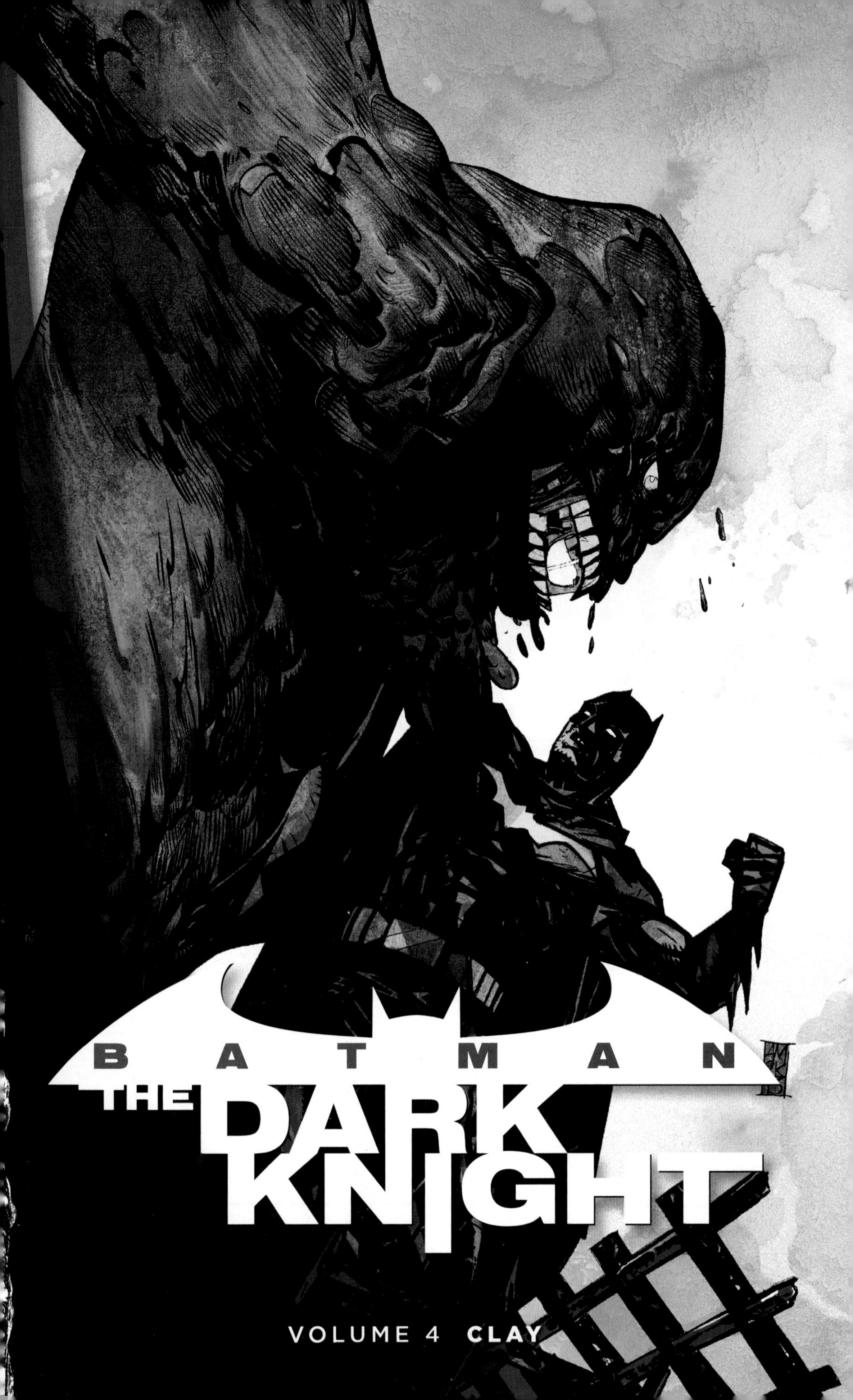
BATMAN
THE DARK KNIGHT
VOLUME 4 CLAY

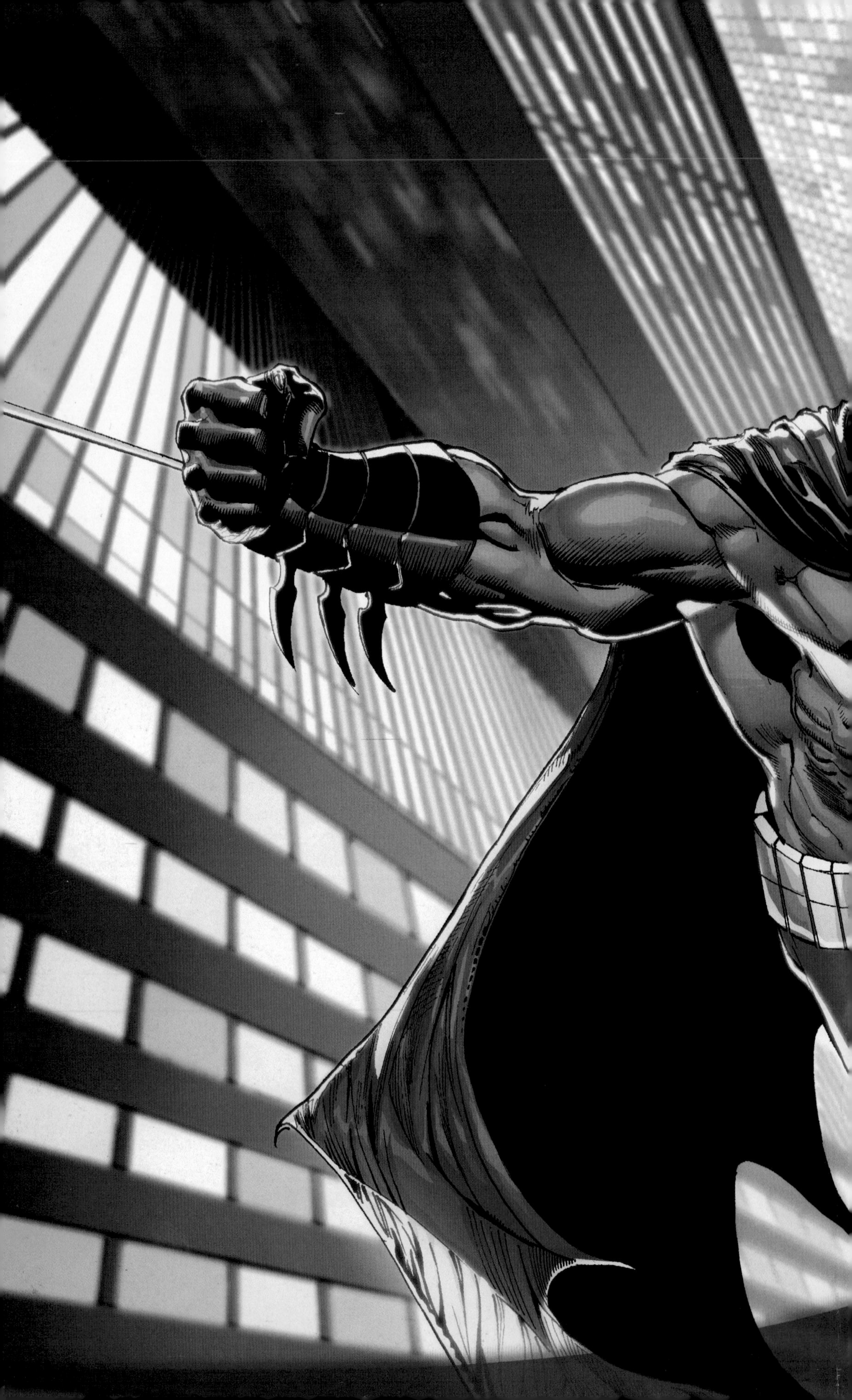

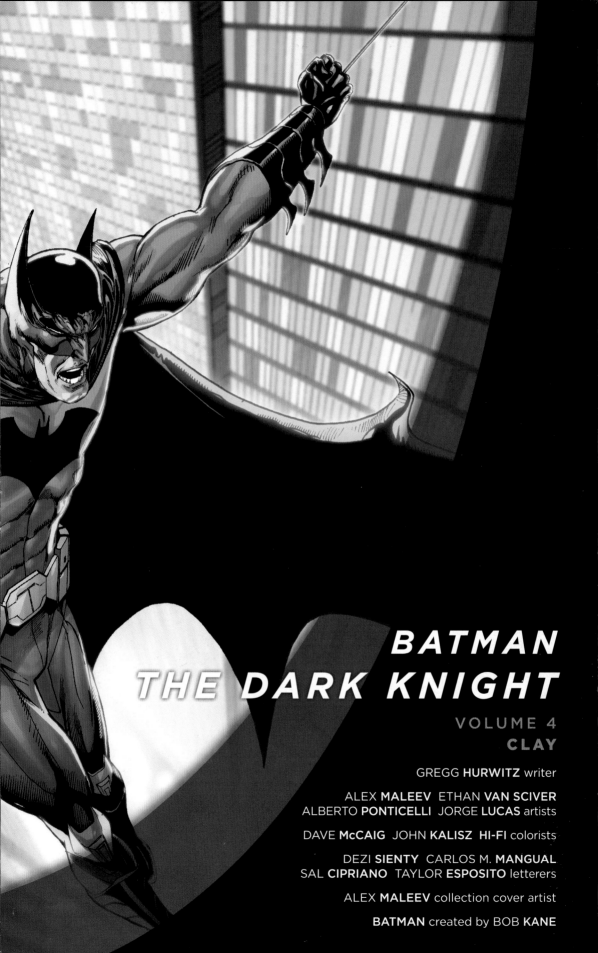

BATMAN
THE DARK KNIGHT

VOLUME 4
CLAY

GREGG **HURWITZ** writer

ALEX **MALEEV** ETHAN **VAN SCIVER**
ALBERTO **PONTICELLI** JORGE **LUCAS** artists

DAVE **McCAIG** JOHN **KALISZ** **HI-FI** colorists

DEZI **SIENTY** CARLOS M. **MANGUAL**
SAL **CIPRIANO** TAYLOR **ESPOSITO** letterers

ALEX **MALEEV** collection cover artist

BATMAN created by BOB **KANE**

MIKE MARTS MARK DOYLE Editors – Original Series DARREN SHAN Assistant Editor – Original Series RACHEL PINNELAS Editor
ROBBIN BROSTERMAN Design Director – Books ROBBIE BIEDERMAN Publication Design

BOB HARRAS Senior VP – Editor-in-Chief, DC Comics

DIANE NELSON President DAN DIDIO and JIM LEE Co-Publishers GEOFF JOHNS Chief Creative Officer
AMIT DESAI Senior VP – Marketing and Franchise Management
AMY GENKINS Senior VP – Business and Legal Affairs NAIRI GARDINER Senior VP – Finance
JEFF BOISON VP – Publishing Planning MARK CHIARELLO VP – Art Direction and Design
JOHN CUNNINGHAM VP – Marketing TERRI CUNNINGHAM VP – Editorial Administration
LARRY GANEM VP – Talent Relations and Services ALISON GILL Senior VP – Manufacturing and Operations
HANK KANALZ Senior VP – Vertigo and Integrated Publishing JAY KOGAN VP – Business and Legal Affairs, Publishing
JACK MAHAN VP – Business Affairs, Talent NICK NAPOLITANO VP – Manufacturing Administration SUE POHJA VP – Book Sales
FRED RUIZ VP – Manufacturing Operations COURTNEY SIMMONS Senior VP – Publicity BOB WAYNE Senior VP – Sales

BATMAN: THE DARK KNIGHT VOLUME 4: CLAY

DC Comics, 1700 Broadway, New York, NY 10019
A Warner Bros. Entertainment Company.
Printed by RR Donnelley, Salem, VA, USA. 6/27/14. First Printing.

HC ISBN: 978-1-4012-4620-4
SC ISBN: 978-1-4012-4930-4

Certified Chain of Custody
20% Certified Forest Content,
80% Certified Sourcing
www.sfiprogram.org
SFI-01042
APPLIES TO TEXT STOCK ONLY

SUSTAINABLE
FORESTRY
INITIATIVE

Library of Congress Cataloging-in-Publication Data

Hurwitz, Gregg Andrew, author.
Batman, the Dark Knight. Volume 4, Clay / Gregg Hurwitz, Alex Maleev.
pages cm. — (The New 52!)
ISBN 978-1-4012-4620-4 (hardback)
1. Graphic novels. I. Maleev, Alexander, illustrator. II. Title. III. Title: Clay.
PN6728.B36H843 2014
741.5'973—dc23
                          2014011609

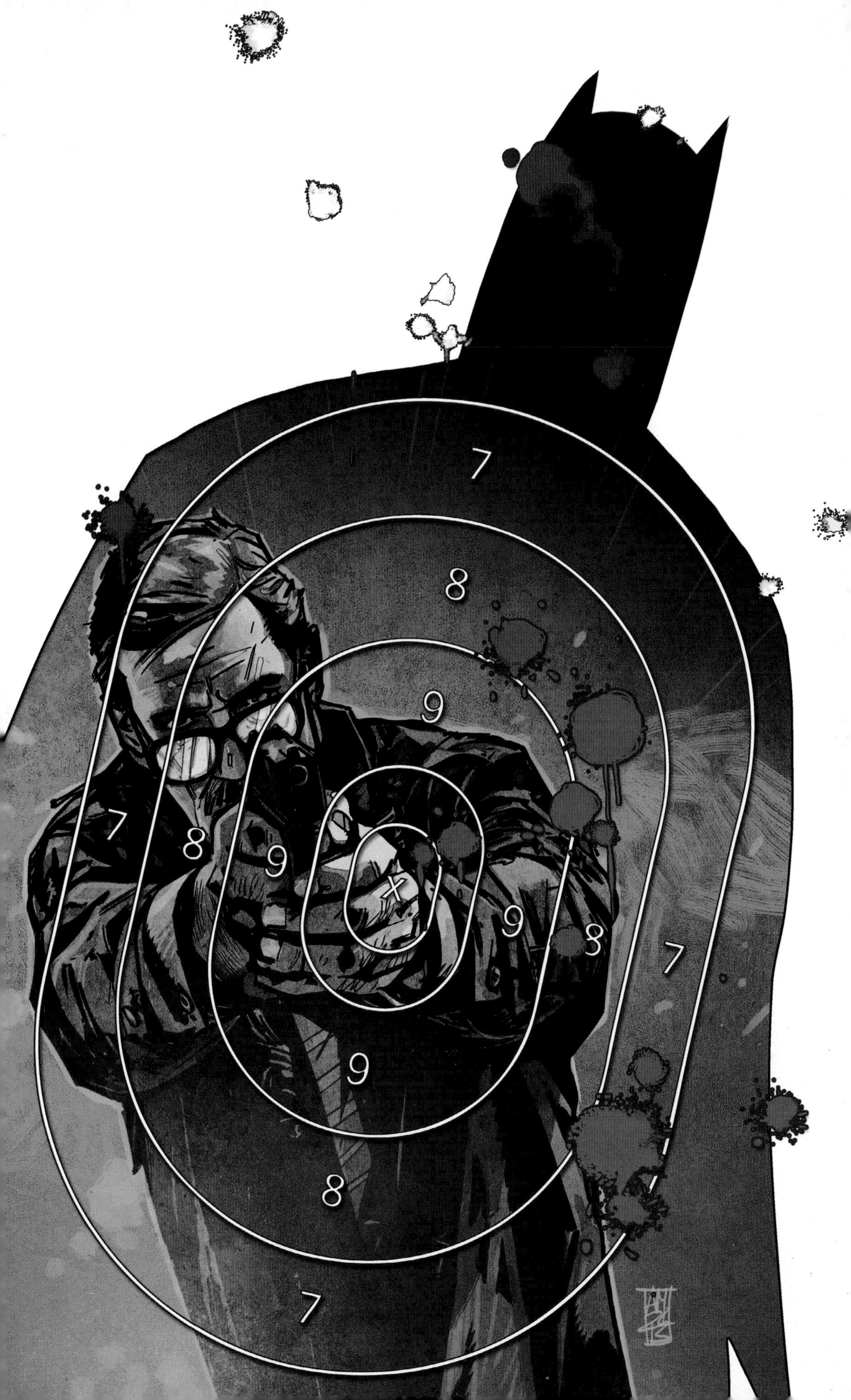

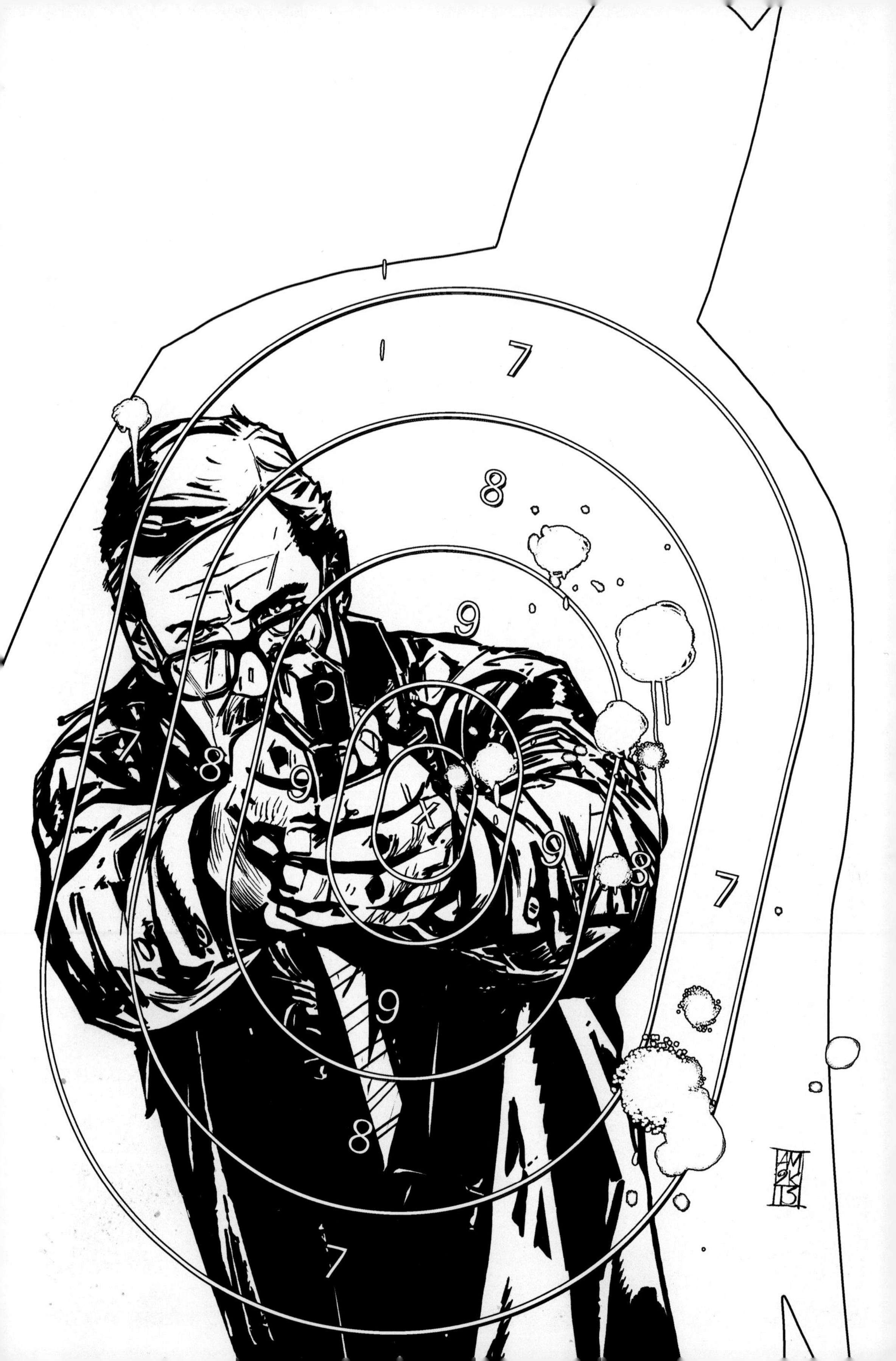

At what point do you *give* up?

How much is too much?

Gotham.

It takes your marriage.

Takes your son's sanity... **His life.**

Takes your daughter's legs-- just blows them right out from under her.

Clayface has reemerged.

Like the city, he morphs from one horror into the next.

All your worst fears, laid out right before you, on that gruesome map of a face.

And you can fight him, yeah, just like you can fight Gotham.

But at some point...

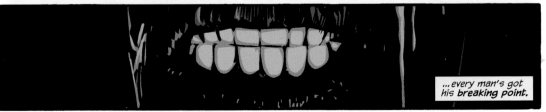

...every man's got his breaking point.

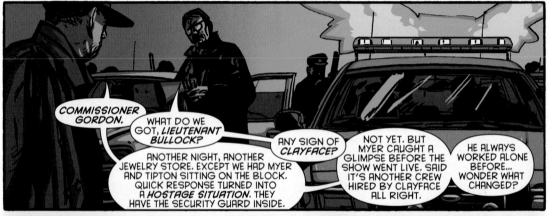

COMMISSIONER GORDON.

WHAT DO WE GOT, *LIEUTENANT BULLOCK?*

ANOTHER NIGHT, ANOTHER JEWELRY STORE. EXCEPT WE HAD MYER AND TIPTON SITTING ON THE BLOCK. QUICK RESPONSE TURNED INTO A *HOSTAGE SITUATION.* THEY HAVE THE SECURITY GUARD INSIDE.

ANY SIGN OF *CLAYFACE?*

NOT YET. BUT MYER CAUGHT A GLIMPSE BEFORE THE SHOW WENT LIVE. SAID IT'S ANOTHER CREW HIRED BY CLAYFACE ALL RIGHT.

HE ALWAYS WORKED ALONE BEFORE... WONDER WHAT CHANGED?

ALL RIGHT. I'M OFFERING YOU AN *UPGRADE.* WE'LL TRADE YOU ONE NIGHT SECURITY GUARD FOR ONE POLICE COMMISSIONER.

YOU CAN'T BE SERIOUS, COMMISSIONER.

I AM *DEAD* SERIOUS.

BUT... WHY?

BECAUSE, HARVEY...

...I'VE DAMN WELL *HAD IT.*

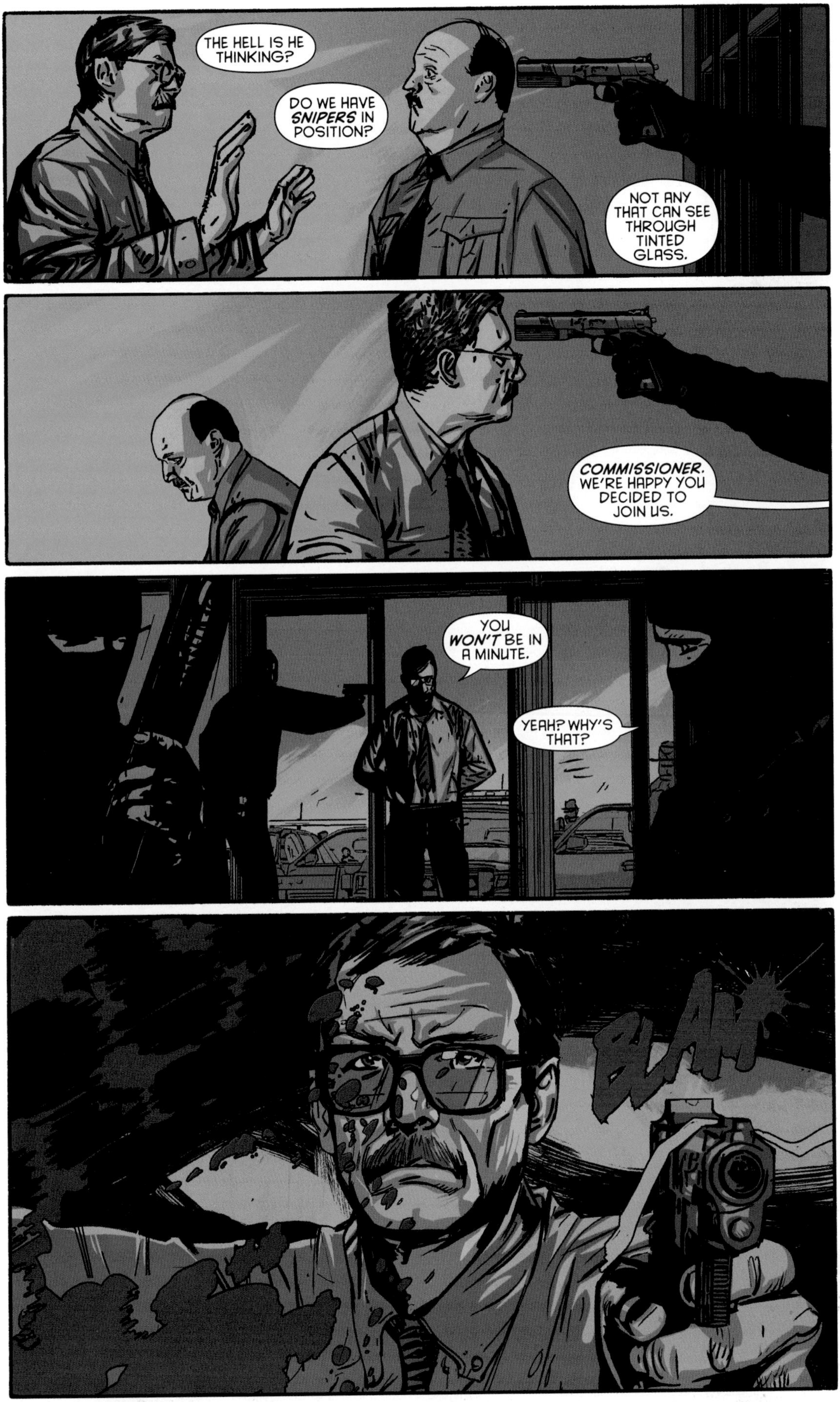
THE HELL IS HE THINKING?
DO WE HAVE *SNIPERS* IN POSITION?
NOT ANY THAT CAN SEE THROUGH TINTED GLASS.
COMMISSIONER. WE'RE HAPPY YOU DECIDED TO JOIN US.
YOU *WON'T* BE IN A MINUTE.
YEAH? WHY'S THAT?
BLAM

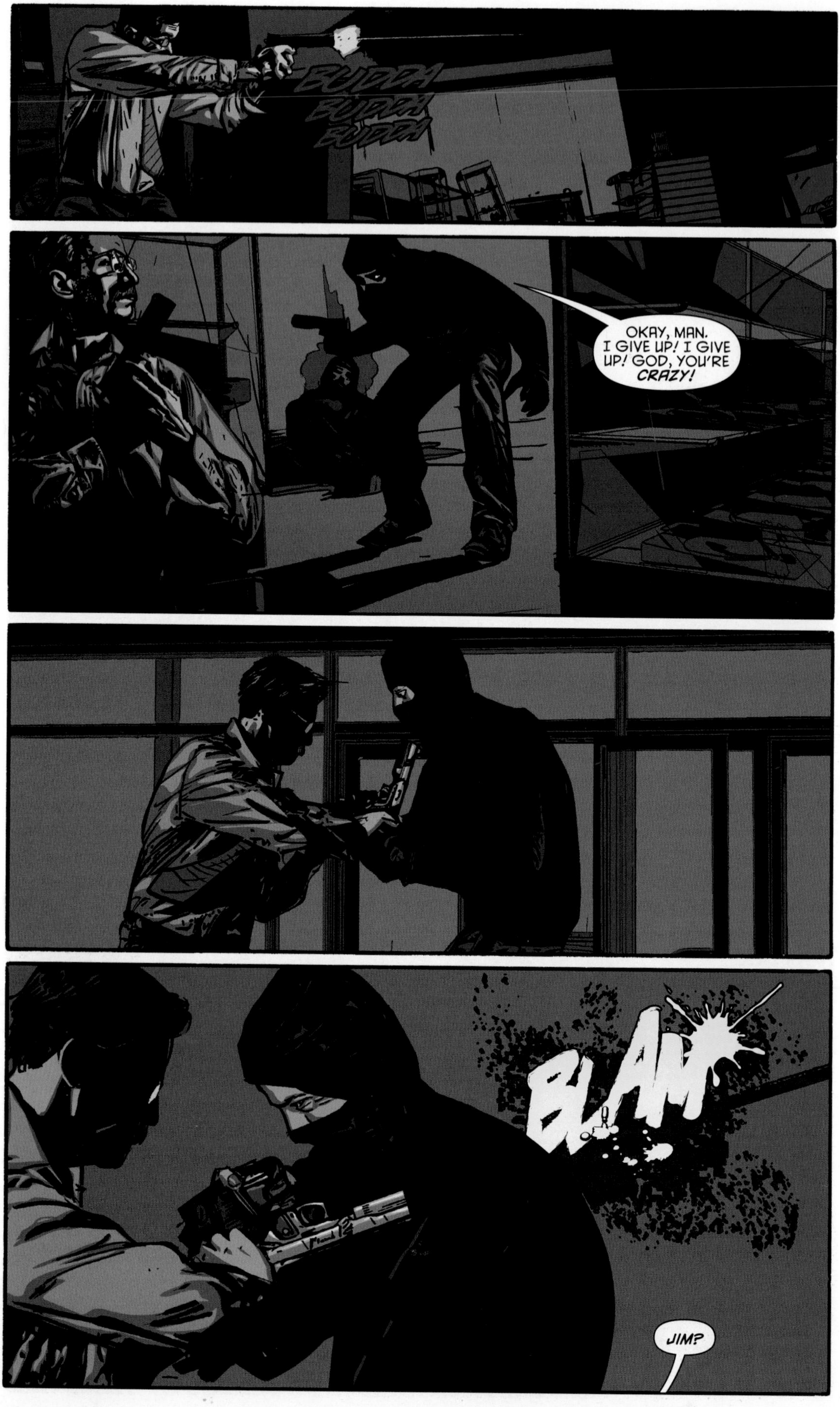
BUDDA BUDDA BUDDA
OKAY, MAN. I GIVE UP! I GIVE UP! GOD, YOU'RE CRAZY!
BLAM
JIM?

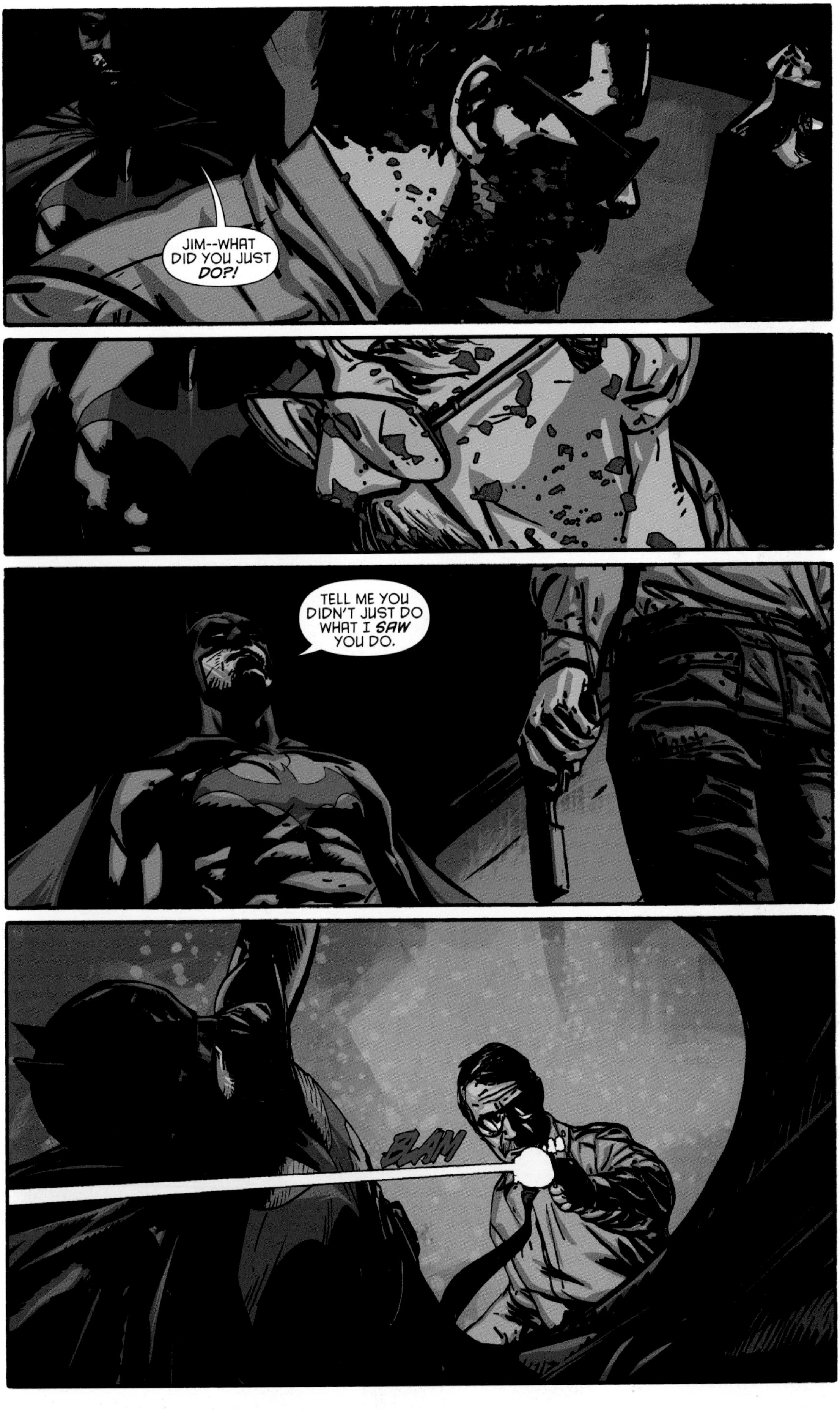
JIM--WHAT DID YOU JUST *DO?!*
TELL ME YOU DIDN'T JUST DO WHAT I *SAW* YOU DO.
BLAM

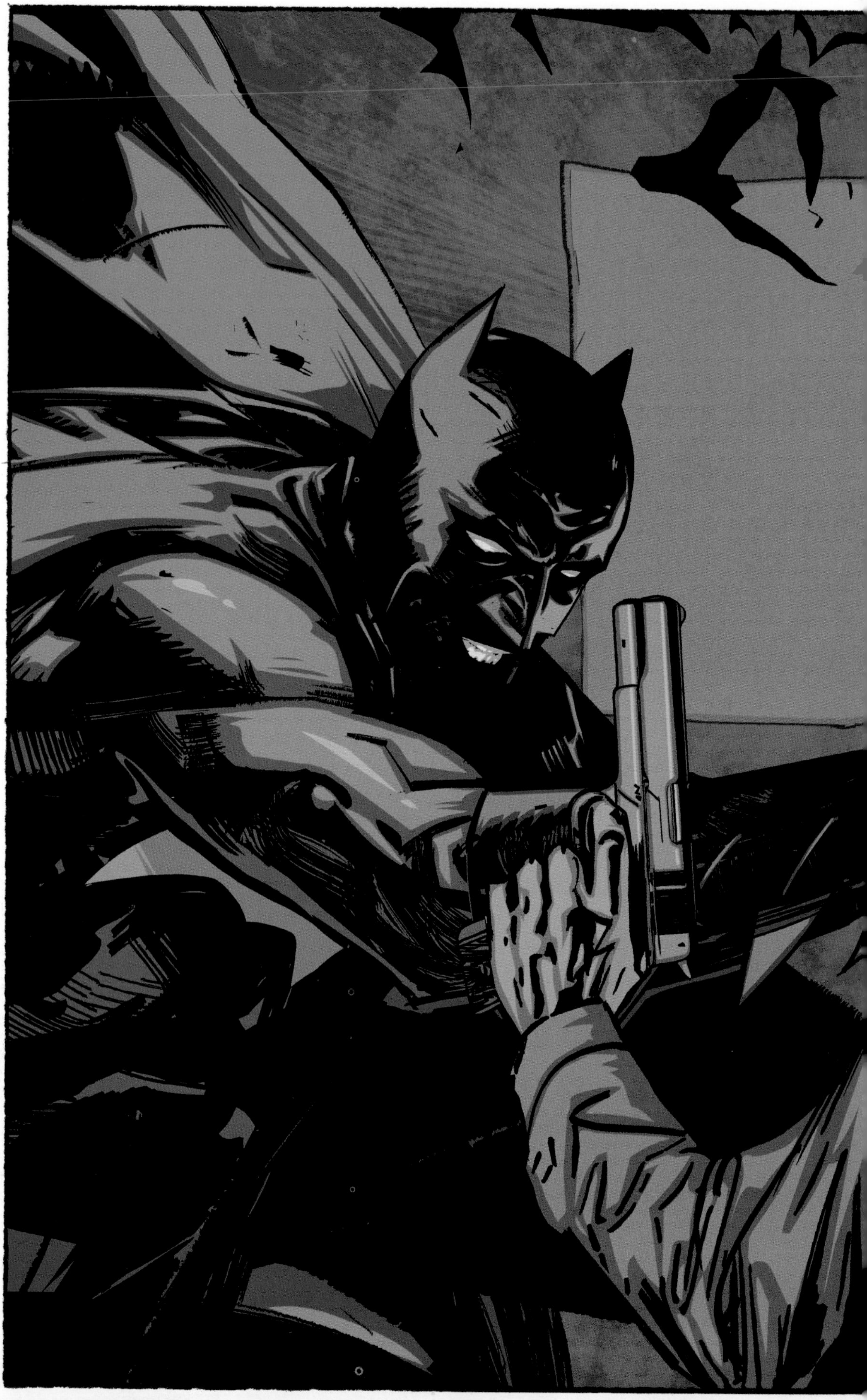

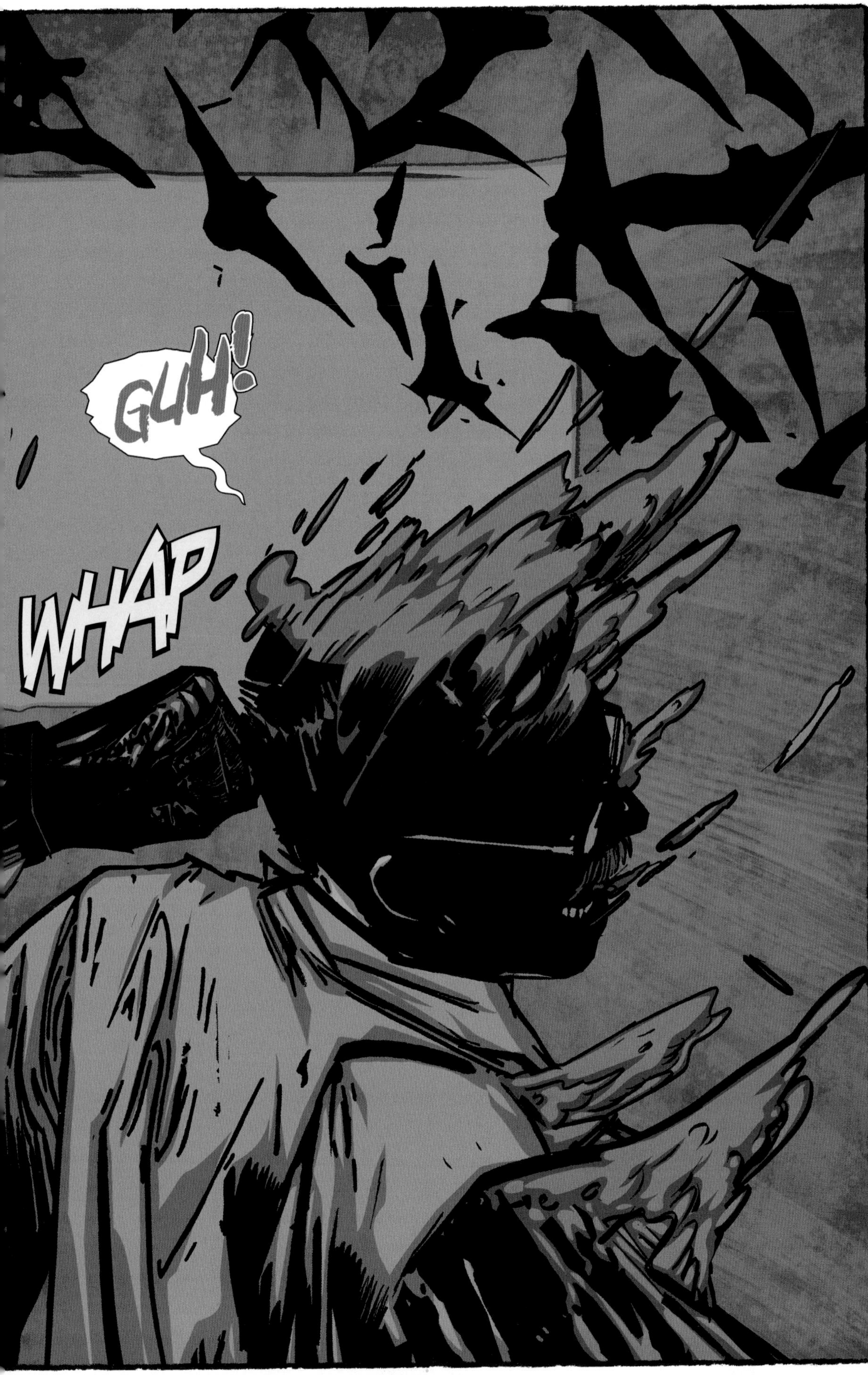
GUH!
WHAP

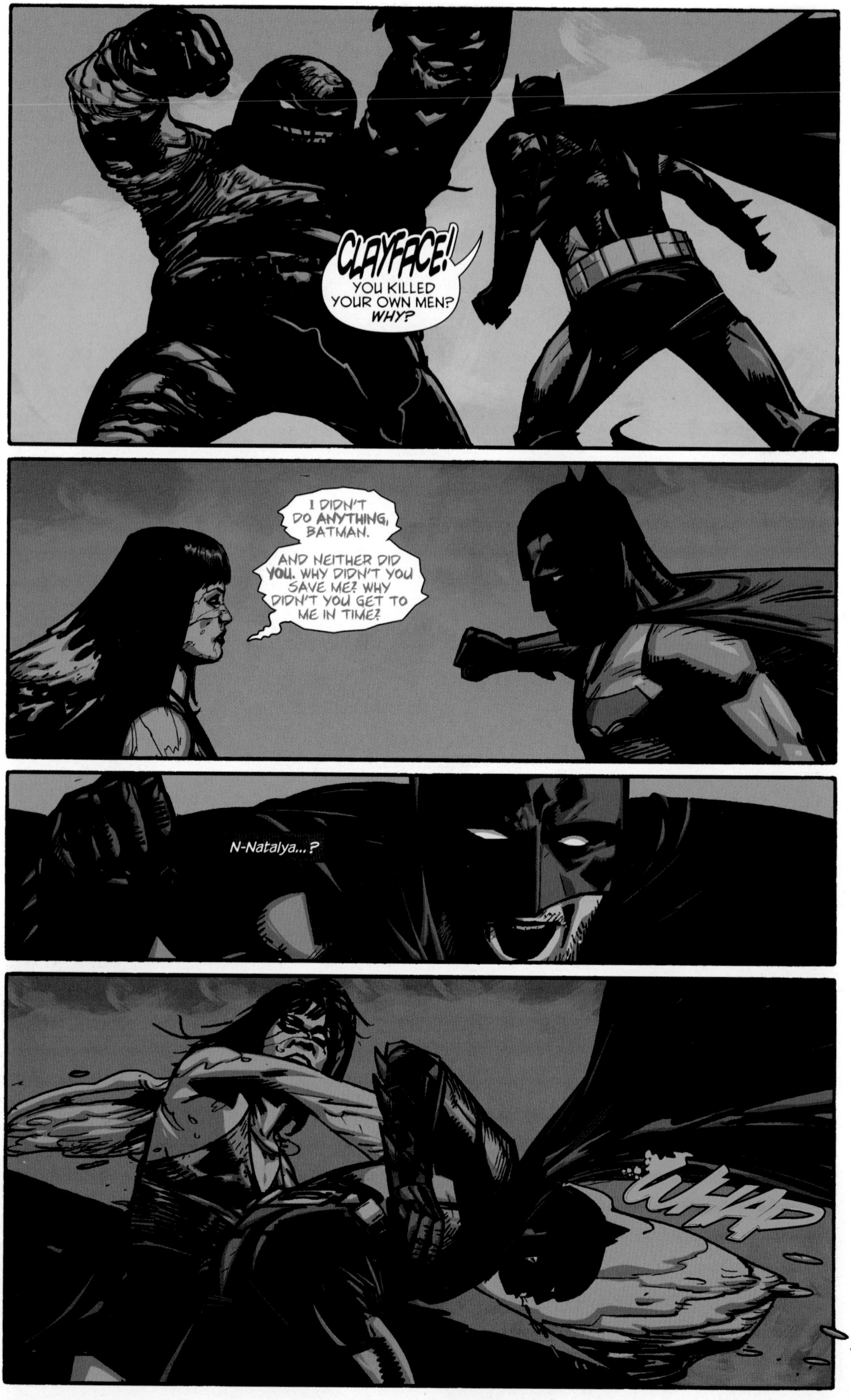
CLAYFACE! YOU KILLED YOUR OWN MEN? WHY?
I DIDN'T DO ANYTHING, BATMAN.
AND NEITHER DID YOU. WHY DIDN'T YOU SAVE ME? WHY DIDN'T YOU GET TO ME IN TIME?
N-Natalya...?
WHAP

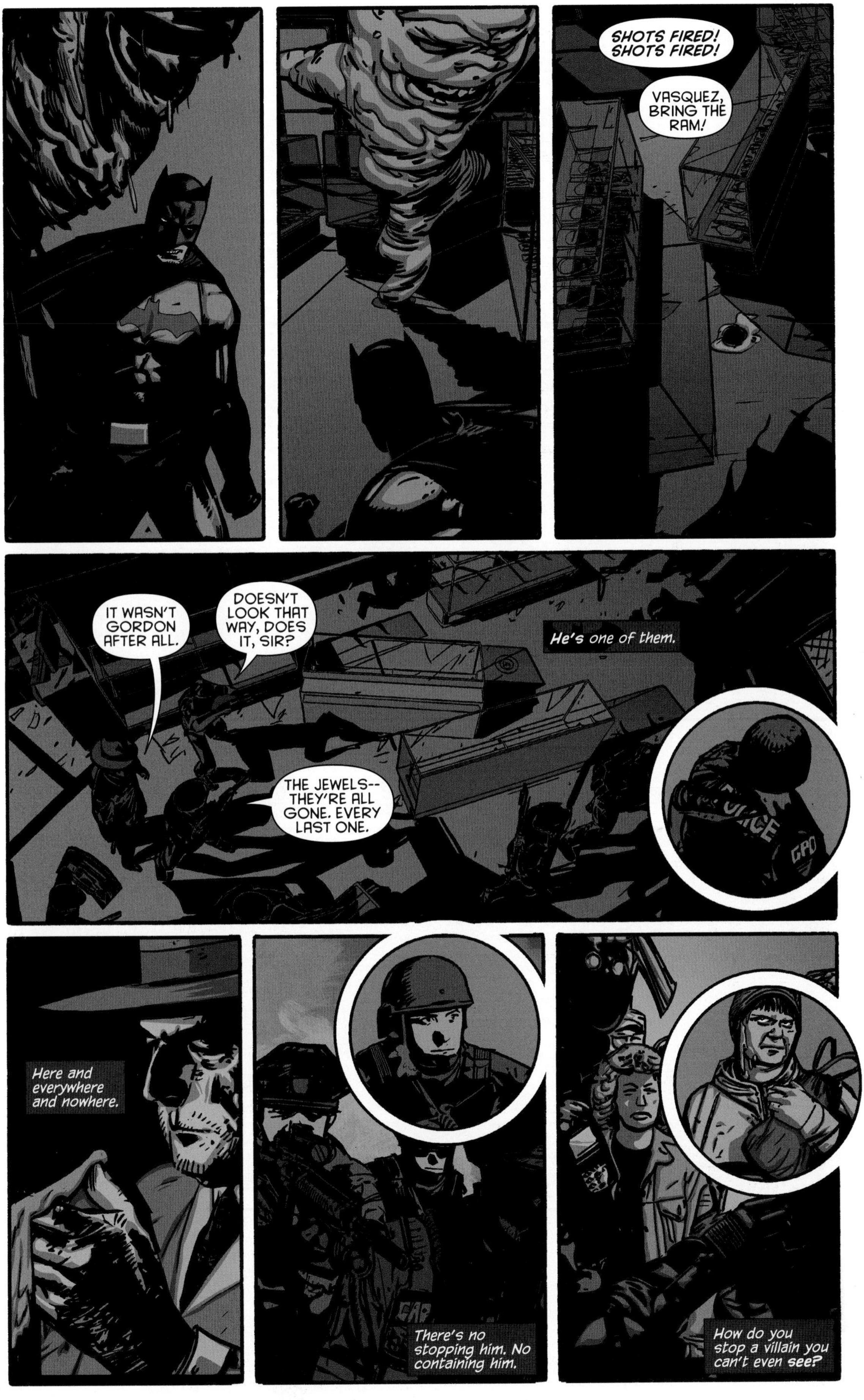
SHOTS FIRED! SHOTS FIRED!
VASQUEZ, BRING THE RAM!
IT WASN'T GORDON AFTER ALL.
DOESN'T LOOK THAT WAY, DOES IT, SIR?
He's one of them.
THE JEWELS-- THEY'RE ALL GONE. EVERY LAST ONE.
POLICE
GPD
Here and everywhere and nowhere.
There's no stopping him. No containing him.
How do you stop a villain you can't even see?

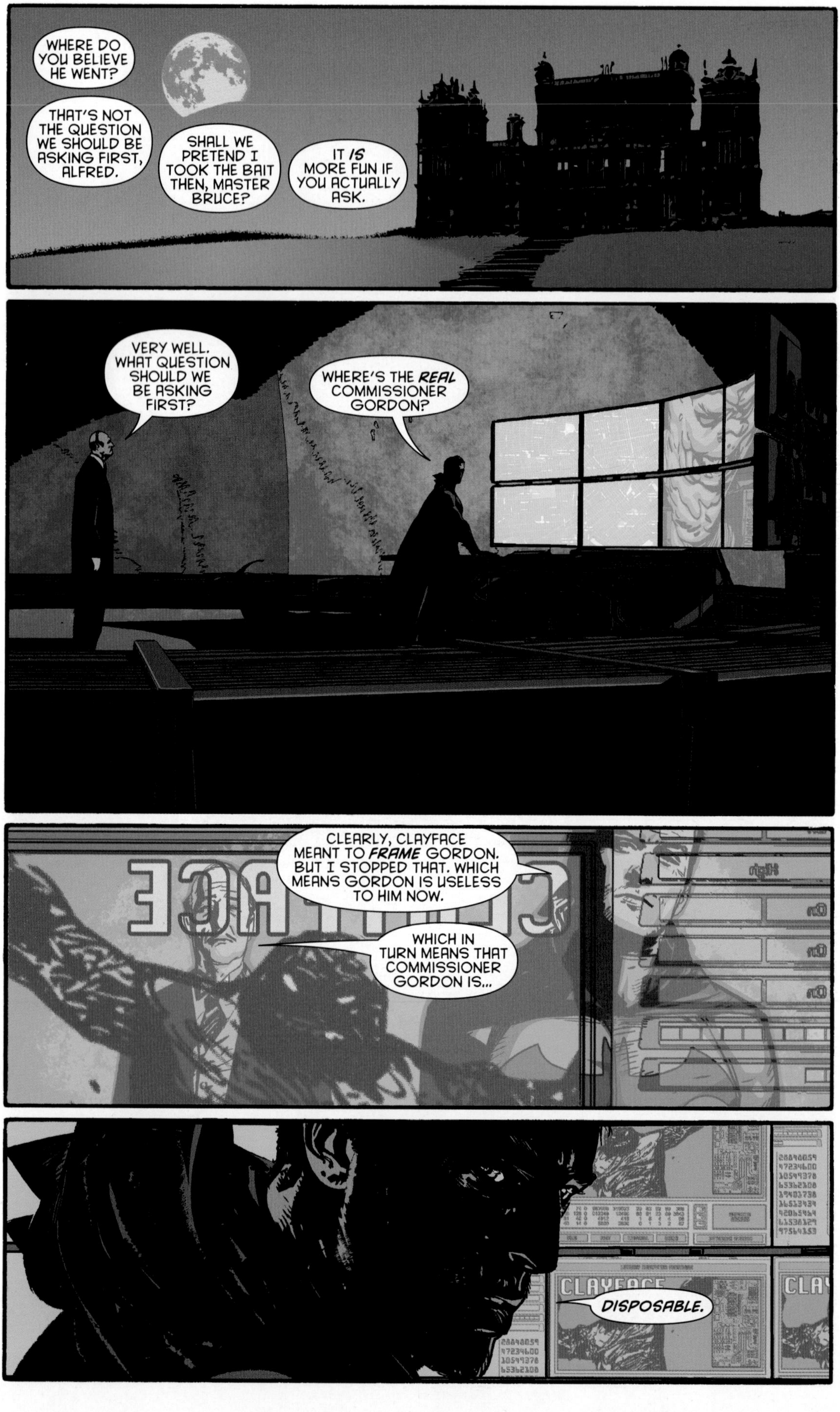
WHERE DO YOU BELIEVE HE WENT?
THAT'S NOT THE QUESTION WE SHOULD BE ASKING FIRST, ALFRED.
SHALL WE PRETEND I TOOK THE BAIT THEN, MASTER BRUCE?
IT *IS* MORE FUN IF YOU ACTUALLY ASK.
VERY WELL. WHAT QUESTION SHOULD WE BE ASKING FIRST?
WHERE'S THE *REAL* COMMISSIONER GORDON?
CLEARLY, CLAYFACE MEANT TO *FRAME* GORDON. BUT I STOPPED THAT. WHICH MEANS GORDON IS USELESS TO HIM NOW.
WHICH IN TURN MEANS THAT COMMISSIONER GORDON IS...
CLAYFACE
DISPOSABLE.

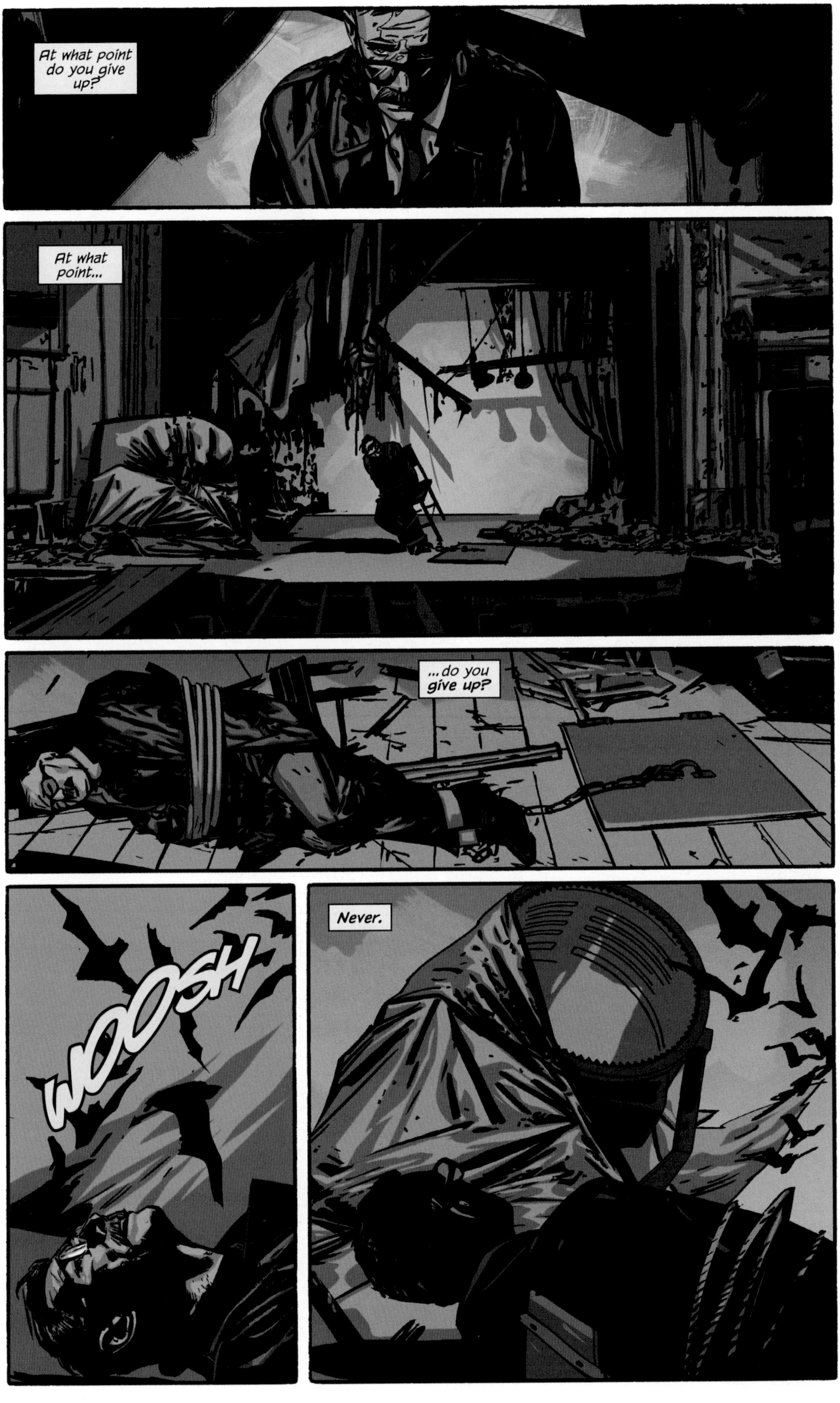
At what point do you give up?
At what point...
...do you give up?
WOOSH
Never.

NO NEW RED FLAGS ON CLAYFACE. SAT FOOTAGE ON HIS LAST-KNOWNS SHOWS ZERO. NOTHING ON WHERE HE MIGHT BE KEEPING GORDON.

FOR HOW... *UNWIELDY* HE IS, HE LEAVES PRECIOUS FEW FOOTPRINTS.

LET'S CHECK THE FIELD FOOTAGE.

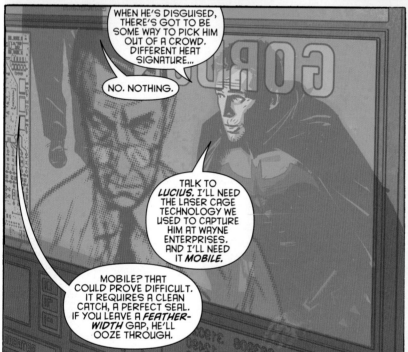

WHEN HE'S DISGUISED, THERE'S GOT TO BE SOME WAY TO PICK HIM OUT OF A CROWD. DIFFERENT HEAT SIGNATURE...

NO. NOTHING.

TALK TO *LUCIUS.* I'LL NEED THE LASER CAGE TECHNOLOGY WE USED TO CAPTURE HIM AT WAYNE ENTERPRISES. AND I'LL NEED IT *MOBILE.*

MOBILE? THAT COULD PROVE DIFFICULT. IT REQUIRES A CLEAN CATCH, A PERFECT SEAL. IF YOU LEAVE A *FEATHER-WIDTH* GAP, HE'LL OOZE THROUGH.

THEN I'D BETTER BE PERFECT.

MAY I ADD ANOTHER QUESTION TO OUR GROWING LIST?

ALWAYS.

WHY DID CLAYFACE KILL HIS OWN HEIST CREW?

PAVING THE WAY FOR HIS OWN ENTER-PRISE?

DOESN'T THAT SEEM A BIT... *AMBITIOUS* FOR HIM?

YOU'RE SAYING HE THREW IN WITH SOMEONE ELSE?

WHICH LEADS TO OUR NEXT QUESTION.

SHALL WE PRETEND I TOOK THE BAIT THEN, ALFRED?

YES, *I'LL* BE GRACIOUS. THE NEXT QUESTION IS...

...WHO TOLD HIM THAT NATALYA KNEW BATMAN?

YOU HESITATED.

I DIDN'T HESITATE.

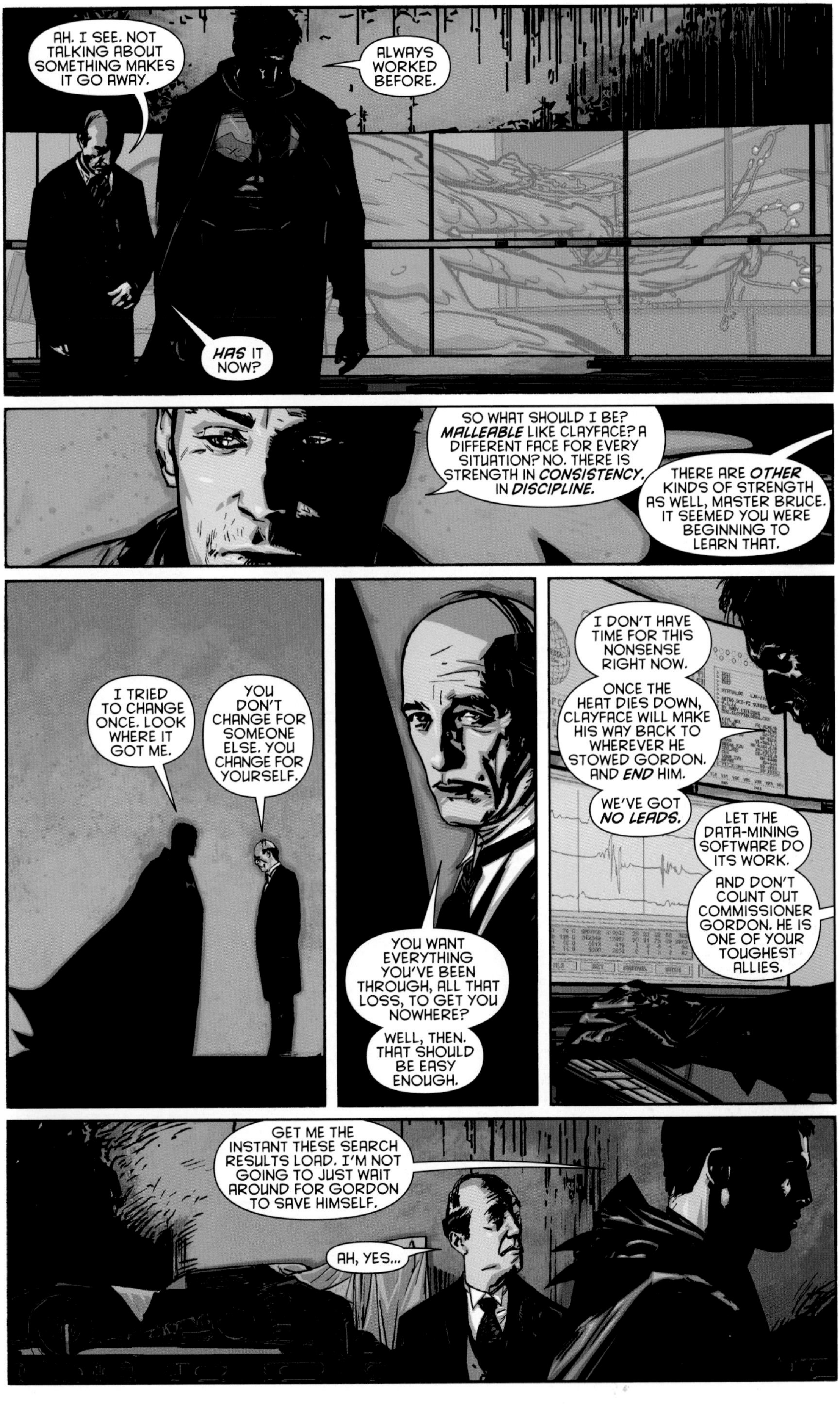
AH. I SEE. NOT TALKING ABOUT SOMETHING MAKES IT GO AWAY.
ALWAYS WORKED BEFORE.
HAS IT NOW?
SO WHAT SHOULD I BE? MALLEABLE LIKE CLAYFACE? A DIFFERENT FACE FOR EVERY SITUATION? NO. THERE IS STRENGTH IN CONSISTENCY. IN DISCIPLINE.
THERE ARE OTHER KINDS OF STRENGTH AS WELL, MASTER BRUCE. IT SEEMED YOU WERE BEGINNING TO LEARN THAT.
I TRIED TO CHANGE ONCE. LOOK WHERE IT GOT ME.
YOU DON'T CHANGE FOR SOMEONE ELSE. YOU CHANGE FOR YOURSELF.
YOU WANT EVERYTHING YOU'VE BEEN THROUGH, ALL THAT LOSS, TO GET YOU NOWHERE?
WELL, THEN. THAT SHOULD BE EASY ENOUGH.
I DON'T HAVE TIME FOR THIS NONSENSE RIGHT NOW.
ONCE THE HEAT DIES DOWN, CLAYFACE WILL MAKE HIS WAY BACK TO WHEREVER HE STOWED GORDON. AND END HIM.
WE'VE GOT NO LEADS.
LET THE DATA-MINING SOFTWARE DO ITS WORK.
AND DON'T COUNT OUT COMMISSIONER GORDON. HE IS ONE OF YOUR TOUGHEST ALLIES.
GET ME THE INSTANT THESE SEARCH RESULTS LOAD. I'M NOT GOING TO JUST WAIT AROUND FOR GORDON TO SAVE HIMSELF.
AH, YES...

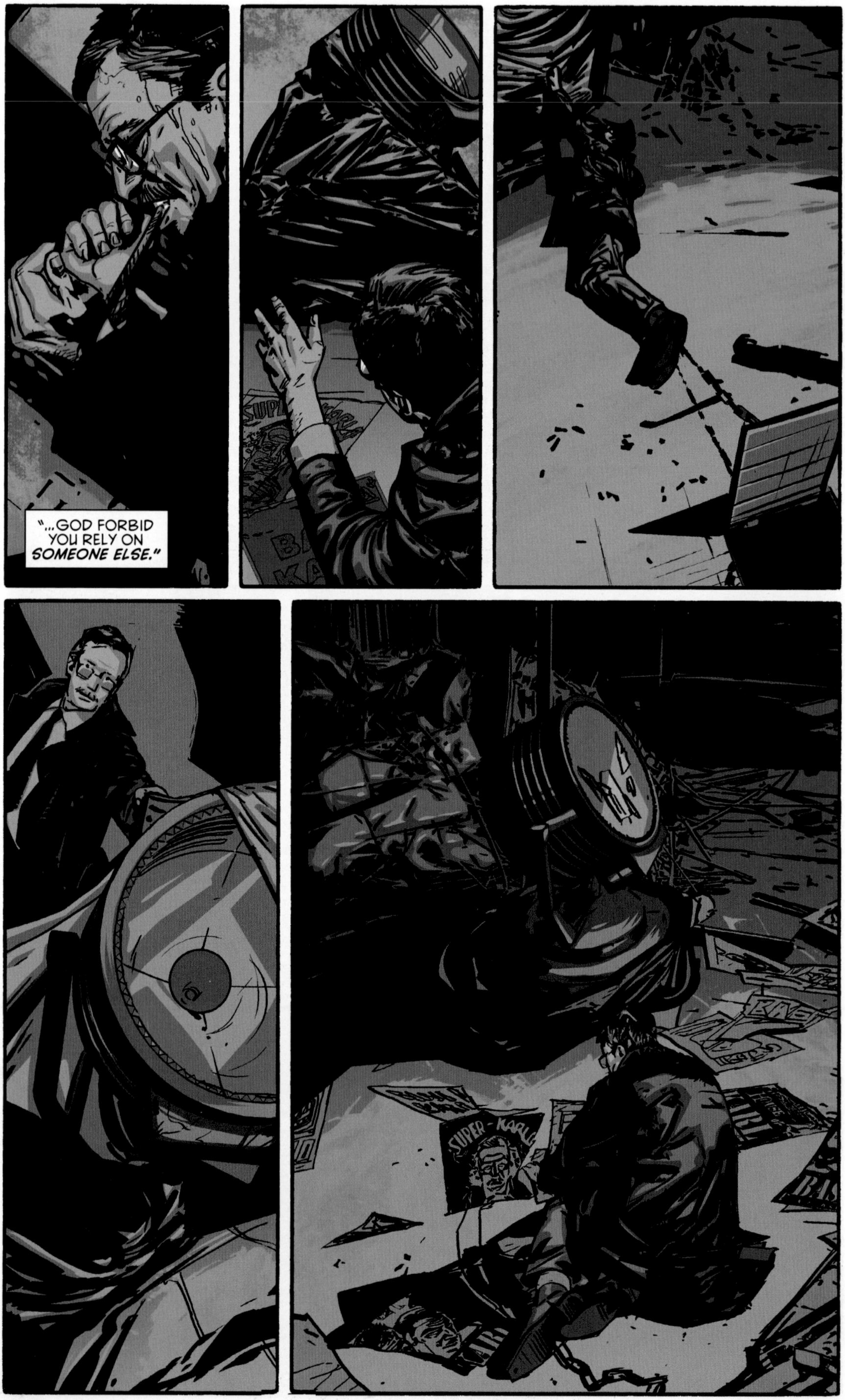
"...GOD FORBID YOU RELY ON SOMEONE ELSE."

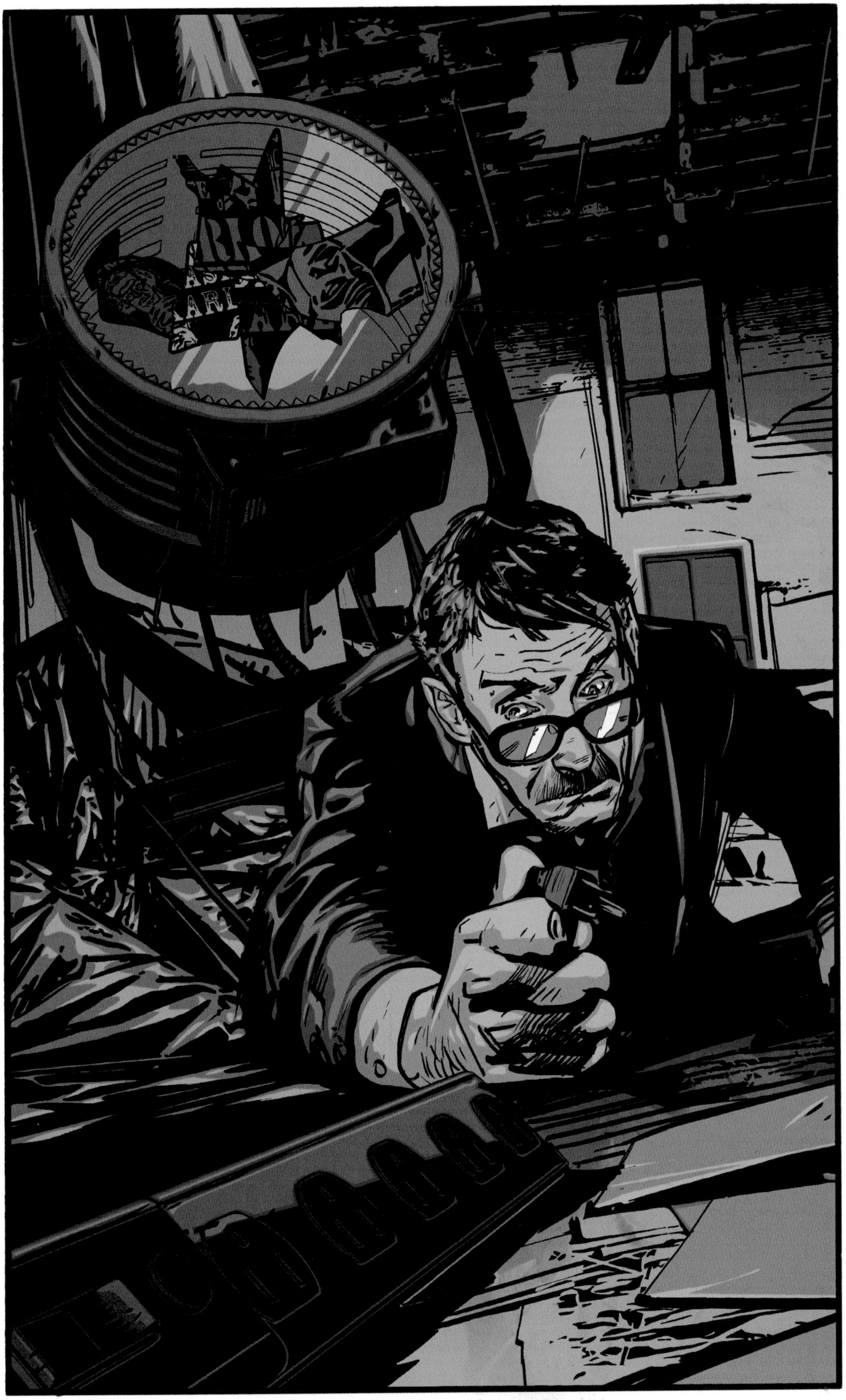

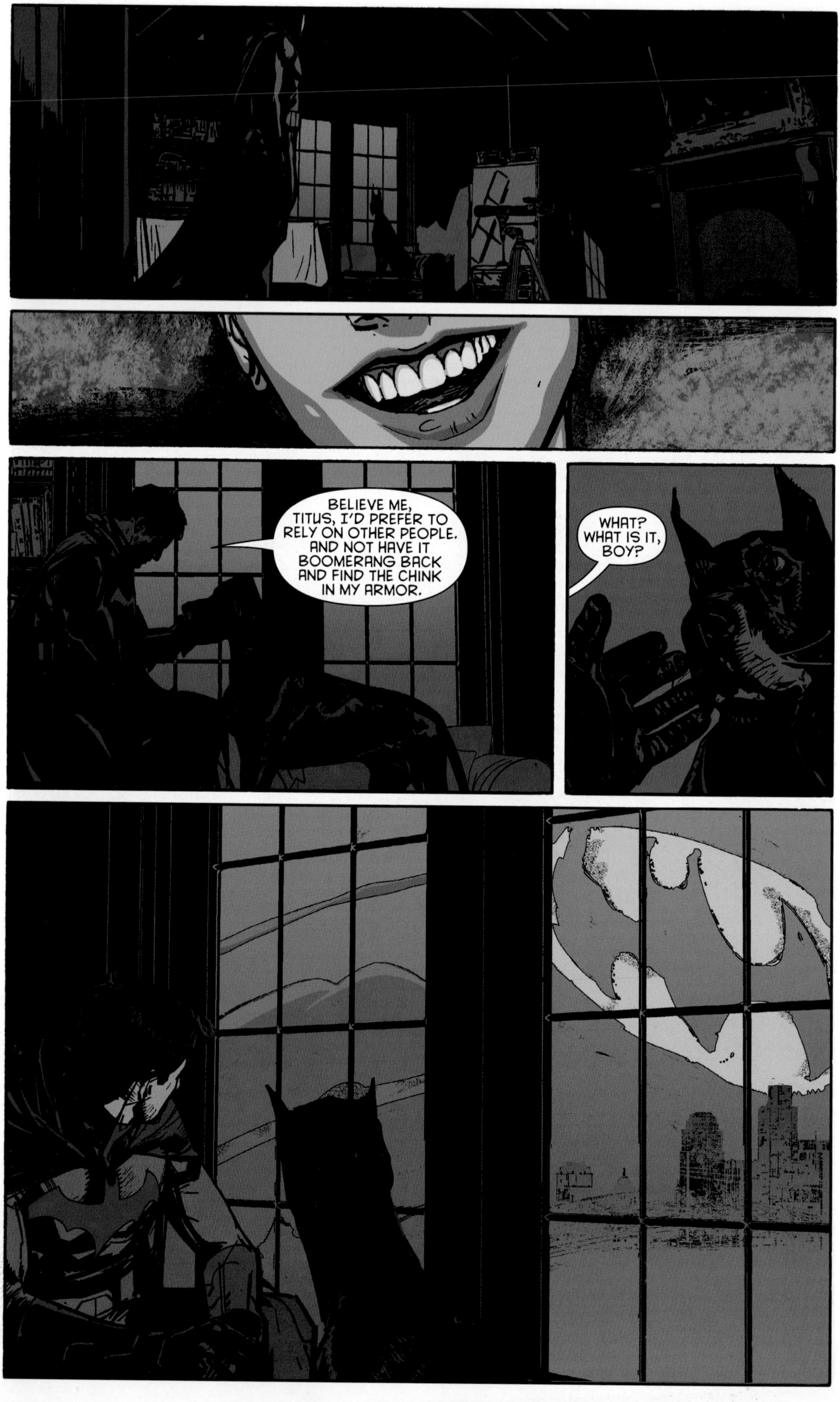
BELIEVE ME, TITUS, I'D PREFER TO RELY ON OTHER PEOPLE. AND NOT HAVE IT BOOMERANG BACK AND FIND THE CHINK IN MY ARMOR.
WHAT? WHAT IS IT, BOY?

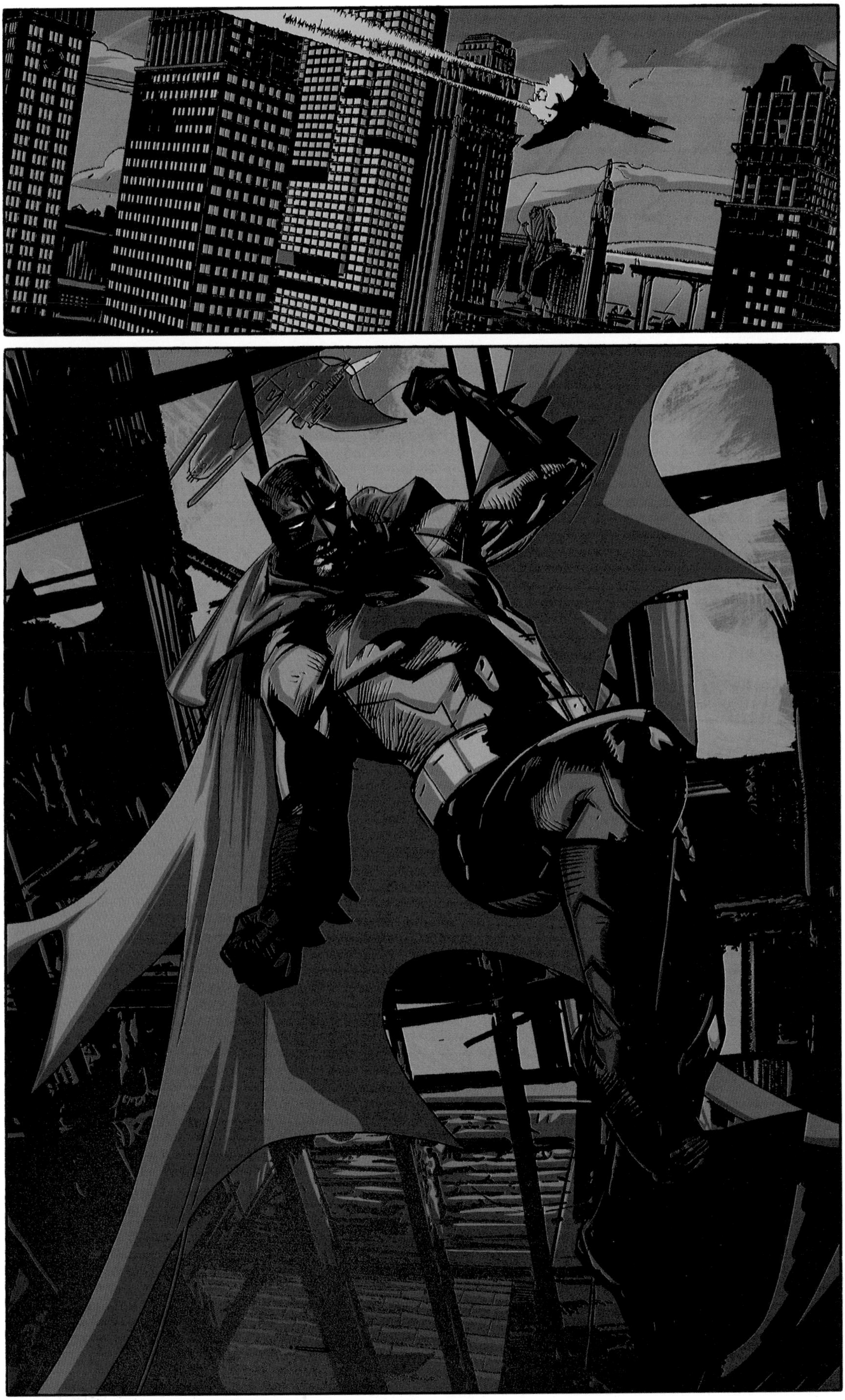

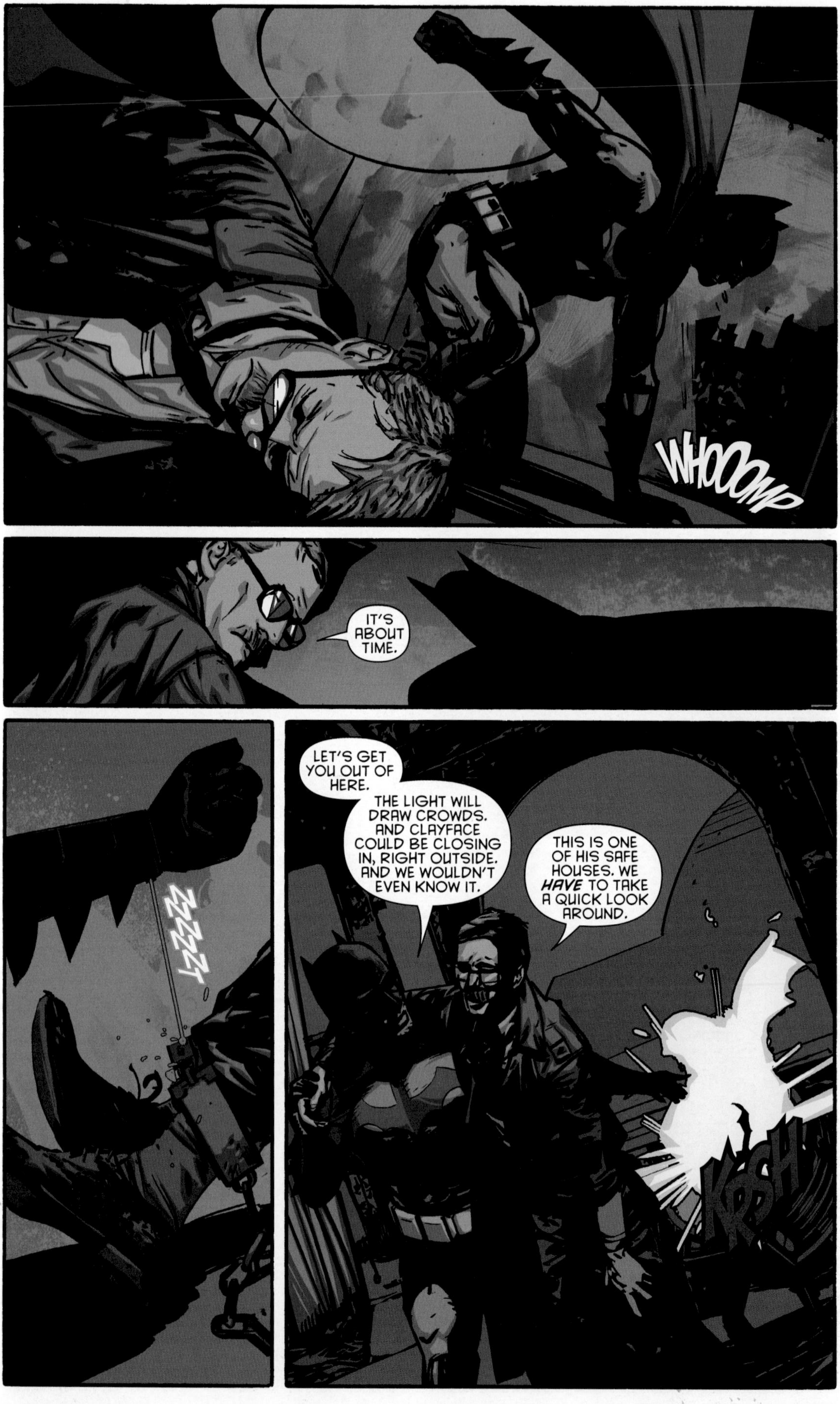
WHOOOOMP
IT'S ABOUT TIME.
ZZZZT
LET'S GET YOU OUT OF HERE.
THE LIGHT WILL DRAW CROWDS. AND CLAYFACE COULD BE CLOSING IN, RIGHT OUTSIDE. AND WE WOULDN'T EVEN KNOW IT.
THIS IS ONE OF HIS SAFE HOUSES. WE *HAVE* TO TAKE A QUICK LOOK AROUND.
KRSH

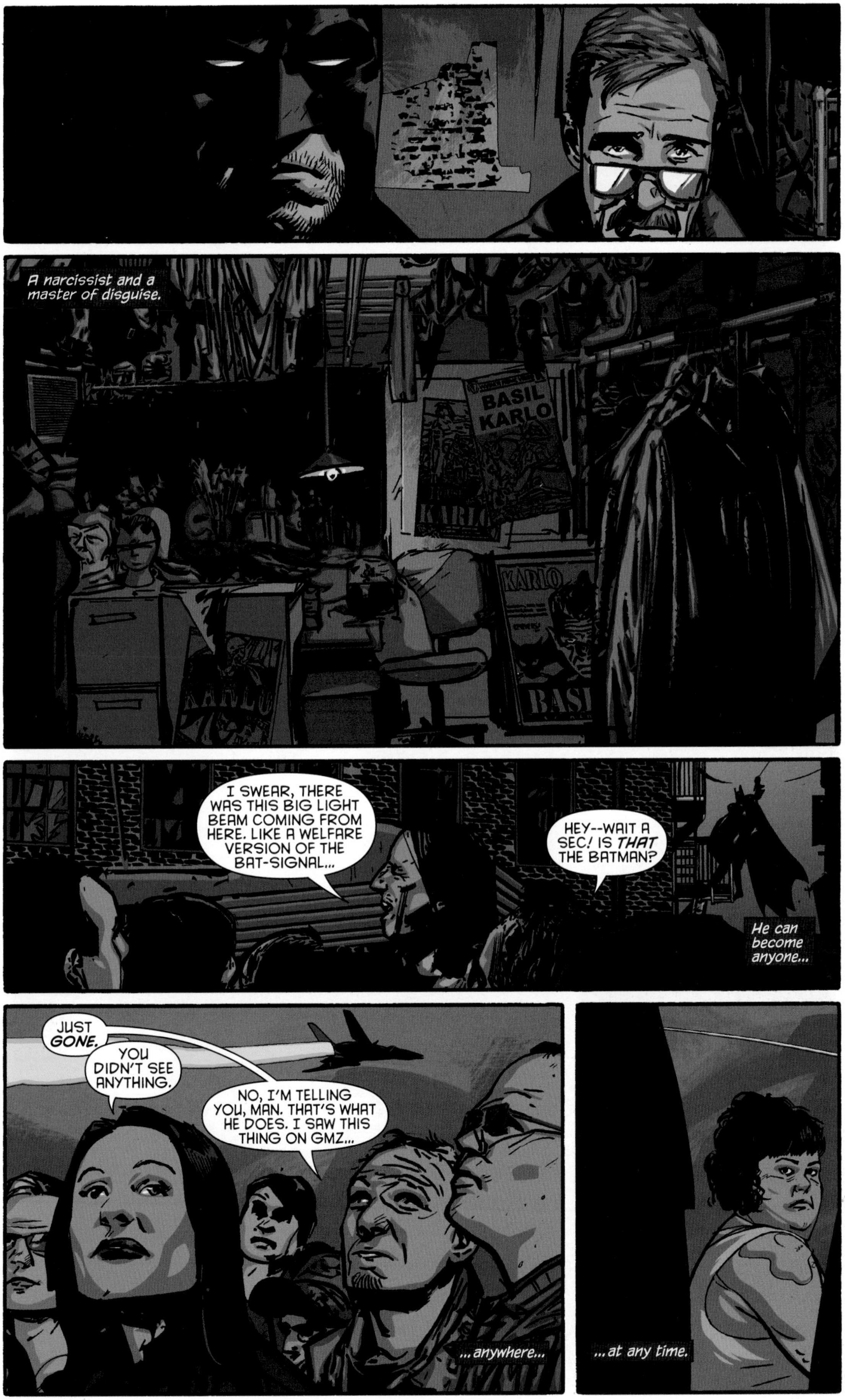

A narcissist and a master of disguise.
BASIL KARLO
KARLO
KARLO
BASIL
KARLO
I SWEAR, THERE WAS THIS BIG LIGHT BEAM COMING FROM HERE. LIKE A WELFARE VERSION OF THE BAT-SIGNAL...
HEY--WAIT A SEC! IS *THAT* THE BATMAN?
He can become anyone...
JUST *GONE.*
YOU DIDN'T SEE ANYTHING.
NO, I'M TELLING YOU, MAN. THAT'S WHAT HE DOES. I SAW THIS THING ON GMZ...
...anywhere...
...at any time.

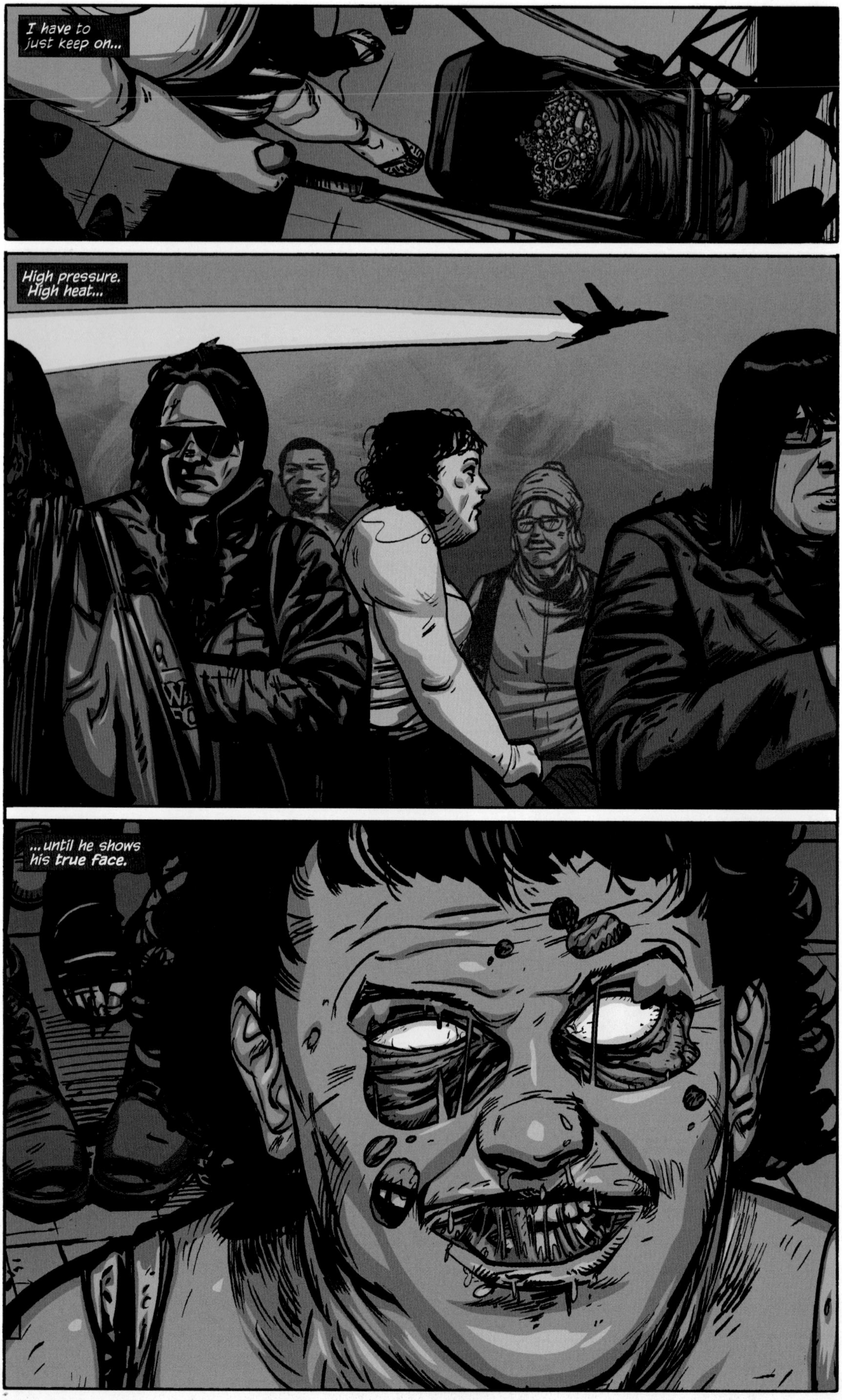
I have to just keep on...
High pressure. High heat...
...until he shows his true face.

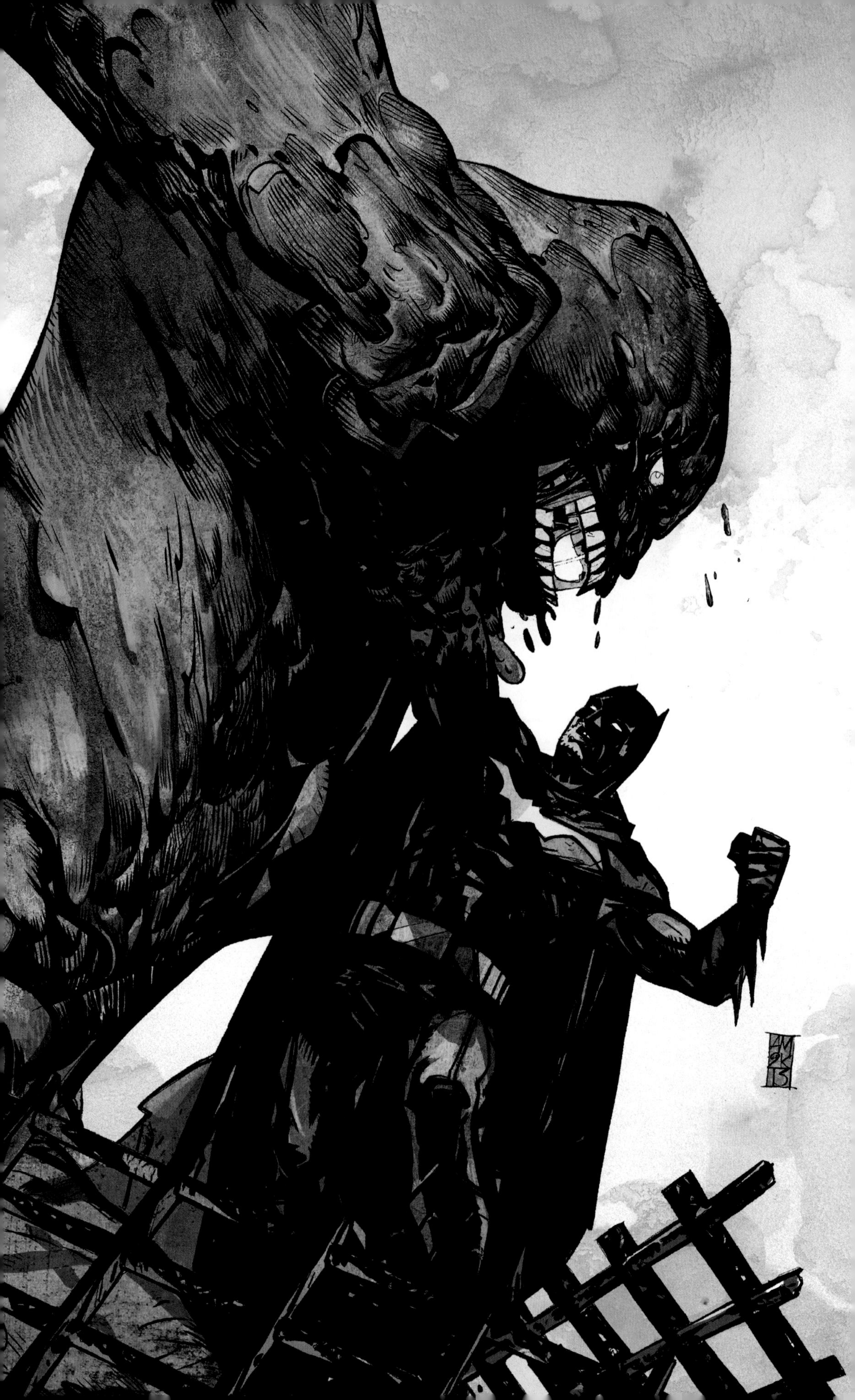

RAMPANT

ALEX MALEEV artist & cover

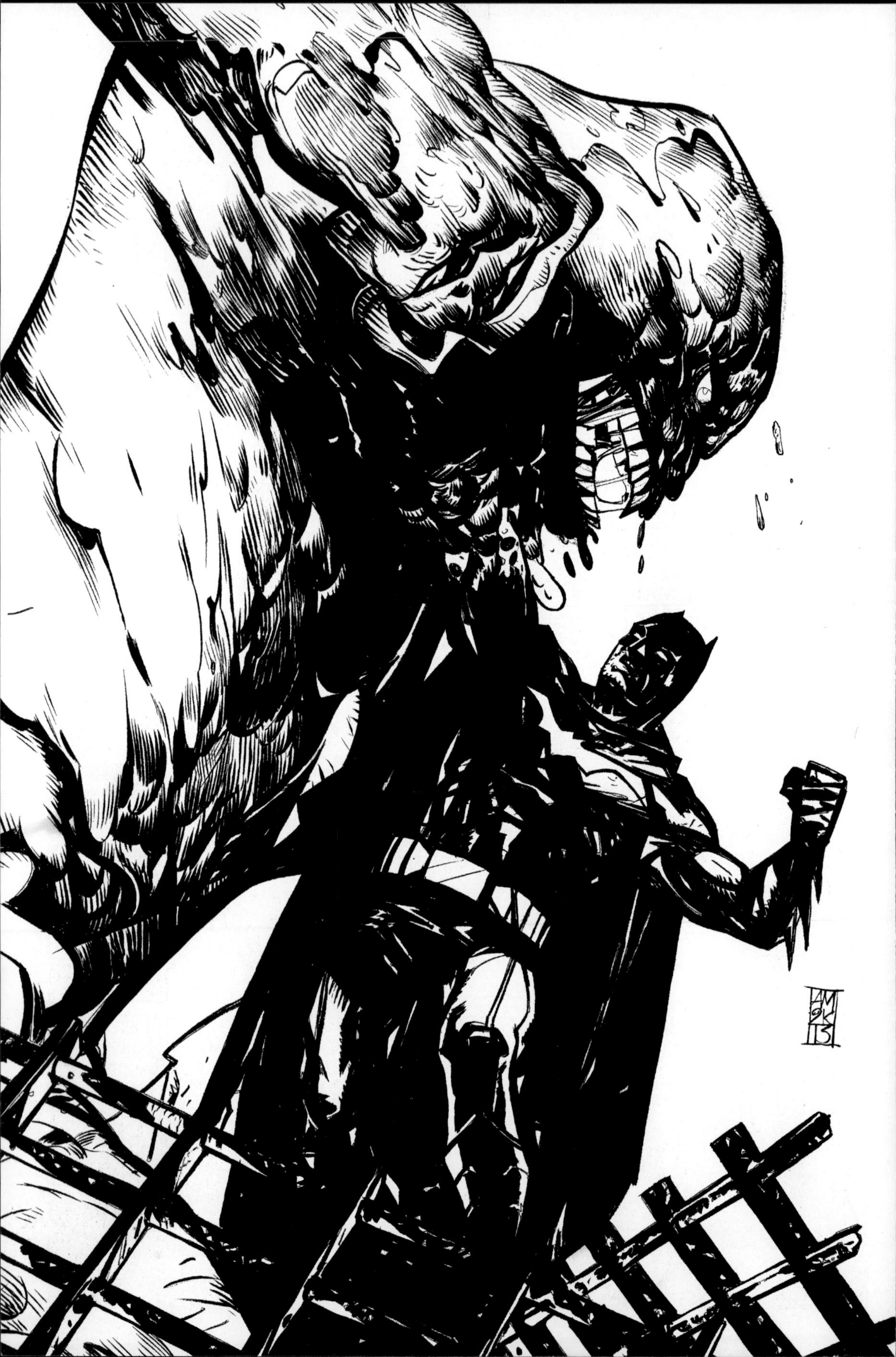

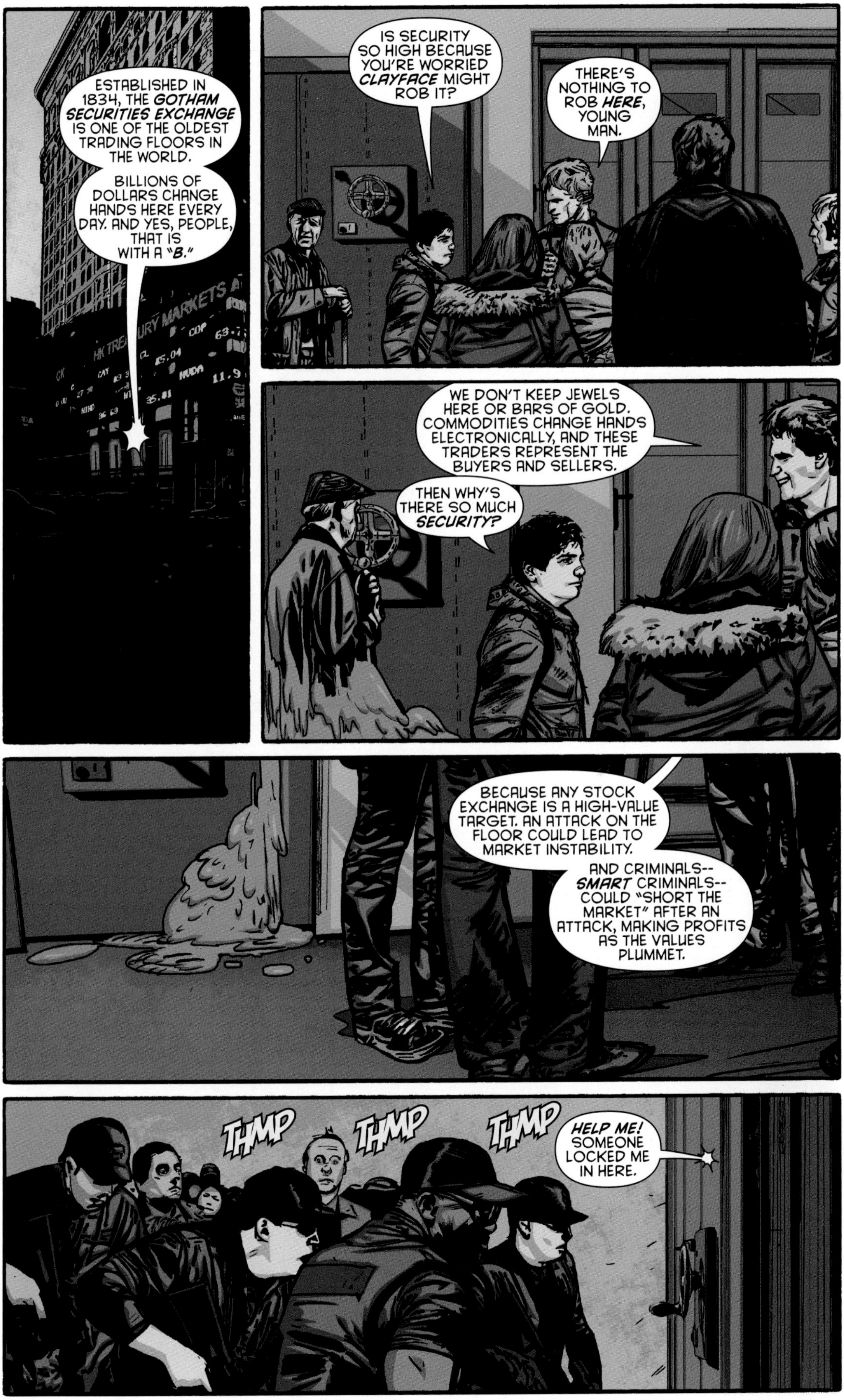
ESTABLISHED IN 1834, THE GOTHAM SECURITIES EXCHANGE IS ONE OF THE OLDEST TRADING FLOORS IN THE WORLD.
BILLIONS OF DOLLARS CHANGE HANDS HERE EVERY DAY. AND YES, PEOPLE, THAT IS WITH A "B."
IS SECURITY SO HIGH BECAUSE YOU'RE WORRIED CLAYFACE MIGHT ROB IT?
THERE'S NOTHING TO ROB HERE, YOUNG MAN.
WE DON'T KEEP JEWELS HERE OR BARS OF GOLD. COMMODITIES CHANGE HANDS ELECTRONICALLY, AND THESE TRADERS REPRESENT THE BUYERS AND SELLERS.
THEN WHY'S THERE SO MUCH SECURITY?
BECAUSE ANY STOCK EXCHANGE IS A HIGH-VALUE TARGET. AN ATTACK ON THE FLOOR COULD LEAD TO MARKET INSTABILITY.
AND CRIMINALS-- SMART CRIMINALS-- COULD "SHORT THE MARKET" AFTER AN ATTACK, MAKING PROFITS AS THE VALUES PLUMMET.
THMP
THMP
THMP
HELP ME! SOMEONE LOCKED ME IN HERE.

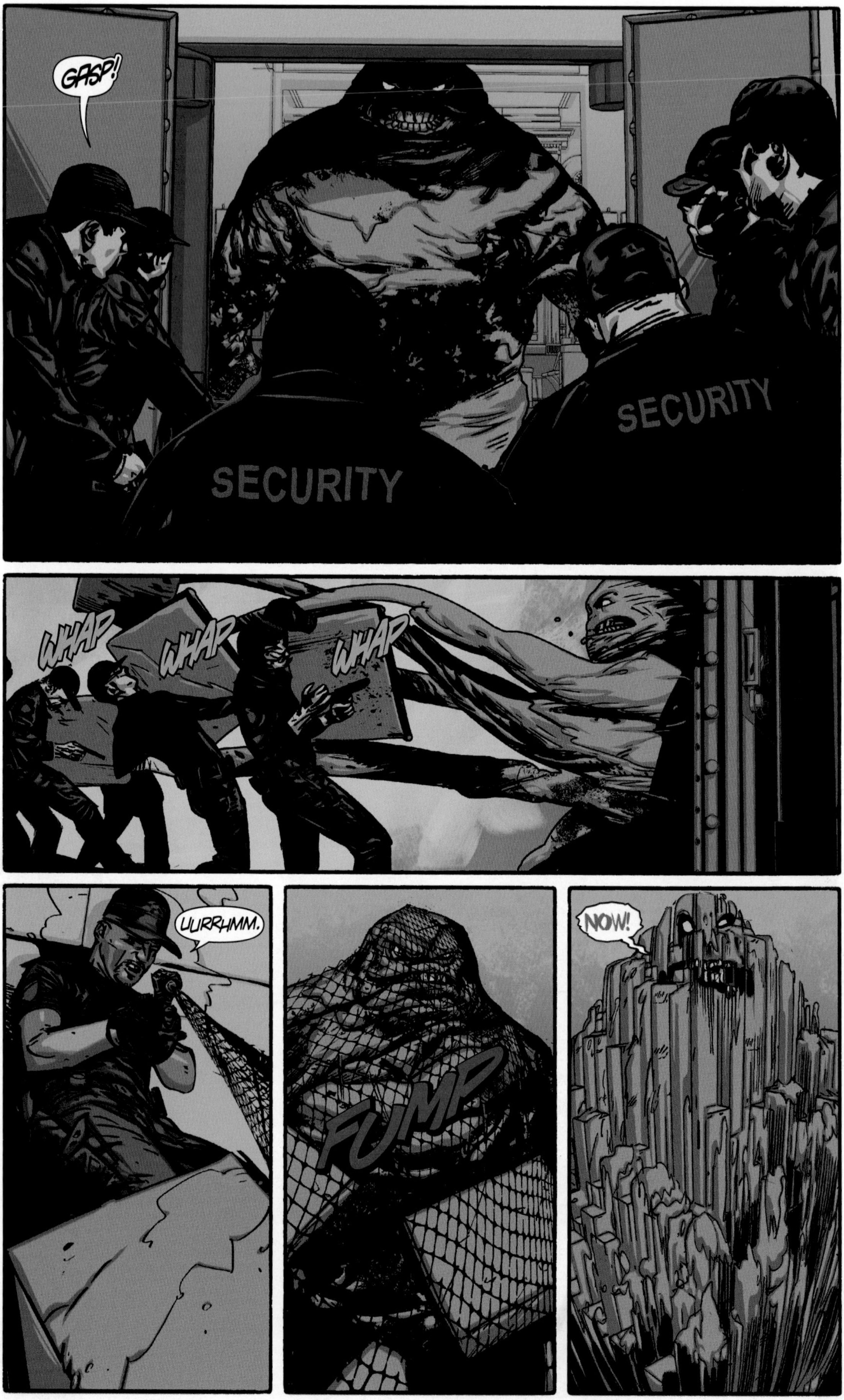
GASP!
SECURITY
SECURITY
WHAP
WHAP
WHAP
UURRHMM.
FUMP
NOW!

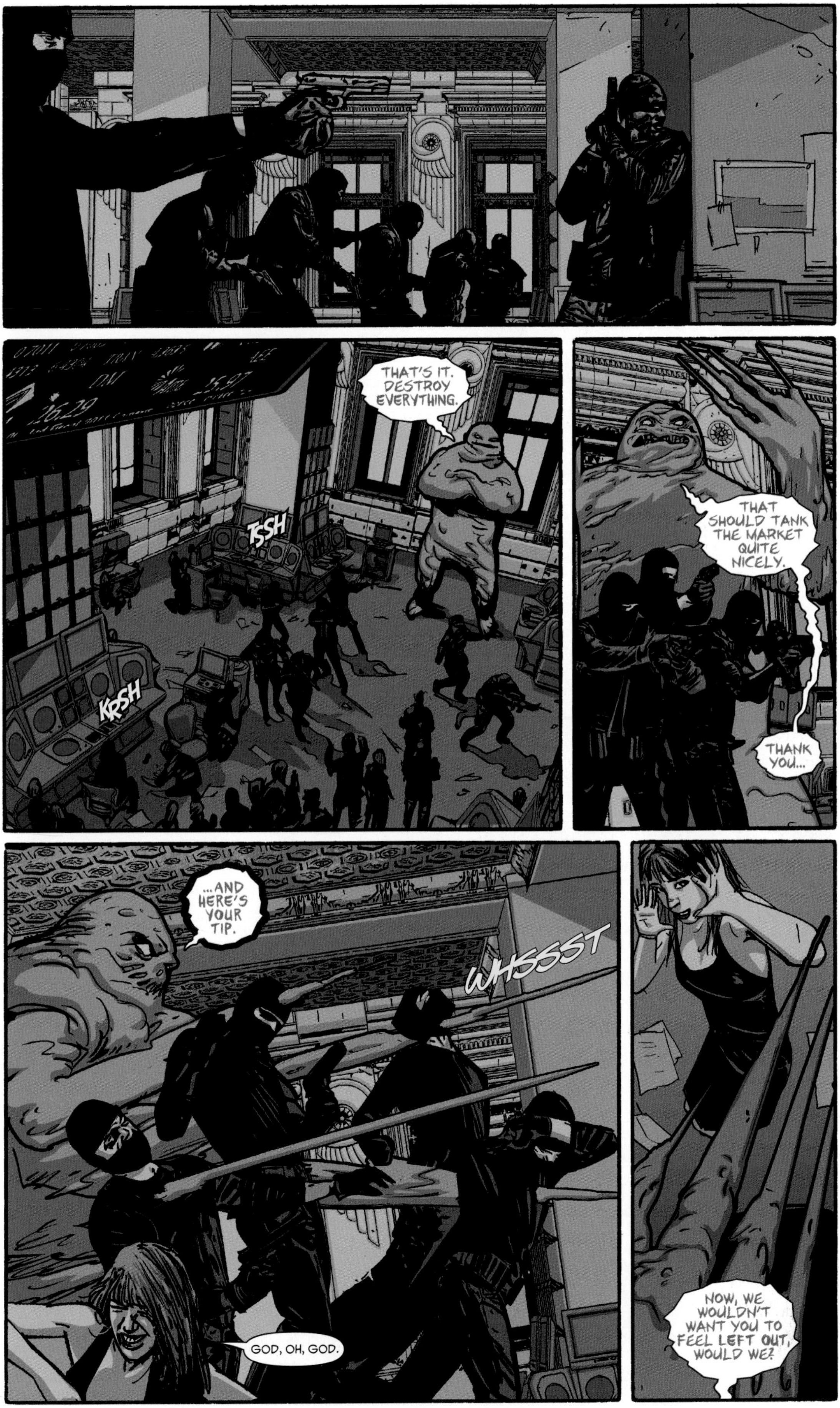

THAT'S IT. DESTROY EVERYTHING.
TSSH
KRSH
THAT SHOULD TANK THE MARKET QUITE NICELY.
THANK YOU...
...AND HERE'S YOUR TIP.
WHSSST
GOD, OH, GOD.
NOW, WE WOULDN'T WANT YOU TO FEEL LEFT OUT, WOULD WE?

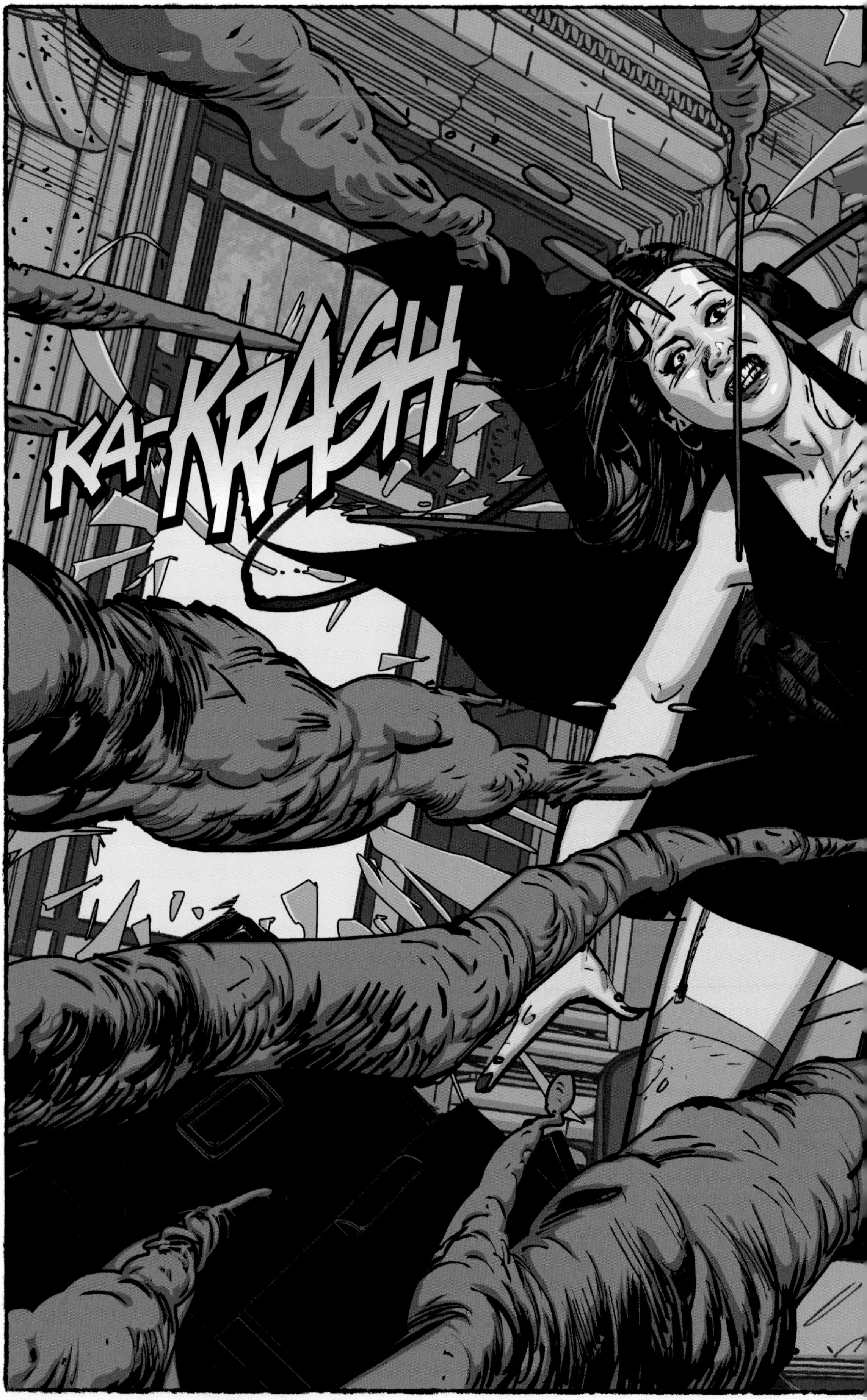
KA-KRASH

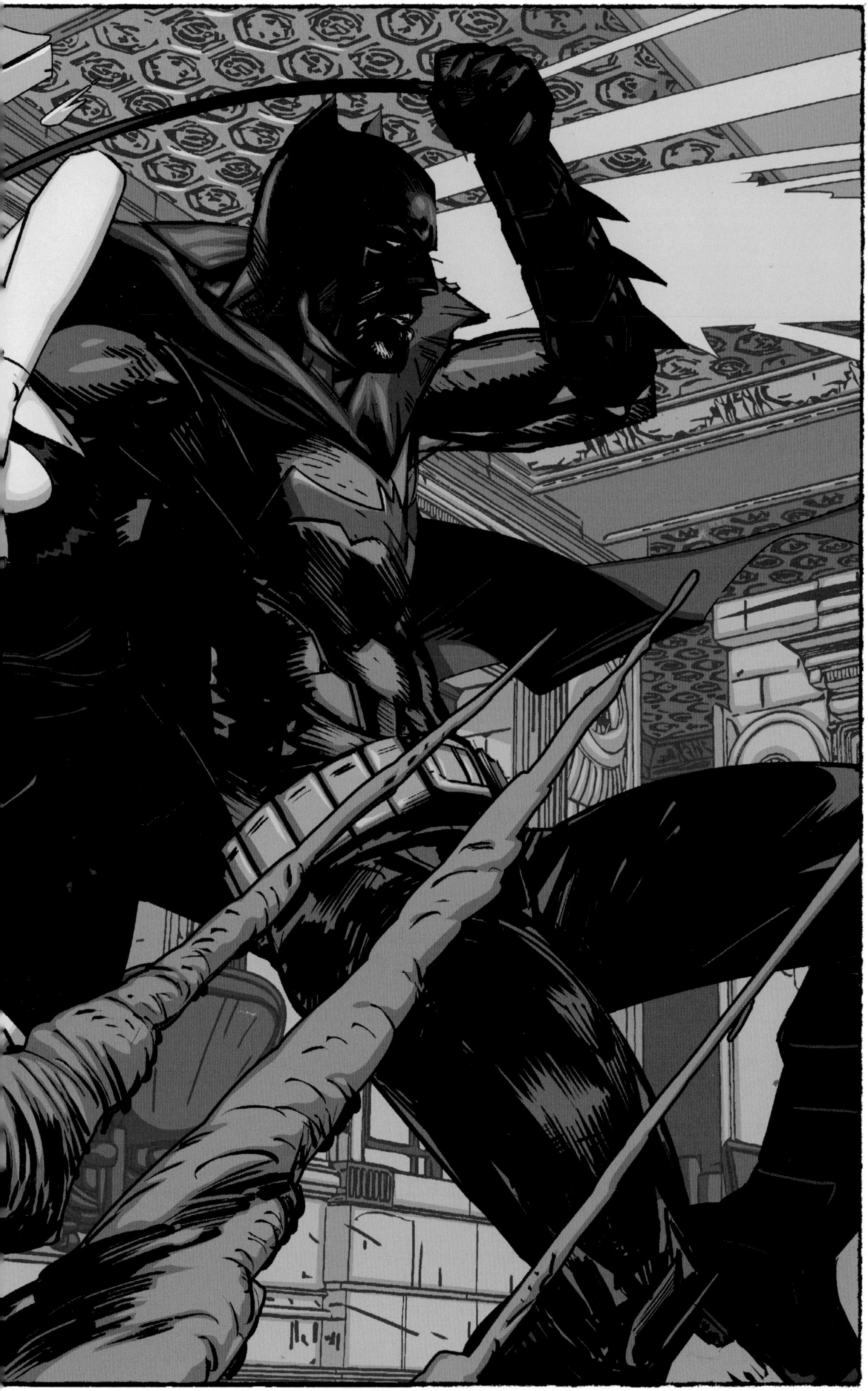

KSSSHHH

UNF.

UFF.

RUN.

FUMP

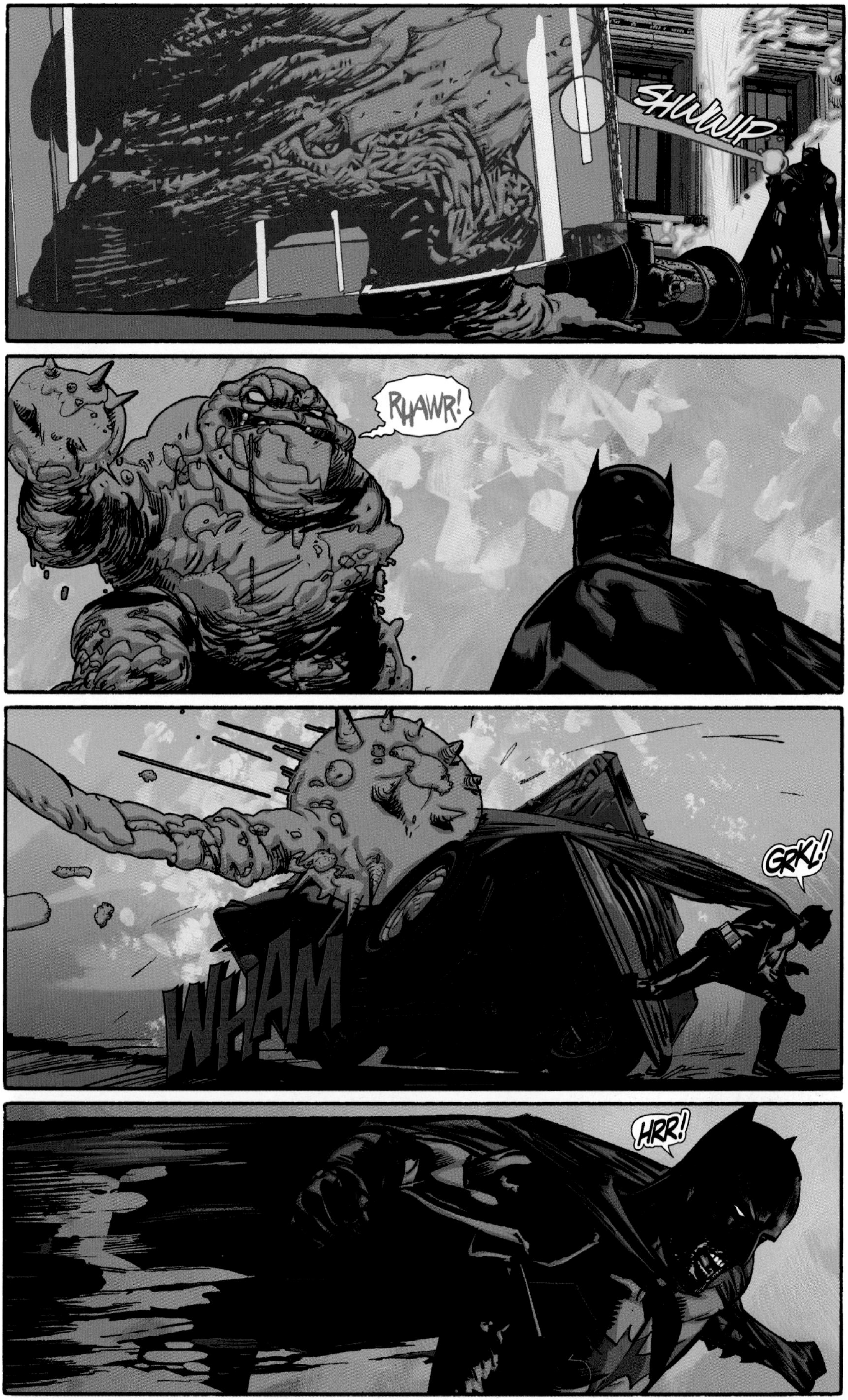
SHUUWIP
RHAWR!
GRKL!
WHAM
HRR!

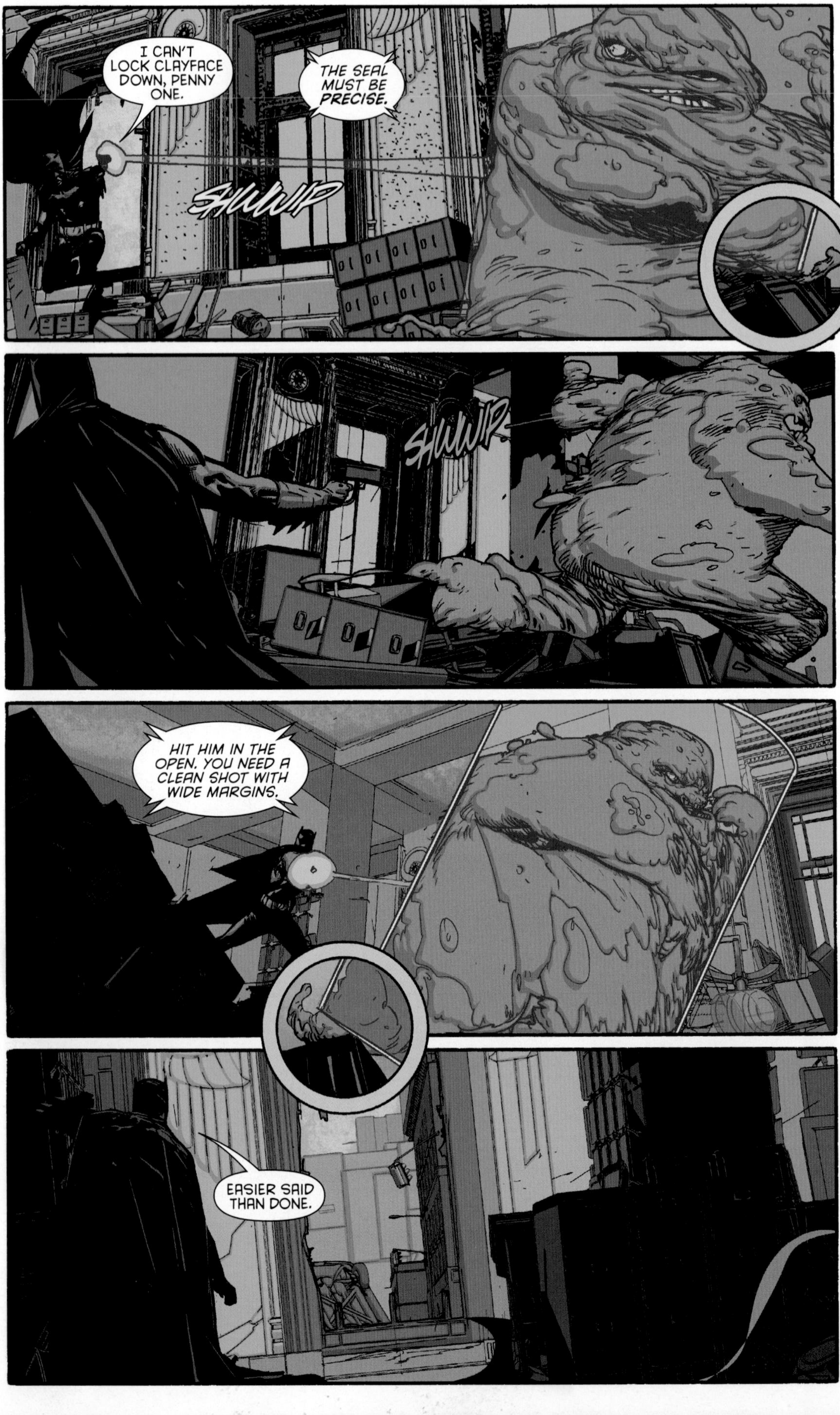
I CAN'T LOCK CLAYFACE DOWN, PENNY ONE.
THE SEAL MUST BE PRECISE.
SHWIP
SHWIP
HIT HIM IN THE OPEN. YOU NEED A CLEAN SHOT WITH WIDE MARGINS.
EASIER SAID THAN DONE.

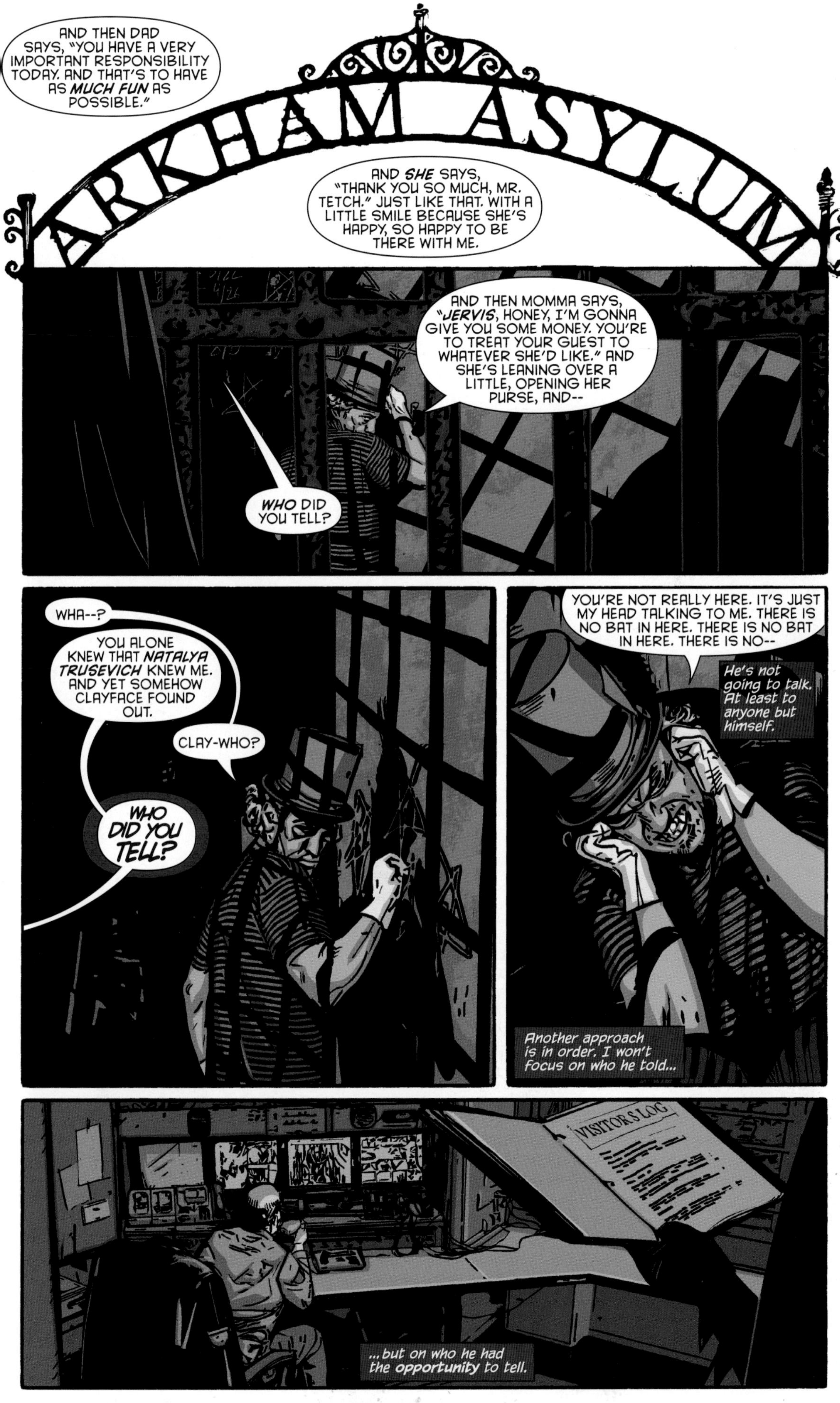

AND THEN DAD SAYS, "YOU HAVE A VERY IMPORTANT RESPONSIBILITY TODAY. AND THAT'S TO HAVE AS ***MUCH FUN*** AS POSSIBLE."
ARKHAM ASYLUM
AND ***SHE*** SAYS, "THANK YOU SO MUCH, MR. TETCH." JUST LIKE THAT. WITH A LITTLE SMILE BECAUSE SHE'S HAPPY, SO HAPPY TO BE THERE WITH ME.
AND THEN MOMMA SAYS, "***JERVIS***, HONEY, I'M GONNA GIVE YOU SOME MONEY. YOU'RE TO TREAT YOUR GUEST TO WHATEVER SHE'D LIKE." AND SHE'S LEANING OVER A LITTLE, OPENING HER PURSE, AND--
WHO DID YOU TELL?
WHA--?
YOU ALONE KNEW THAT ***NATALYA TRUSEVICH*** KNEW ME. AND YET SOMEHOW CLAYFACE FOUND OUT.
CLAY-WHO?
WHO DID YOU TELL?
YOU'RE NOT REALLY HERE. IT'S JUST MY HEAD TALKING TO ME. THERE IS NO BAT IN HERE. THERE IS NO BAT IN HERE. THERE IS NO--
He's not going to talk. At least to anyone but himself.
Another approach is in order. I won't focus on who he told...
VISITORS LOG
*...but on who he had the **opportunity** to tell.*

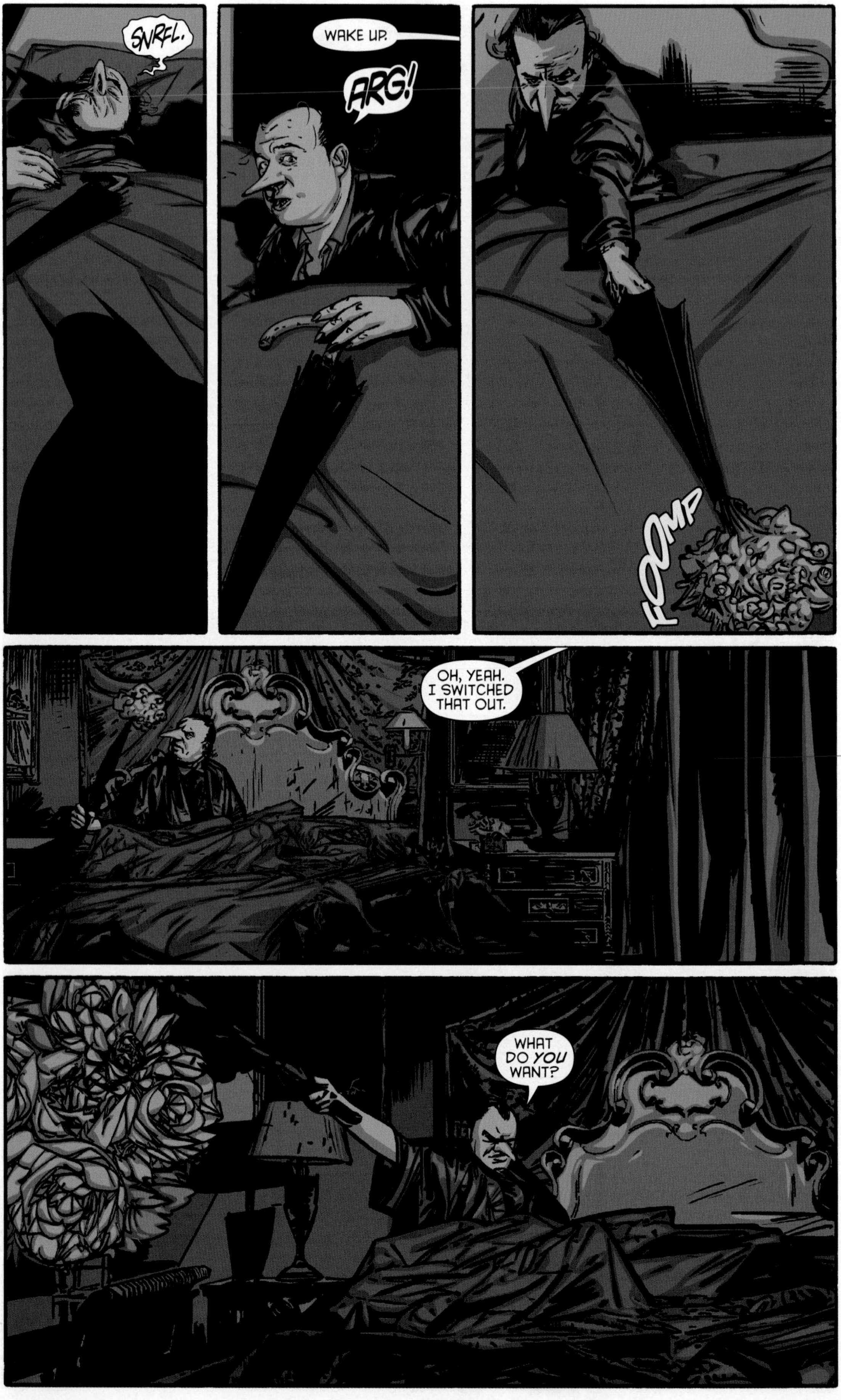
SNRFL.
WAKE UP.
ARG!
FOOMP
OH, YEAH. I SWITCHED THAT OUT.
WHAT DO *YOU* WANT?

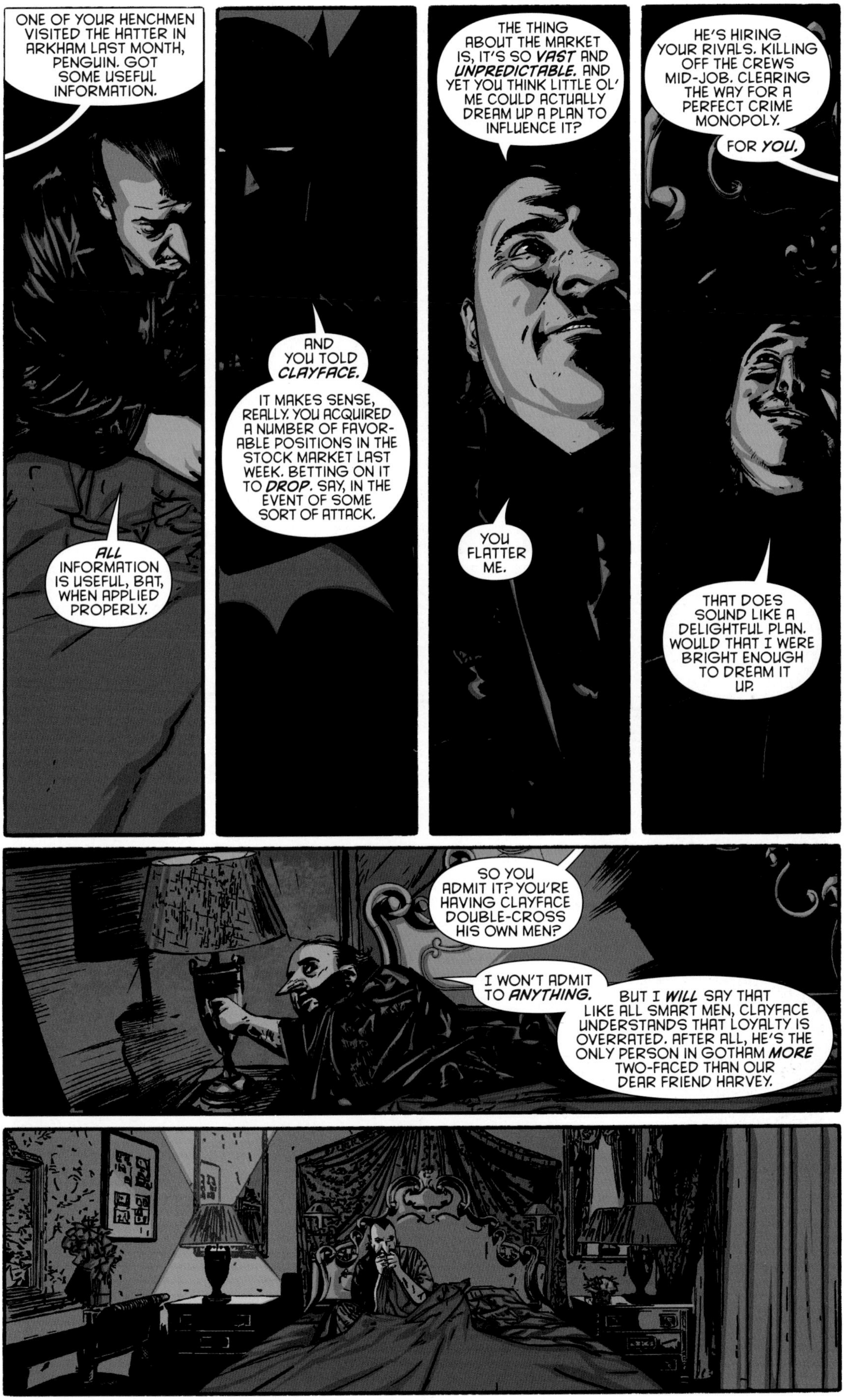
ONE OF YOUR HENCHMEN VISITED THE HATTER IN ARKHAM LAST MONTH, PENGUIN. GOT SOME USEFUL INFORMATION.
ALL INFORMATION IS USEFUL, BAT, WHEN APPLIED PROPERLY.
AND YOU TOLD CLAYFACE.
IT MAKES SENSE, REALLY. YOU ACQUIRED A NUMBER OF FAVOR-ABLE POSITIONS IN THE STOCK MARKET LAST WEEK. BETTING ON IT TO DROP. SAY, IN THE EVENT OF SOME SORT OF ATTACK.
THE THING ABOUT THE MARKET IS, IT'S SO VAST AND UNPREDICTABLE. AND YET YOU THINK LITTLE OL' ME COULD ACTUALLY DREAM UP A PLAN TO INFLUENCE IT?
YOU FLATTER ME.
HE'S HIRING YOUR RIVALS. KILLING OFF THE CREWS MID-JOB. CLEARING THE WAY FOR A PERFECT CRIME MONOPOLY.
FOR YOU.
THAT DOES SOUND LIKE A DELIGHTFUL PLAN. WOULD THAT I WERE BRIGHT ENOUGH TO DREAM IT UP.
SO YOU ADMIT IT? YOU'RE HAVING CLAYFACE DOUBLE-CROSS HIS OWN MEN?
I WON'T ADMIT TO ANYTHING.
BUT I WILL SAY THAT LIKE ALL SMART MEN, CLAYFACE UNDERSTANDS THAT LOYALTY IS OVERRATED. AFTER ALL, HE'S THE ONLY PERSON IN GOTHAM MORE TWO-FACED THAN OUR DEAR FRIEND HARVEY.

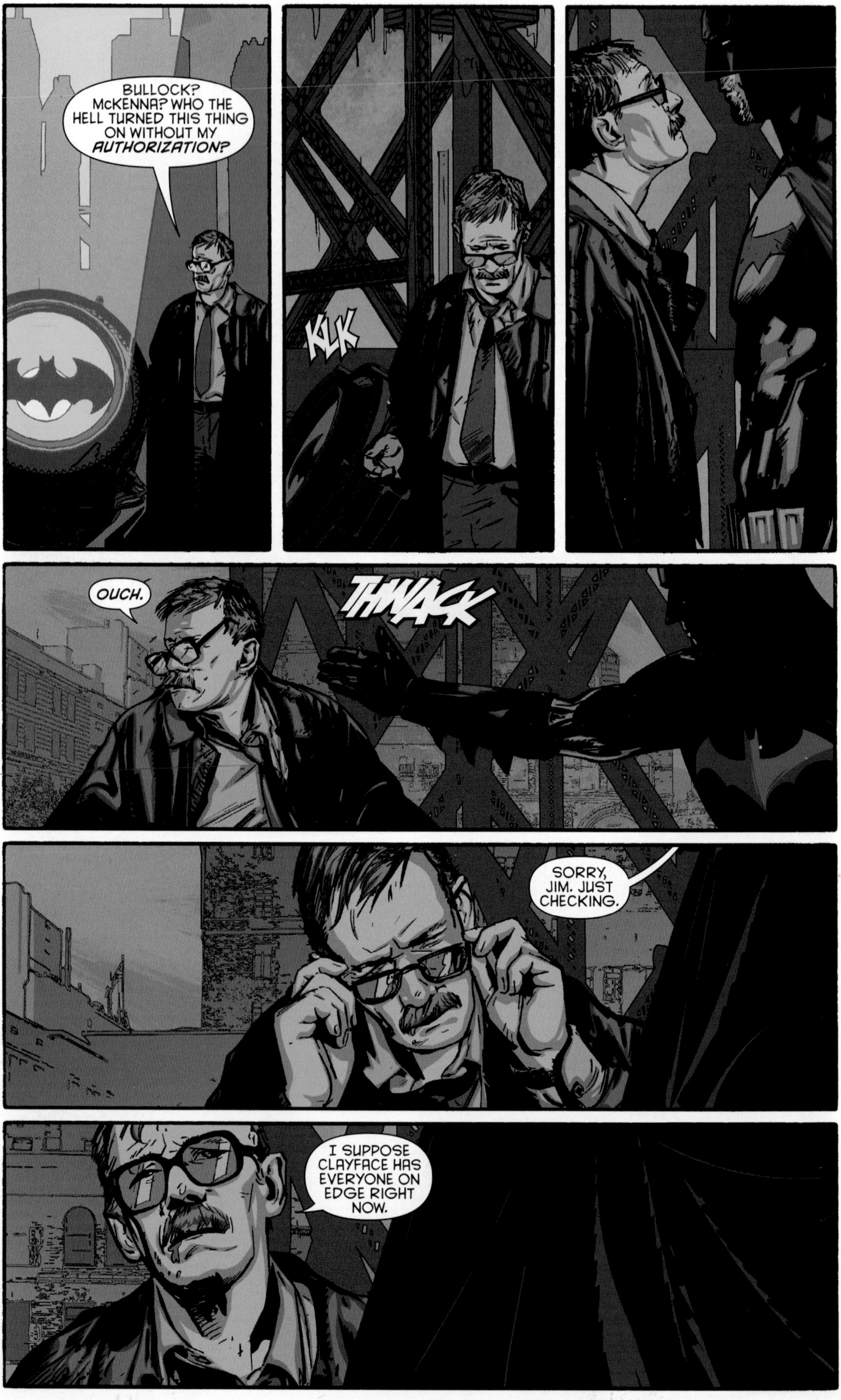
BULLOCK? McKENNA? WHO THE HELL TURNED THIS THING ON WITHOUT MY AUTHORIZATION?
KLIK
OUCH.
THWACK
SORRY, JIM. JUST CHECKING.
I SUPPOSE CLAYFACE HAS EVERYONE ON EDGE RIGHT NOW.

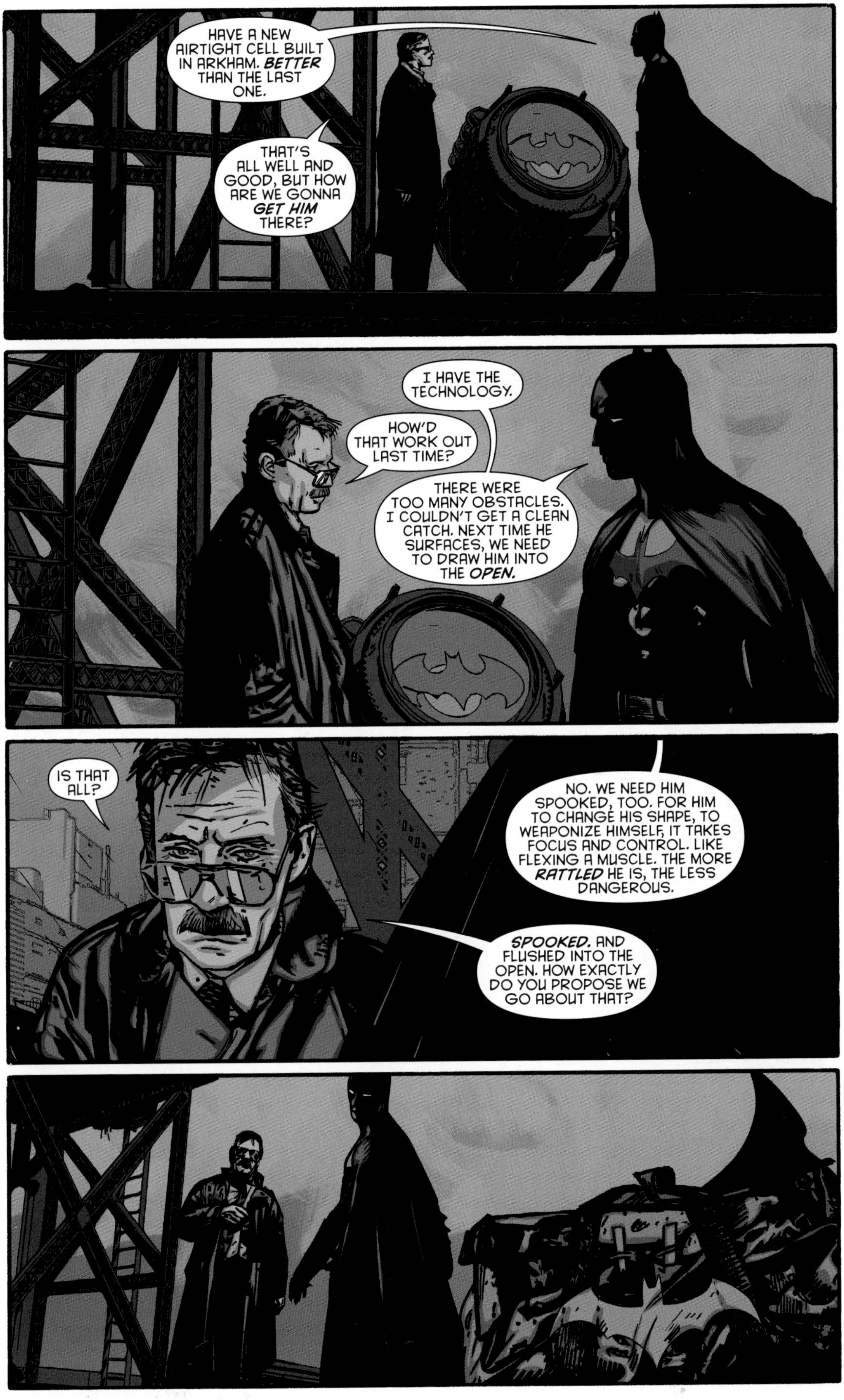
HAVE A NEW AIRTIGHT CELL BUILT IN ARKHAM. BETTER THAN THE LAST ONE.
THAT'S ALL WELL AND GOOD, BUT HOW ARE WE GONNA GET HIM THERE?
I HAVE THE TECHNOLOGY.
HOW'D THAT WORK OUT LAST TIME?
THERE WERE TOO MANY OBSTACLES. I COULDN'T GET A CLEAN CATCH. NEXT TIME HE SURFACES, WE NEED TO DRAW HIM INTO THE OPEN.
IS THAT ALL?
NO. WE NEED HIM SPOOKED, TOO. FOR HIM TO CHANGE HIS SHAPE, TO WEAPONIZE HIMSELF, IT TAKES FOCUS AND CONTROL. LIKE FLEXING A MUSCLE. THE MORE RATTLED HE IS, THE LESS DANGEROUS.
SPOOKED. AND FLUSHED INTO THE OPEN. HOW EXACTLY DO YOU PROPOSE WE GO ABOUT THAT?

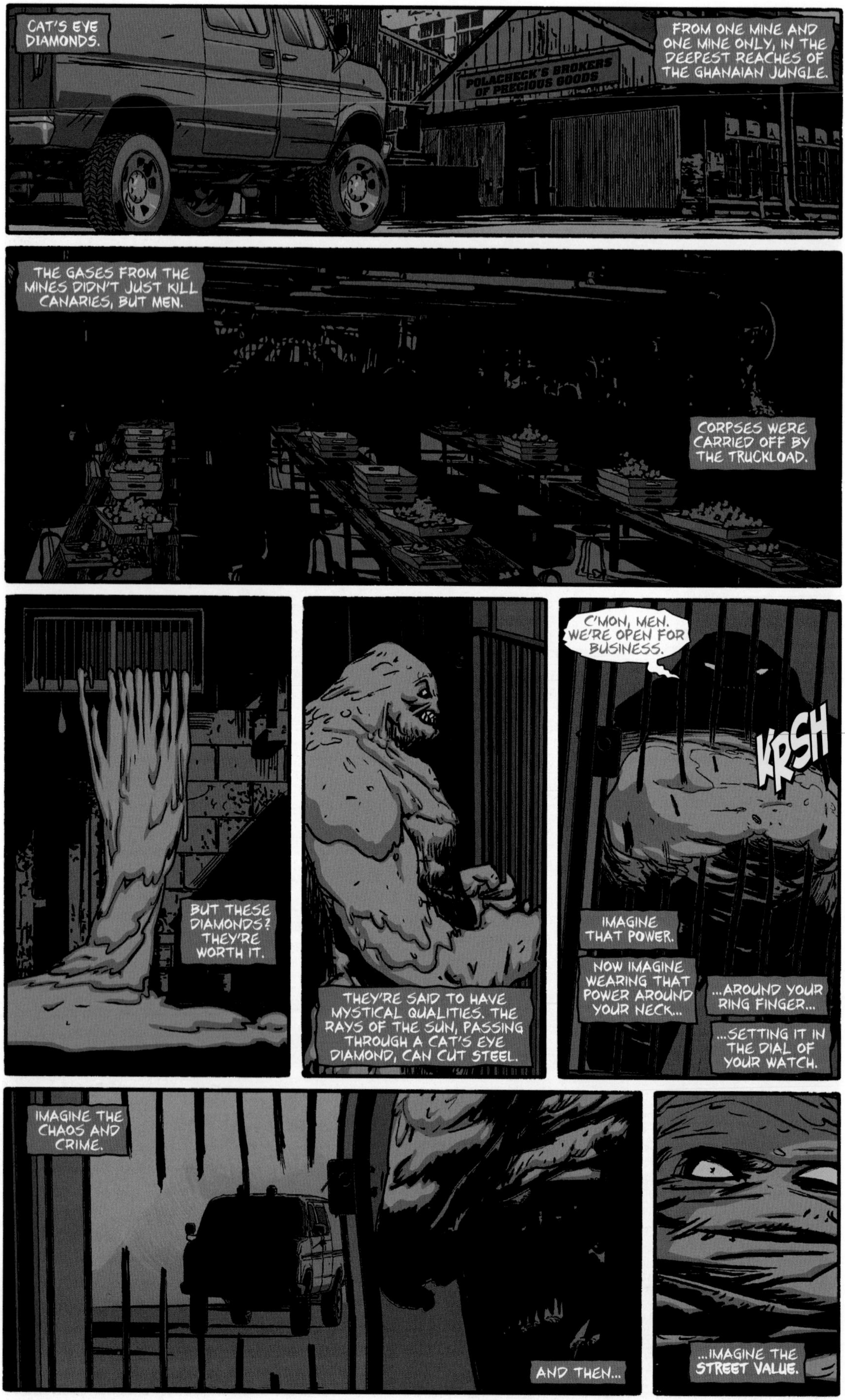
CAT'S EYE DIAMONDS.
POLACHECK'S BROKERS OF PRECIOUS GOODS
FROM ONE MINE AND ONE MINE ONLY, IN THE DEEPEST REACHES OF THE GHANAIAN JUNGLE.
THE GASES FROM THE MINES DIDN'T JUST KILL CANARIES, BUT MEN.
CORPSES WERE CARRIED OFF BY THE TRUCKLOAD.
BUT THESE DIAMONDS? THEY'RE WORTH IT.
THEY'RE SAID TO HAVE MYSTICAL QUALITIES. THE RAYS OF THE SUN, PASSING THROUGH A CAT'S EYE DIAMOND, CAN CUT STEEL.
C'MON, MEN. WE'RE OPEN FOR BUSINESS.
KRSH
IMAGINE THAT POWER.
NOW IMAGINE WEARING THAT POWER AROUND YOUR NECK...
...AROUND YOUR RING FINGER...
...SETTING IT IN THE DIAL OF YOUR WATCH.
IMAGINE THE CHAOS AND CRIME.
AND THEN...
...IMAGINE THE STREET VALUE.

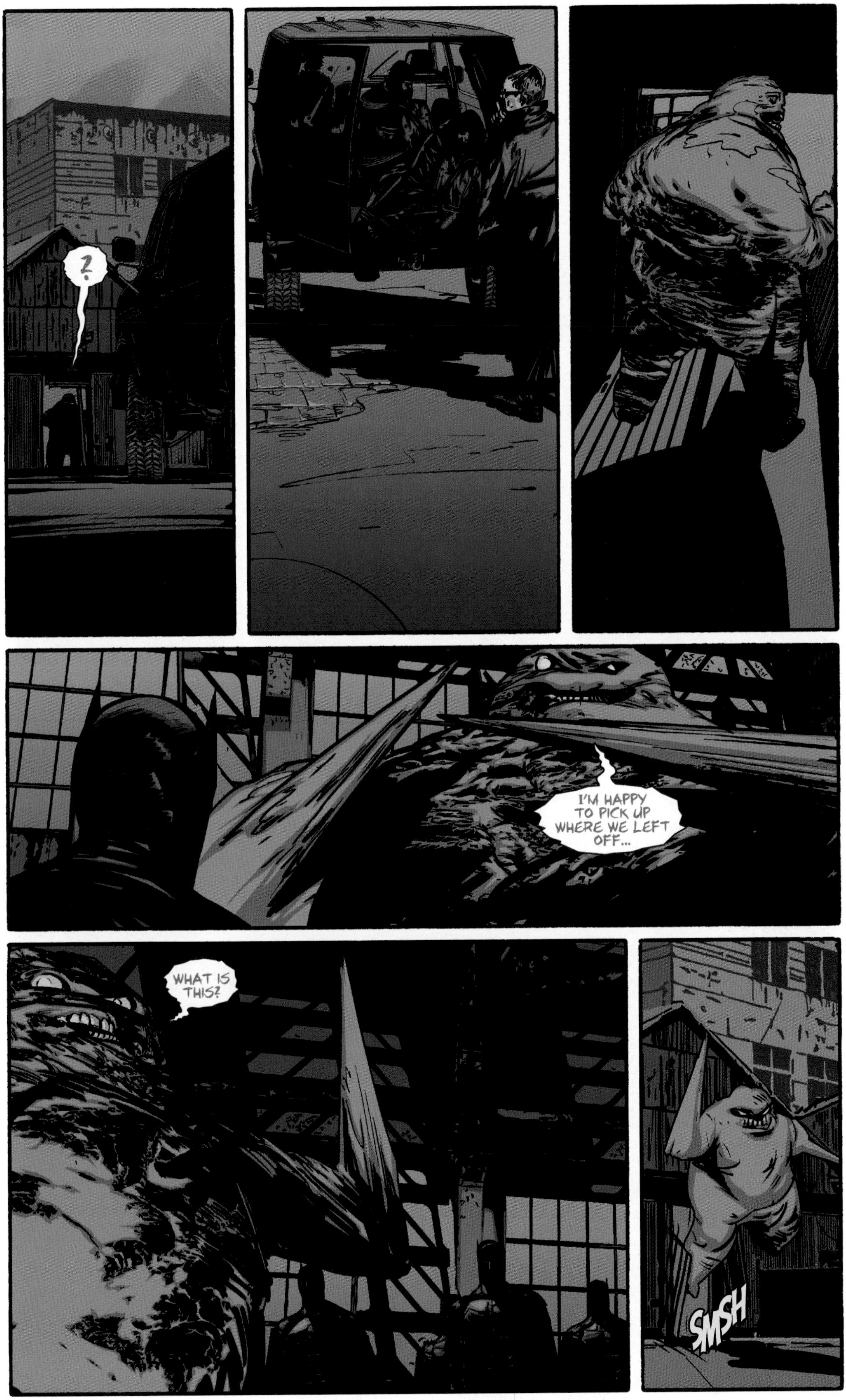
?
I'M HAPPY TO PICK UP WHERE WE LEFT OFF...
WHAT IS THIS?
SMSH

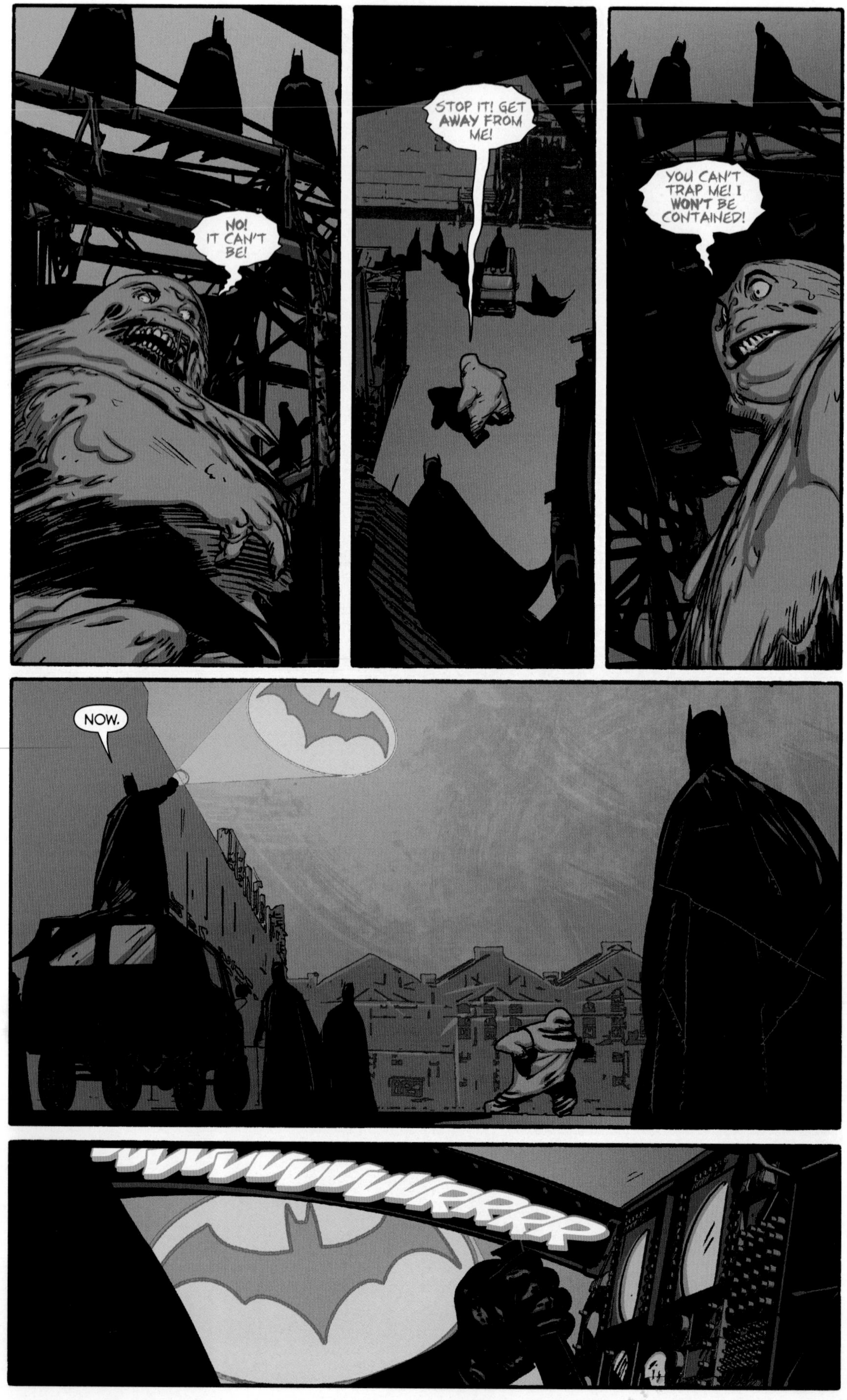
NO! IT CAN'T BE!
STOP IT! GET AWAY FROM ME!
YOU CAN'T TRAP ME! I WON'T BE CONTAINED!
NOW.
VVVVVVVVVVVRRRRR

VVVVVVVVRRRRR

THIS MIGHT ACTUALLY WORK.

SIX STAKEOUTS LATER...

SHWWIP

RAAARGH!

JJJJJTT

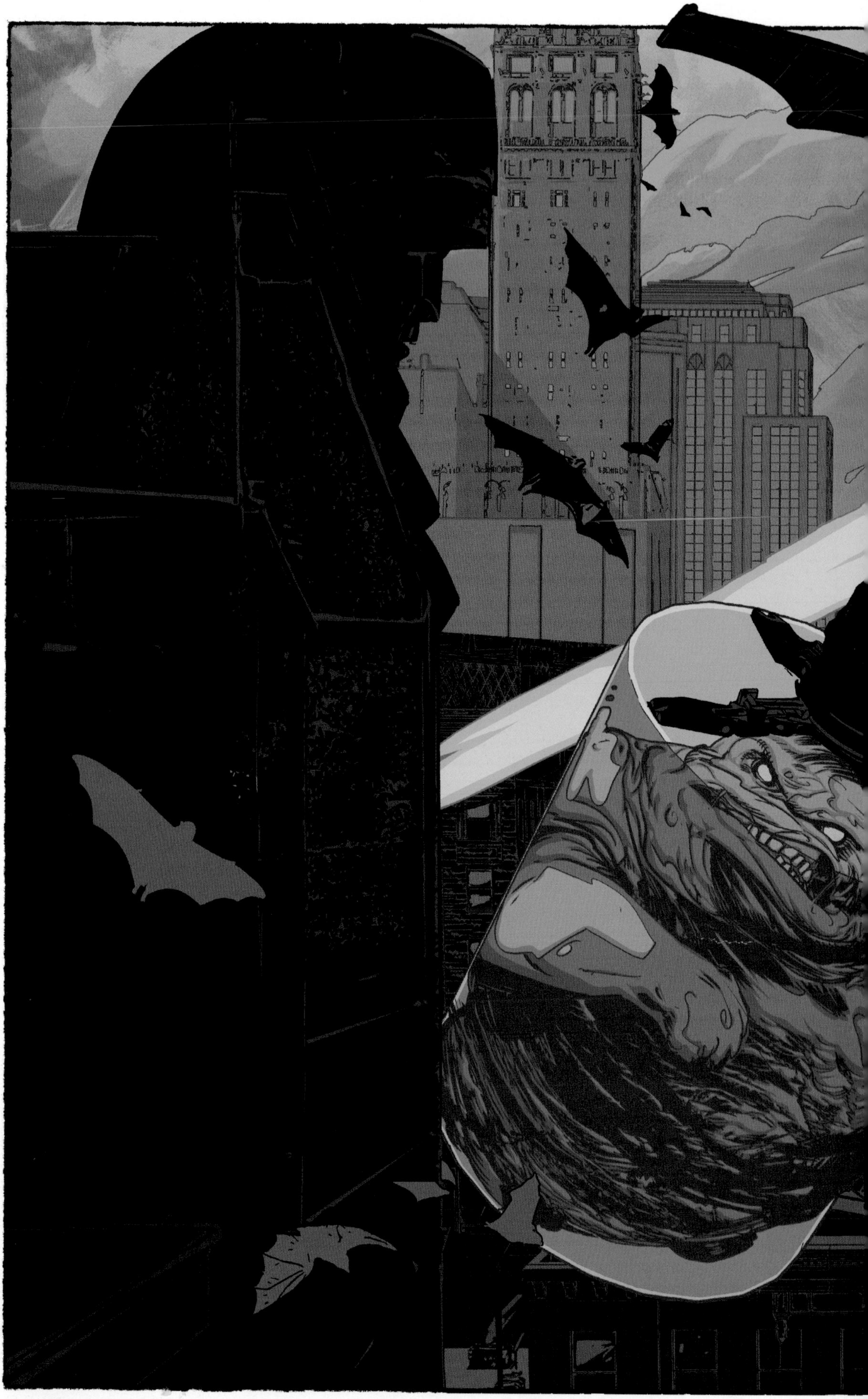

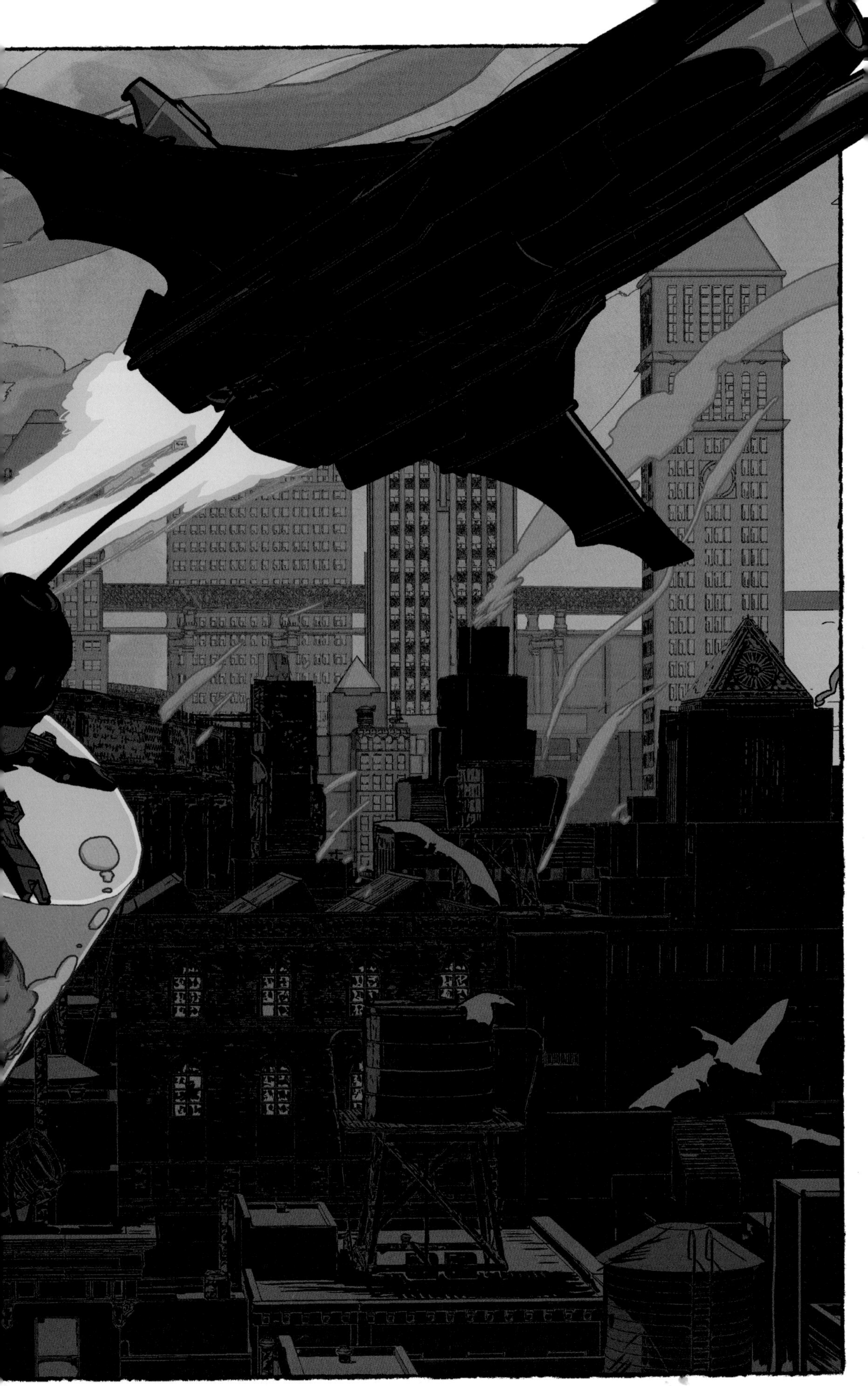

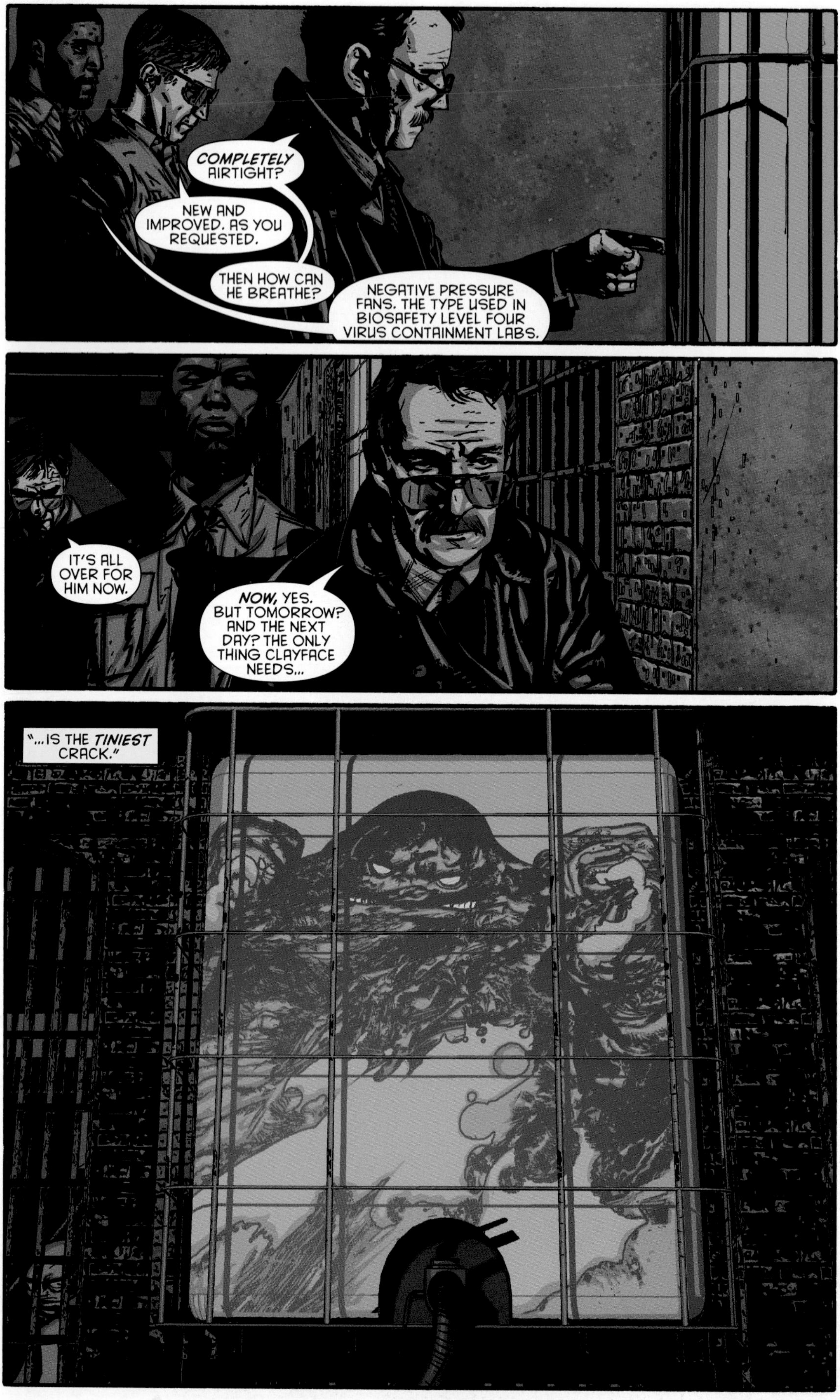
COMPLETELY AIRTIGHT?
NEW AND IMPROVED. AS YOU REQUESTED.
THEN HOW CAN HE BREATHE?
NEGATIVE PRESSURE FANS. THE TYPE USED IN BIOSAFETY LEVEL FOUR VIRUS CONTAINMENT LABS.
IT'S ALL OVER FOR HIM NOW.
NOW, YES. BUT TOMORROW? AND THE NEXT DAY? THE ONLY THING CLAYFACE NEEDS...
"...IS THE TINIEST CRACK."

CAPTIVE AUDIENCE
ALEX MALEEV artist & cover

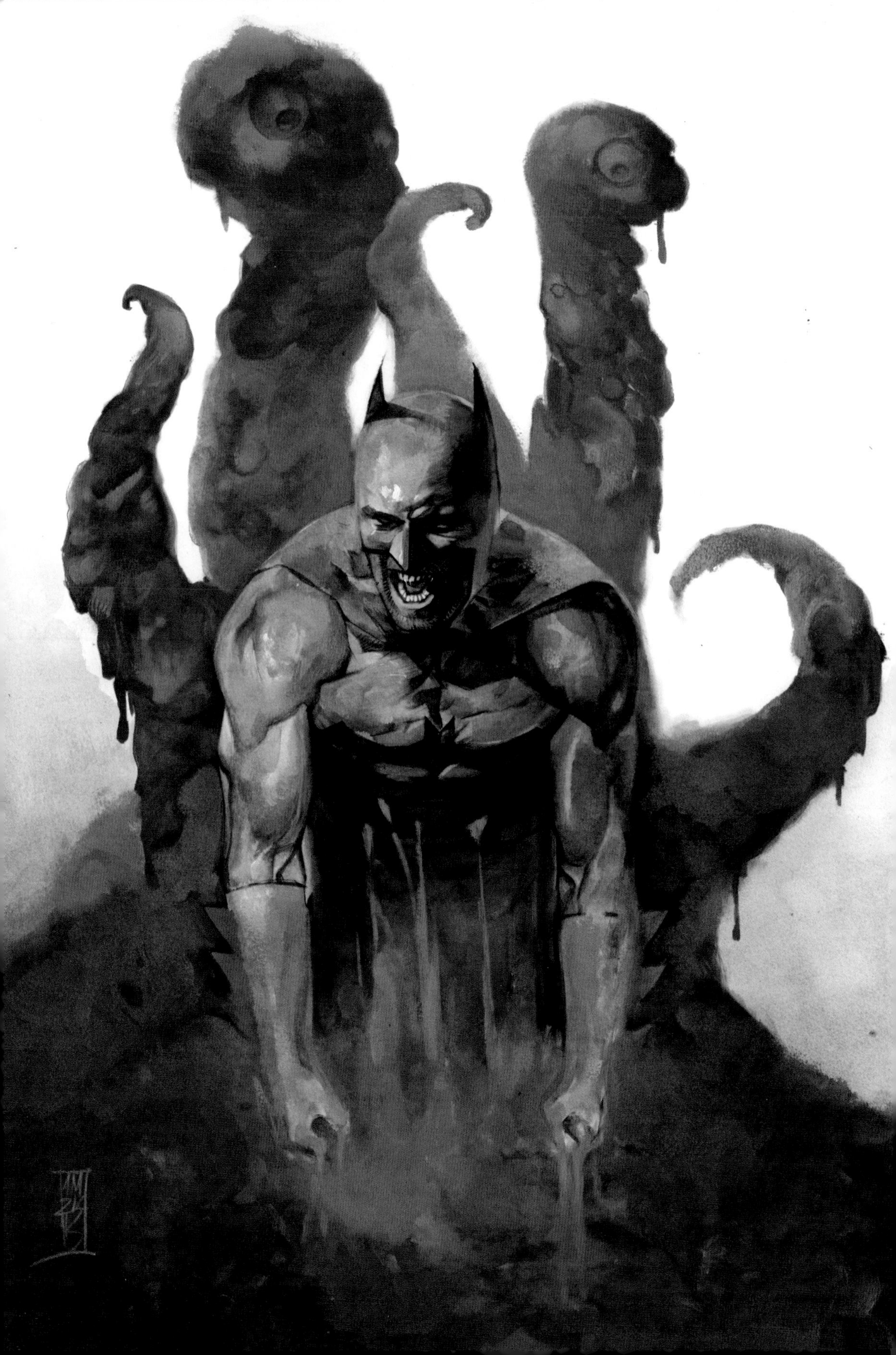

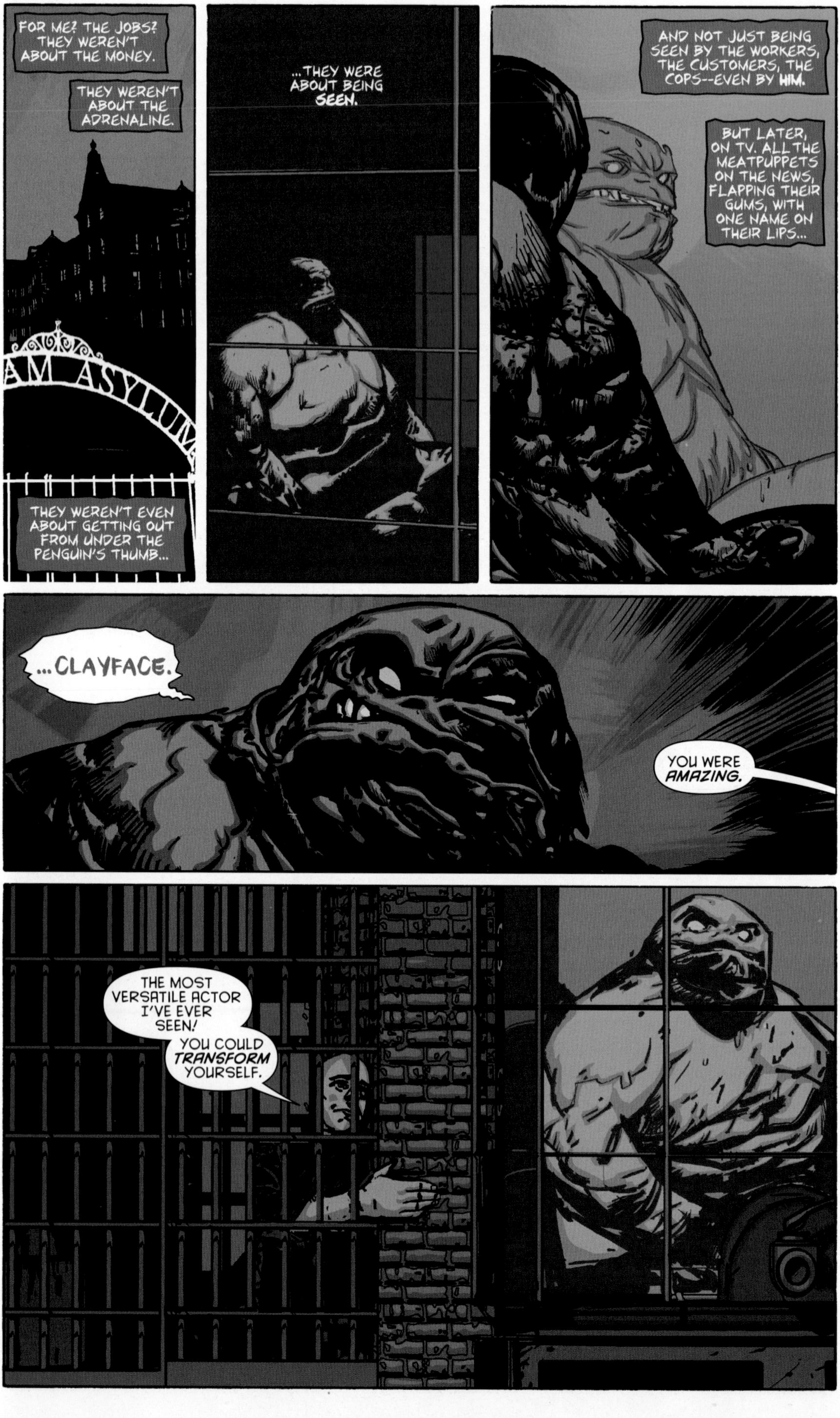
FOR ME? THE JOBS? THEY WEREN'T ABOUT THE MONEY.
THEY WEREN'T ABOUT THE ADRENALINE.
AM ASYLUM
THEY WEREN'T EVEN ABOUT GETTING OUT FROM UNDER THE PENGUIN'S THUMB...
...THEY WERE ABOUT BEING SEEN.
AND NOT JUST BEING SEEN BY THE WORKERS, THE CUSTOMERS, THE COPS--EVEN BY HIM.
BUT LATER, ON TV. ALL THE MEATPUPPETS ON THE NEWS, FLAPPING THEIR GUMS, WITH ONE NAME ON THEIR LIPS...
...CLAYFACE.
YOU WERE AMAZING.
THE MOST VERSATILE ACTOR I'VE EVER SEEN!
YOU COULD TRANSFORM YOURSELF.

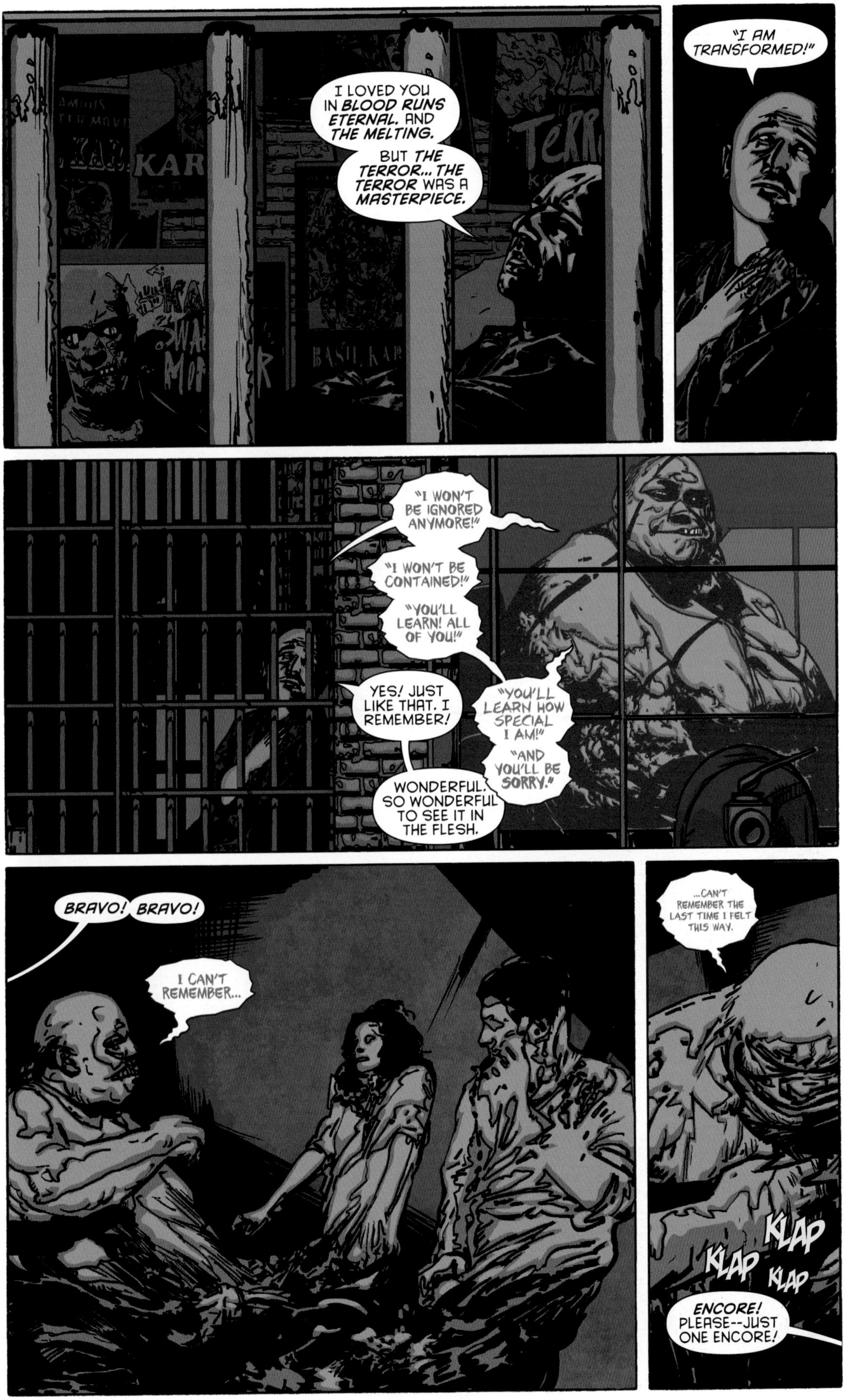
I LOVED YOU IN BLOOD RUNS ETERNAL. AND THE MELTING.
BUT THE TERROR... THE TERROR WAS A MASTERPIECE.
"I AM TRANSFORMED!"
"I WON'T BE IGNORED ANYMORE!"
"I WON'T BE CONTAINED!"
"YOU'LL LEARN! ALL OF YOU!"
"YOU'LL LEARN HOW SPECIAL I AM!"
"AND YOU'LL BE SORRY."
YES! JUST LIKE THAT. I REMEMBER!
WONDERFUL. SO WONDERFUL TO SEE IT IN THE FLESH.
BRAVO! BRAVO!
I CAN'T REMEMBER...
...CAN'T REMEMBER THE LAST TIME I FELT THIS WAY.
KLAP KLAP KLAP
ENCORE! PLEASE--JUST ONE ENCORE!

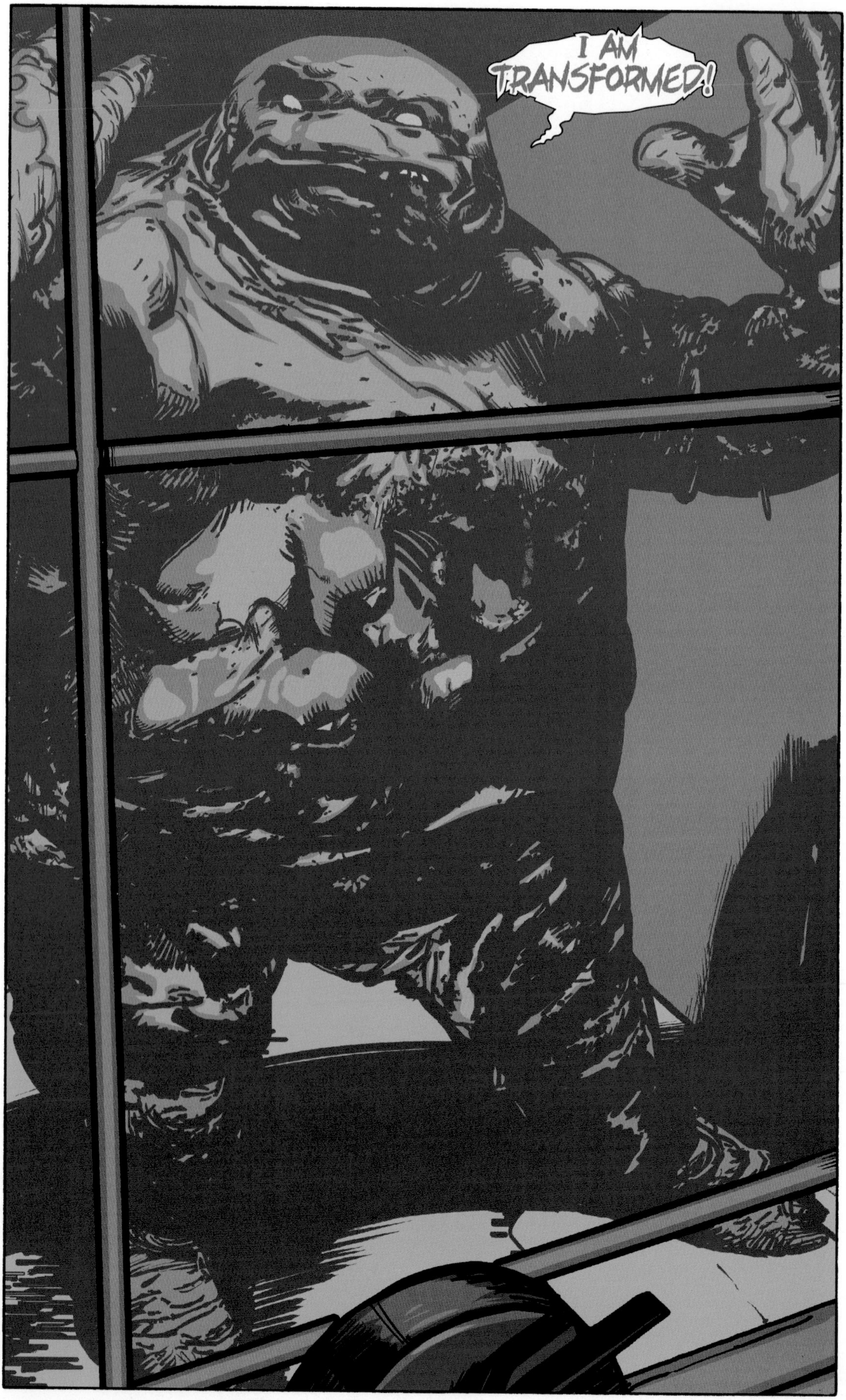
I AM TRANSFORMED!

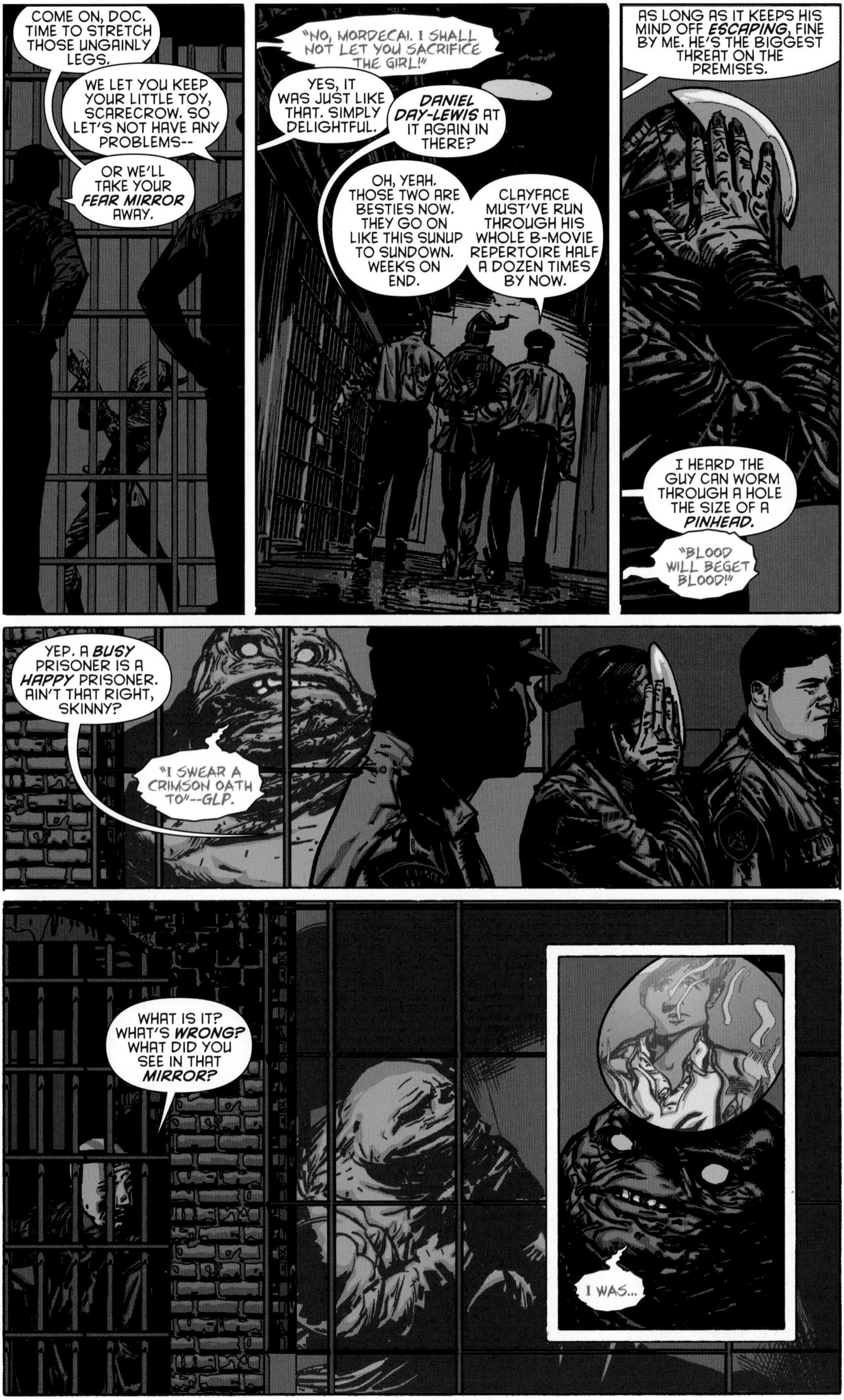

COME ON, DOC. TIME TO STRETCH THOSE UNGAINLY LEGS.
WE LET YOU KEEP YOUR LITTLE TOY, SCARECROW. SO LET'S NOT HAVE ANY PROBLEMS--
OR WE'LL TAKE YOUR FEAR MIRROR AWAY.
"NO, MORDECAI. I SHALL NOT LET YOU SACRIFICE THE GIRL!"
YES, IT WAS JUST LIKE THAT. SIMPLY DELIGHTFUL.
DANIEL DAY-LEWIS AT IT AGAIN IN THERE?
OH, YEAH. THOSE TWO ARE BESTIES NOW. THEY GO ON LIKE THIS SUNUP TO SUNDOWN. WEEKS ON END.
CLAYFACE MUST'VE RUN THROUGH HIS WHOLE B-MOVIE REPERTOIRE HALF A DOZEN TIMES BY NOW.
AS LONG AS IT KEEPS HIS MIND OFF ESCAPING, FINE BY ME. HE'S THE BIGGEST THREAT ON THE PREMISES.
I HEARD THE GUY CAN WORM THROUGH A HOLE THE SIZE OF A PINHEAD.
"BLOOD WILL BEGET BLOOD!"
YEP. A BUSY PRISONER IS A HAPPY PRISONER. AIN'T THAT RIGHT, SKINNY?
"I SWEAR A CRIMSON OATH TO"--GLP.
WHAT IS IT? WHAT'S WRONG? WHAT DID YOU SEE IN THAT MIRROR?
I WAS...

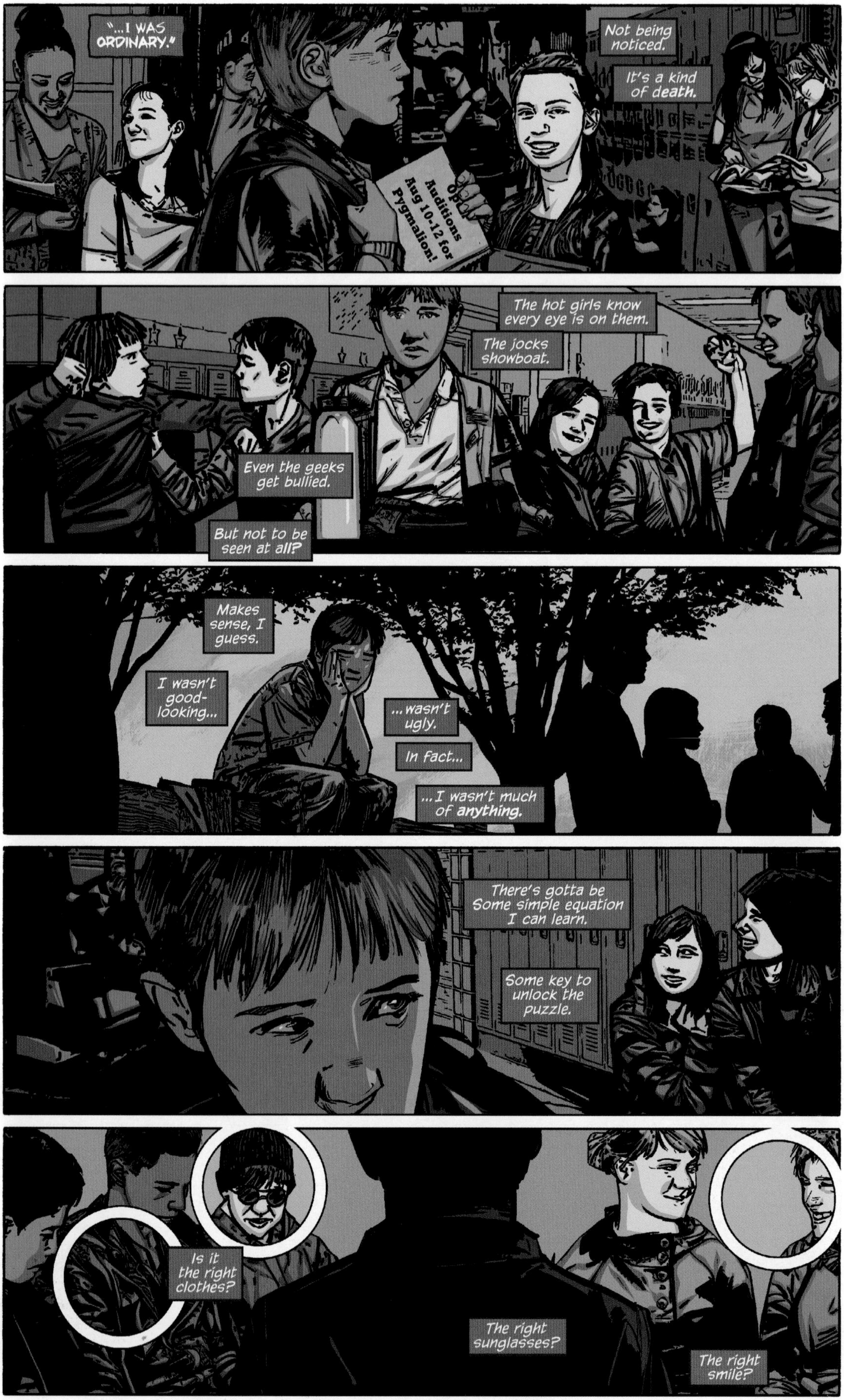
"...I WAS ORDINARY."
Op
Auditions
Aug 10-12 for
Pygmalion!
Not being noticed.
It's a kind of death.
The hot girls know every eye is on them.
The jocks showboat.
Even the geeks get bullied.
But not to be seen at all?
Makes sense, I guess.
I wasn't good-looking...
...wasn't ugly.
In fact...
...I wasn't much of anything.
There's gotta be Some simple equation I can learn.
Some key to unlock the puzzle.
Is it the right clothes?
The right sunglasses?
The right smile?

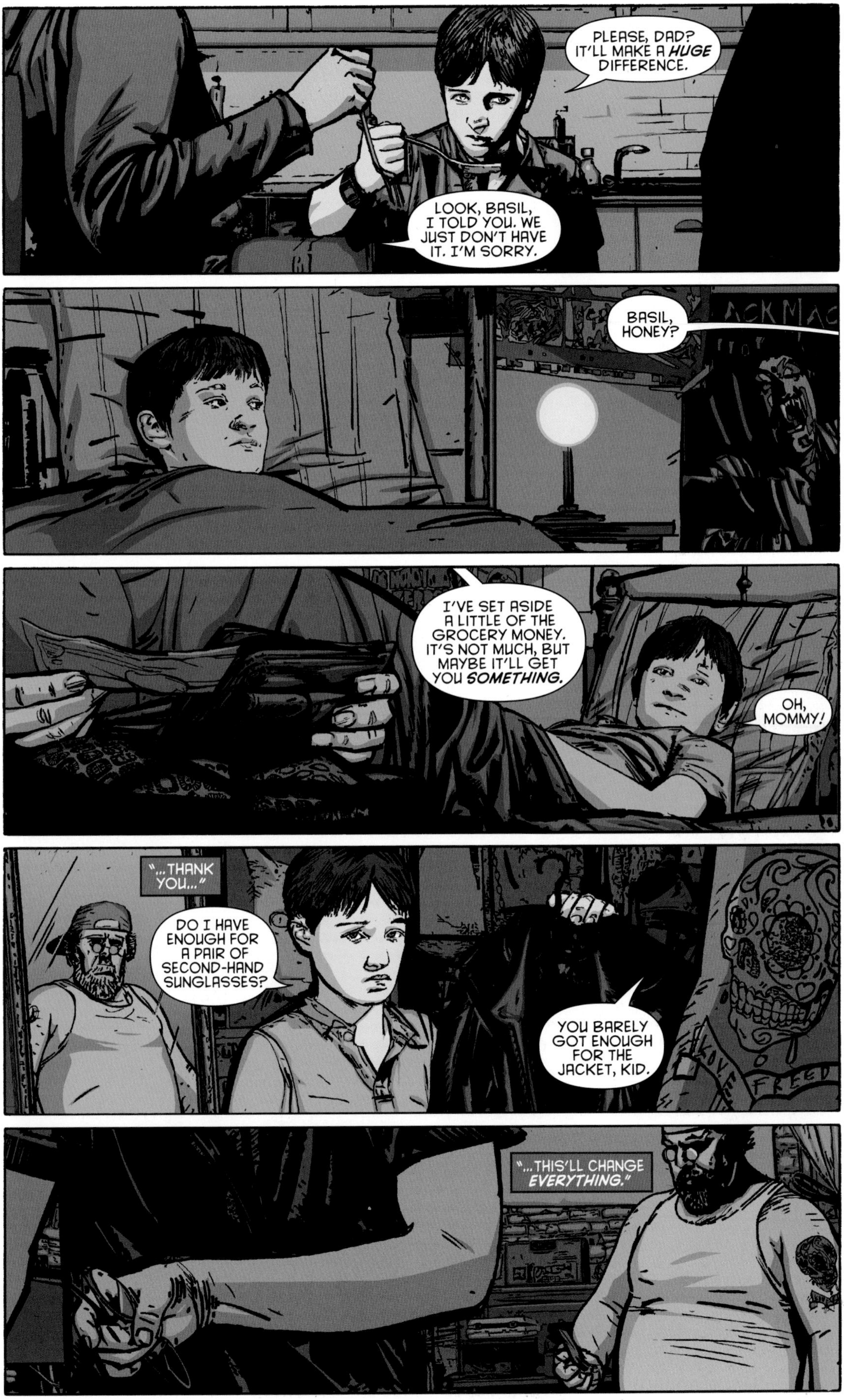
PLEASE, DAD? IT'LL MAKE A *HUGE* DIFFERENCE.
LOOK, BASIL, I TOLD YOU. WE JUST DON'T HAVE IT. I'M SORRY.
BASIL, HONEY?
I'VE SET ASIDE A LITTLE OF THE GROCERY MONEY. IT'S NOT MUCH, BUT MAYBE IT'LL GET YOU *SOMETHING.*
OH, MOMMY!
"...THANK YOU..."
DO I HAVE ENOUGH FOR A PAIR OF SECOND-HAND SUNGLASSES?
YOU BARELY GOT ENOUGH FOR THE JACKET, KID.
"...THIS'LL CHANGE *EVERYTHING.*"

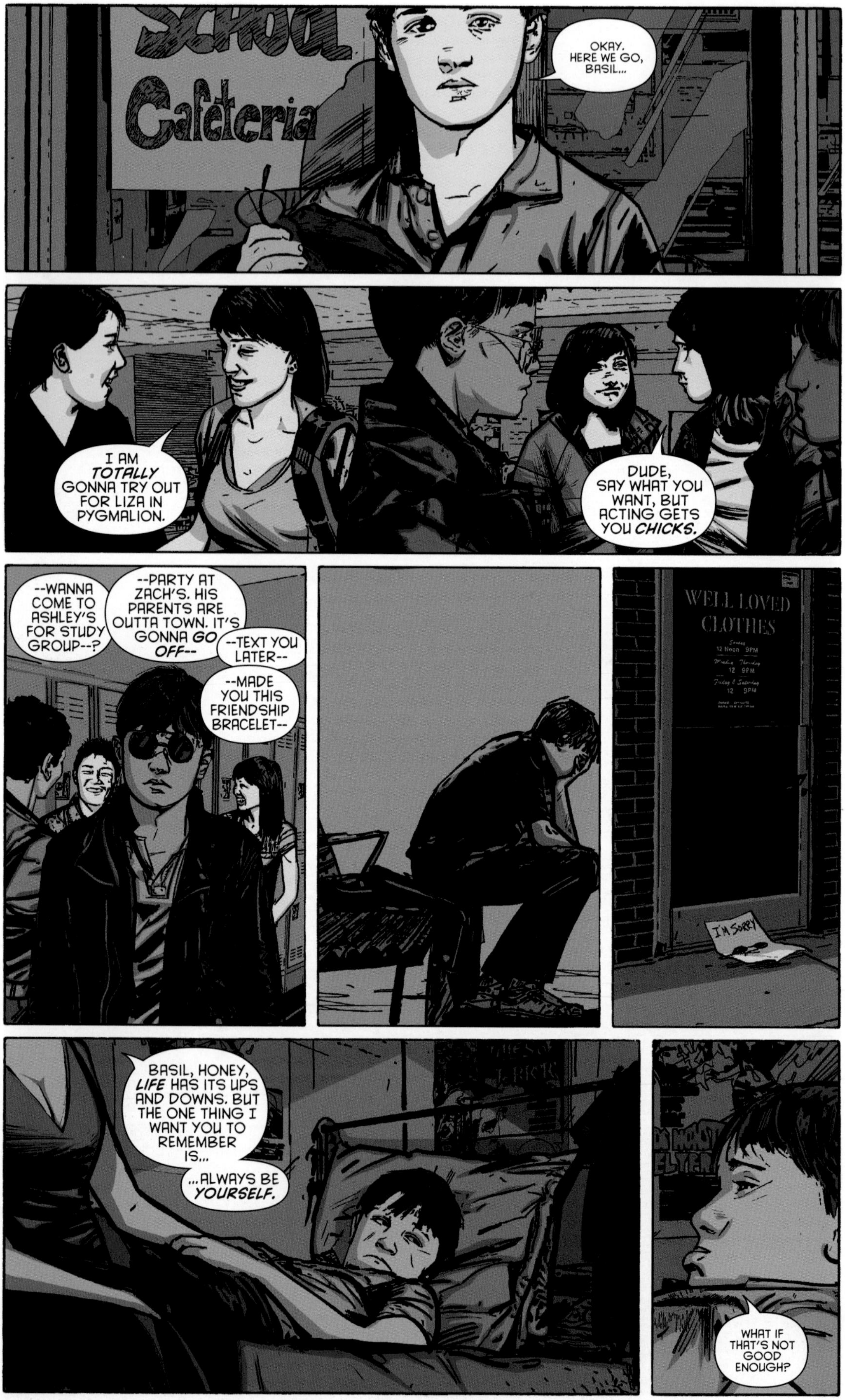
SCHOOL
Cafeteria
OKAY. HERE WE GO, BASIL...
I AM *TOTALLY* GONNA TRY OUT FOR LIZA IN PYGMALION.
DUDE, SAY WHAT YOU WANT, BUT ACTING GETS YOU *CHICKS*.
--WANNA COME TO ASHLEY'S FOR STUDY GROUP--?
--PARTY AT ZACH'S. HIS PARENTS ARE OUTTA TOWN. IT'S GONNA *GO OFF*--
--TEXT YOU LATER--
--MADE YOU THIS FRIENDSHIP BRACELET--
WELL LOVED CLOTHES
I'M SORRY
BASIL, HONEY, *LIFE* HAS ITS UPS AND DOWNS. BUT THE ONE THING I WANT YOU TO REMEMBER IS...
...ALWAYS BE *YOURSELF*.
WHAT IF THAT'S NOT GOOD ENOUGH?

AUDITIONS
TODAY!!!

*I won't
be ignored
anymore.*

*I won't be
contained.*

NEXT!

COME ON,
NOW. WE HAVE
A HALF MILE OF
KIDS TO SEE.

AHEM.

*You'll
learn.*

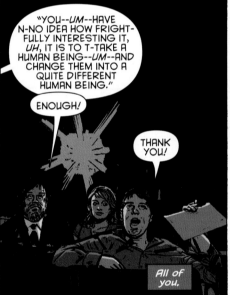

"YOU--*UM*--HAVE
N-NO IDEA HOW FRIGHT-
FULLY INTERESTING IT,
UH, IT IS TO T-TAKE A
HUMAN BEING--*UM*--AND
CHANGE THEM INTO A
QUITE DIFFERENT
HUMAN BEING."

ENOUGH!

THANK
YOU!

*All of
you.*

I'M SORRY. I
CAN DO BETTER.
JUST GIVE ME
ONE CHANCE
TO--

LOOK, KID,
YOU'RE JUST NOT...
INTERESTING.

*You'll learn how
special I am.*

I'M
SORRY--
THERE'S
JUST NOTHING
SPECIAL ABOUT
YOU.

*And you'll
be sorry.*

"ONCE THE PORTAL HAS OPENED, MY LOVELY, THERE'S NO TELLING WHAT WILL POUR FORTH!"

THAT'S ENOUGH. THANK YOU.

I caught word that there was a magic man in Gotham...

BASIL, LOOK...

...YOU'RE IN HERE ALL THE TIME. AND I'D BE REMISS NOT TO TELL YOU...

...a man who could get anything you wanted...

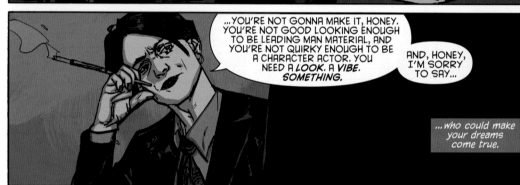

...YOU'RE NOT GONNA MAKE IT, HONEY. YOU'RE NOT GOOD LOOKING ENOUGH TO BE LEADING MAN MATERIAL, AND YOU'RE NOT QUIRKY ENOUGH TO BE A CHARACTER ACTOR. YOU NEED A *LOOK*. A *VIBE*. *SOMETHING*.

AND, HONEY, I'M SORRY TO SAY...

...who could make your dreams come true.

"...YOU DON'T HAVE IT."

A devil of flesh and blood, ready to make a deal. Which was good.

Because I was ready, too...

EXCUSE ME, SIR?

...ready to do anything.

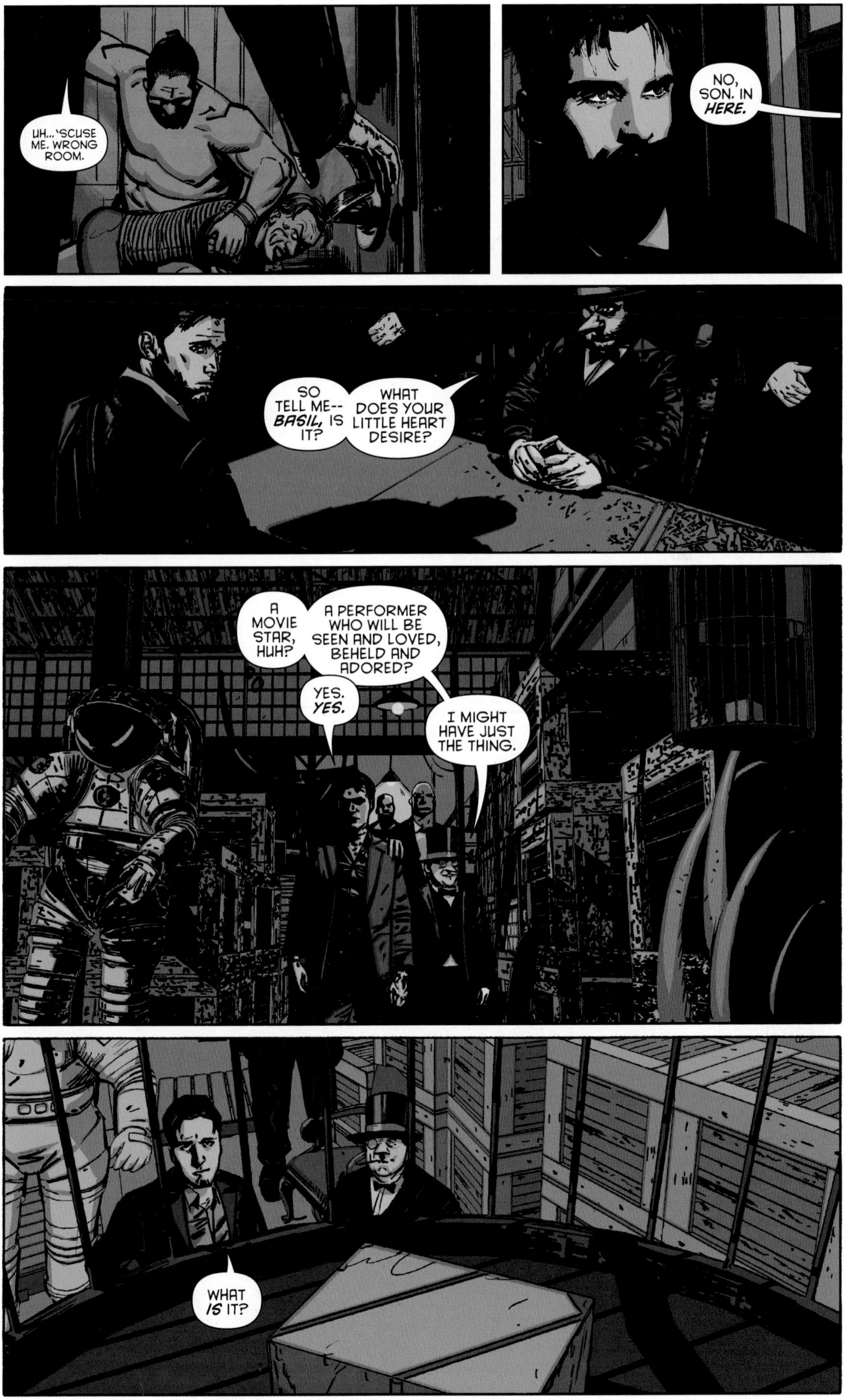
UH...'SCUSE ME. WRONG ROOM.
NO, SON. IN *HERE.*
SO TELL ME-- *BASIL,* IS IT?
WHAT DOES YOUR LITTLE HEART DESIRE?
A MOVIE STAR, HUH?
A PERFORMER WHO WILL BE SEEN AND LOVED, BEHELD AND ADORED?
YES. *YES.*
I MIGHT HAVE JUST THE THING.
WHAT *IS* IT?

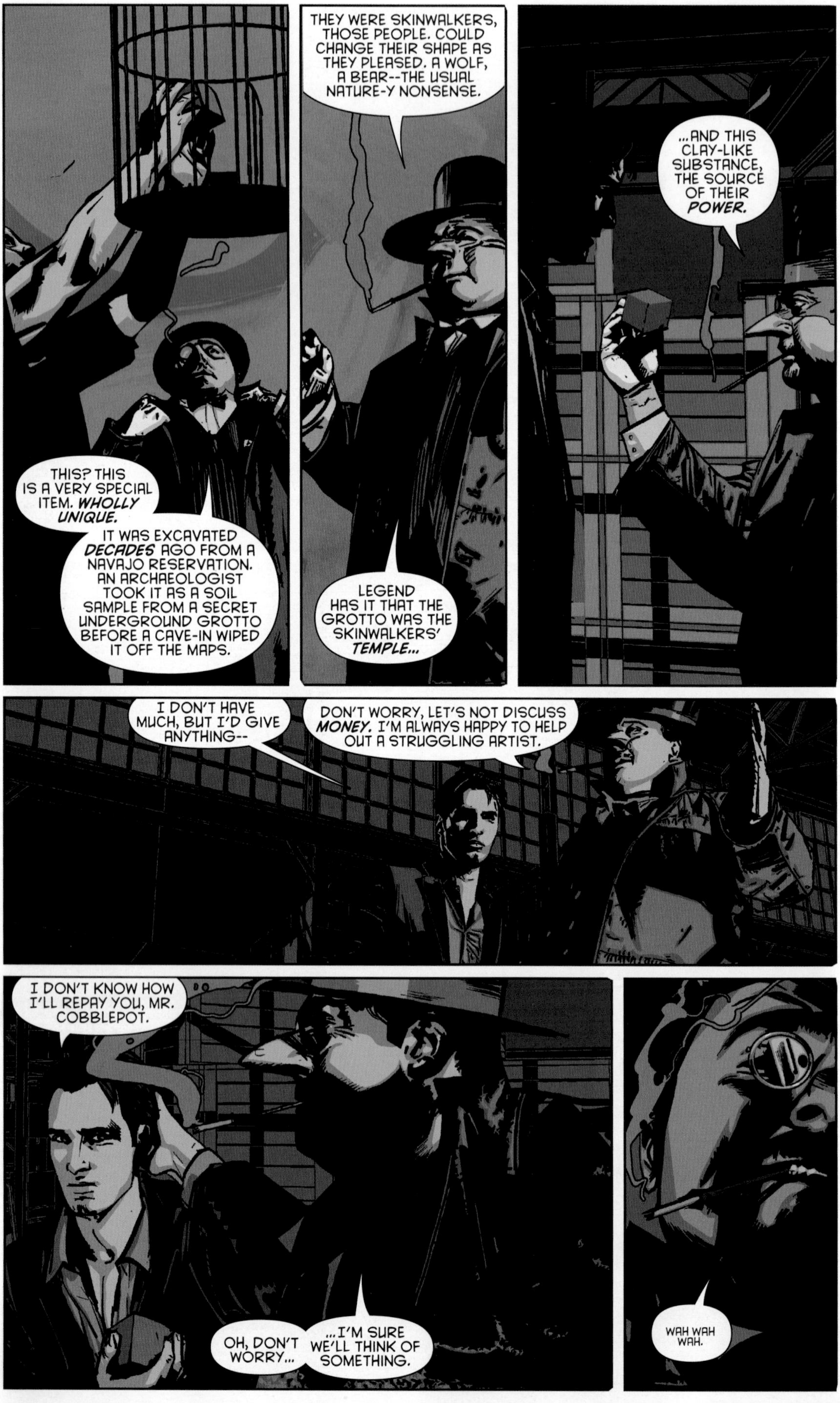
THIS? THIS IS A VERY SPECIAL ITEM. *WHOLLY UNIQUE.*
IT WAS EXCAVATED *DECADES* AGO FROM A NAVAJO RESERVATION. AN ARCHAEOLOGIST TOOK IT AS A SOIL SAMPLE FROM A SECRET UNDERGROUND GROTTO BEFORE A CAVE-IN WIPED IT OFF THE MAPS.
THEY WERE SKINWALKERS, THOSE PEOPLE. COULD CHANGE THEIR SHAPE AS THEY PLEASED. A WOLF, A BEAR--THE USUAL NATURE-Y NONSENSE.
LEGEND HAS IT THAT THE GROTTO WAS THE SKINWALKERS' *TEMPLE...*
...AND THIS CLAY-LIKE SUBSTANCE, THE SOURCE OF THEIR *POWER.*
I DON'T HAVE MUCH, BUT I'D GIVE ANYTHING--
DON'T WORRY, LET'S NOT DISCUSS *MONEY.* I'M ALWAYS HAPPY TO HELP OUT A STRUGGLING ARTIST.
I DON'T KNOW HOW I'LL REPAY YOU, MR. COBBLEPOT.
OH, DON'T WORRY...
...I'M SURE WE'LL THINK OF SOMETHING.
WAH WAH WAH.

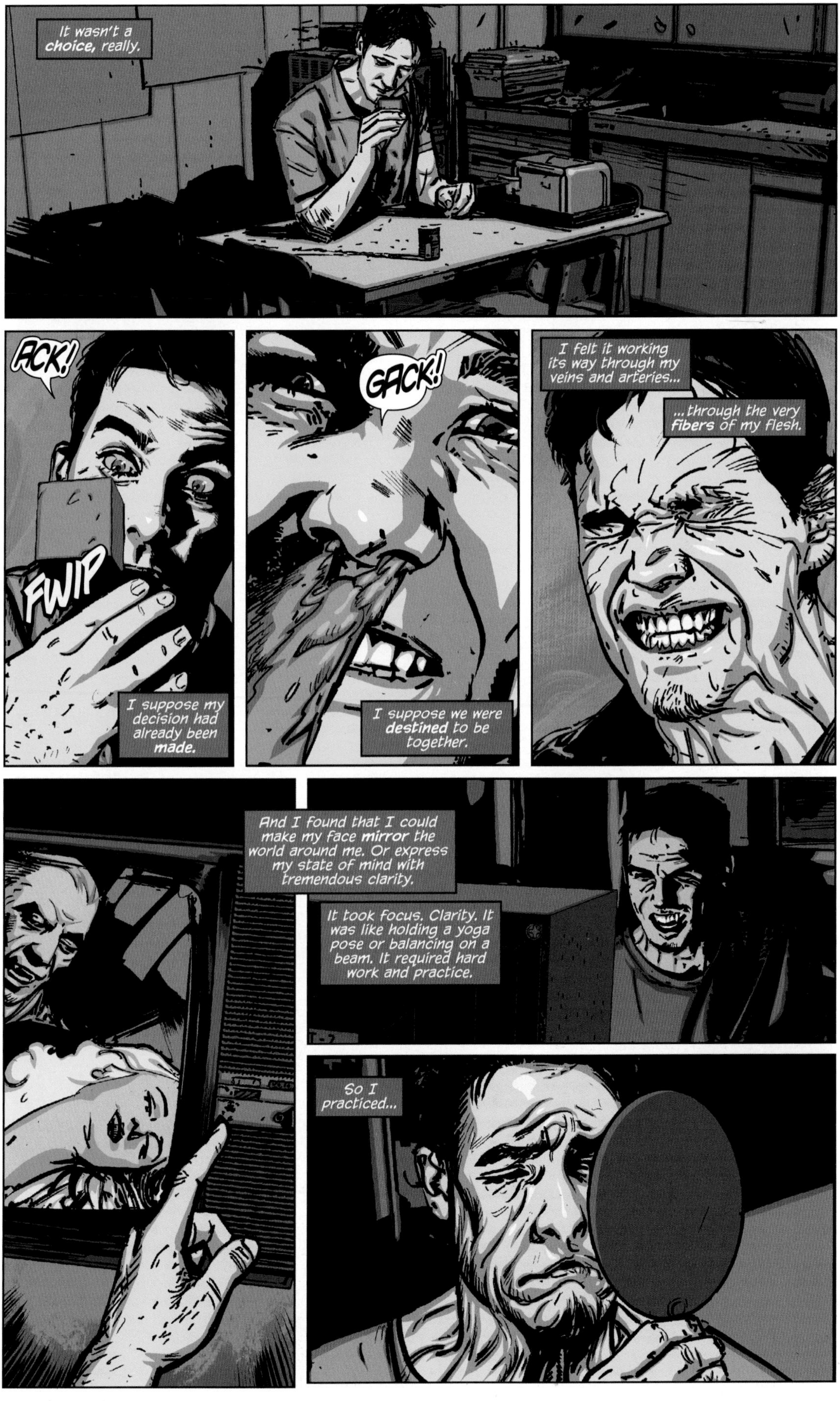
It wasn't a choice, really.
ACK!
FWIP
I suppose my decision had already been made.
GACK!
I suppose we were destined to be together.
I felt it working its way through my veins and arteries...
...through the very fibers of my flesh.
And I found that I could make my face mirror the world around me. Or express my state of mind with tremendous clarity.
It took focus. Clarity. It was like holding a yoga pose or balancing on a beam. It required hard work and practice.
So I practiced...

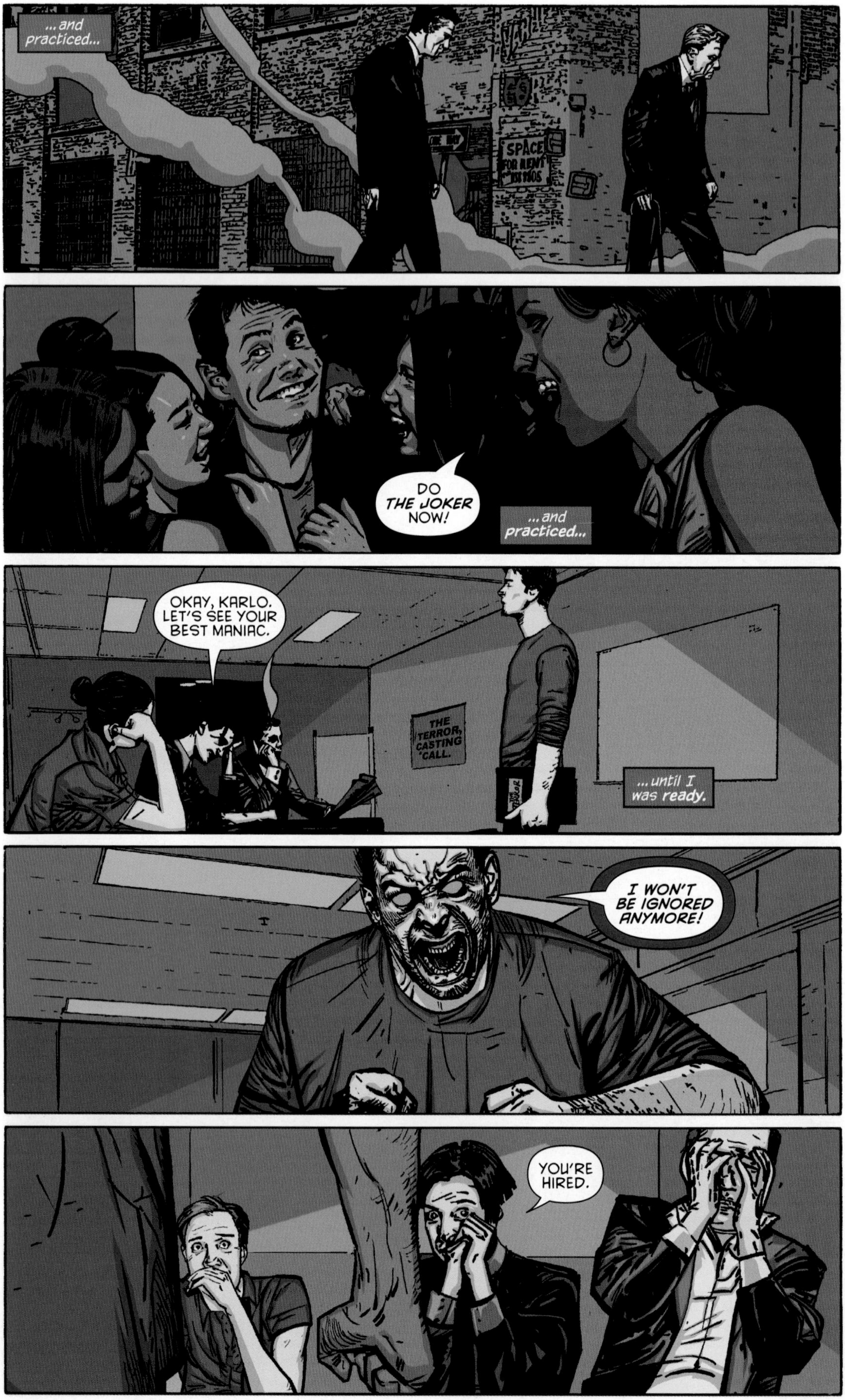
...and practiced...
DO THE JOKER NOW!
...and practiced...
OKAY, KARLO. LET'S SEE YOUR BEST MANIAC.
THE TERROR, CASTING CALL.
...until I was ready.
I WON'T BE IGNORED ANYMORE!
YOU'RE HIRED.

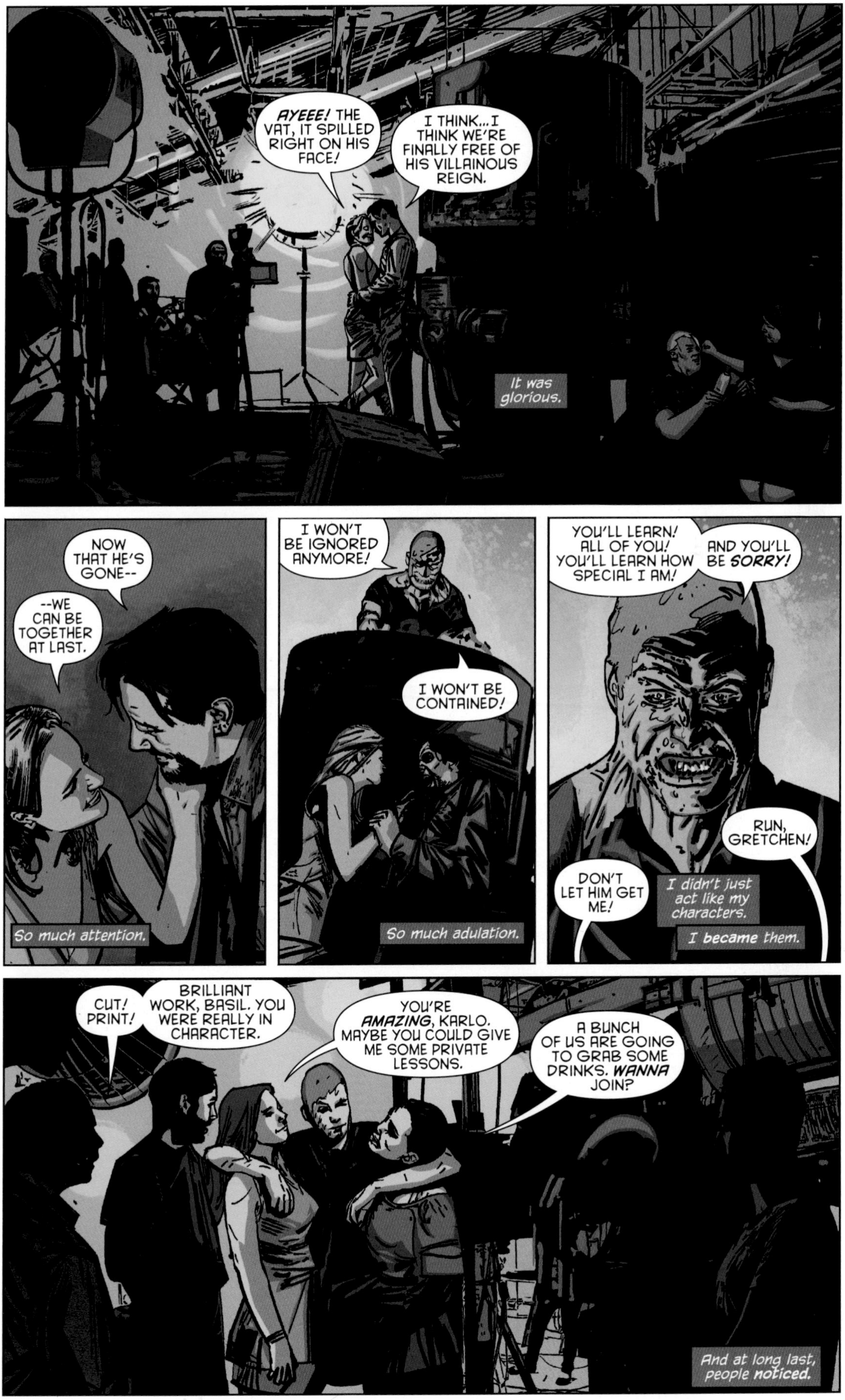
AYEEE! THE VAT, IT SPILLED RIGHT ON HIS FACE!
I THINK... I THINK WE'RE FINALLY FREE OF HIS VILLAINOUS REIGN.
It was glorious.
NOW THAT HE'S GONE--
--WE CAN BE TOGETHER AT LAST.
So much attention.
I WON'T BE IGNORED ANYMORE!
I WON'T BE CONTAINED!
So much adulation.
YOU'LL LEARN! ALL OF YOU! YOU'LL LEARN HOW SPECIAL I AM!
AND YOU'LL BE SORRY!
RUN, GRETCHEN!
DON'T LET HIM GET ME!
I didn't just act like my characters.
I became them.
CUT! PRINT!
BRILLIANT WORK, BASIL. YOU WERE REALLY IN CHARACTER.
YOU'RE AMAZING, KARLO. MAYBE YOU COULD GIVE ME SOME PRIVATE LESSONS.
A BUNCH OF US ARE GOING TO GRAB SOME DRINKS. WANNA JOIN?
And at long last, people noticed.

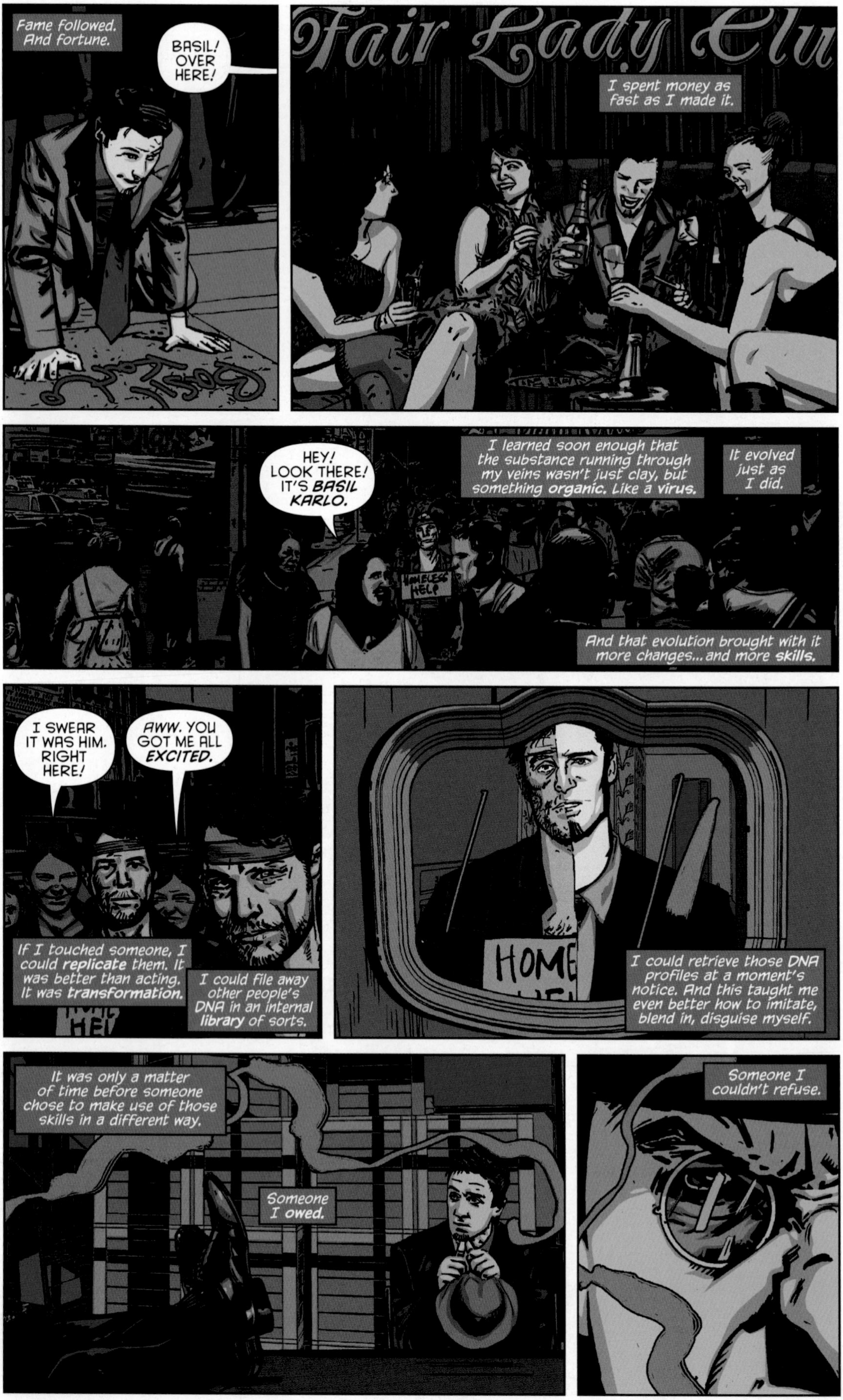

Fame followed. And fortune.
BASIL! OVER HERE!
Fair Lady Clu
I spent money as fast as I made it.
HEY! LOOK THERE! IT'S BASIL KARLO.
I learned soon enough that the substance running through my veins wasn't just clay, but something organic. Like a virus.
It evolved just as I did.
HOMELESS HELP
And that evolution brought with it more changes...and more skills.
I SWEAR IT WAS HIM. RIGHT HERE!
AWW. YOU GOT ME ALL EXCITED.
If I touched someone, I could replicate them. It was better than acting. It was transformation.
I could file away other people's DNA in an internal library of sorts.
HOME
I could retrieve those DNA profiles at a moment's notice. And this taught me even better how to imitate, blend in, disguise myself.
It was only a matter of time before someone chose to make use of those skills in a different way.
Someone I owed.
Someone I couldn't refuse.

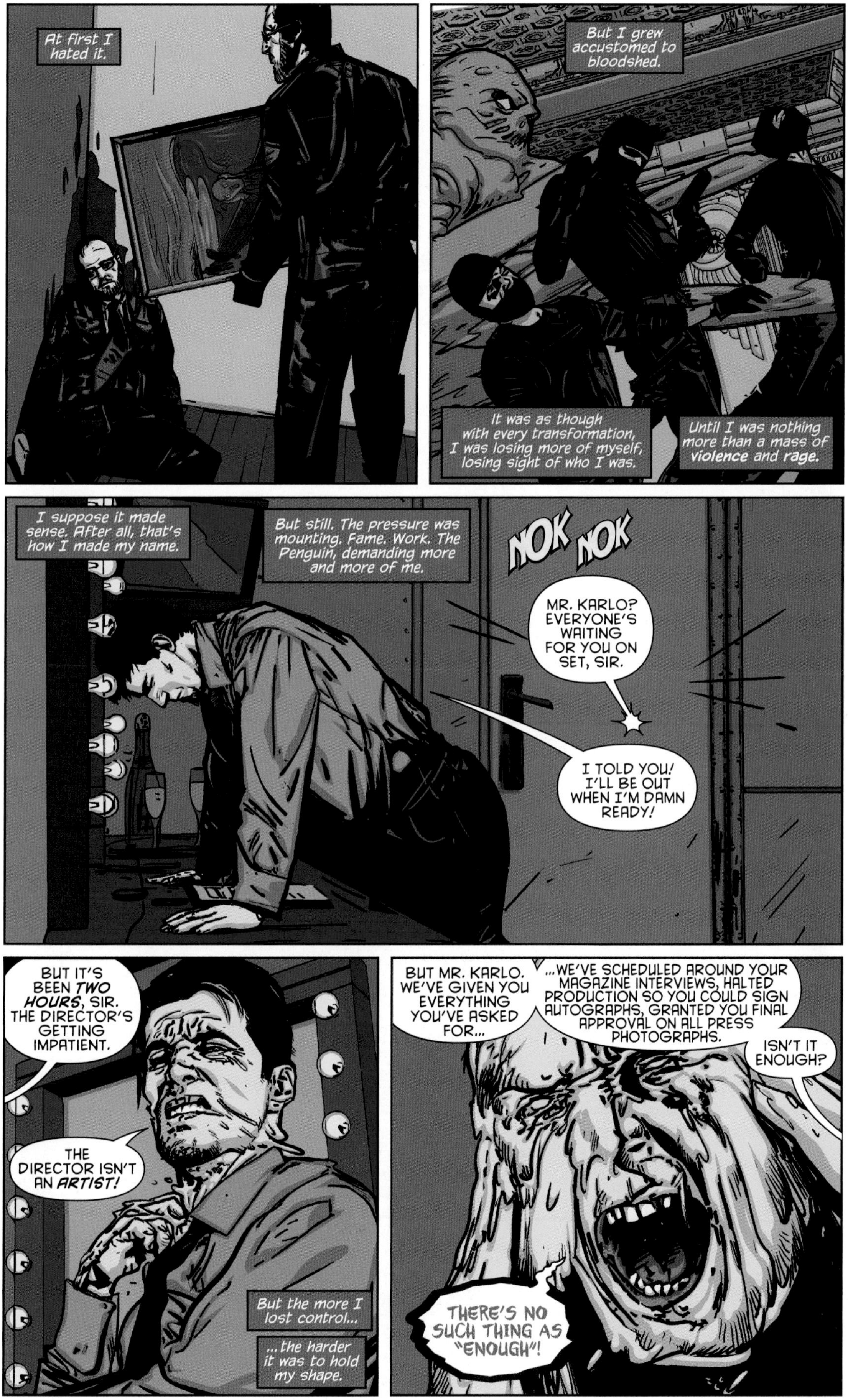

At first I hated it.
But I grew accustomed to bloodshed.
It was as though with every transformation, I was losing more of myself, losing sight of who I was.
Until I was nothing more than a mass of violence and rage.
I suppose it made sense. After all, that's how I made my name.
But still. The pressure was mounting. Fame. Work. The Penguin, demanding more and more of me.
NOK NOK
MR. KARLO? EVERYONE'S WAITING FOR YOU ON SET, SIR.
I TOLD YOU! I'LL BE OUT WHEN I'M DAMN READY!
BUT IT'S BEEN TWO HOURS, SIR. THE DIRECTOR'S GETTING IMPATIENT.
THE DIRECTOR ISN'T AN ARTIST!
But the more I lost control...
...the harder it was to hold my shape.
BUT MR. KARLO. WE'VE GIVEN YOU EVERYTHING YOU'VE ASKED FOR...
...WE'VE SCHEDULED AROUND YOUR MAGAZINE INTERVIEWS, HALTED PRODUCTION SO YOU COULD SIGN AUTOGRAPHS, GRANTED YOU FINAL APPROVAL ON ALL PRESS PHOTOGRAPHS.
ISN'T IT ENOUGH?
THERE'S NO SUCH THING AS "ENOUGH"!

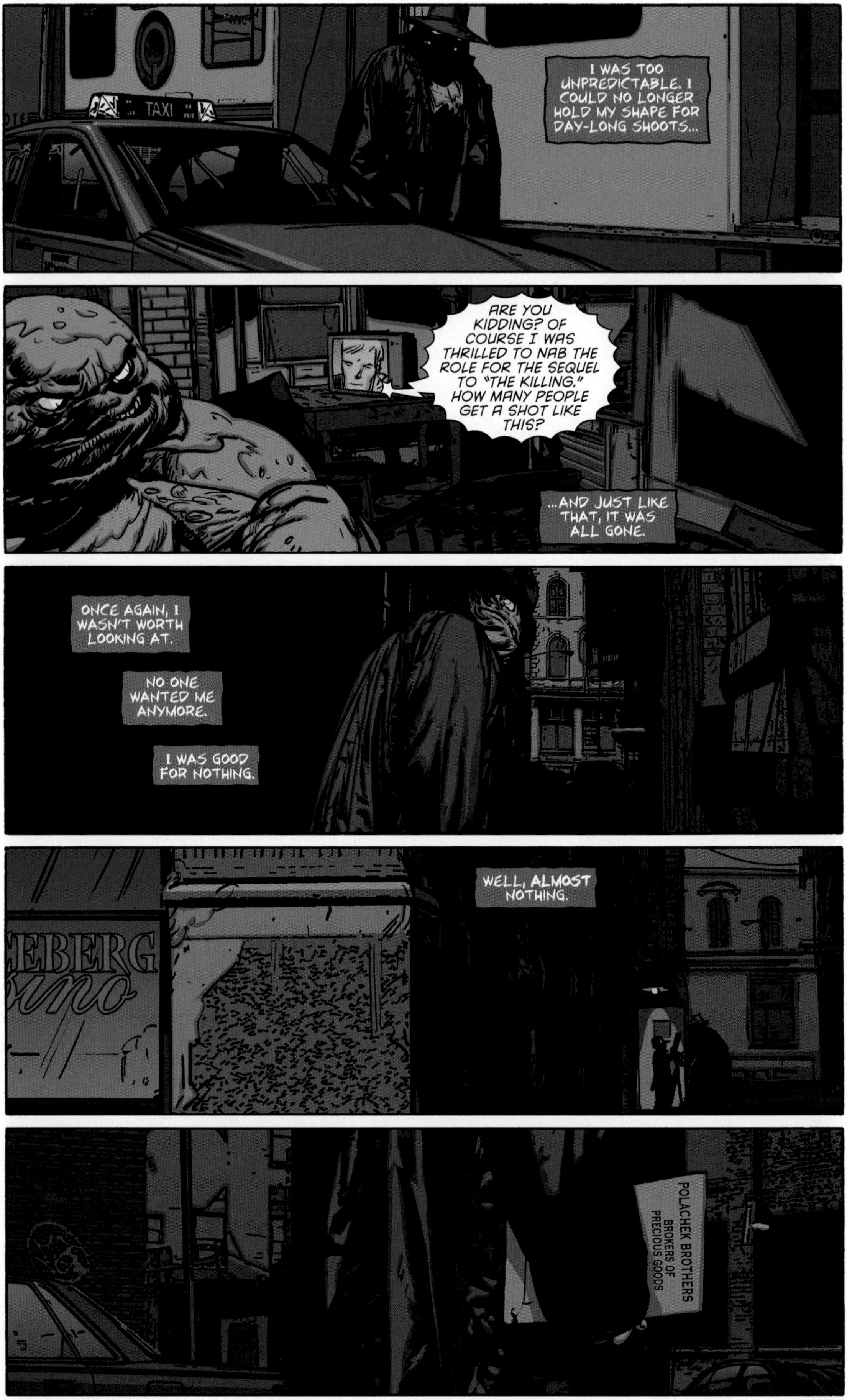
TAXI
I WAS TOO UNPREDICTABLE. I COULD NO LONGER HOLD MY SHAPE FOR DAY-LONG SHOOTS...
ARE YOU KIDDING? OF COURSE I WAS THRILLED TO NAB THE ROLE FOR THE SEQUEL TO "THE KILLING." HOW MANY PEOPLE GET A SHOT LIKE THIS?
...AND JUST LIKE THAT, IT WAS ALL GONE.
ONCE AGAIN, I WASN'T WORTH LOOKING AT.
NO ONE WANTED ME ANYMORE.
I WAS GOOD FOR NOTHING.
WELL, ALMOST NOTHING.
POLACHEK BROTHERS
BROKERS OF PRECIOUS GOODS

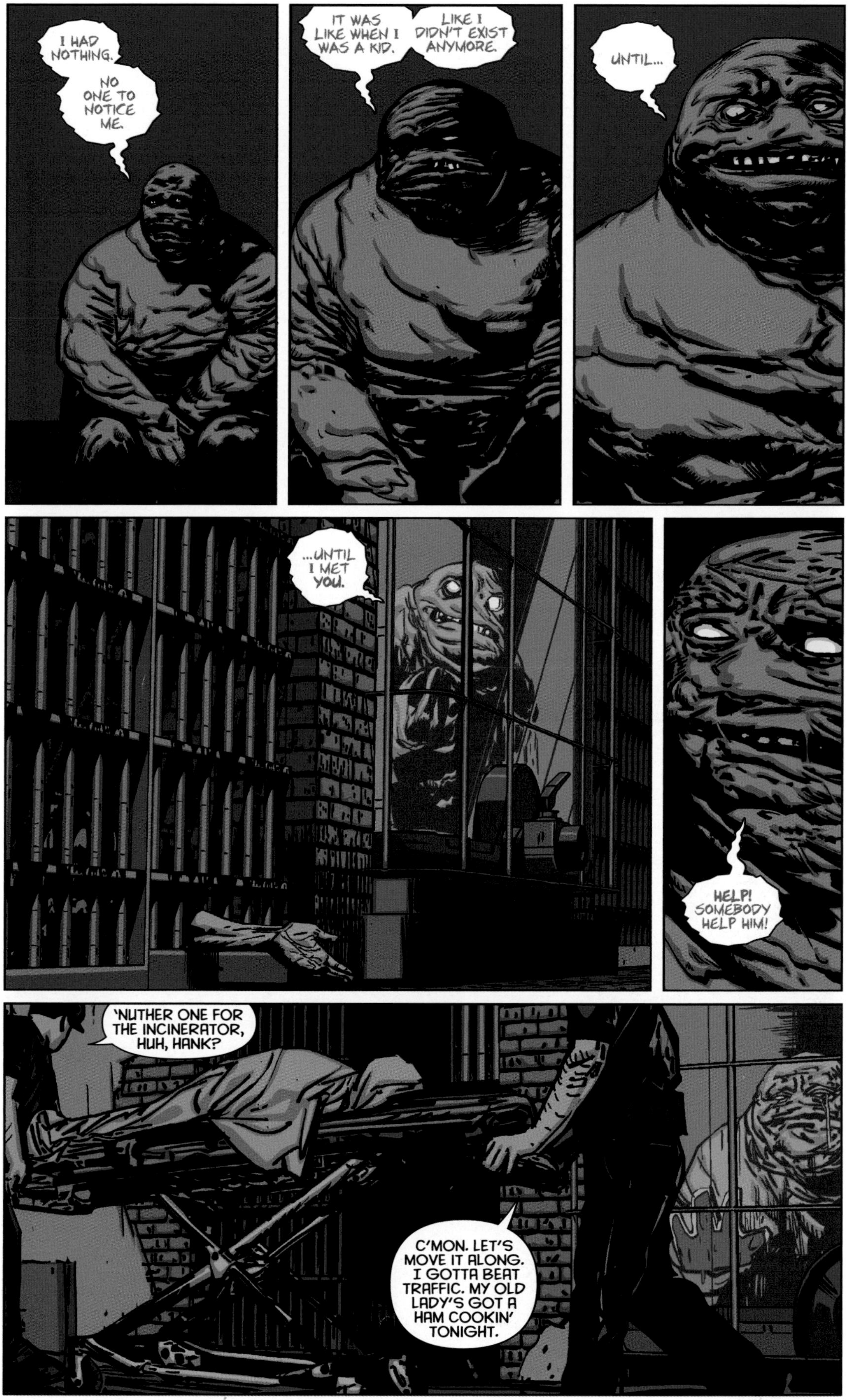
I HAD NOTHING.
NO ONE TO NOTICE ME.
IT WAS LIKE WHEN I WAS A KID.
LIKE I DIDN'T EXIST ANYMORE.
UNTIL...
...UNTIL I MET YOU.
HELP! SOMEBODY HELP HIM!
'NUTHER ONE FOR THE INCINERATOR, HUH, HANK?
C'MON. LET'S MOVE IT ALONG. I GOTTA BEAT TRAFFIC. MY OLD LADY'S GOT A HAM COOKIN' TONIGHT.

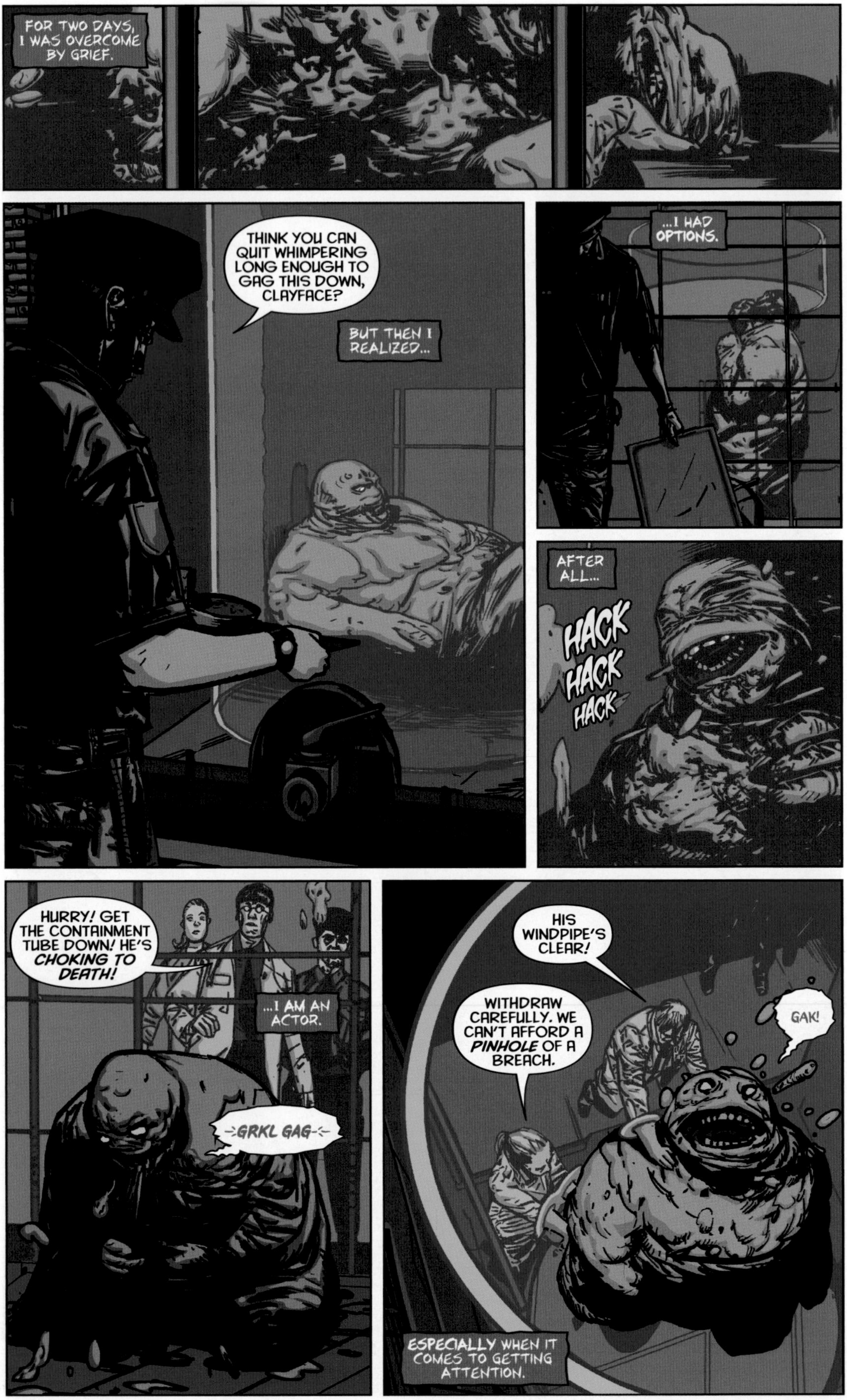
FOR TWO DAYS, I WAS OVERCOME BY GRIEF.
THINK YOU CAN QUIT WHIMPERING LONG ENOUGH TO GAG THIS DOWN, CLAYFACE?
BUT THEN I REALIZED...
...I HAD OPTIONS.
AFTER ALL...
HACK HACK HACK
HURRY! GET THE CONTAINMENT TUBE DOWN! HE'S *CHOKING TO DEATH!*
...I AM AN ACTOR.
GRKL GAG
HIS WINDPIPE'S CLEAR!
WITHDRAW CAREFULLY. WE CAN'T AFFORD A *PINHOLE* OF A BREACH.
GAK!
ESPECIALLY WHEN IT COMES TO GETTING ATTENTION.

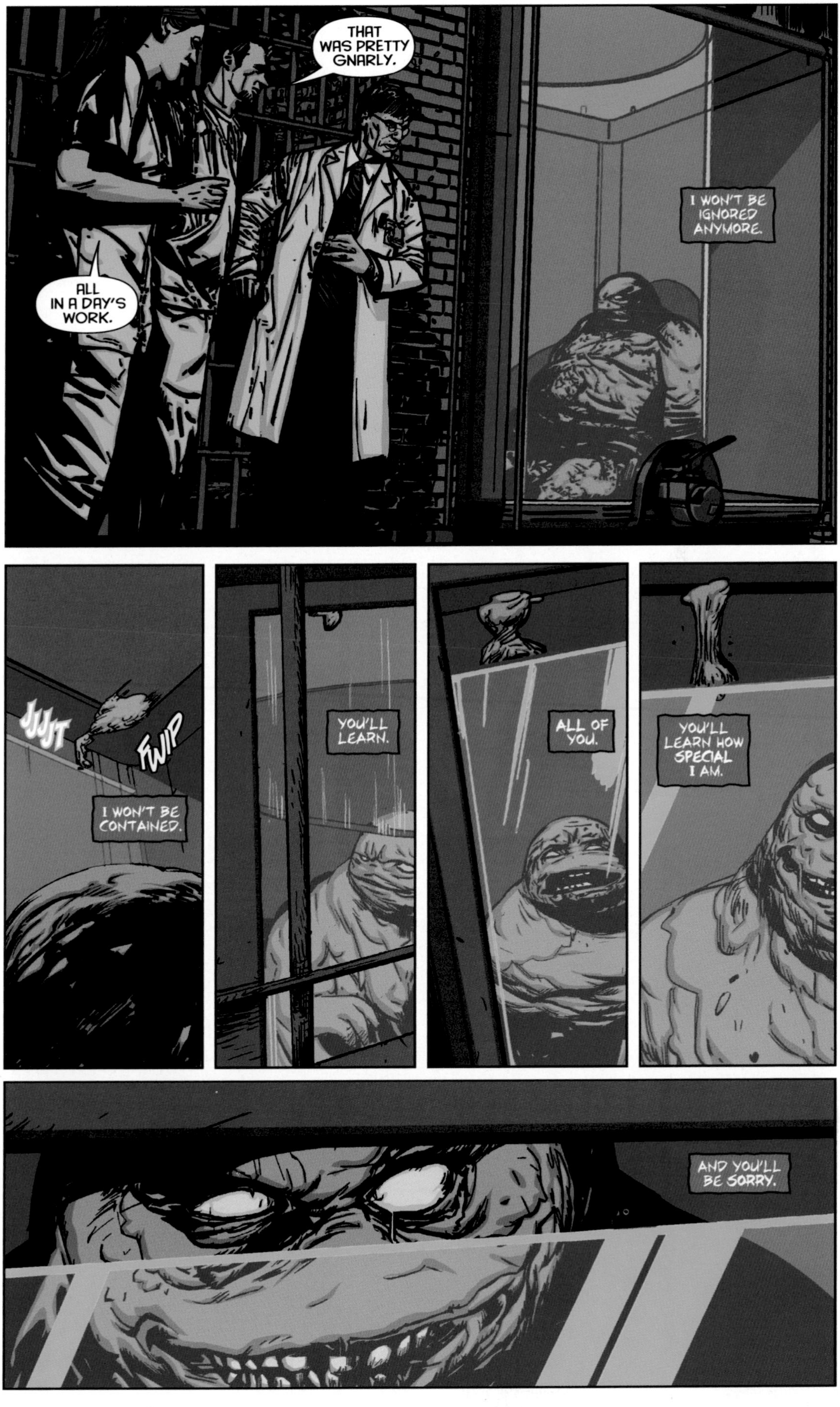
THAT WAS PRETTY GNARLY.
ALL IN A DAY'S WORK.
I WON'T BE IGNORED ANYMORE.
JJJJT
FWIP
I WON'T BE CONTAINED.
YOU'LL LEARN.
ALL OF YOU.
YOU'LL LEARN HOW SPECIAL I AM.
AND YOU'LL BE SORRY.

FULL HOUSE

ALEX MALEEV artist & cover

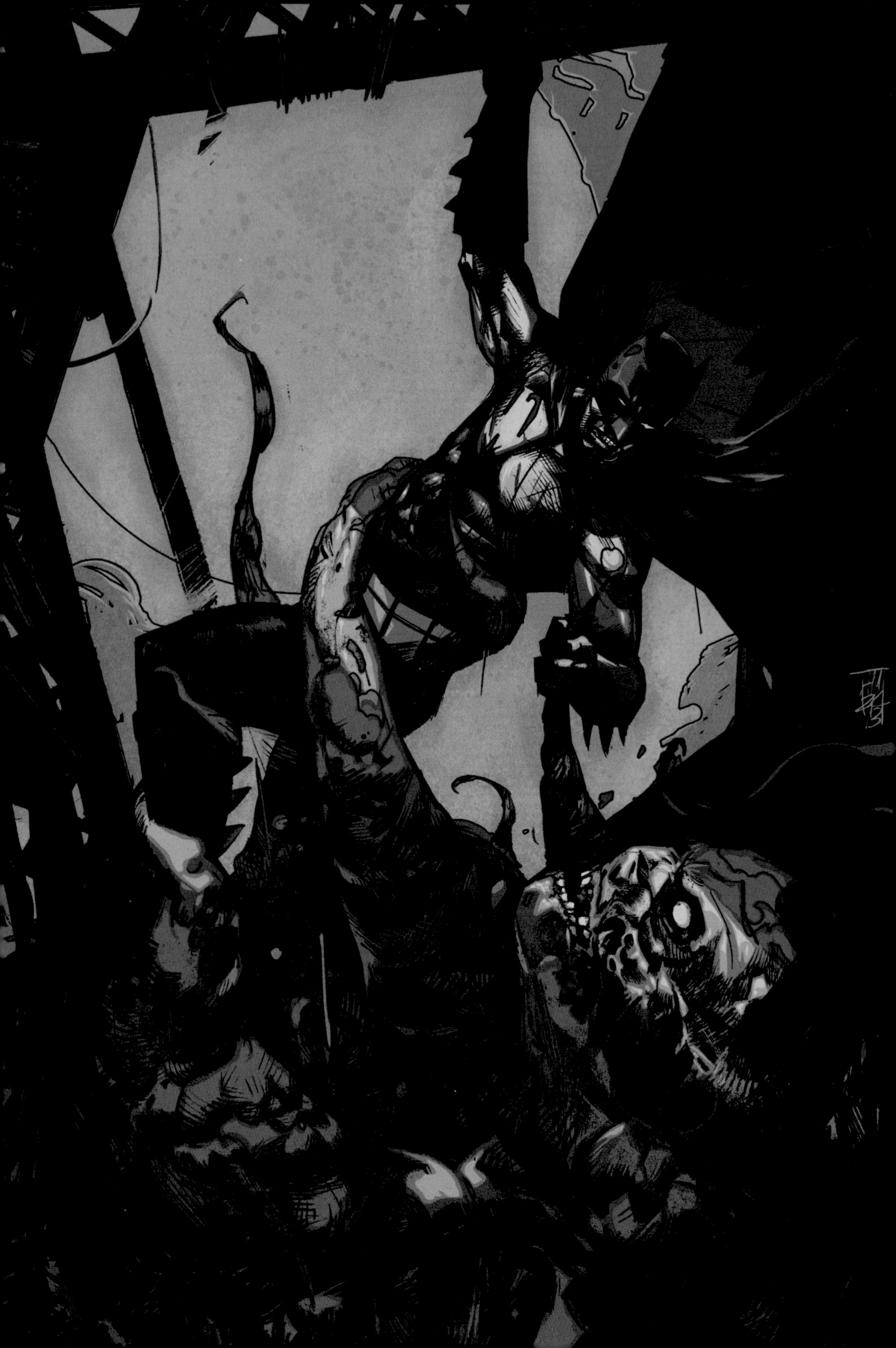

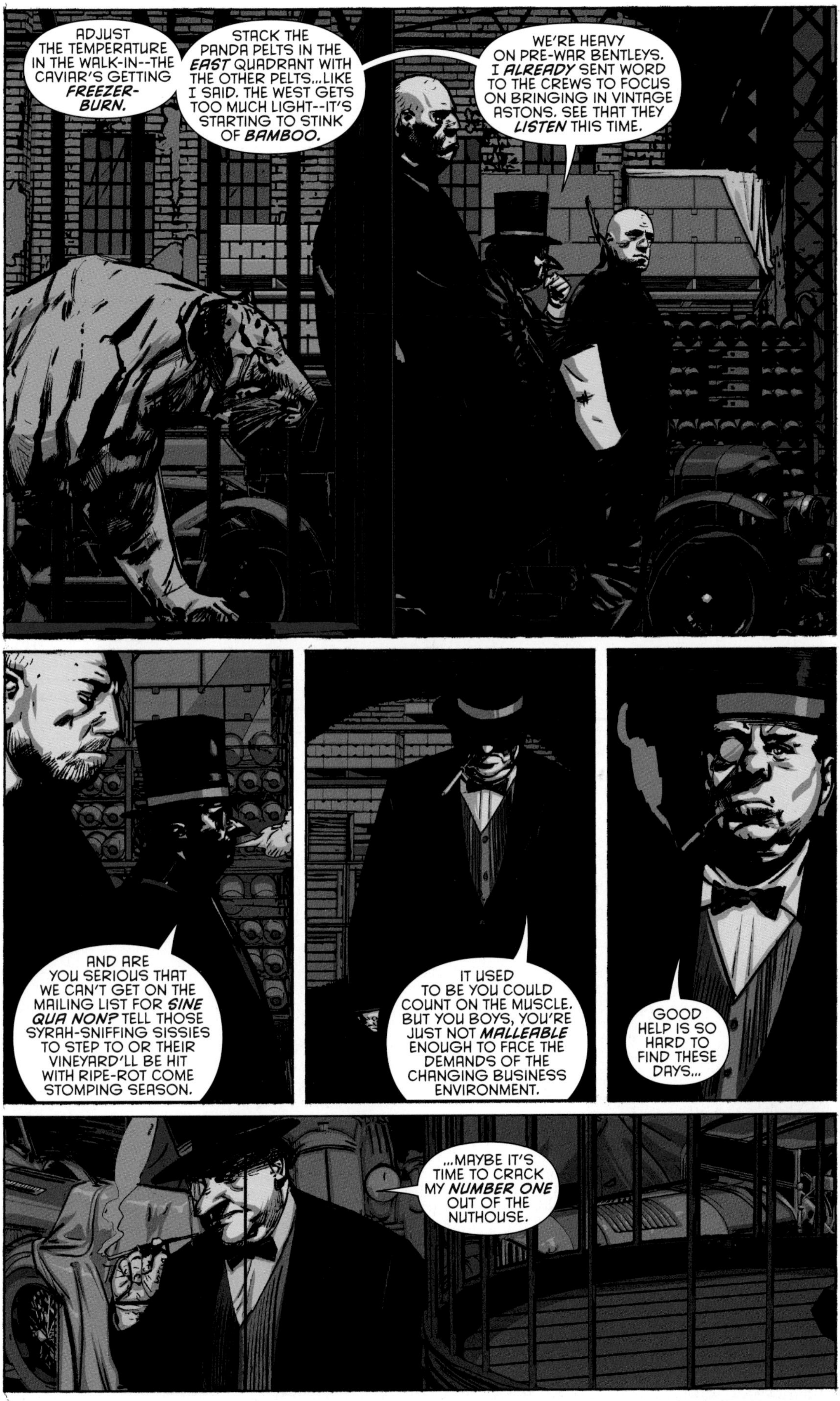
ADJUST THE TEMPERATURE IN THE WALK-IN--THE CAVIAR'S GETTING FREEZER-BURN.
STACK THE PANDA PELTS IN THE EAST QUADRANT WITH THE OTHER PELTS...LIKE I SAID. THE WEST GETS TOO MUCH LIGHT--IT'S STARTING TO STINK OF BAMBOO.
WE'RE HEAVY ON PRE-WAR BENTLEYS. I ALREADY SENT WORD TO THE CREWS TO FOCUS ON BRINGING IN VINTAGE ASTONS. SEE THAT THEY LISTEN THIS TIME.
AND ARE YOU SERIOUS THAT WE CAN'T GET ON THE MAILING LIST FOR SINE QUA NON? TELL THOSE SYRAH-SNIFFING SISSIES TO STEP TO OR THEIR VINEYARD'LL BE HIT WITH RIPE-ROT COME STOMPING SEASON.
IT USED TO BE YOU COULD COUNT ON THE MUSCLE. BUT YOU BOYS, YOU'RE JUST NOT MALLEABLE ENOUGH TO FACE THE DEMANDS OF THE CHANGING BUSINESS ENVIRONMENT.
GOOD HELP IS SO HARD TO FIND THESE DAYS...
...MAYBE IT'S TIME TO CRACK MY NUMBER ONE OUT OF THE NUTHOUSE.

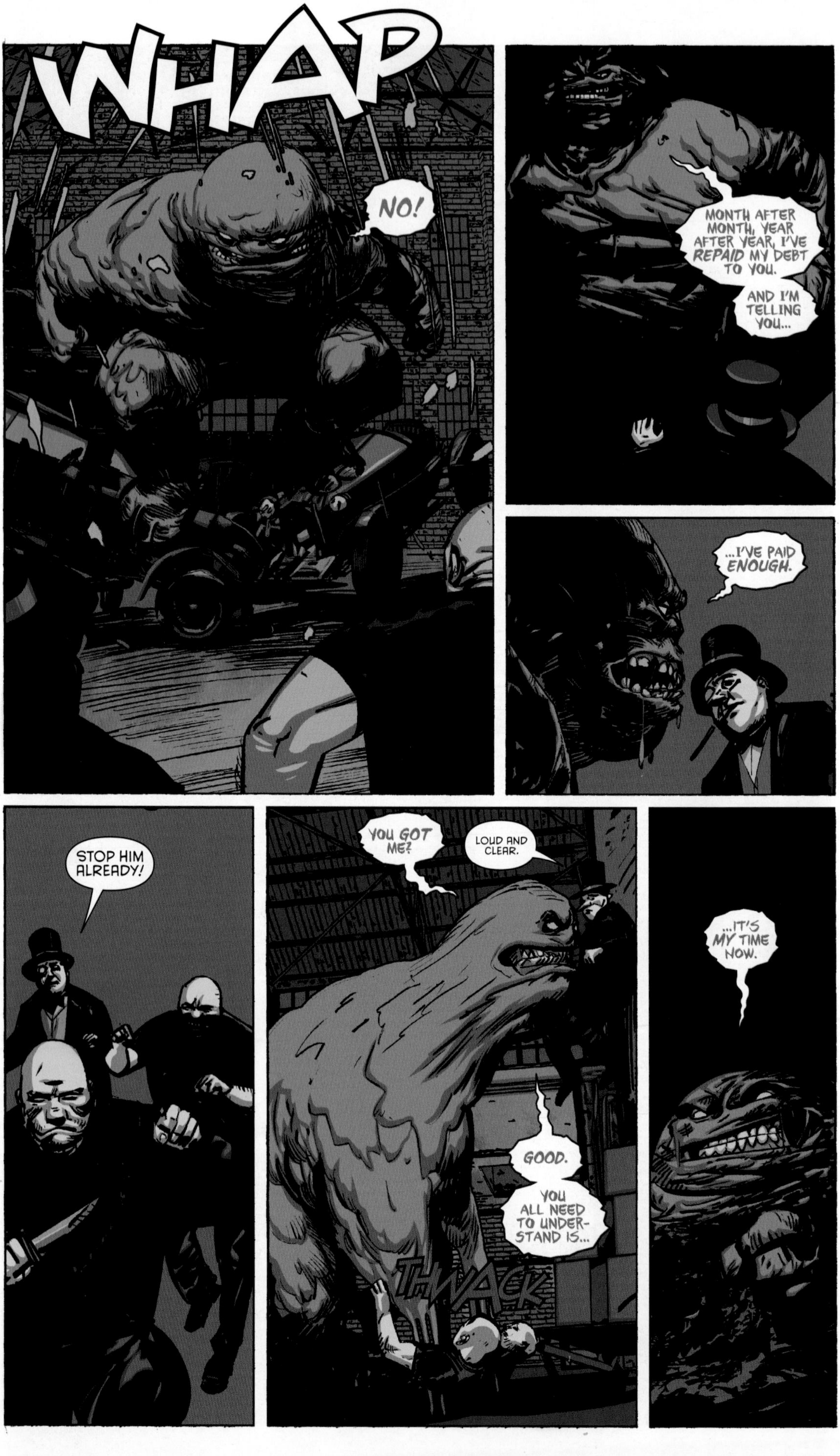
WHAP
NO!
MONTH AFTER MONTH, YEAR AFTER YEAR, I'VE REPAID MY DEBT TO YOU.
AND I'M TELLING YOU...
...I'VE PAID ENOUGH.
STOP HIM ALREADY!
YOU GOT ME?
LOUD AND CLEAR.
GOOD.
YOU ALL NEED TO UNDER-STAND IS...
THWACK
...IT'S MY TIME NOW.

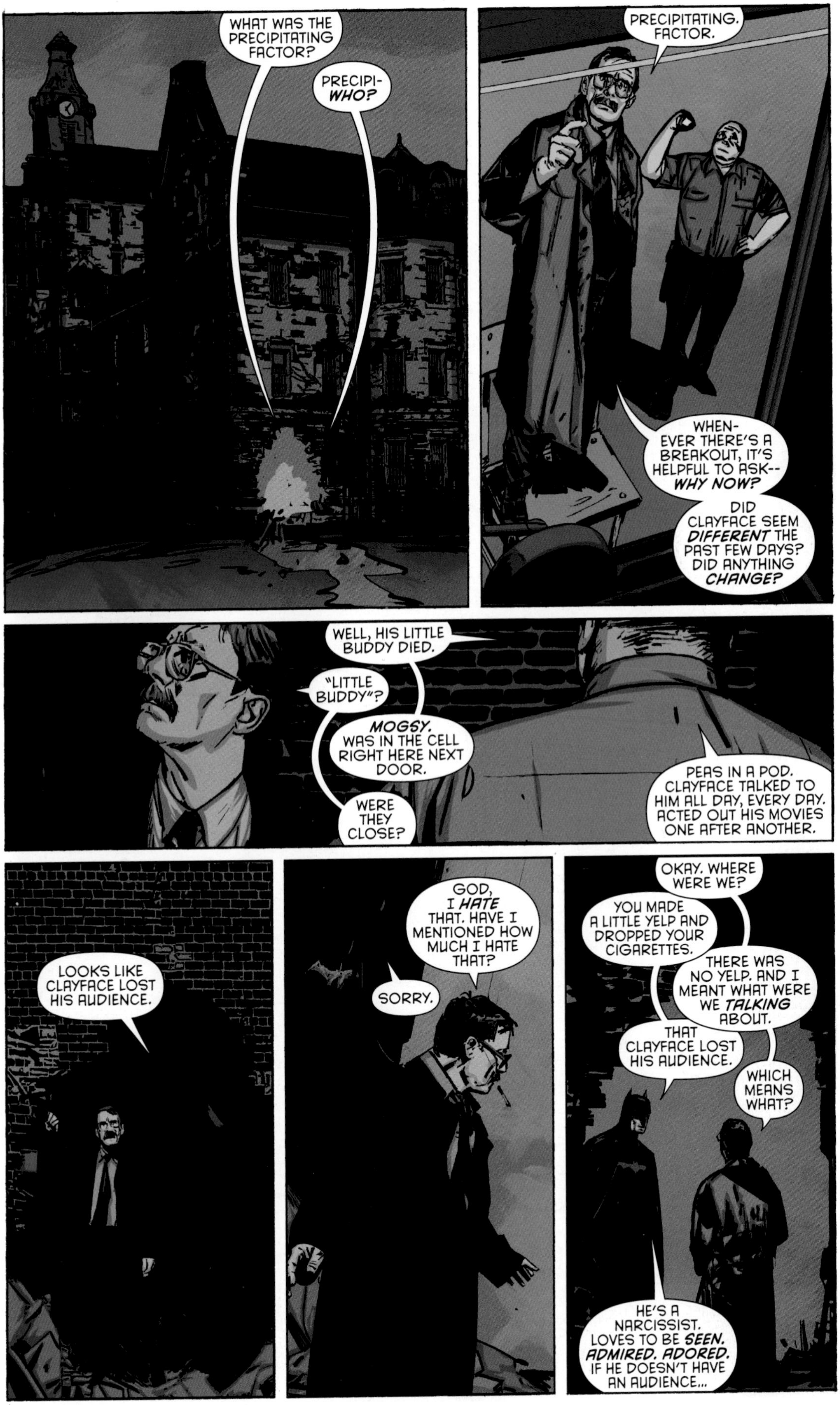
WHAT WAS THE PRECIPITATING FACTOR?
PRECIPI-*WHO?*
PRECIPITATING. FACTOR.
WHEN-EVER THERE'S A BREAKOUT, IT'S HELPFUL TO ASK-- *WHY NOW?*
DID CLAYFACE SEEM *DIFFERENT* THE PAST FEW DAYS? DID ANYTHING *CHANGE?*
WELL, HIS LITTLE BUDDY DIED.
"LITTLE BUDDY"?
MOGSY. WAS IN THE CELL RIGHT HERE NEXT DOOR.
WERE THEY CLOSE?
PEAS IN A POD. CLAYFACE TALKED TO HIM ALL DAY, EVERY DAY. ACTED OUT HIS MOVIES ONE AFTER ANOTHER.
LOOKS LIKE CLAYFACE LOST HIS AUDIENCE.
GOD, I *HATE* THAT. HAVE I MENTIONED HOW MUCH I HATE THAT?
SORRY.
OKAY. WHERE WERE WE?
YOU MADE A LITTLE YELP AND DROPPED YOUR CIGARETTES.
THERE WAS NO YELP. AND I MEANT WHAT WERE WE *TALKING* ABOUT.
THAT CLAYFACE LOST HIS AUDIENCE.
WHICH MEANS WHAT?
HE'S A NARCISSIST. LOVES TO BE *SEEN. ADMIRED. ADORED.* IF HE DOESN'T HAVE AN AUDIENCE...

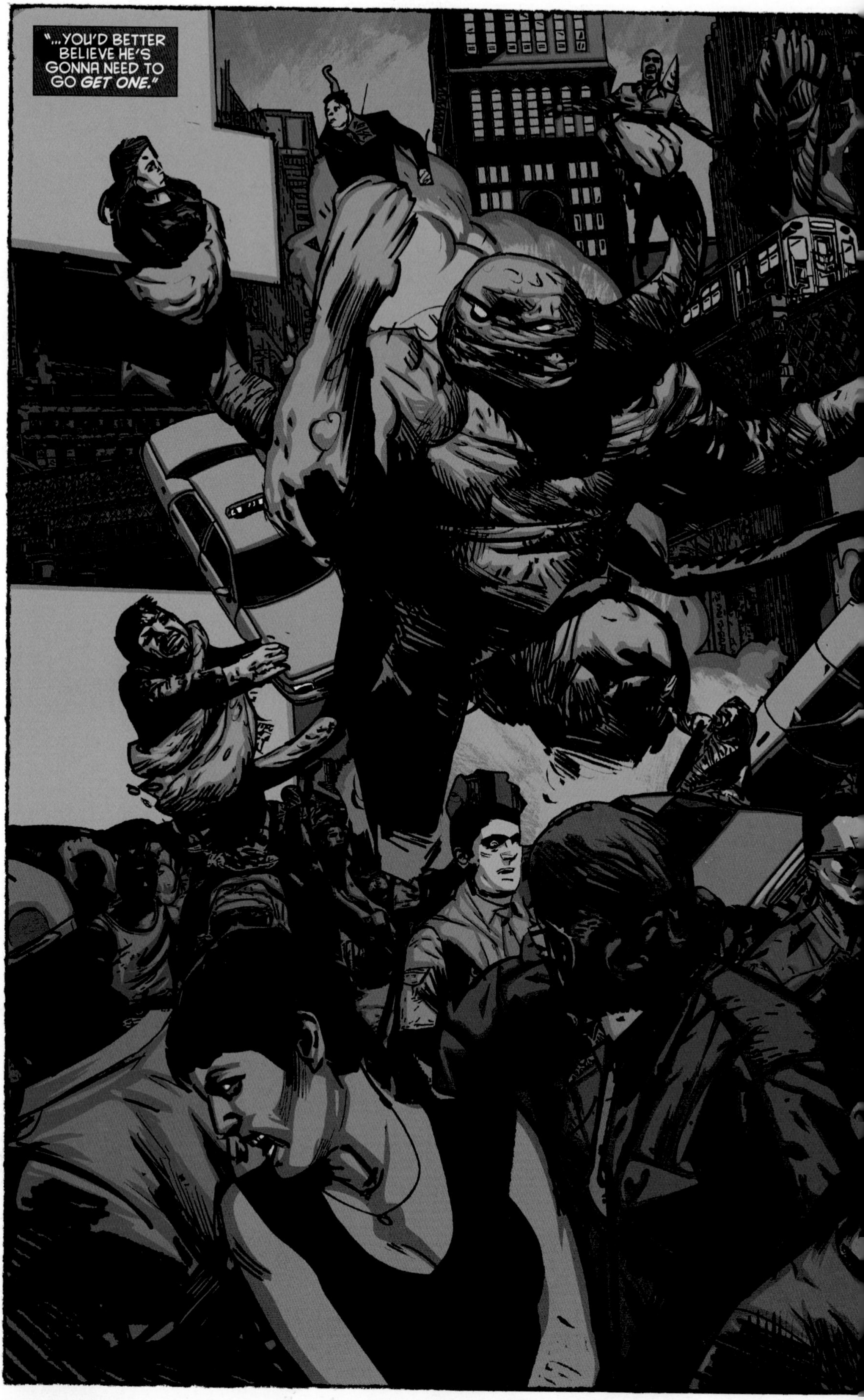
"...YOU'D BETTER BELIEVE HE'S GONNA NEED TO GO GET ONE."

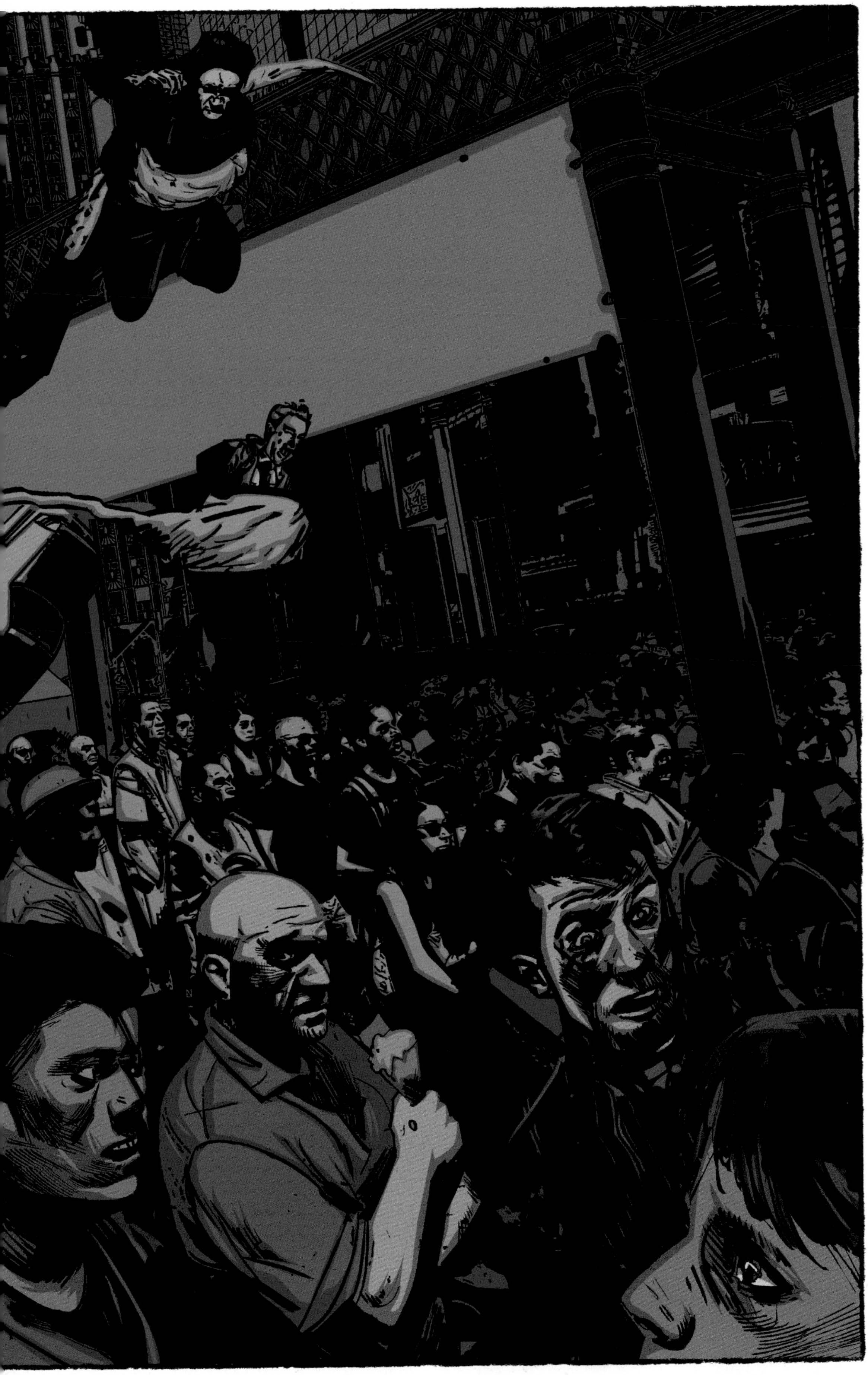

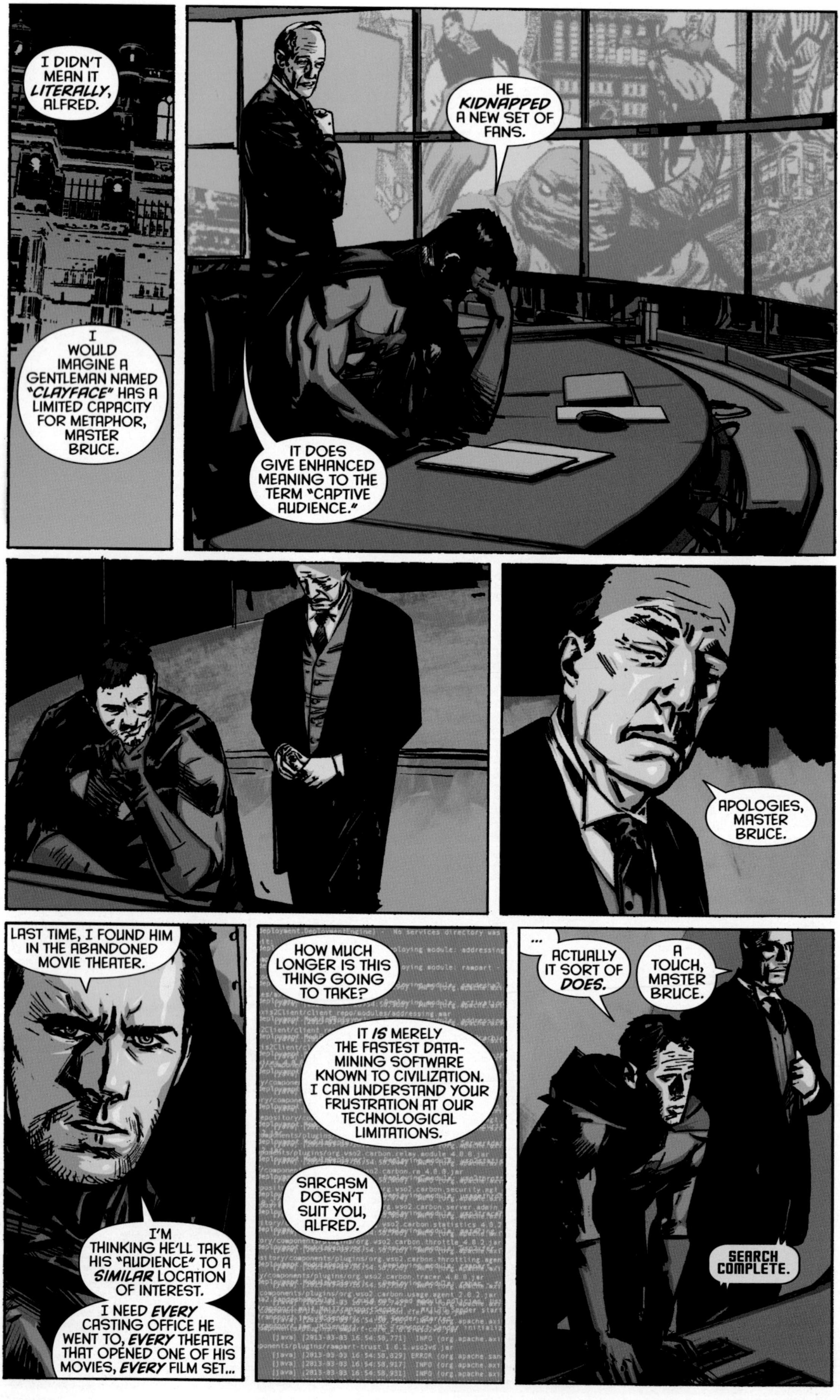
I DIDN'T MEAN IT *LITERALLY*, ALFRED.
HE *KIDNAPPED* A NEW SET OF FANS.
I WOULD IMAGINE A GENTLEMAN NAMED "*CLAYFACE*" HAS A LIMITED CAPACITY FOR METAPHOR, MASTER BRUCE.
IT DOES GIVE ENHANCED MEANING TO THE TERM "CAPTIVE AUDIENCE."
APOLOGIES, MASTER BRUCE.
LAST TIME, I FOUND HIM IN THE ABANDONED MOVIE THEATER.
I'M THINKING HE'LL TAKE HIS "AUDIENCE" TO A *SIMILAR* LOCATION OF INTEREST.
I NEED *EVERY* CASTING OFFICE HE WENT TO, *EVERY* THEATER THAT OPENED ONE OF HIS MOVIES, *EVERY* FILM SET...
HOW MUCH LONGER IS THIS THING GOING TO TAKE?
IT *IS* MERELY THE FASTEST DATA-MINING SOFTWARE KNOWN TO CIVILIZATION. I CAN UNDERSTAND YOUR FRUSTRATION AT OUR TECHNOLOGICAL LIMITATIONS.
SARCASM DOESN'T SUIT YOU, ALFRED.
...
ACTUALLY IT SORT OF *DOES.*
A TOUCH, MASTER BRUCE.
SEARCH COMPLETE.

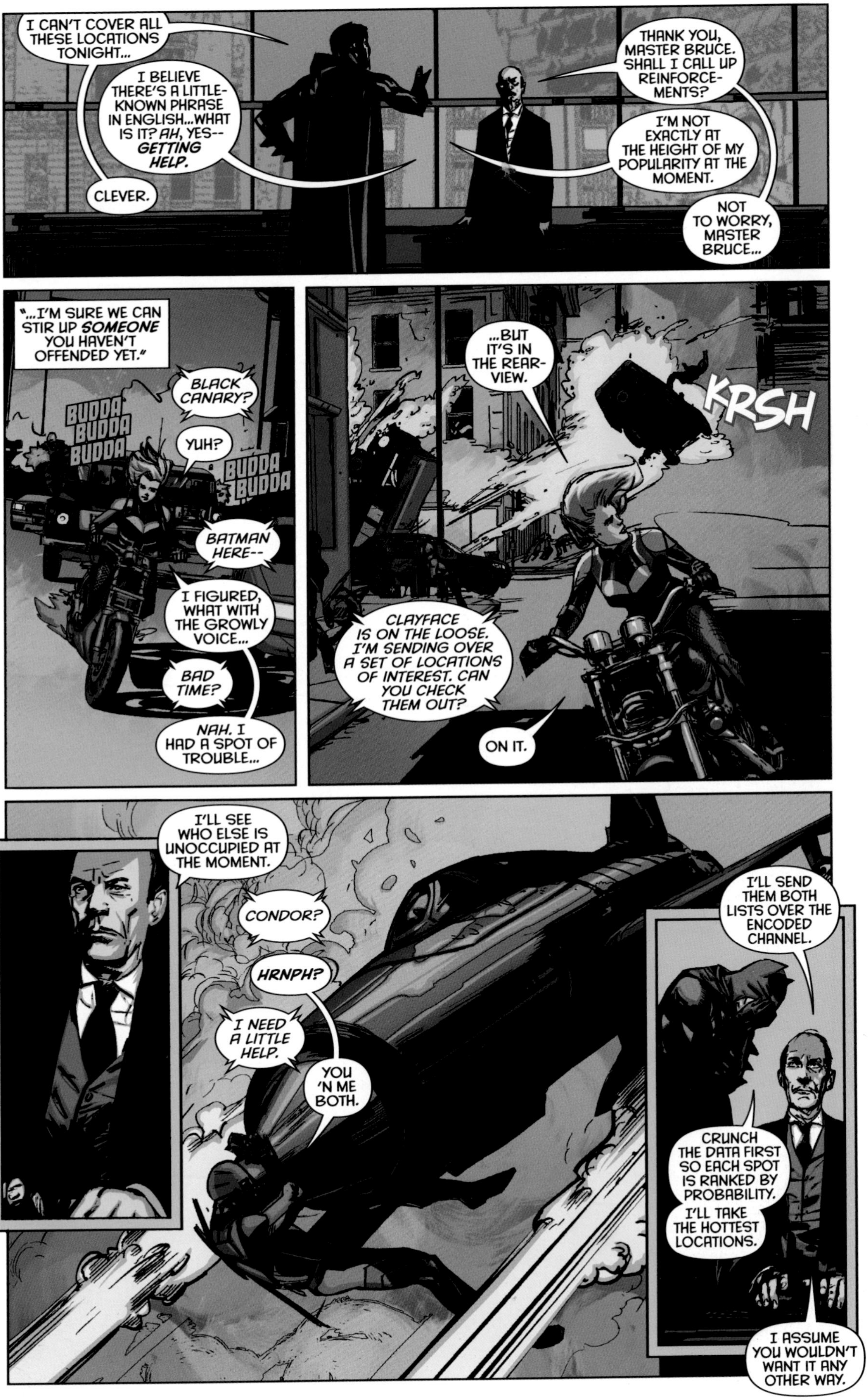
I CAN'T COVER ALL THESE LOCATIONS TONIGHT...
CLEVER.
I BELIEVE THERE'S A LITTLE-KNOWN PHRASE IN ENGLISH...WHAT IS IT? AH, YES-- GETTING HELP.
THANK YOU, MASTER BRUCE. SHALL I CALL UP REINFORCEMENTS?
I'M NOT EXACTLY AT THE HEIGHT OF MY POPULARITY AT THE MOMENT.
NOT TO WORRY, MASTER BRUCE...
"...I'M SURE WE CAN STIR UP SOMEONE YOU HAVEN'T OFFENDED YET."
BUDDA BUDDA BUDDA
BLACK CANARY?
YUH?
BUDDA BUDDA
BATMAN HERE--
I FIGURED, WHAT WITH THE GROWLY VOICE...
BAD TIME?
NAH. I HAD A SPOT OF TROUBLE...
...BUT IT'S IN THE REAR-VIEW.
KRSH
CLAYFACE IS ON THE LOOSE. I'M SENDING OVER A SET OF LOCATIONS OF INTEREST. CAN YOU CHECK THEM OUT?
ON IT.
I'LL SEE WHO ELSE IS UNOCCUPIED AT THE MOMENT.
CONDOR?
HRNPH?
I NEED A LITTLE HELP.
YOU 'N ME BOTH.
I'LL SEND THEM BOTH LISTS OVER THE ENCODED CHANNEL.
CRUNCH THE DATA FIRST SO EACH SPOT IS RANKED BY PROBABILITY.
I'LL TAKE THE HOTTEST LOCATIONS.
I ASSUME YOU WOULDN'T WANT IT ANY OTHER WAY.

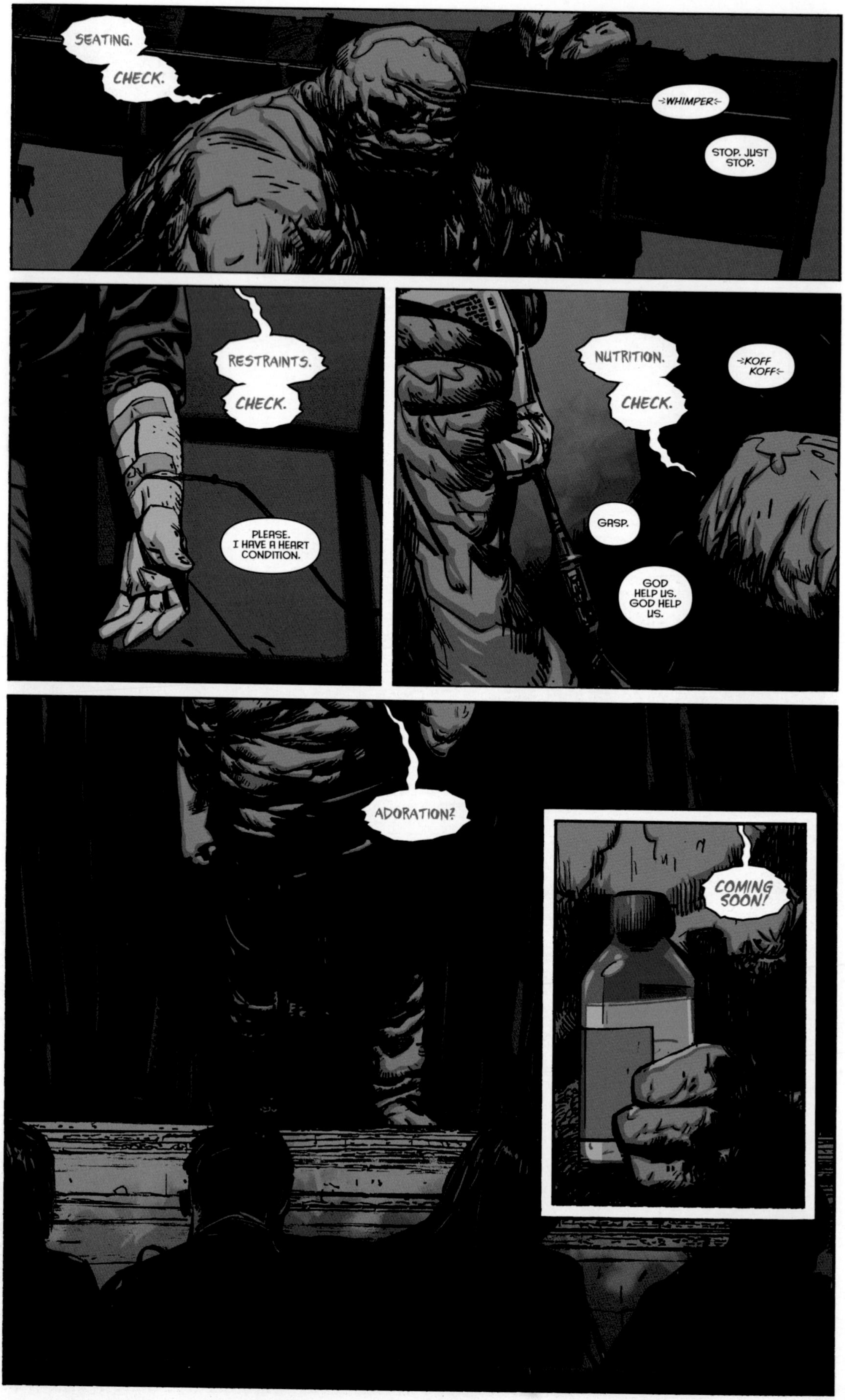
SEATING.
CHECK.
WHIMPER
STOP. JUST STOP.
RESTRAINTS.
CHECK.
PLEASE. I HAVE A HEART CONDITION.
NUTRITION.
CHECK.
KOFF KOFF
GASP.
GOD HELP US. GOD HELP US.
ADORATION?
COMING SOON!

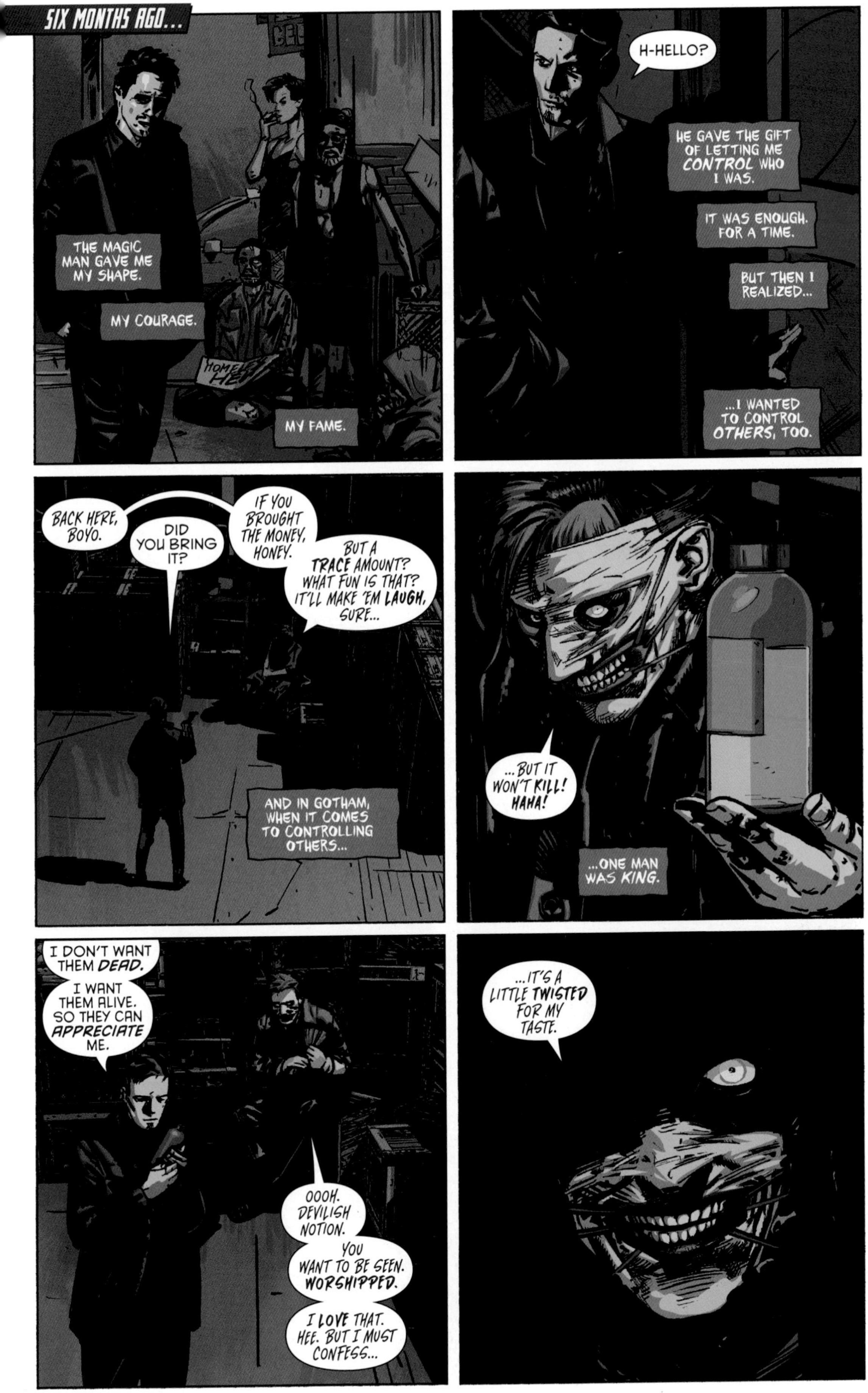
SIX MONTHS AGO...
THE MAGIC MAN GAVE ME MY SHAPE.
MY COURAGE.
MY FAME.
H-HELLO?
HE GAVE THE GIFT OF LETTING ME CONTROL WHO I WAS.
IT WAS ENOUGH. FOR A TIME.
BUT THEN I REALIZED...
...I WANTED TO CONTROL OTHERS, TOO.
BACK HERE, BOYO.
DID YOU BRING IT?
IF YOU BROUGHT THE MONEY, HONEY.
BUT A TRACE AMOUNT? WHAT FUN IS THAT? IT'LL MAKE 'EM LAUGH, SURE...
AND IN GOTHAM, WHEN IT COMES TO CONTROLLING OTHERS...
...BUT IT WON'T KILL! HAHA!
...ONE MAN WAS KING.
I DON'T WANT THEM DEAD.
I WANT THEM ALIVE. SO THEY CAN APPRECIATE ME.
OOOH. DEVILISH NOTION.
YOU WANT TO BE SEEN. WORSHIPPED.
I LOVE THAT. HEE. BUT I MUST CONFESS...
...IT'S A LITTLE TWISTED FOR MY TASTE.

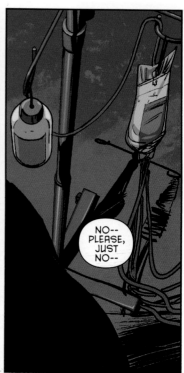

LET US GO.

MY WRIST-- THE STRAP IS CUTTING INTO MY WRIST...

IS THAT--?

WAIT. JUST WAIT. CAN WE TALK ABOUT THIS?

→SOB SOB←

NO-- PLEASE, JUST NO--

HANG ON!

--CAN'T MOVE--

KEEP IT AWAY! KEEP IT AWAY FROM ME!

STOP IT! PLEASE STOP IT BEFORE--

GOD, NOOO!

PLEASE, PLEASE--

WA HA HA. HA HA HA. HA HA HA HA!

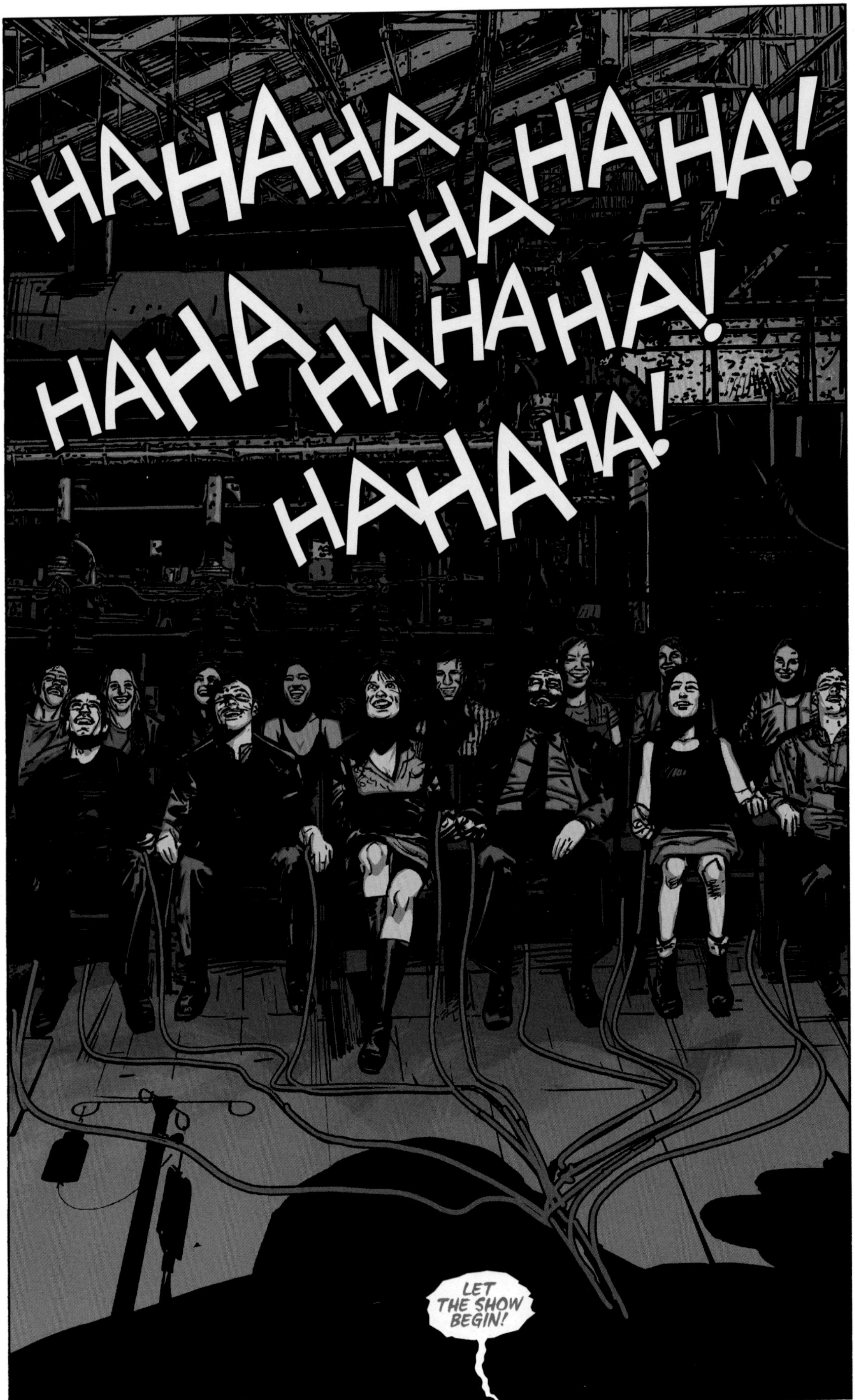
HAHAHA
HA
HAHAHA!
HAHA
HAHAHAHA!
HAHAHA!
LET THE SHOW BEGIN!

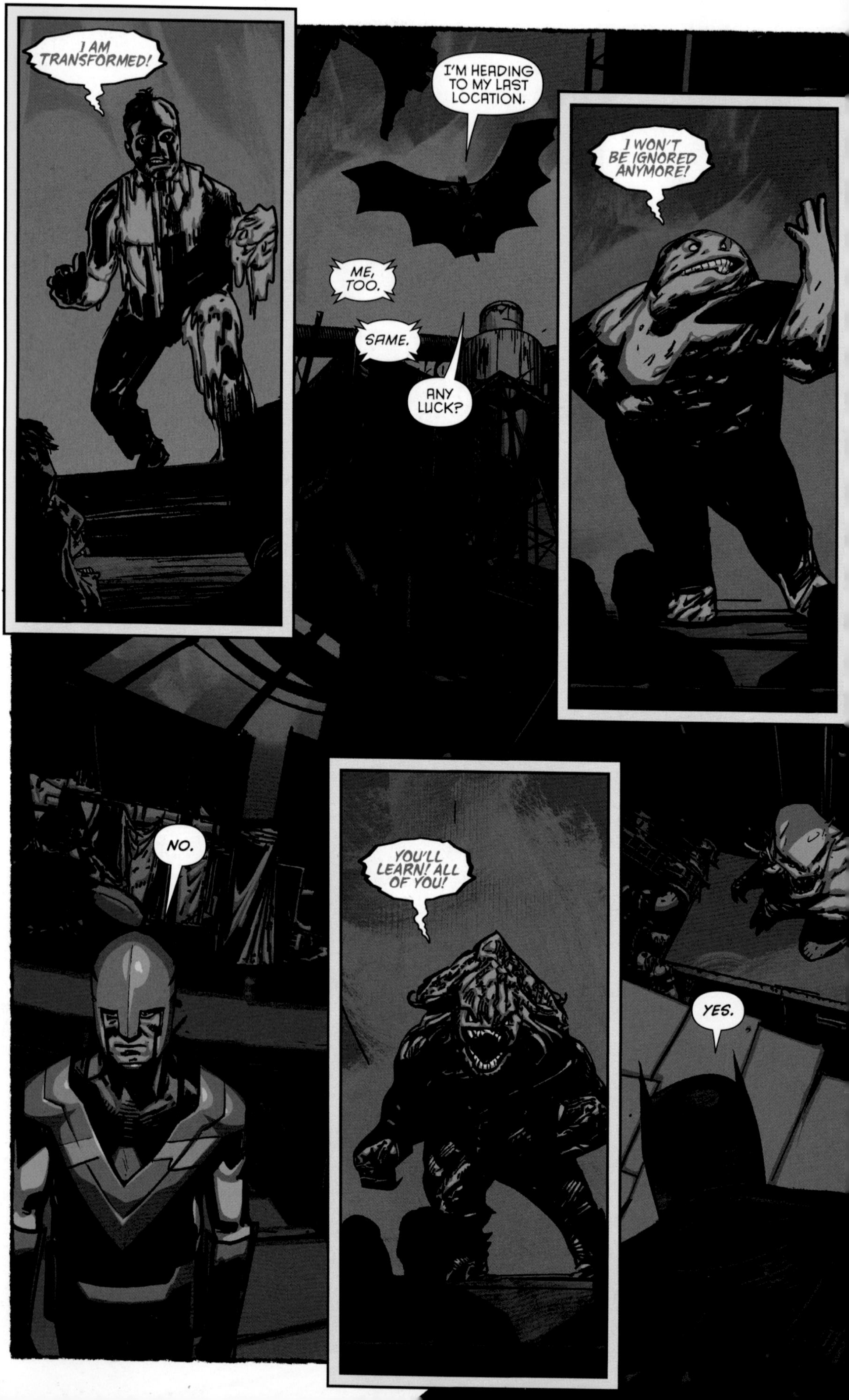
I AM TRANSFORMED!
I'M HEADING TO MY LAST LOCATION.
ME, TOO.
SAME.
ANY LUCK?
I WON'T BE IGNORED ANYMORE!
NO.
YOU'LL LEARN! ALL OF YOU!
YES.

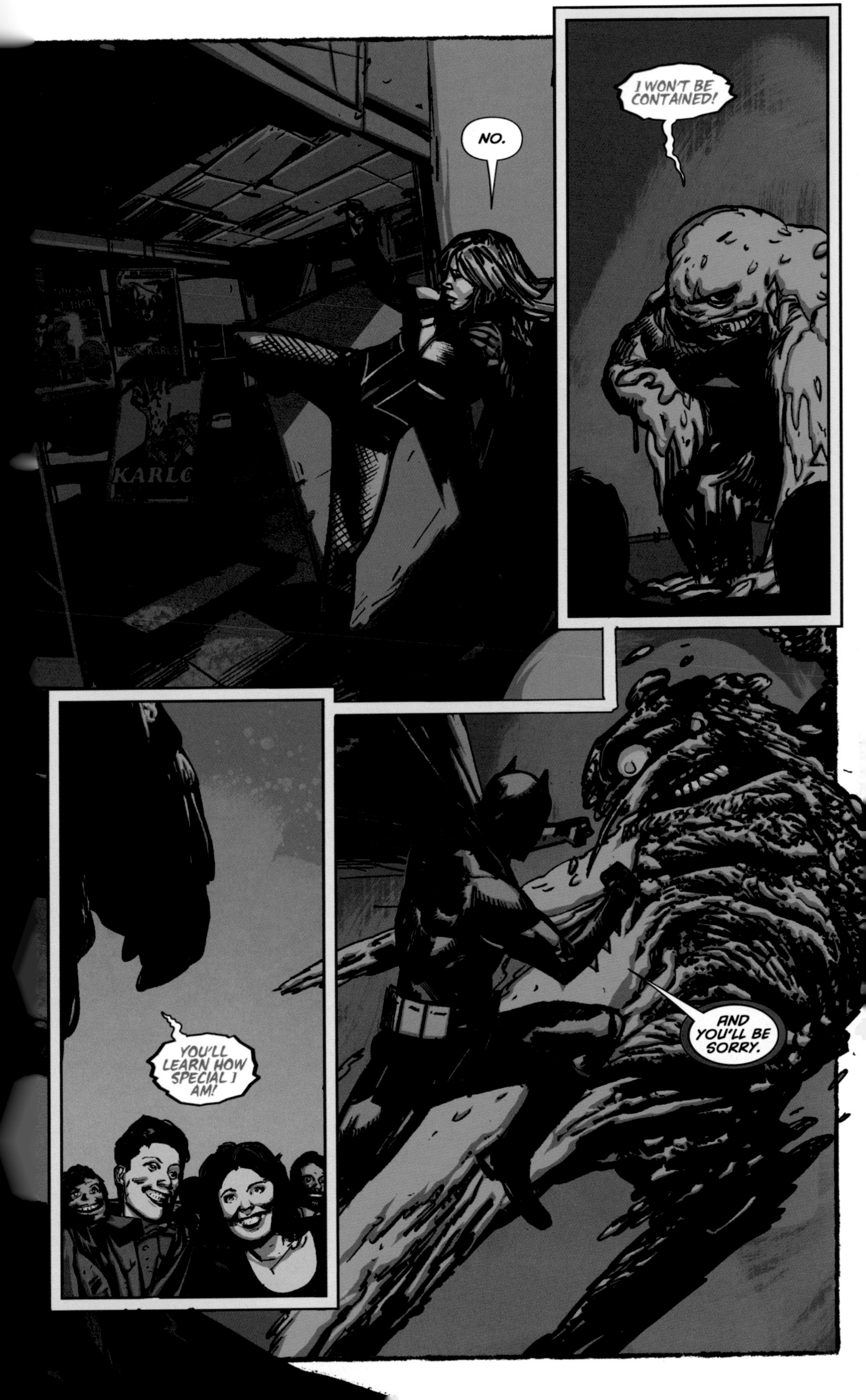
NO.
I WON'T BE CONTAINED!
YOU'LL LEARN HOW SPECIAL I AM!
AND YOU'LL BE SORRY.

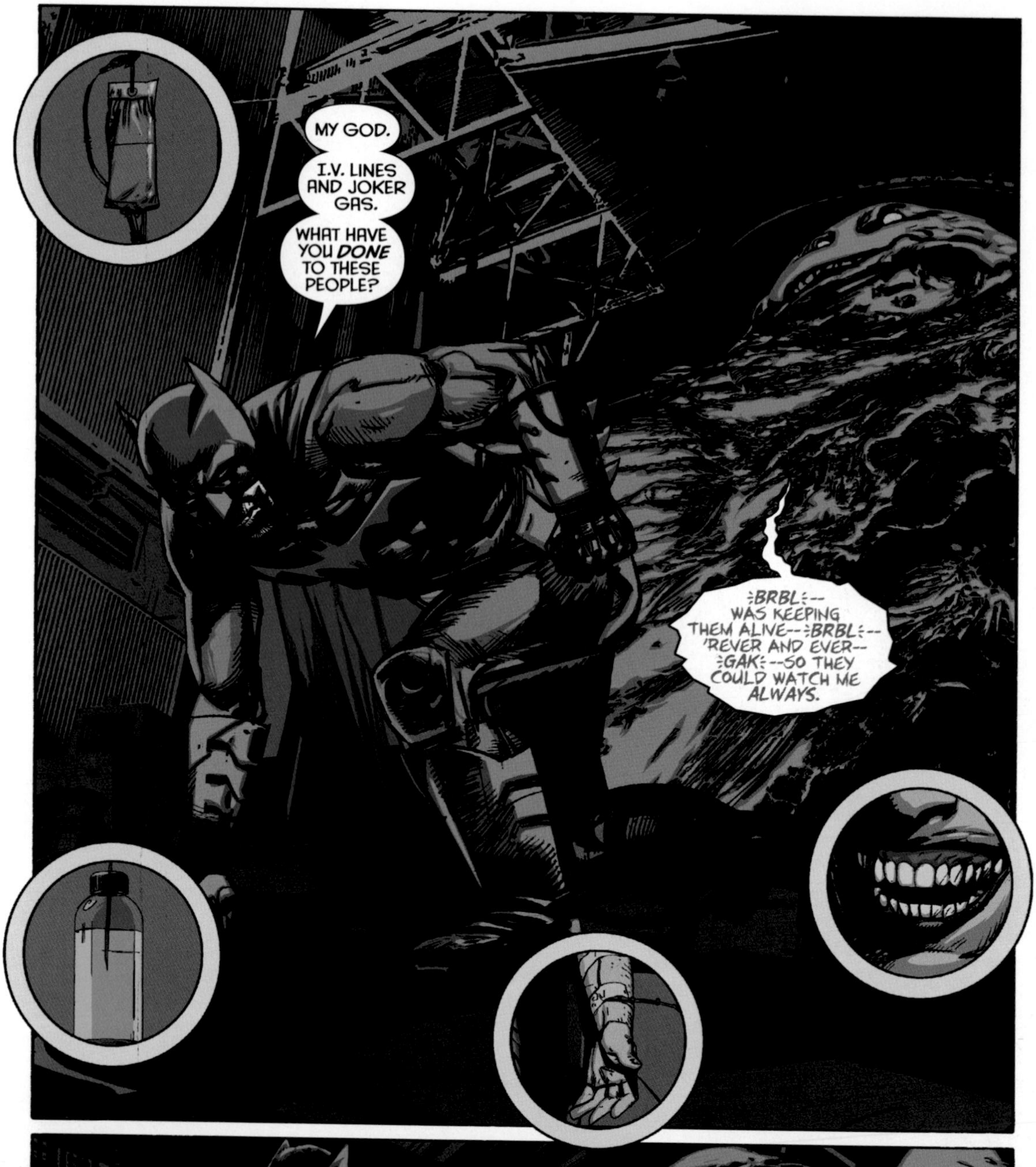
MY GOD.
I.V. LINES AND JOKER GAS.
WHAT HAVE YOU DONE TO THESE PEOPLE?
:BRBL:-- WAS KEEPING THEM ALIVE--:BRBL:-- 'REVER AND EVER-- :GAK:--SO THEY COULD WATCH ME ALWAYS.
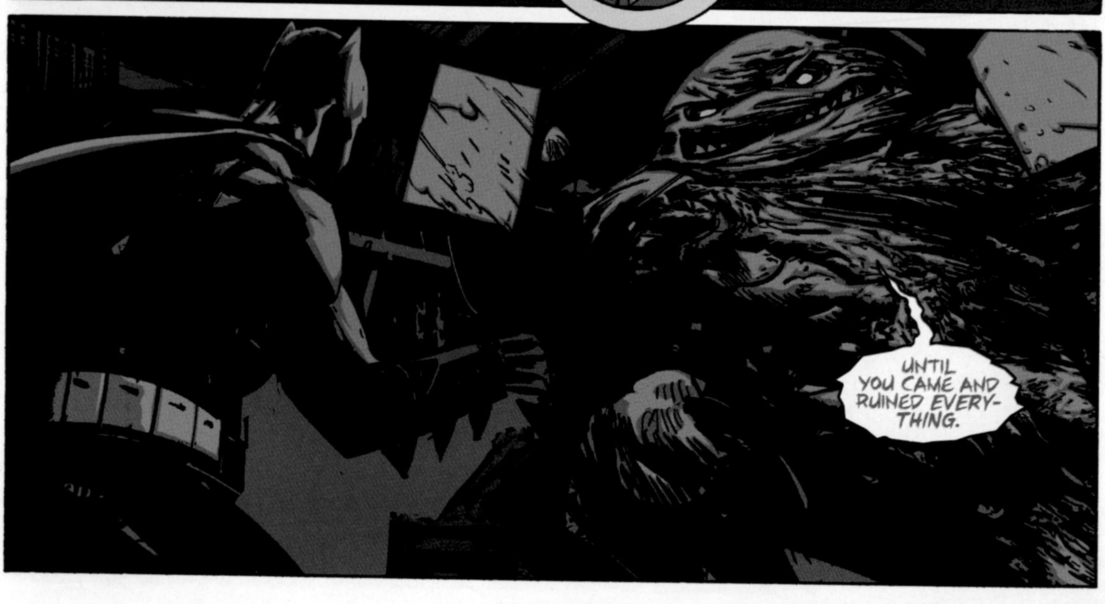
UNTIL YOU CAME AND RUINED EVERY-THING.

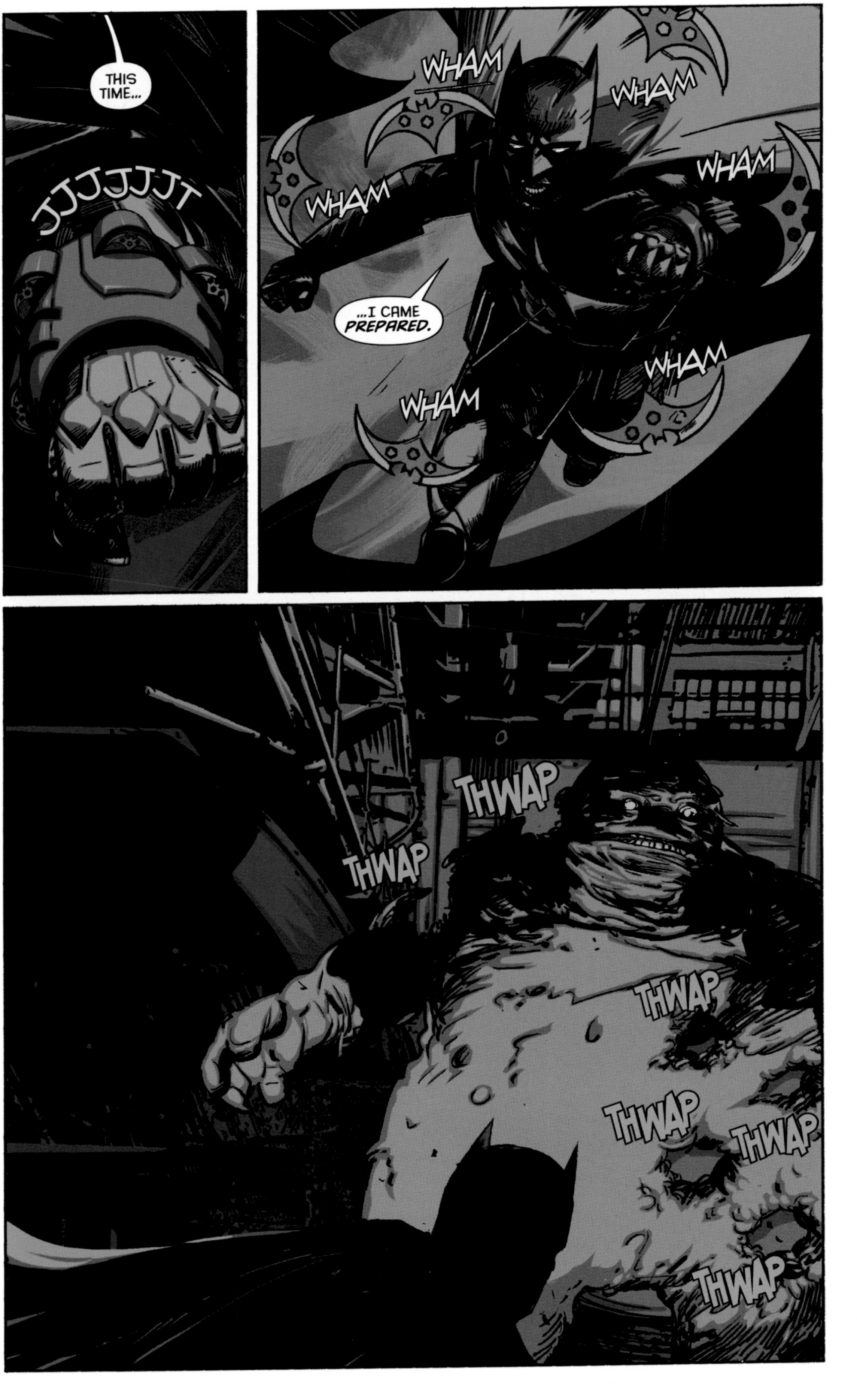
THIS TIME...
JJJJJJT
WHAM
WHAM
WHAM
WHAM
...I CAME PREPARED.
WHAM
WHAM
THWAP
THWAP
THWAP
THWAP
THWAP
THWAP

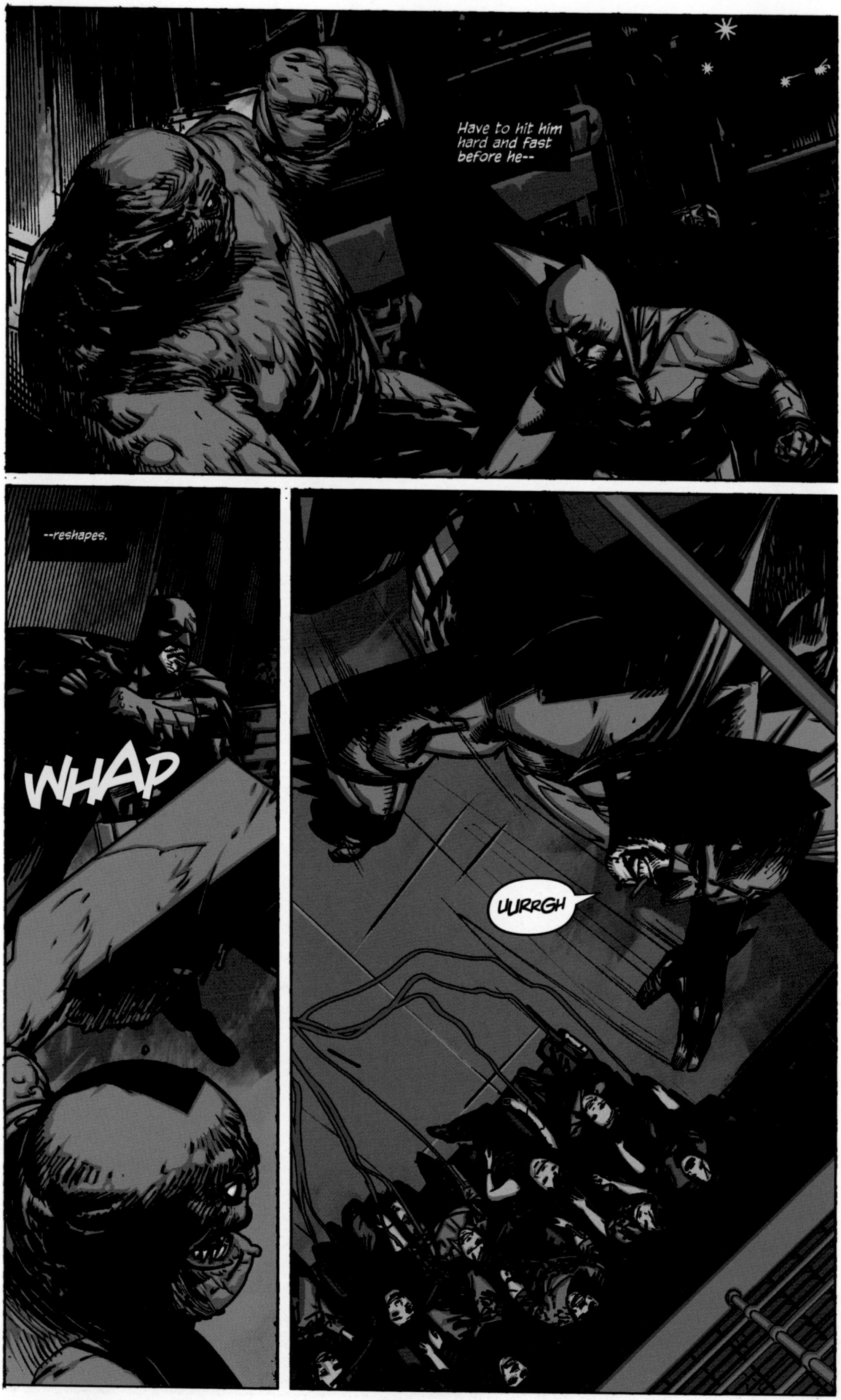
Have to hit him hard and fast before he--
--reshapes.
WHAP
UURRGH

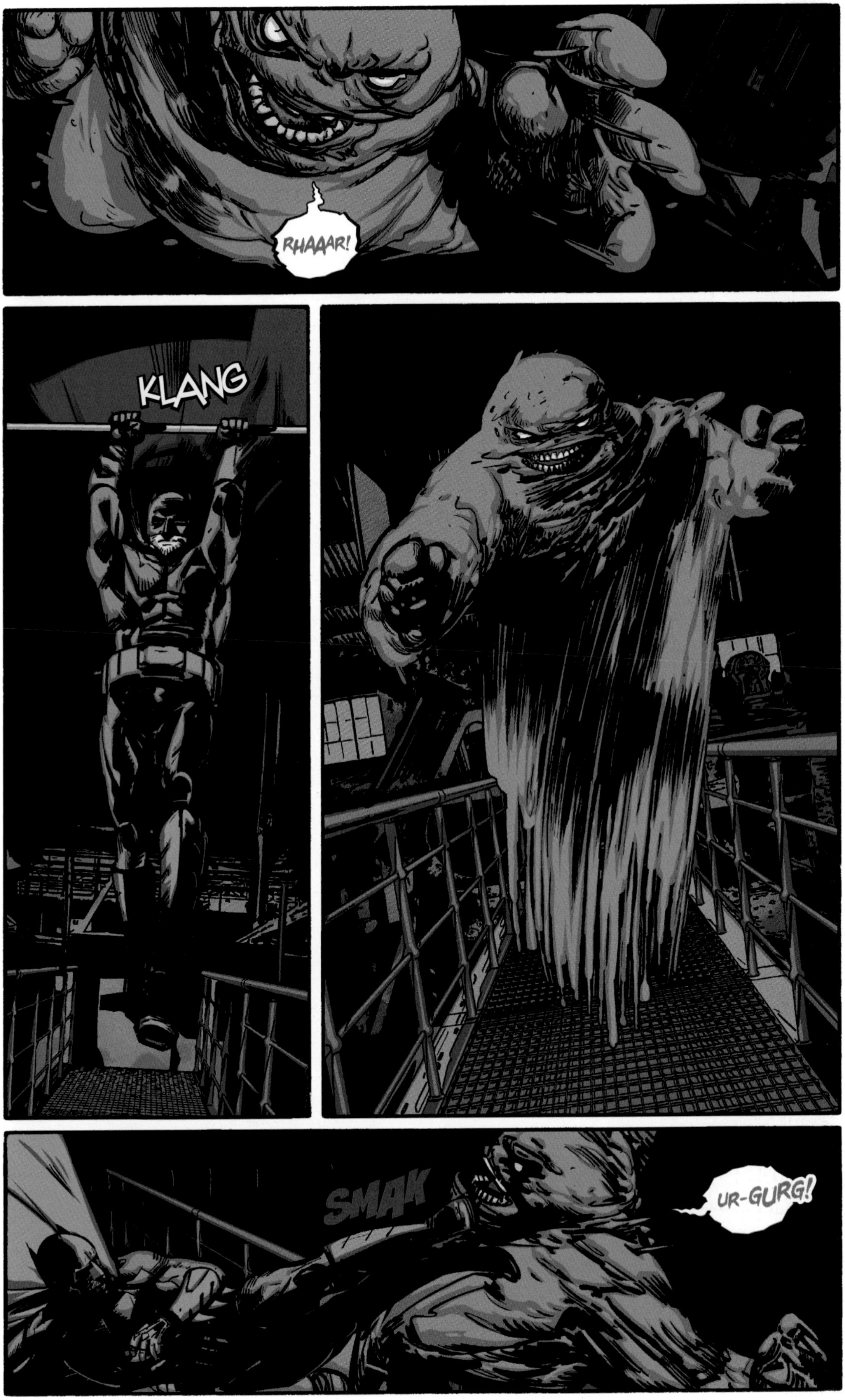
RHAAAR!
KLANG
SMAK
UR-GURG!

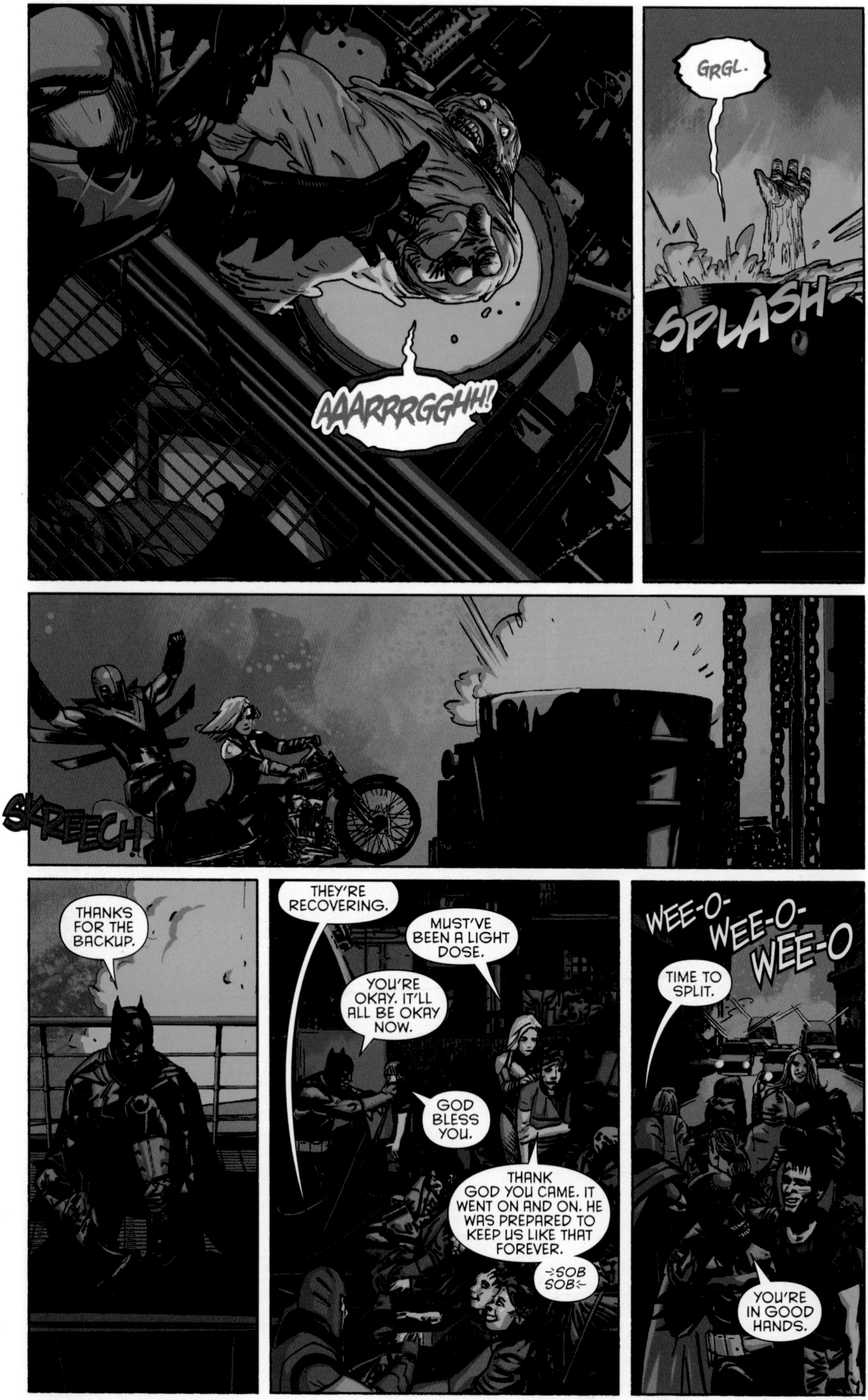
AAARRRGGHH!
GRGL.
SPLASH
SKREEECH
THANKS FOR THE BACKUP.
THEY'RE RECOVERING.
MUST'VE BEEN A LIGHT DOSE.
YOU'RE OKAY. IT'LL ALL BE OKAY NOW.
GOD BLESS YOU.
THANK GOD YOU CAME. IT WENT ON AND ON. HE WAS PREPARED TO KEEP US LIKE THAT FOREVER.
SOB SOB
WEE-O- WEE-O- WEE-O
TIME TO SPLIT.
YOU'RE IN GOOD HANDS.

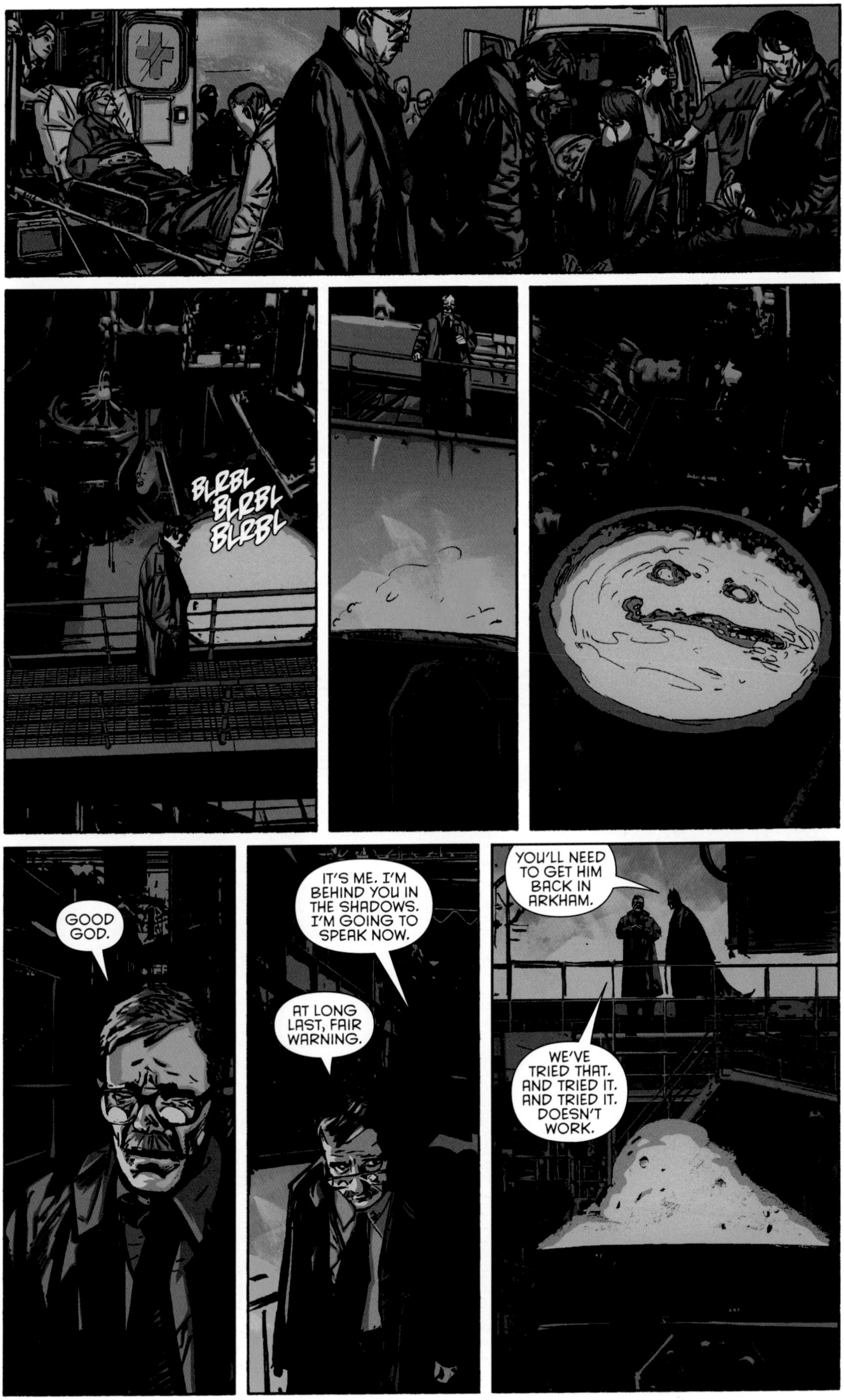
BLRBL
BLRBL
BLRBL
GOOD GOD.
IT'S ME. I'M BEHIND YOU IN THE SHADOWS. I'M GOING TO SPEAK NOW.
AT LONG LAST, FAIR WARNING.
YOU'LL NEED TO GET HIM BACK IN ARKHAM.
WE'VE TRIED THAT. AND TRIED IT. AND TRIED IT. DOESN'T WORK.

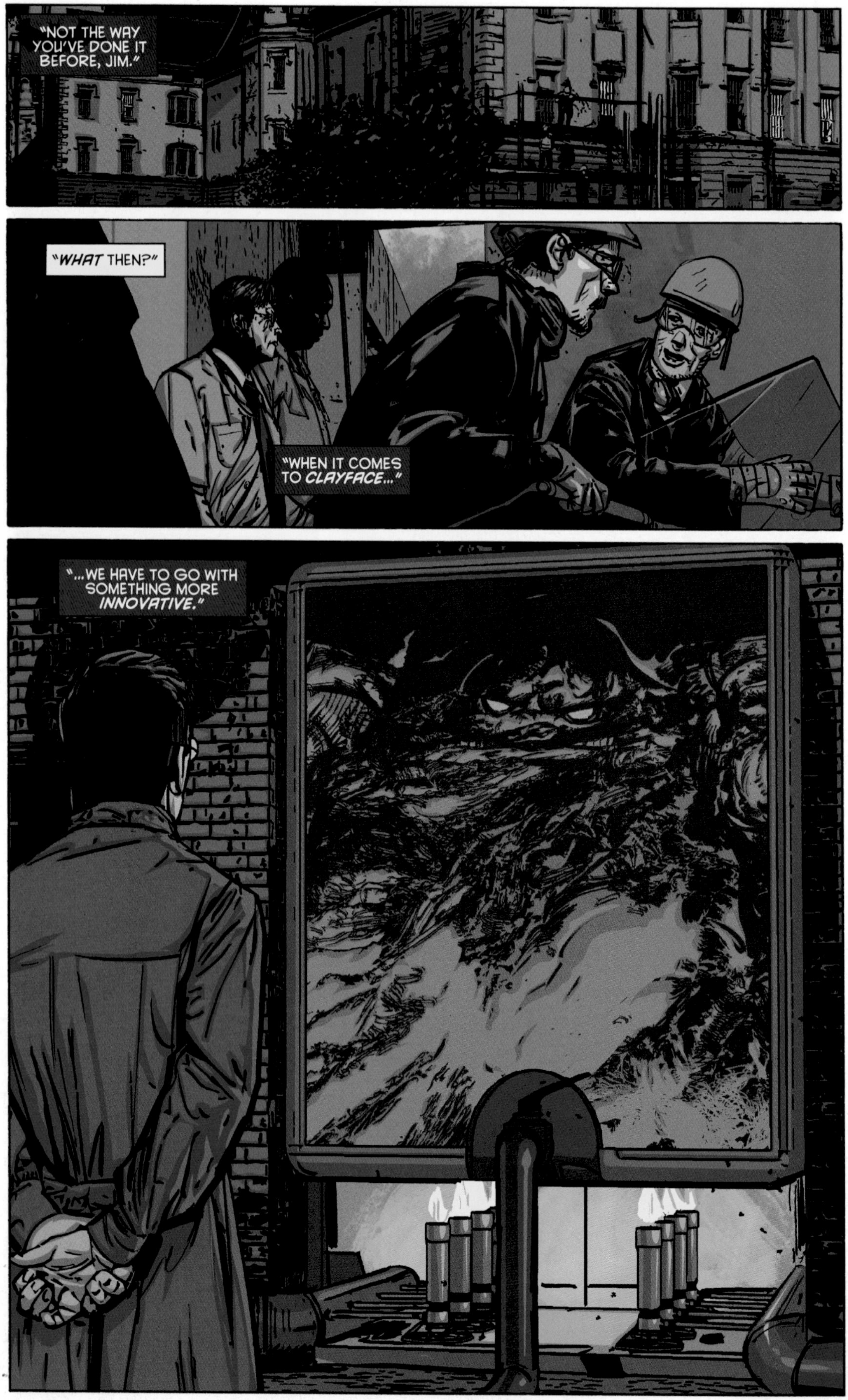
"NOT THE WAY YOU'VE DONE IT BEFORE, JIM."
"*WHAT* THEN?"
"WHEN IT COMES TO *CLAYFACE*..."
"...WE HAVE TO GO WITH SOMETHING MORE *INNOVATIVE*."

ALBERTO PONTICELLI artist cover art by Chris Burnham & Nathan Fairbairn

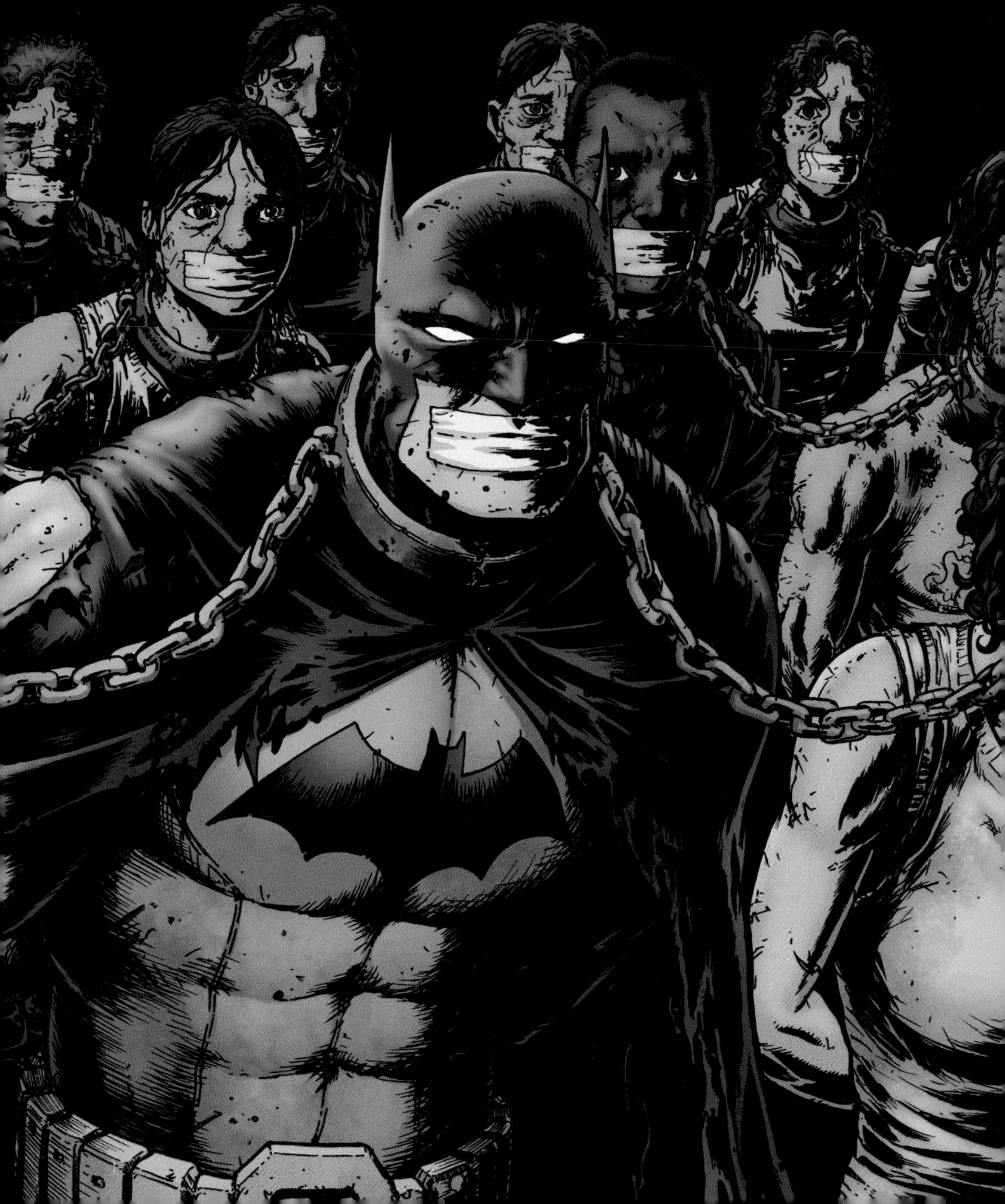

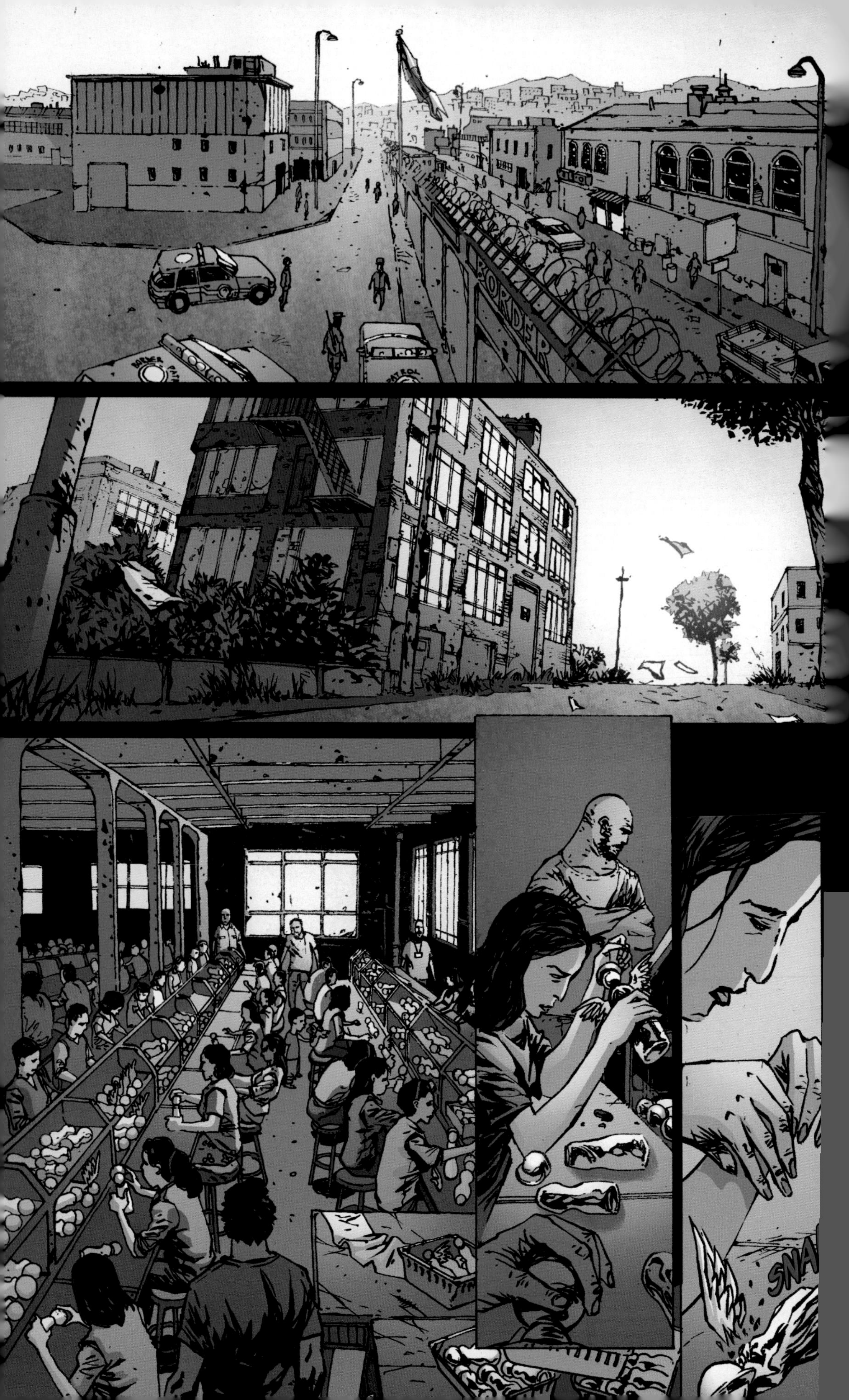
BORDER
SNA

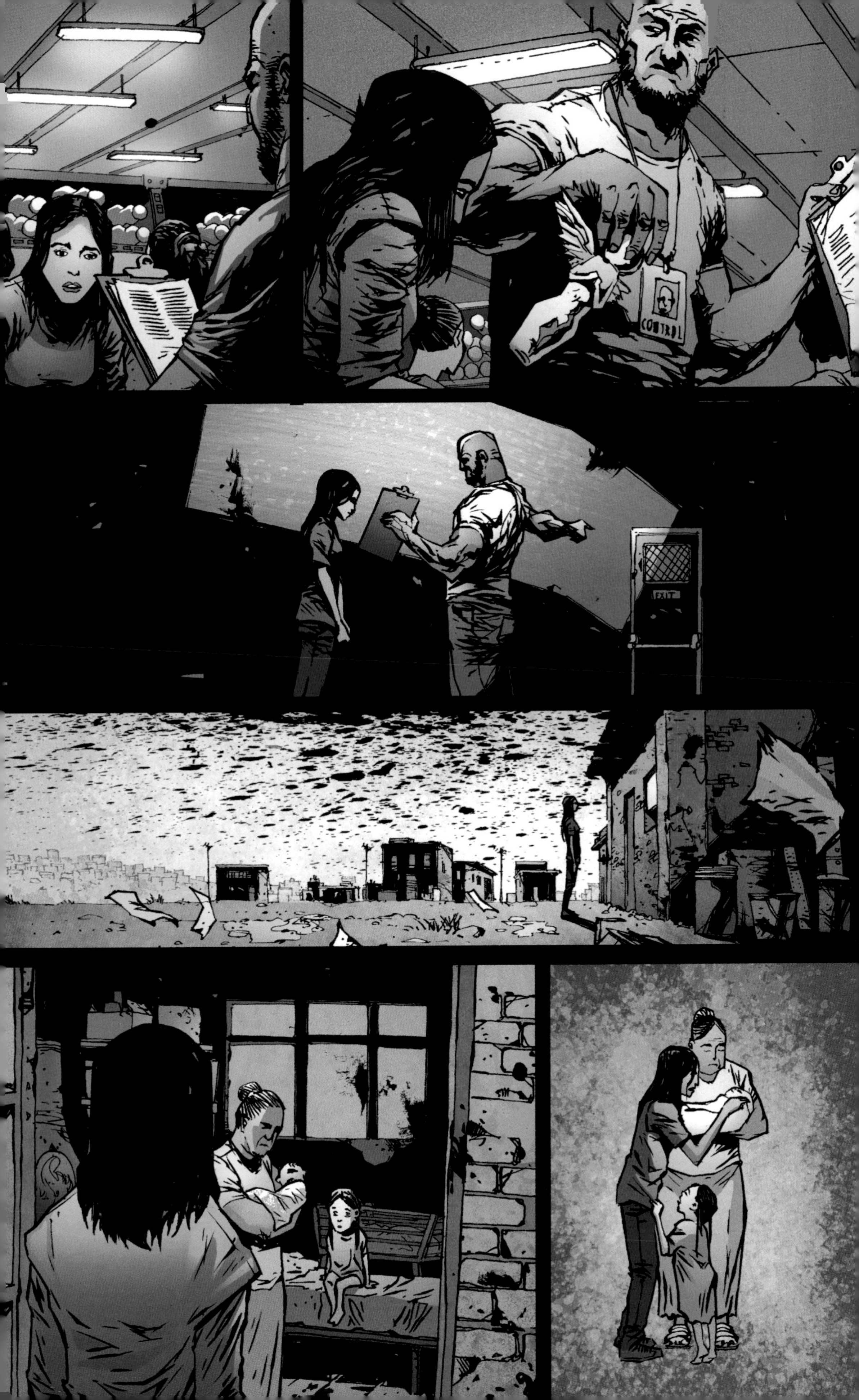
CONTROL
EXIT

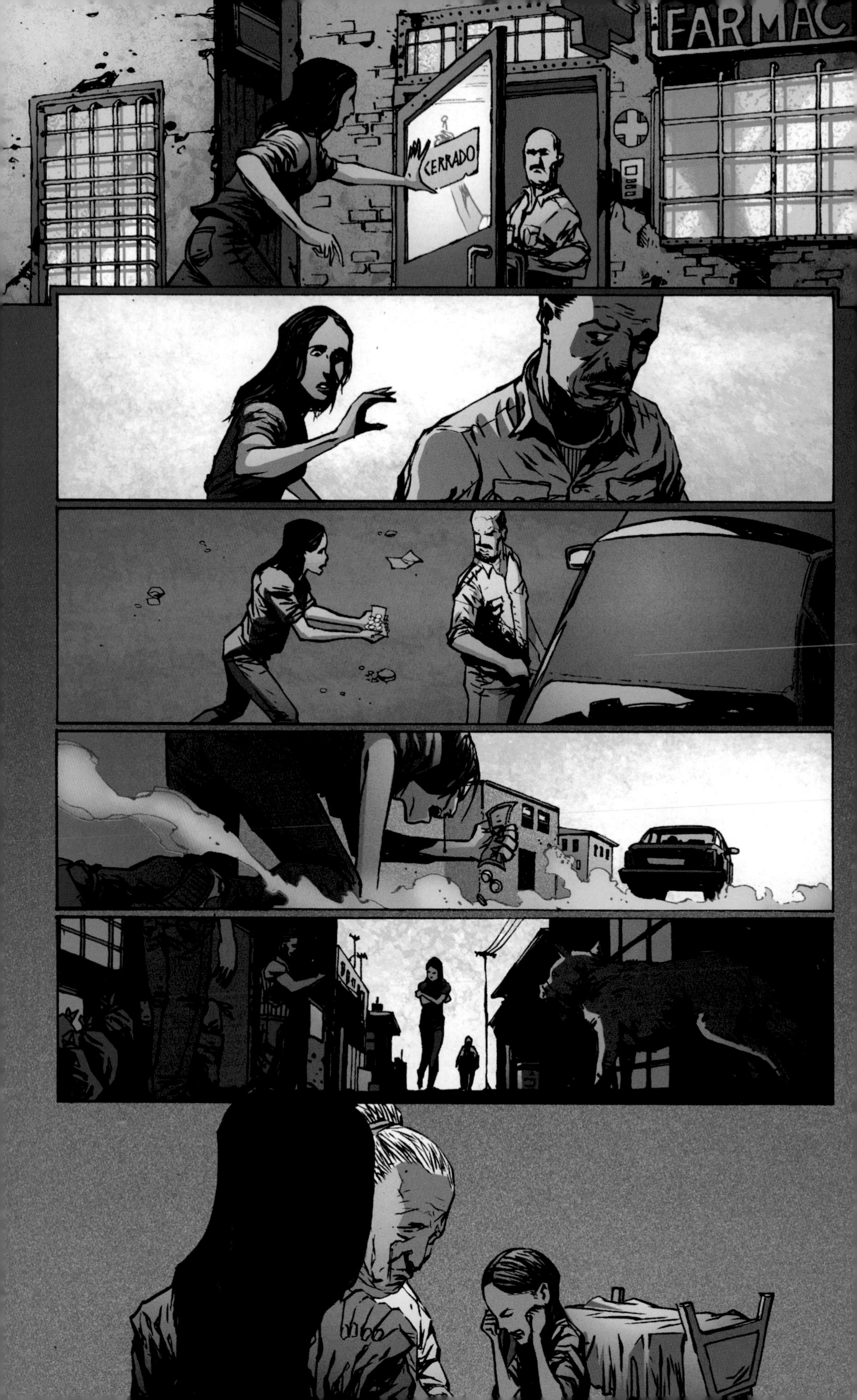
FARMAC
CERRADO

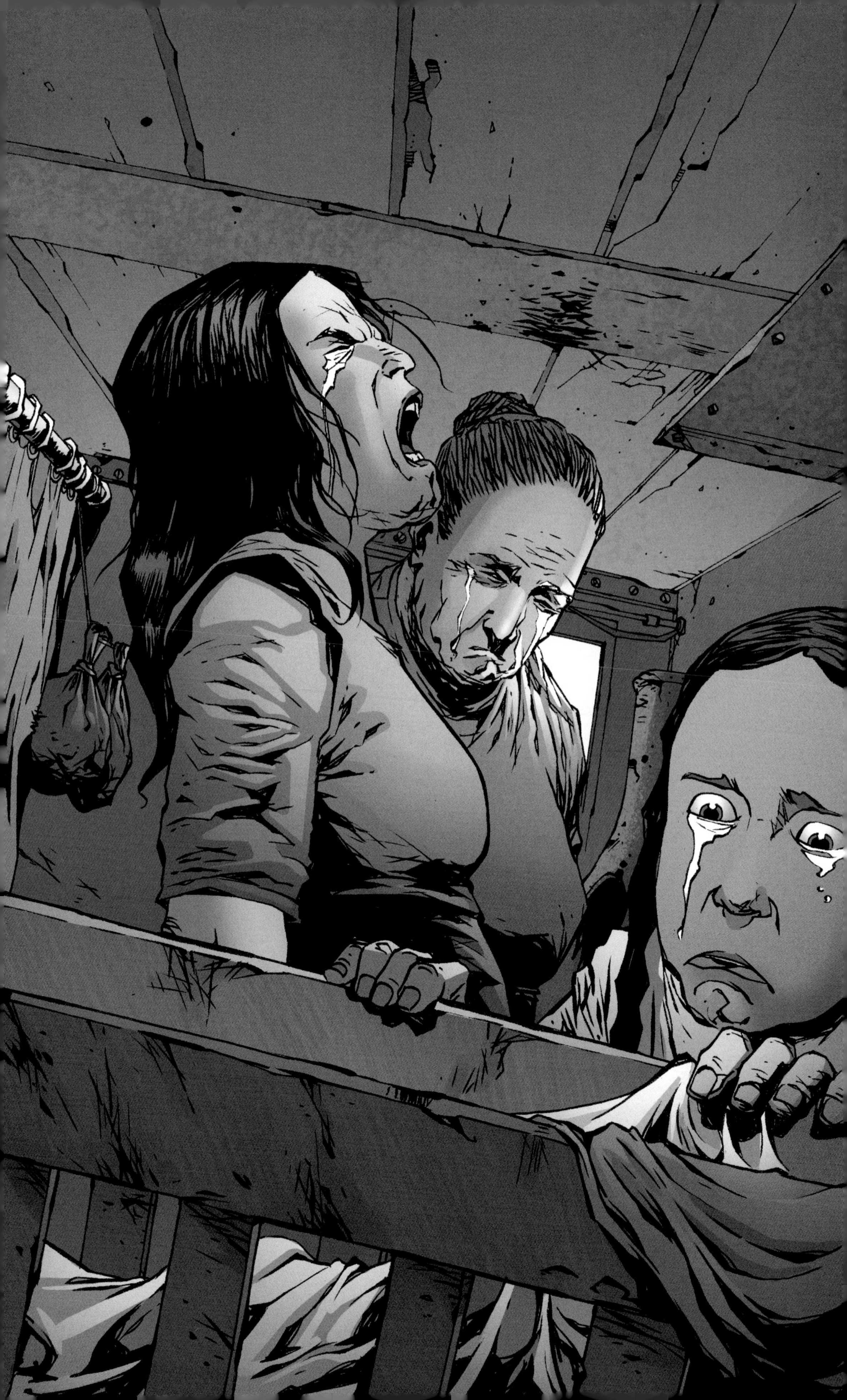

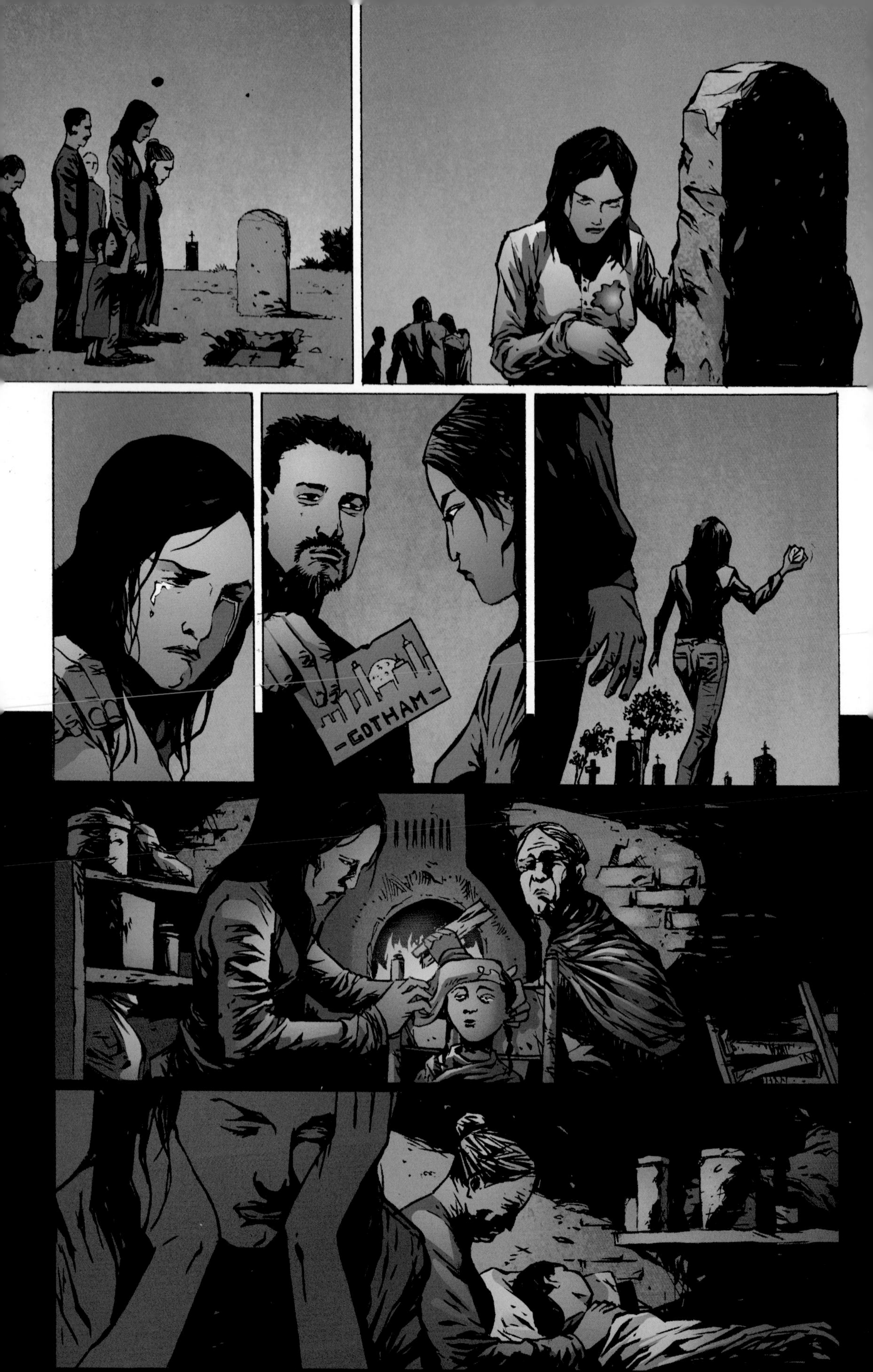
GOTHAM

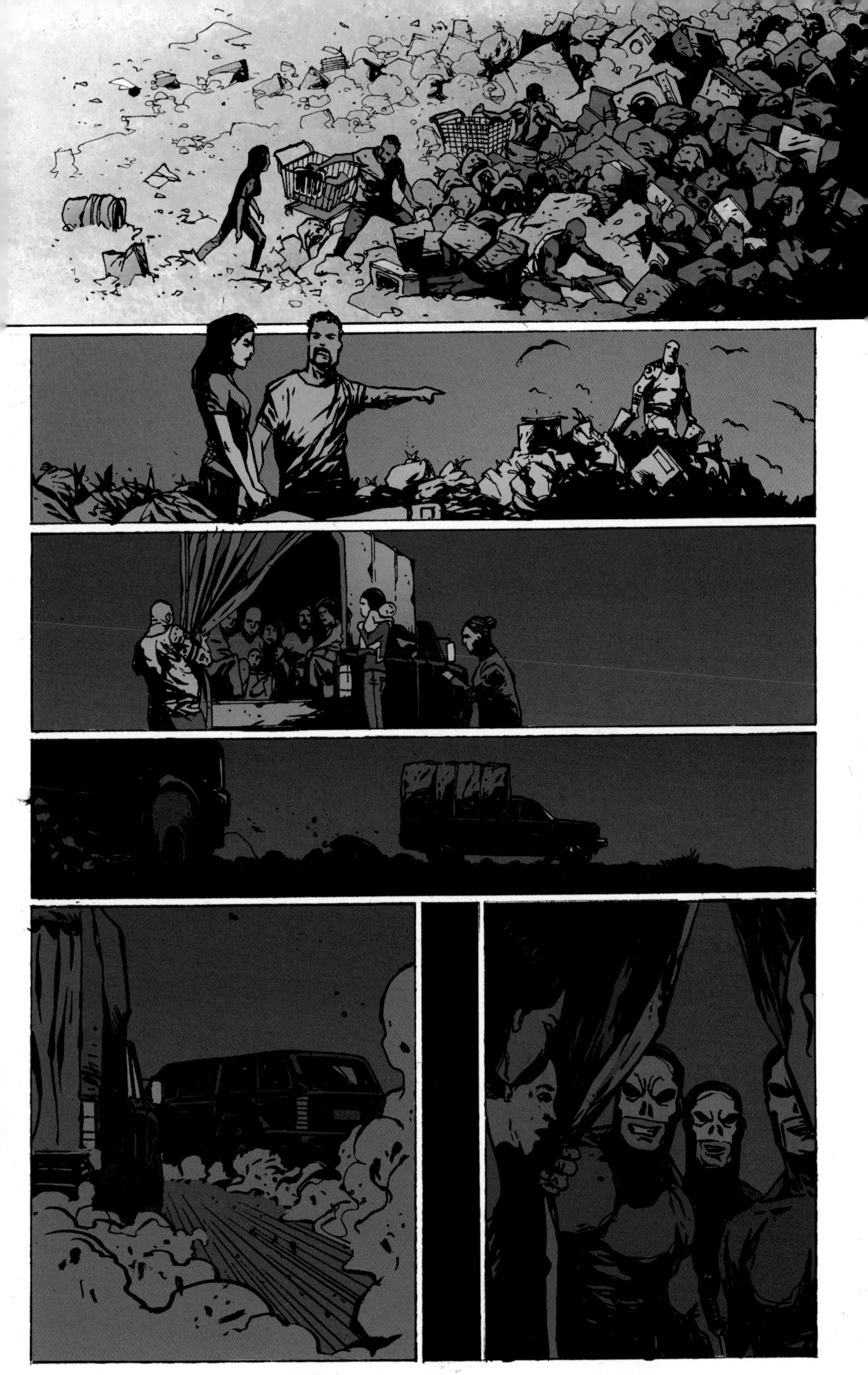

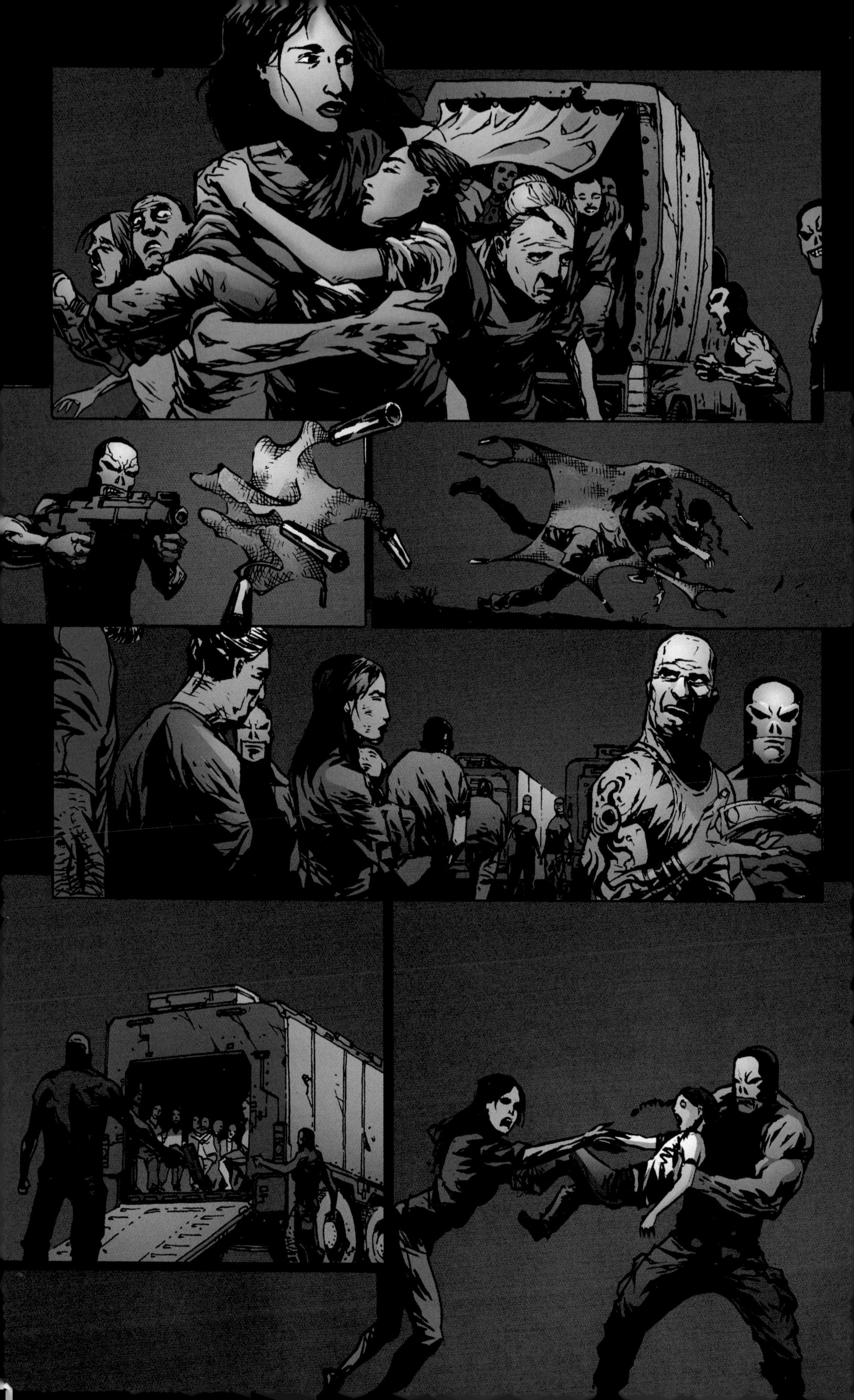

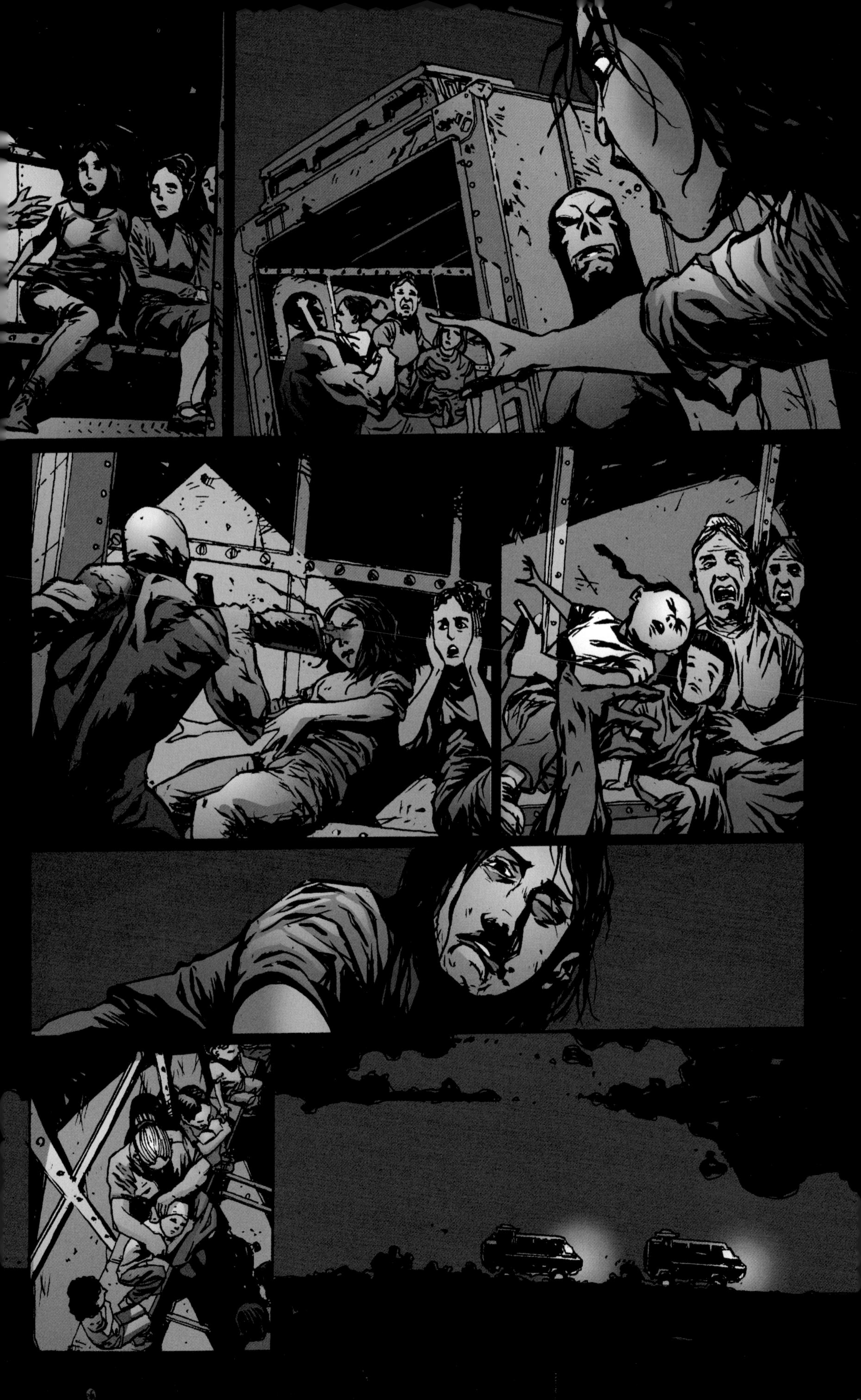

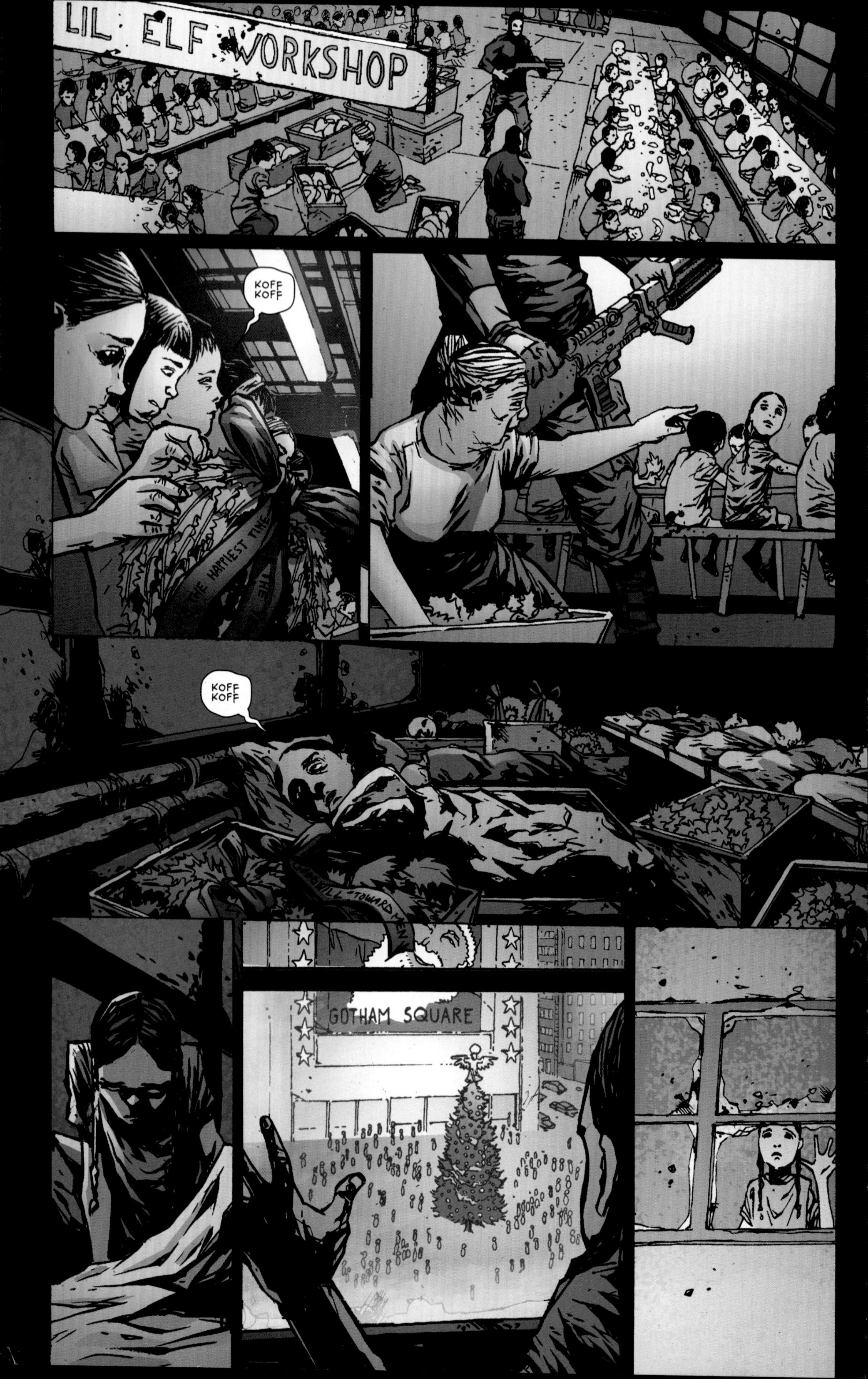
LIL ELF WORKSHOP
KOFF KOFF
THE HAPPIEST TIME
KOFF KOFF
GOTHAM SQUARE

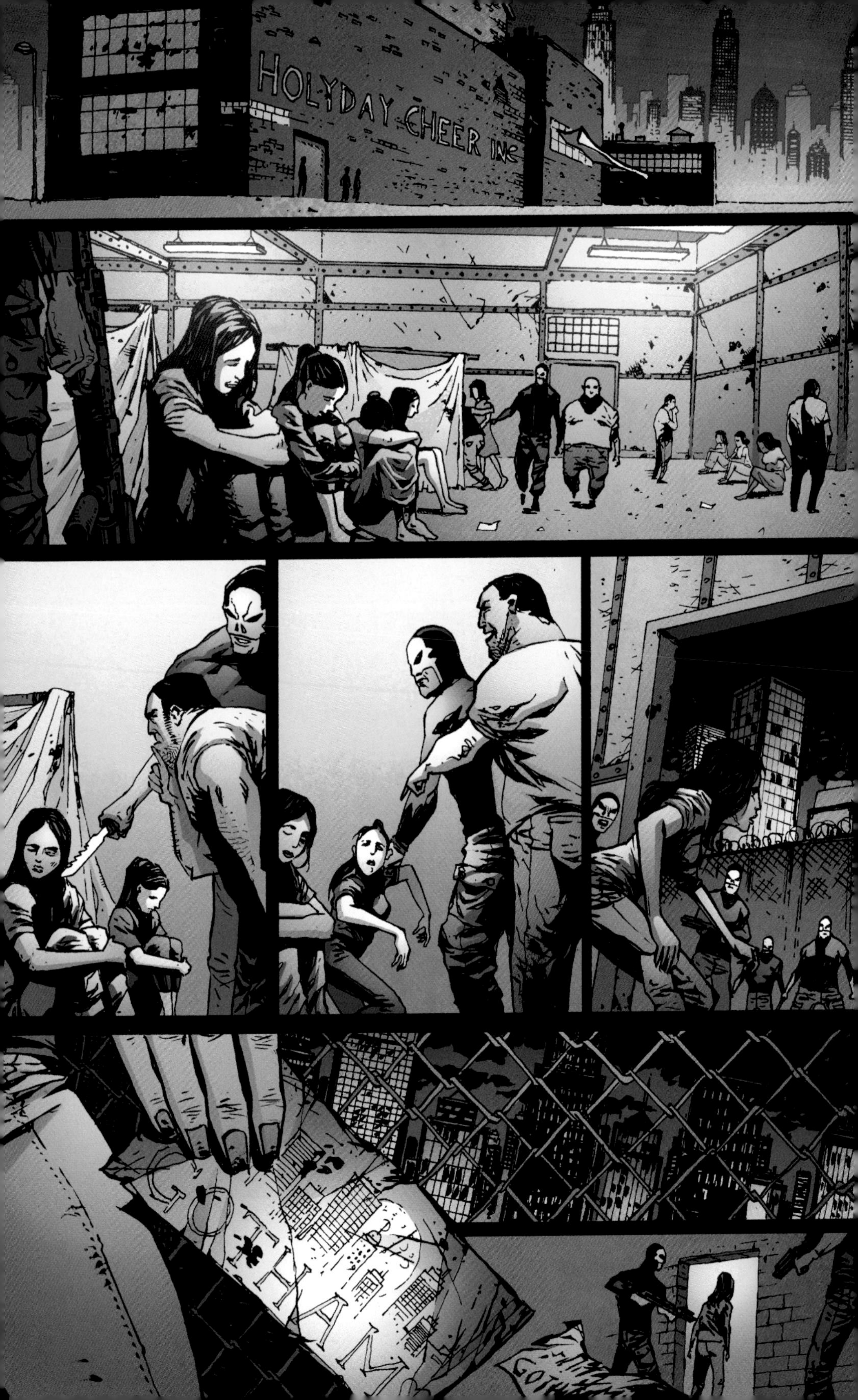
HOLYDAY CHEER INC
GOTHAM

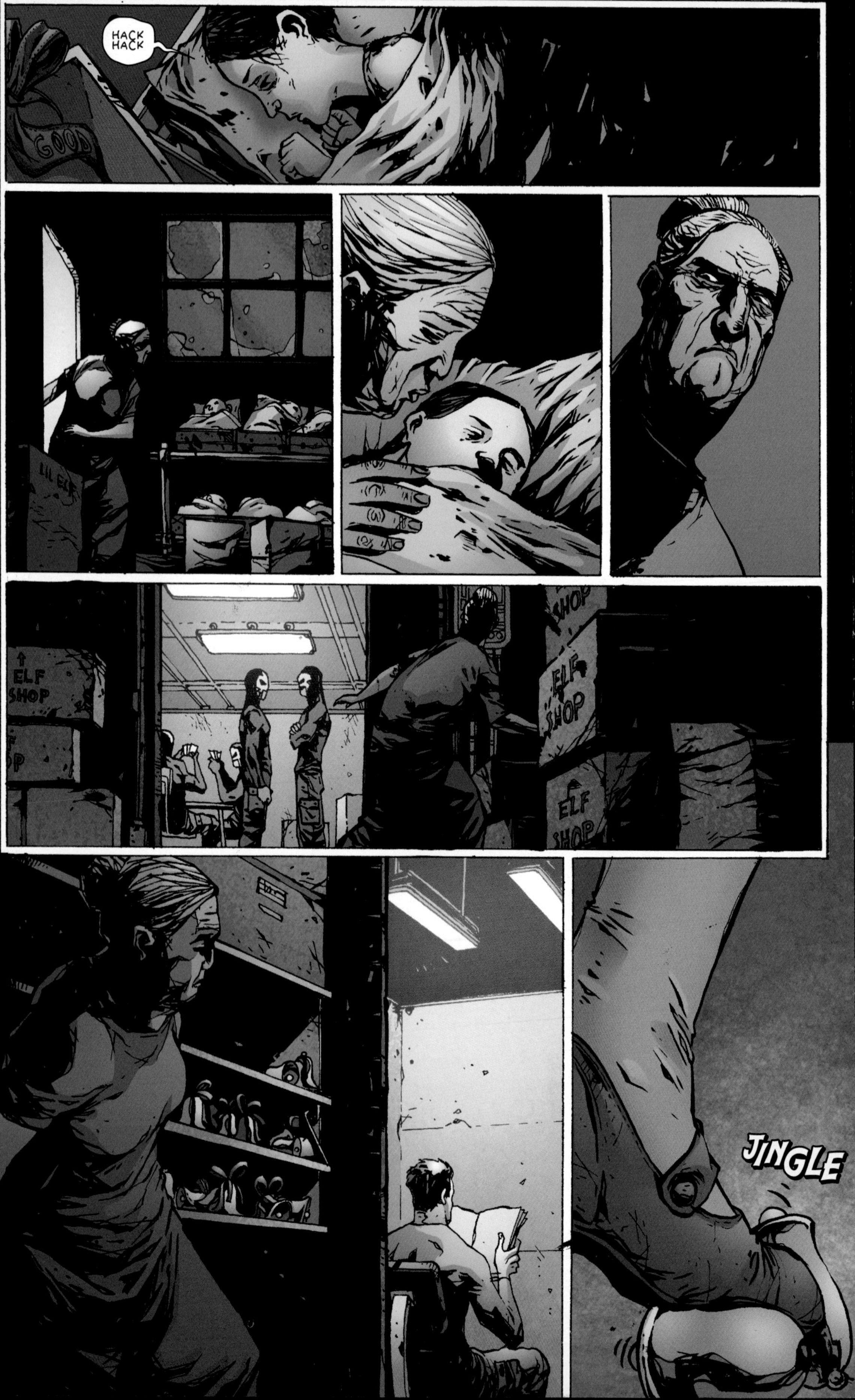

HACK HACK
GOOD
LIL ELF
ELF SHOP
ELF SHOP
ELF SHOP
JINGLE

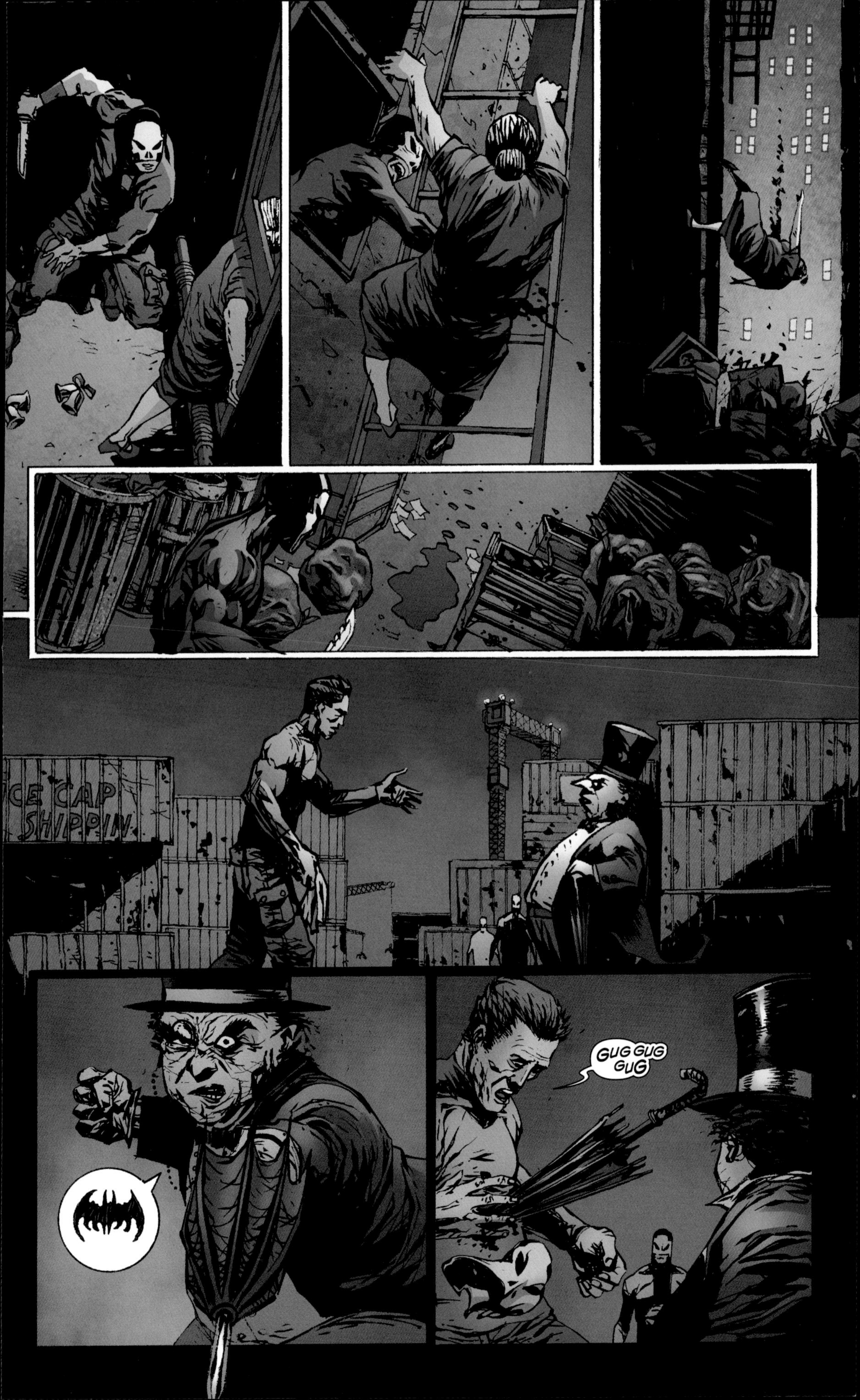
ICE CAP
SHIPPIN
GUG GUG
GUG

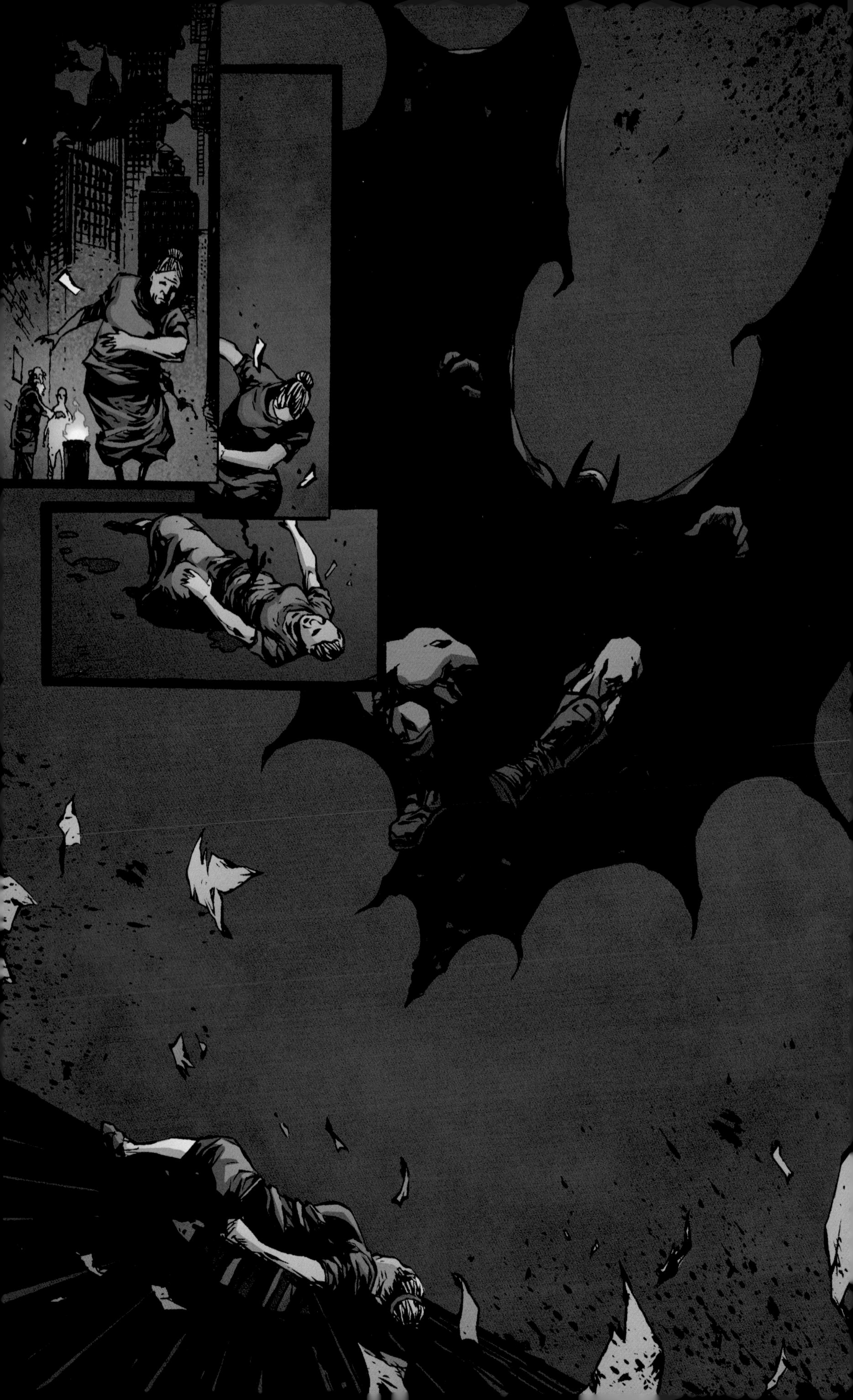

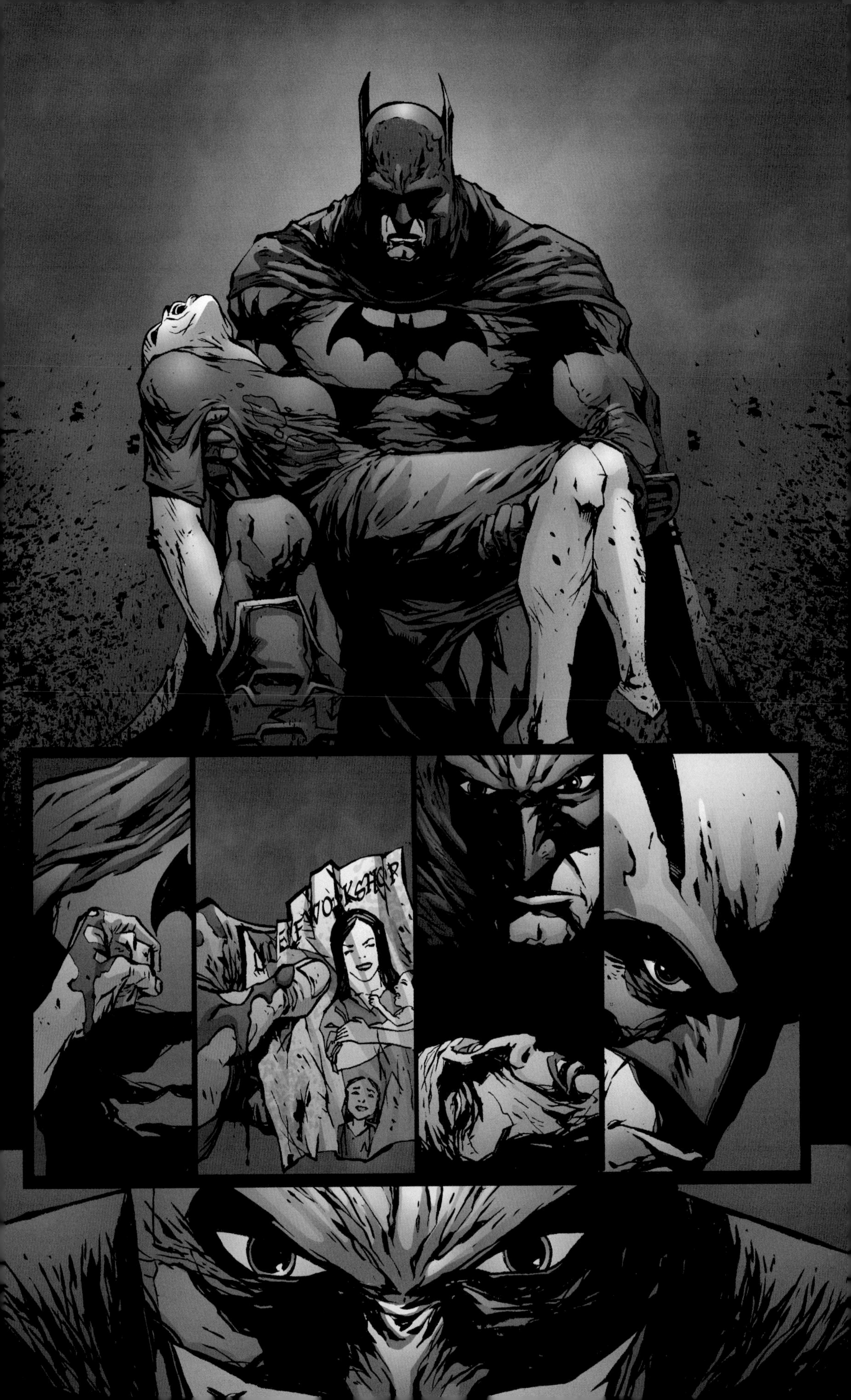

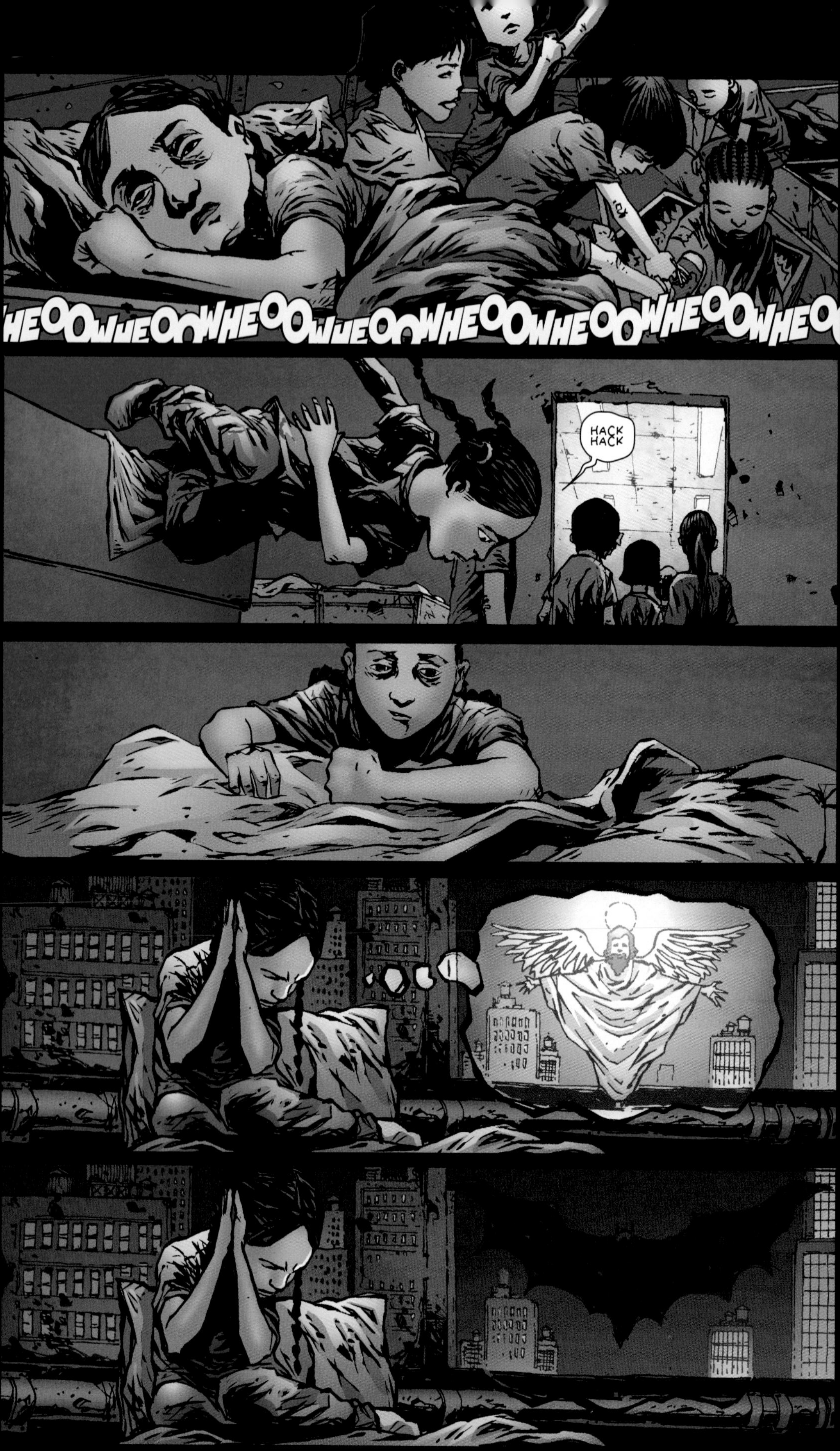
WHEOOWHEOOWHEOOWHEOOWHEOOWHEOOWHEO
HACK HACK

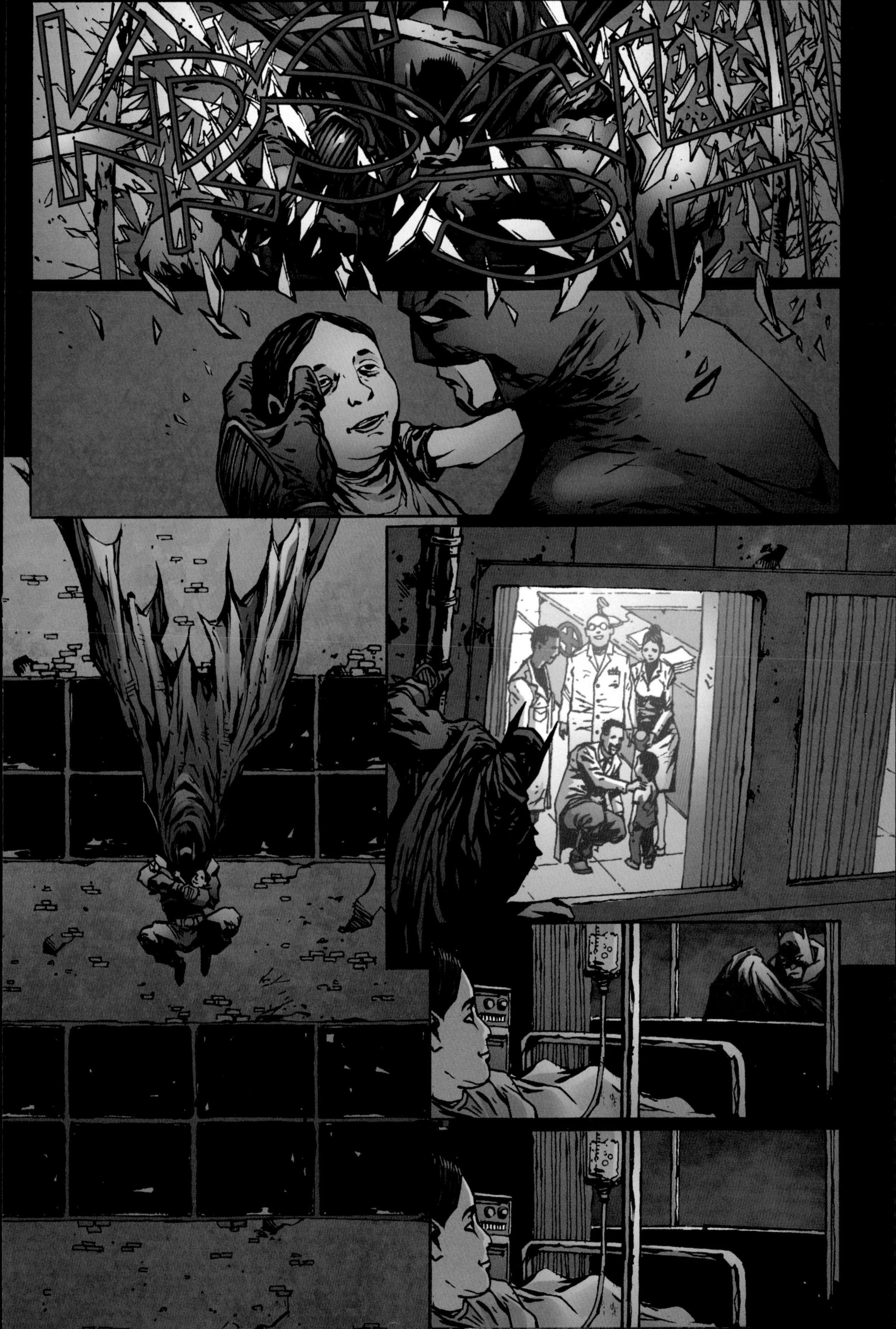
KRSSH

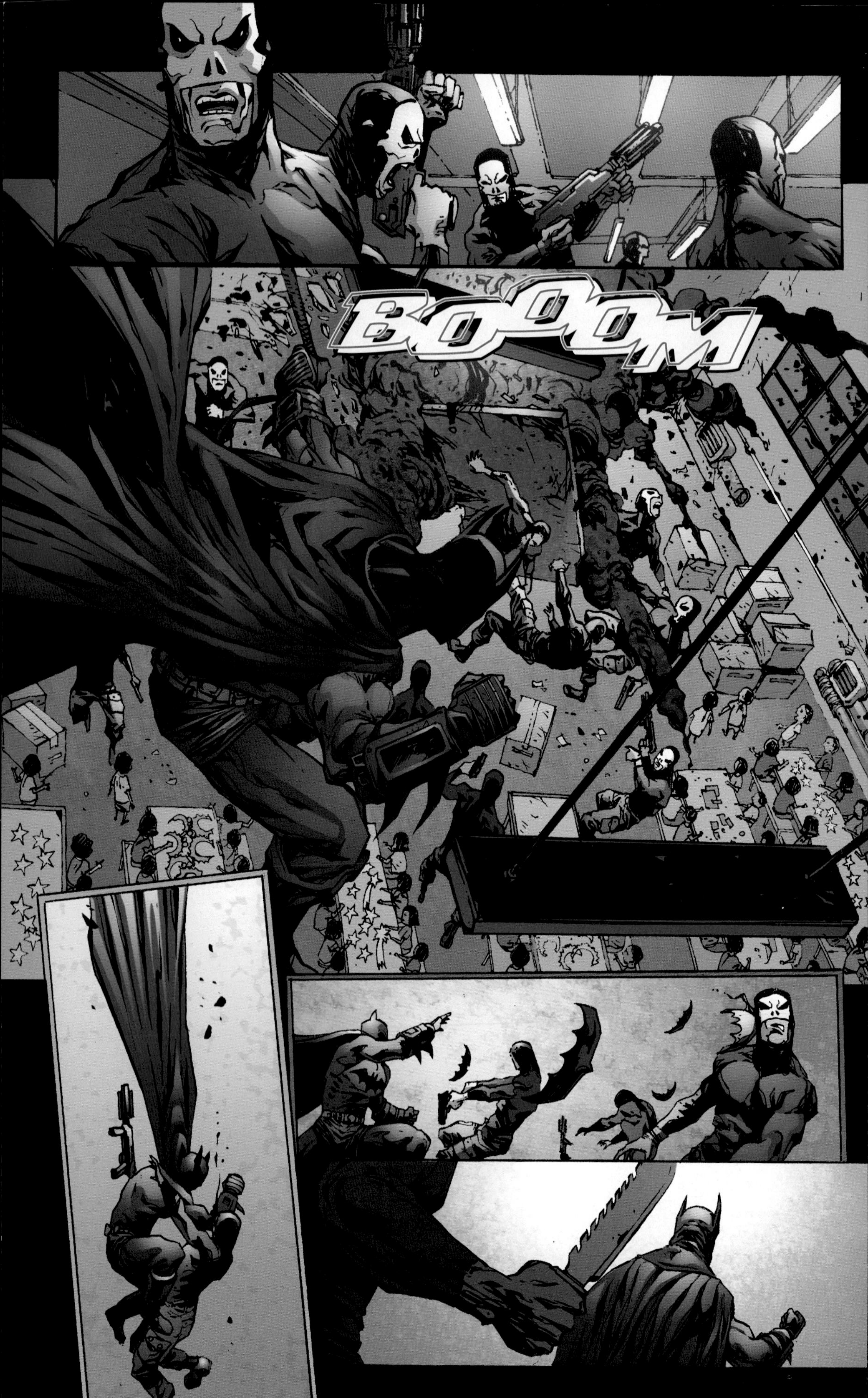
BOOOM

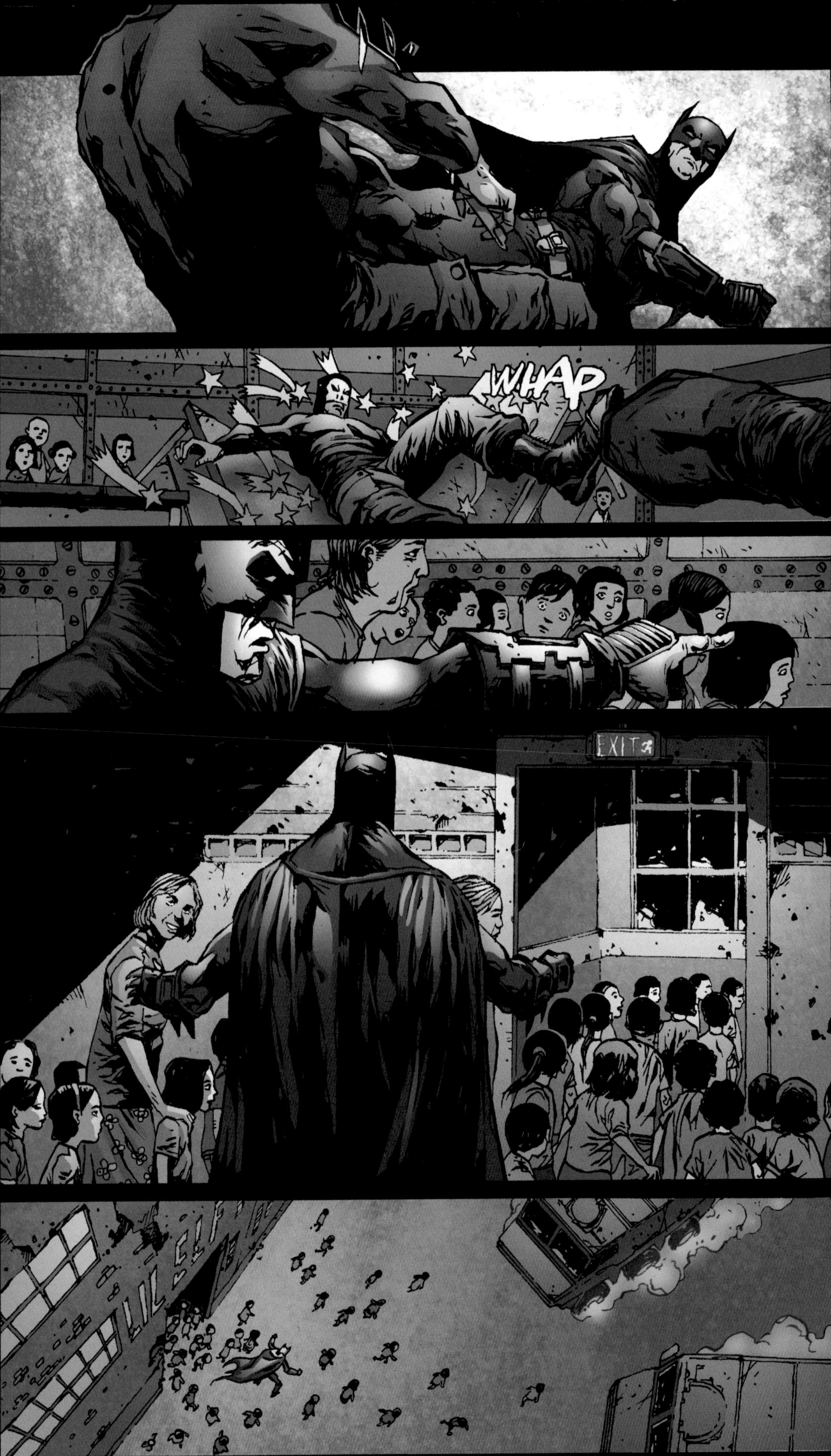
WHAP
EXIT

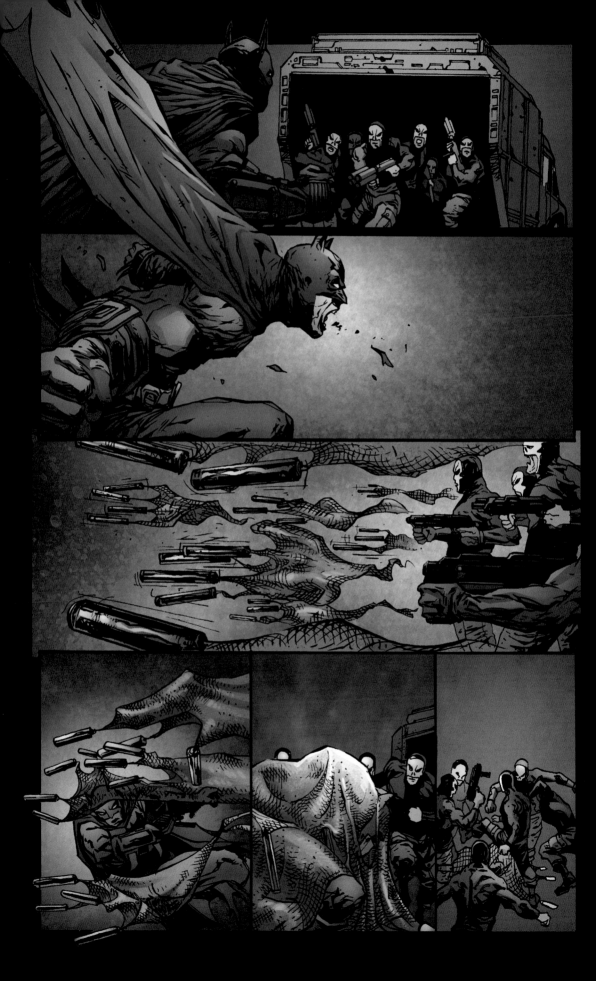

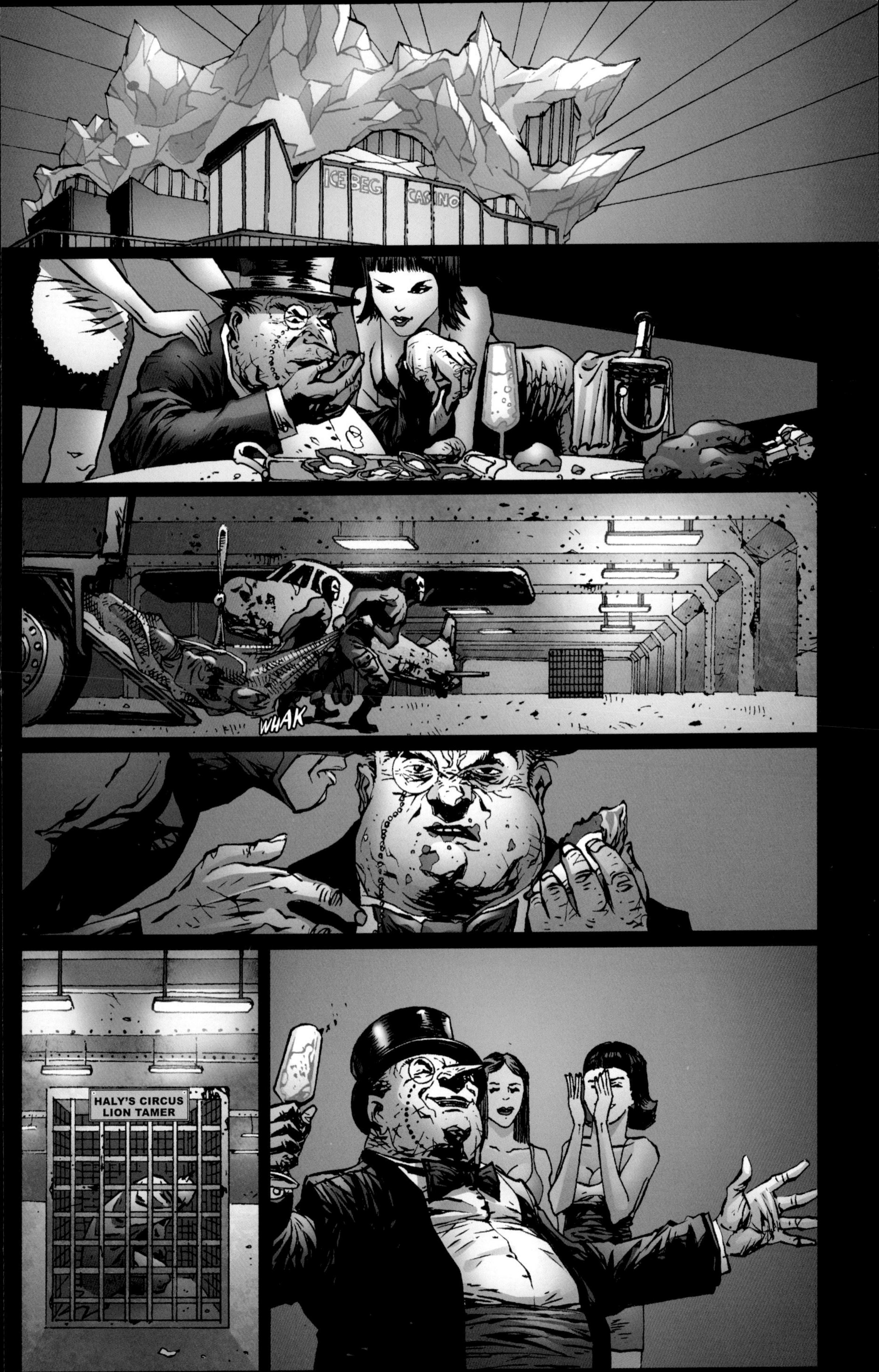
ICEBERG CASINO
WHAK
HALY'S CIRCUS
LION TAMER

ANGEL OF DARKNESS

ALBERTO PONTICELLI artist cover art by **Chris Burnham & Nathan Fairbairn**

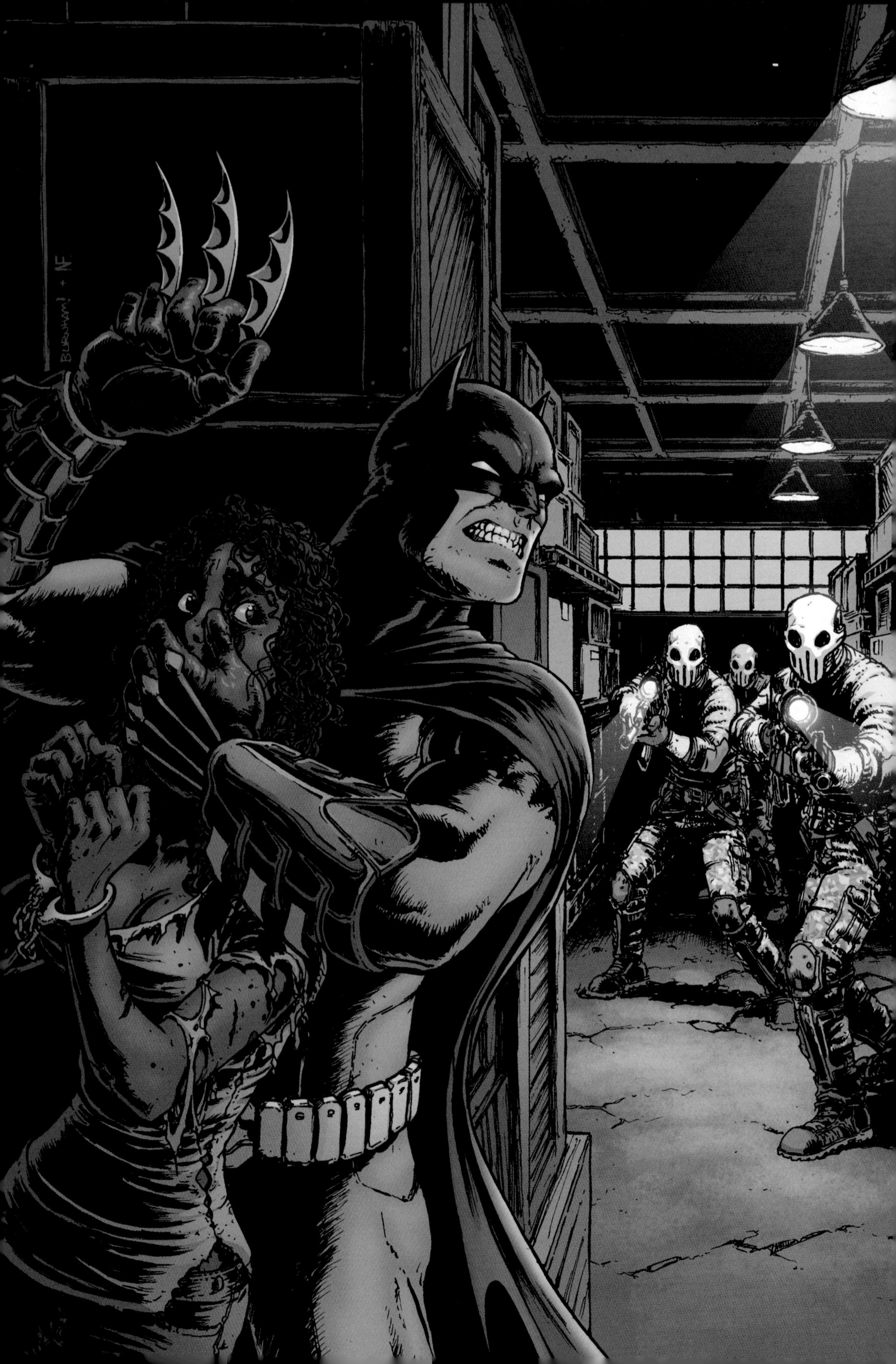
BURNHAM! + NF

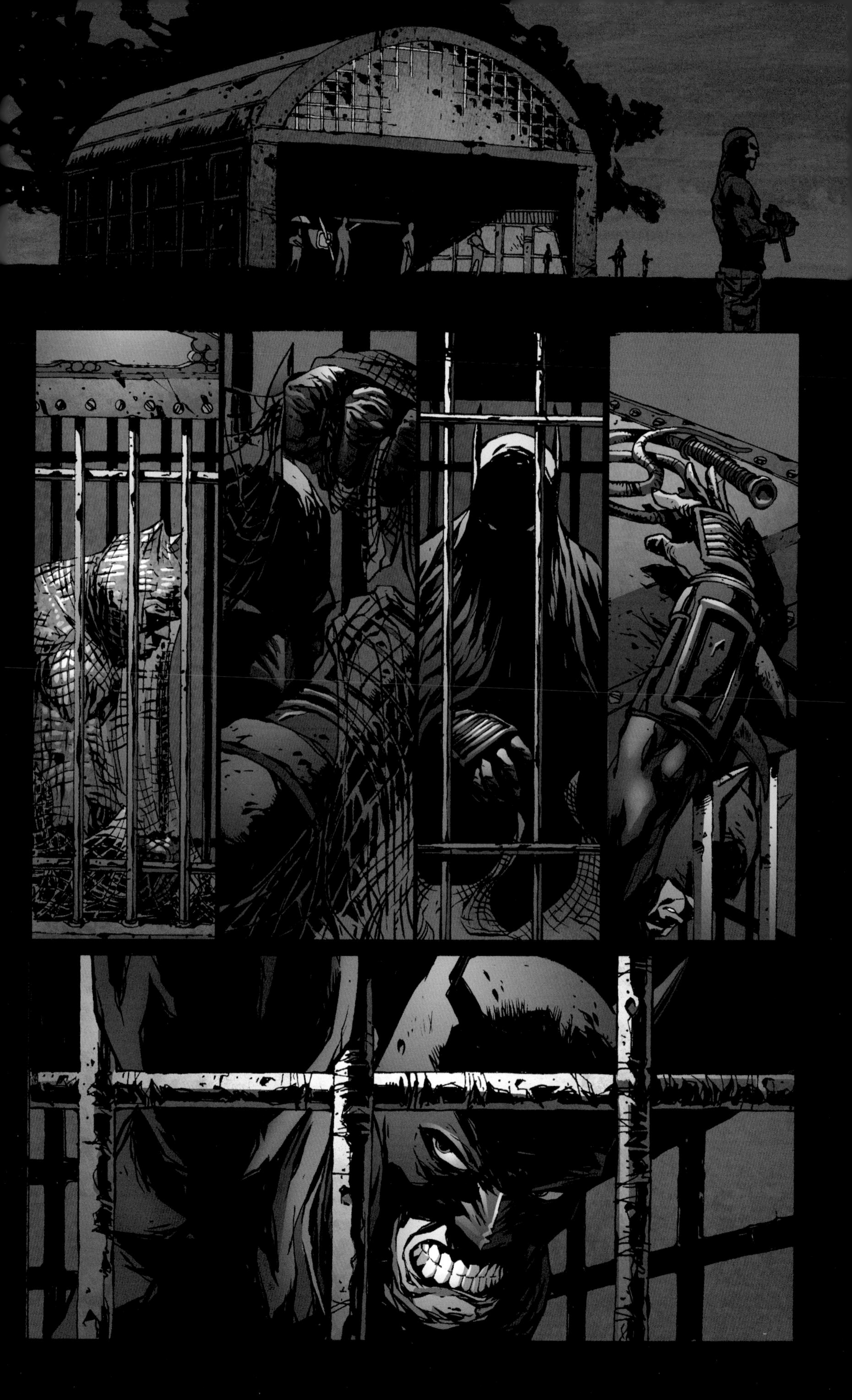

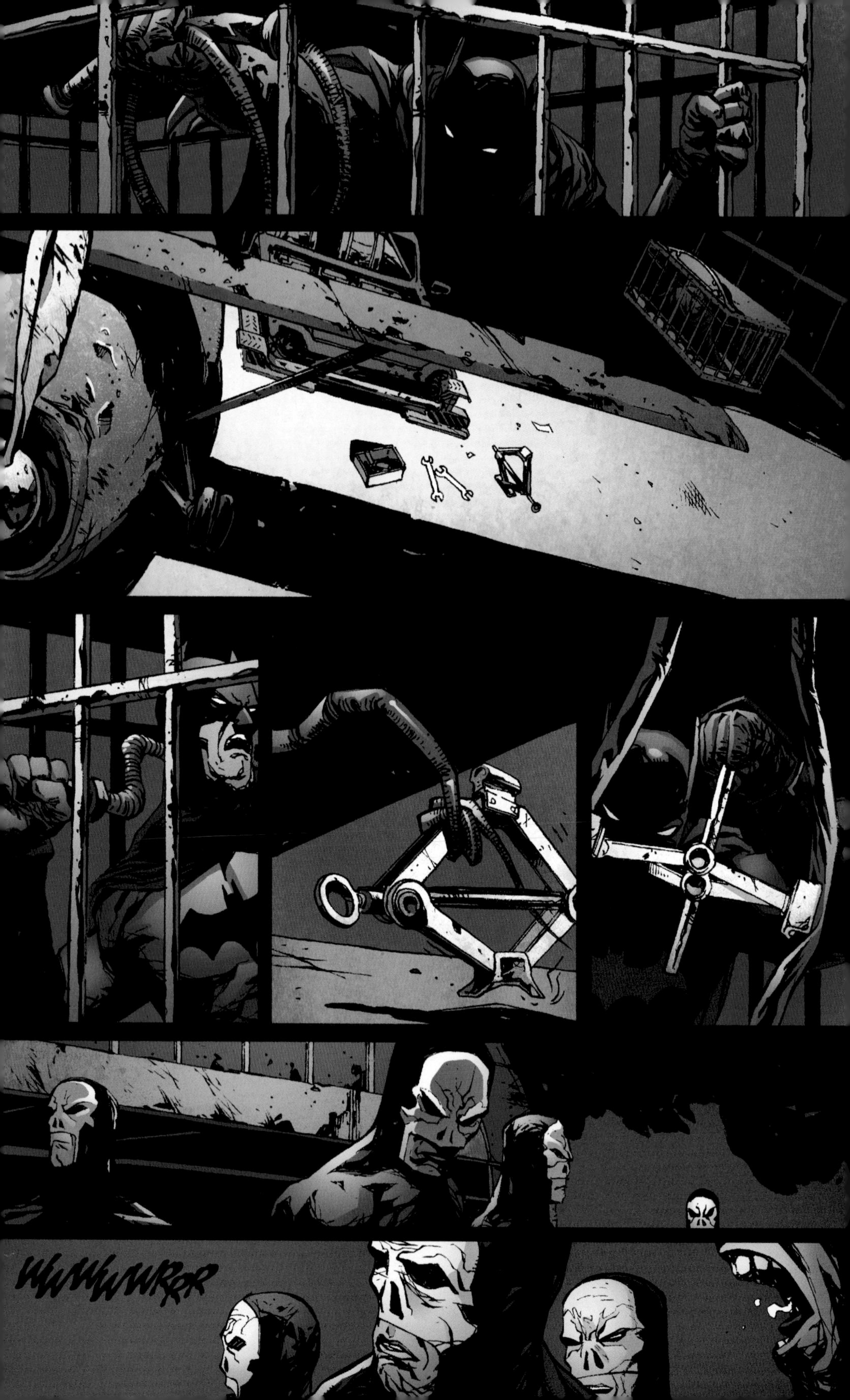
WWWWWRRR

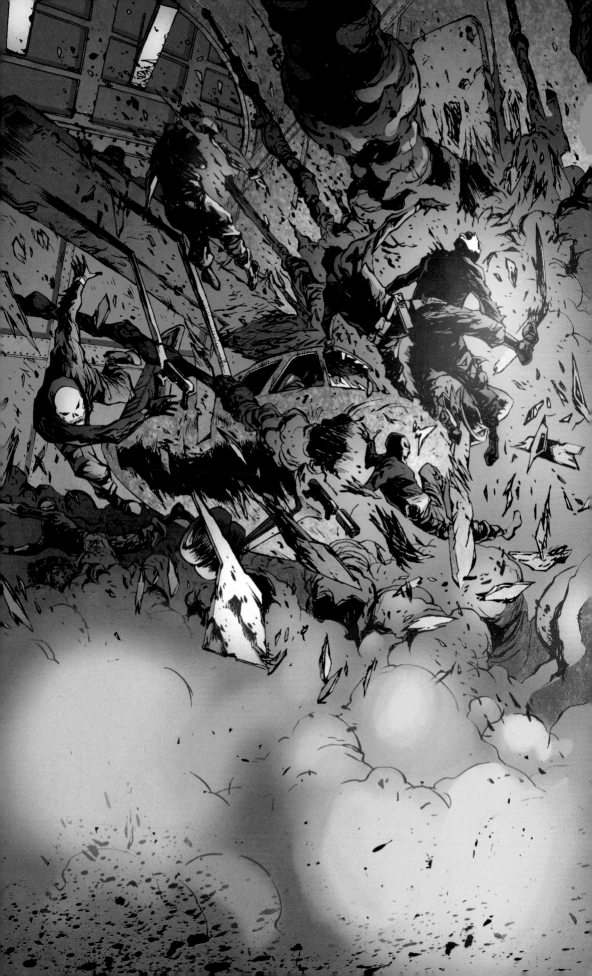

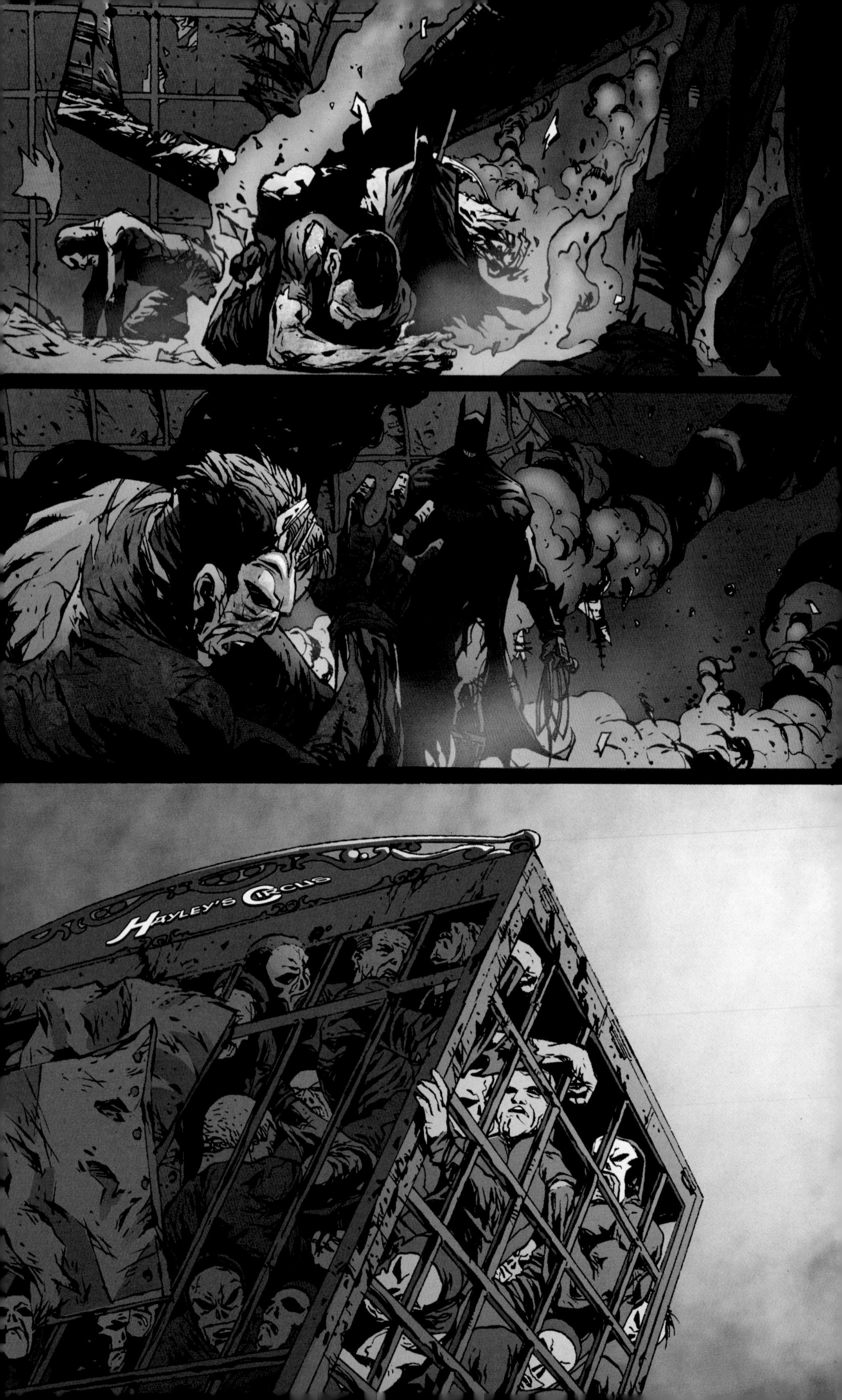
HAYLEY'S CIRCUS

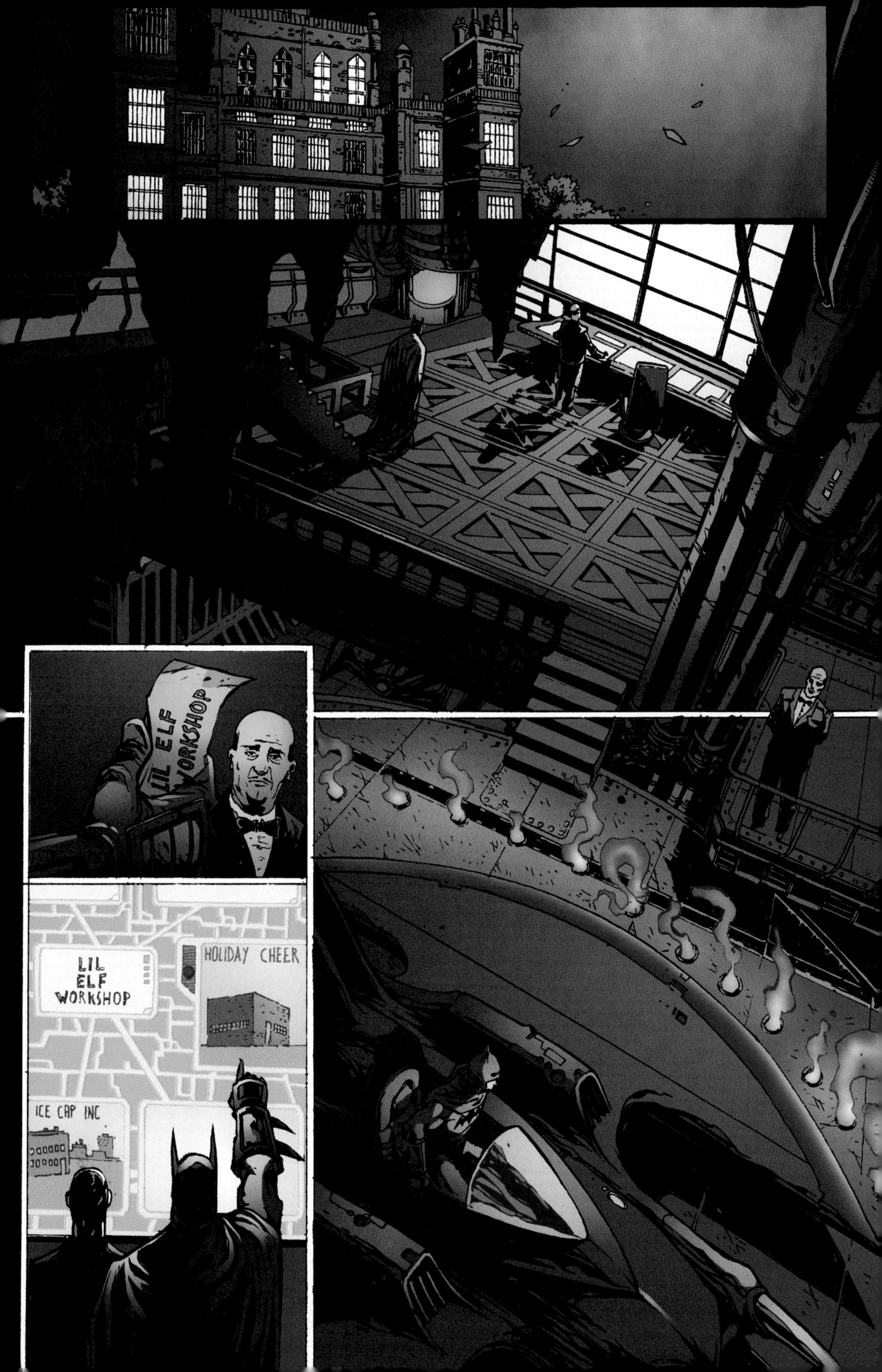
LIL ELF WORKSHOP
LIL ELF WORKSHOP
HOLIDAY CHEER
ICE CAP INC

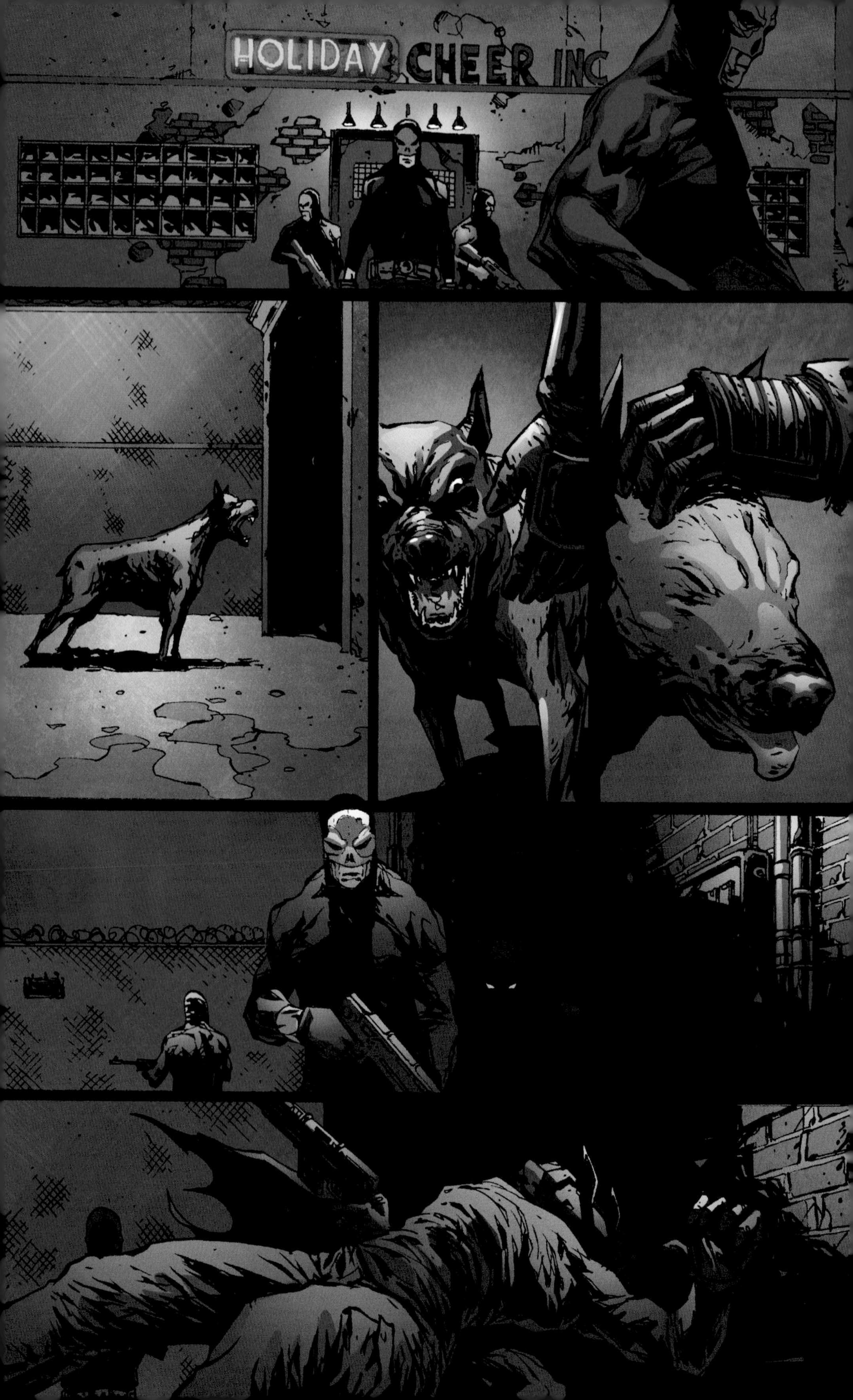
HOLIDAY CHEER INC

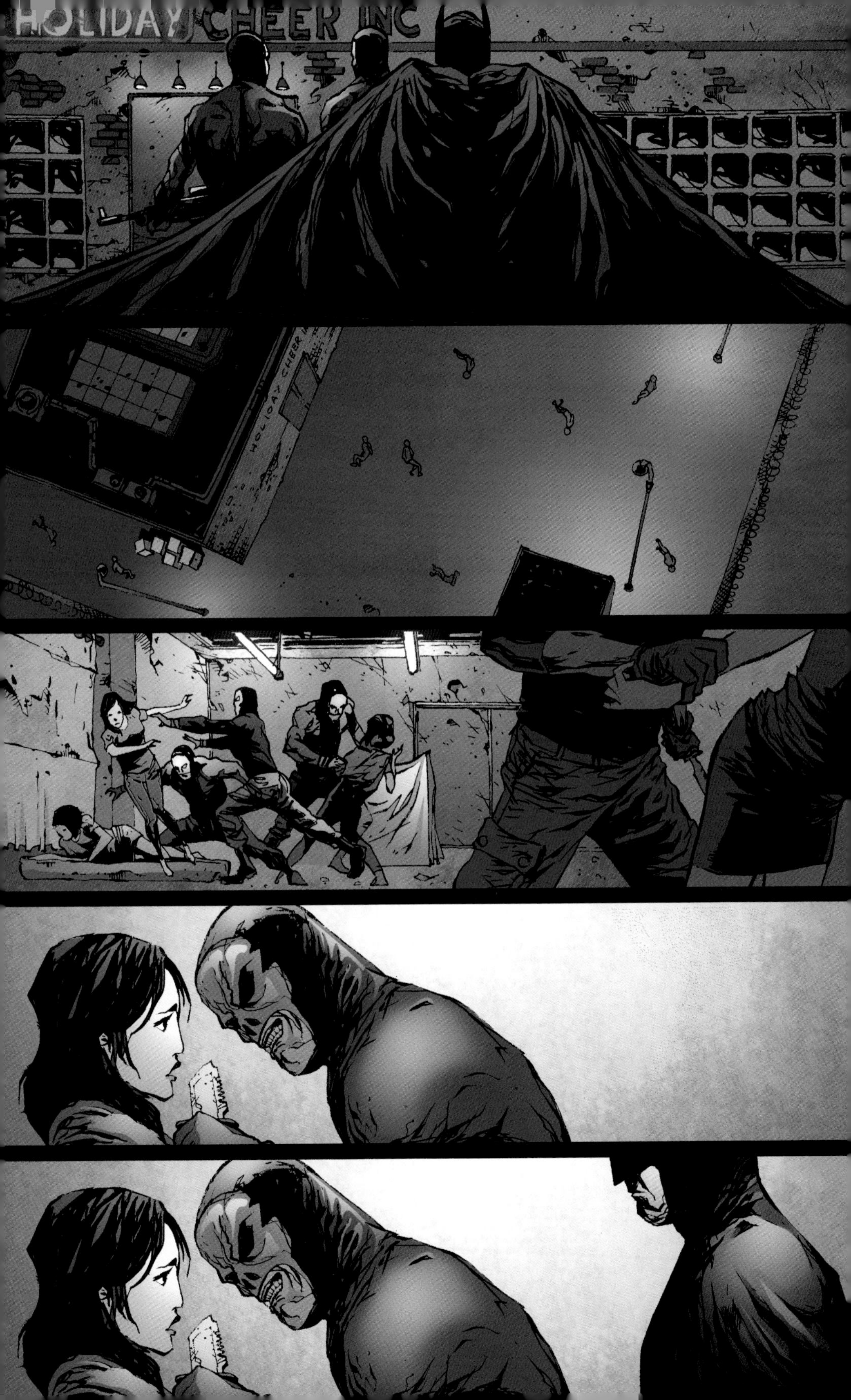
HOLIDAY CHEER INC

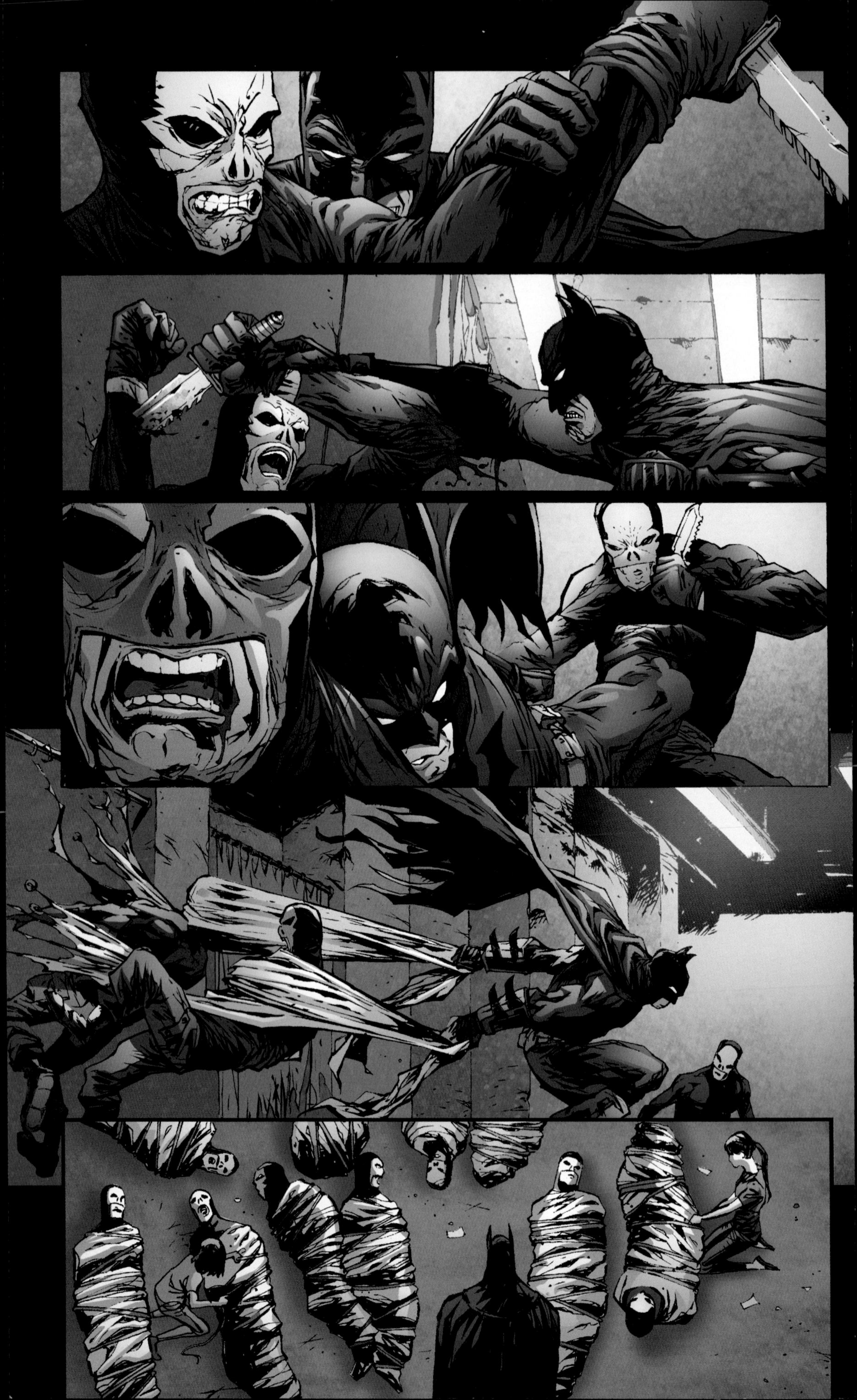

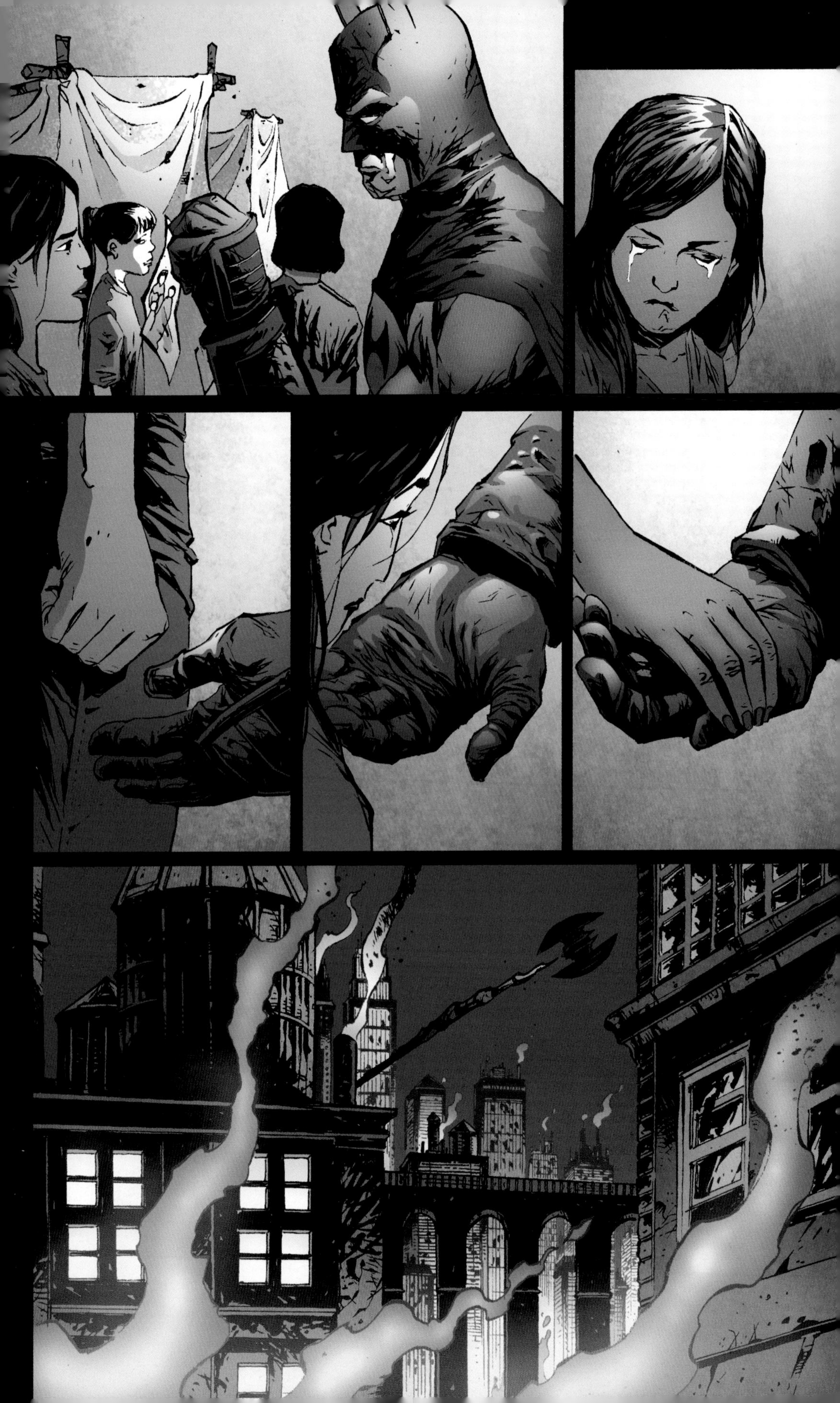

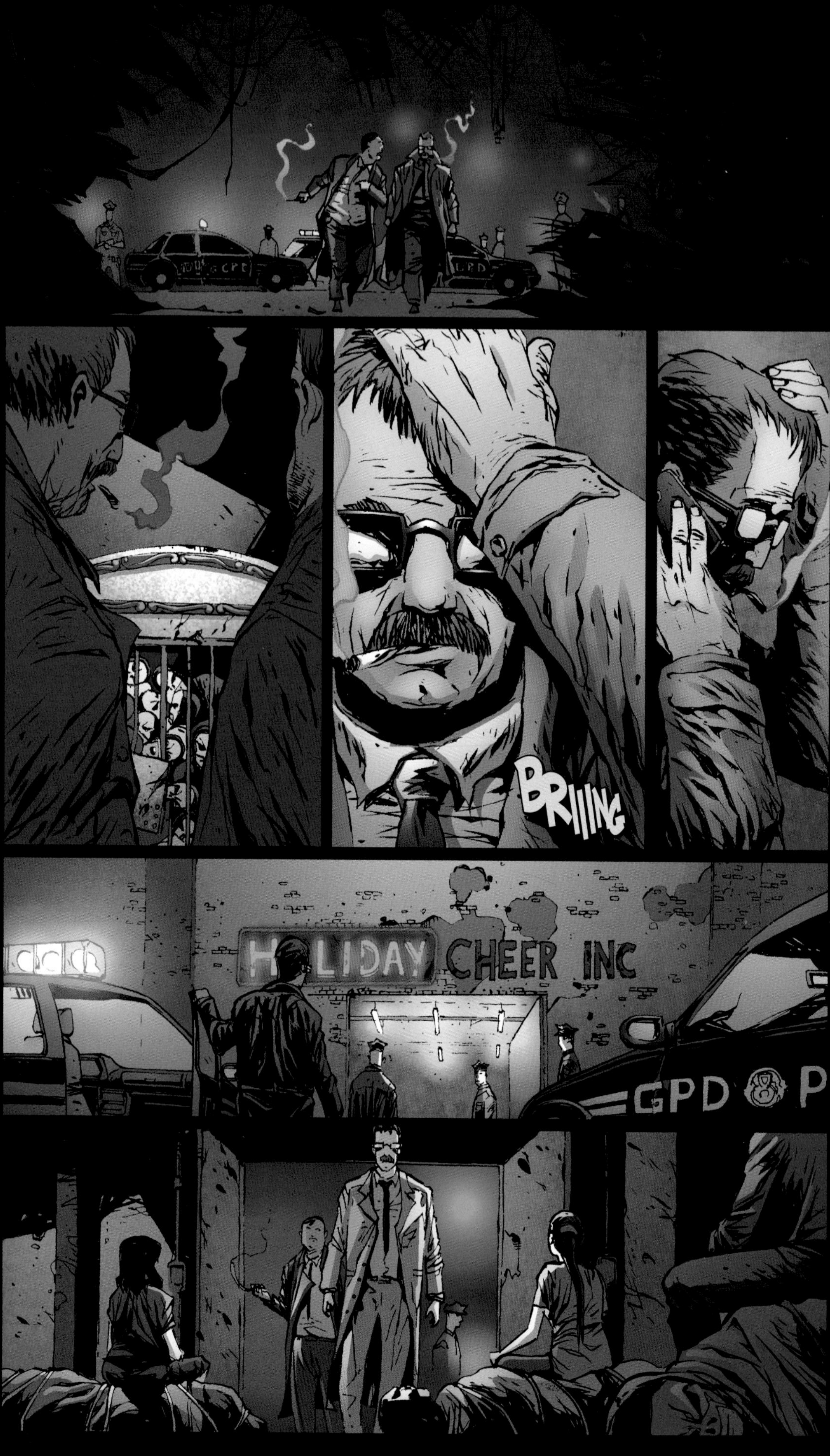
BRIIIING
HOLIDAY CHEER INC
GPD

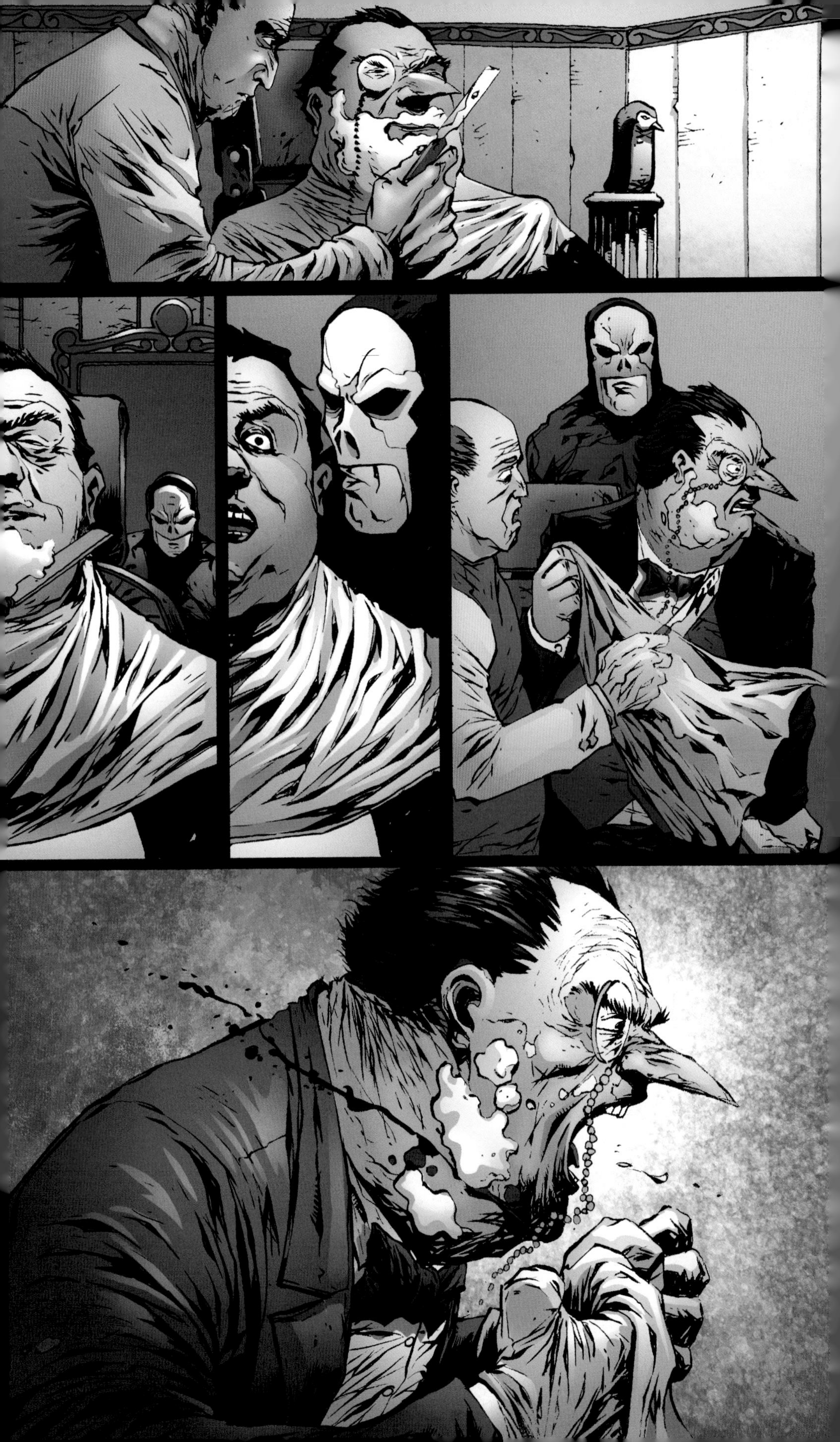

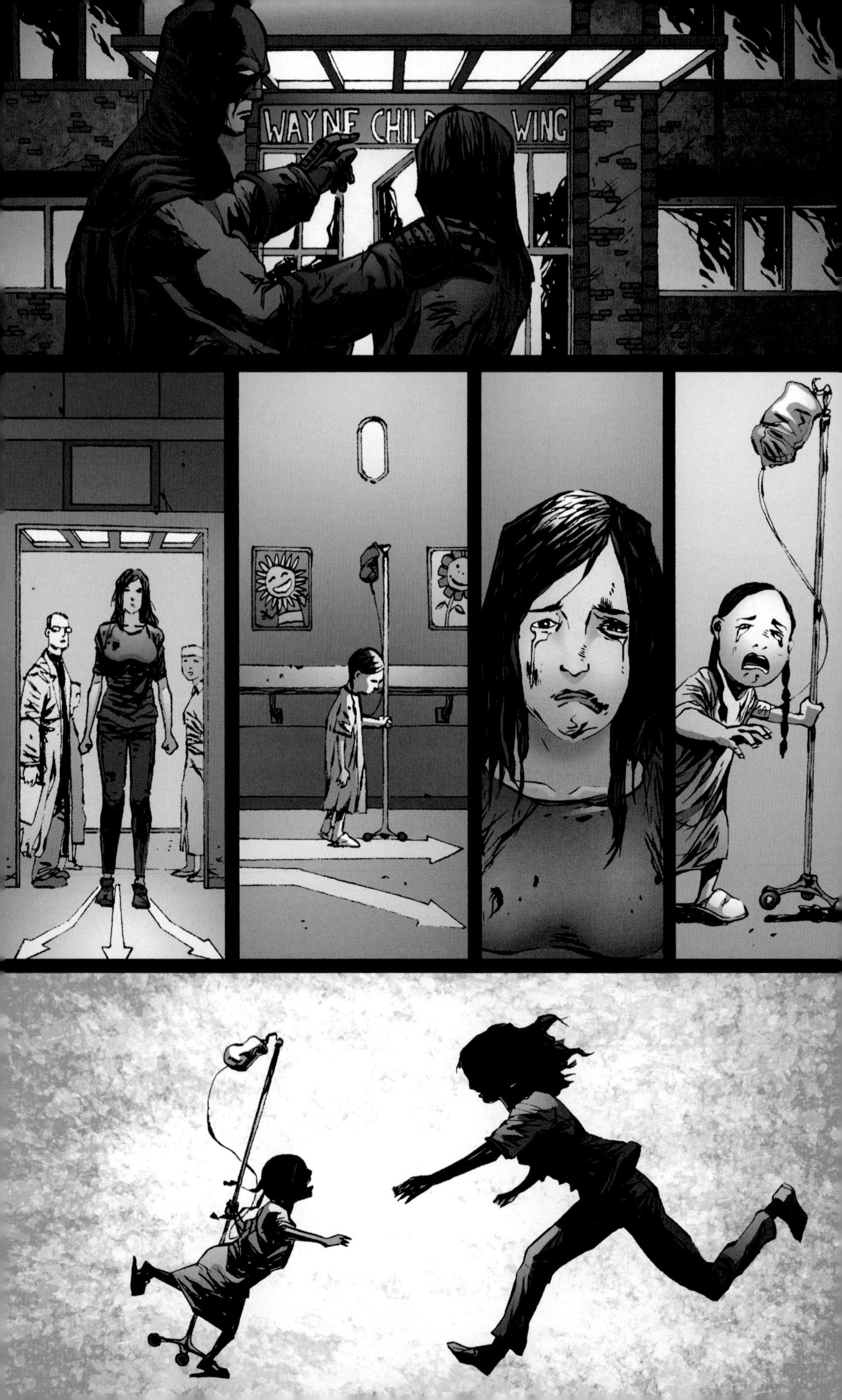

WAYNE CHILD
WING

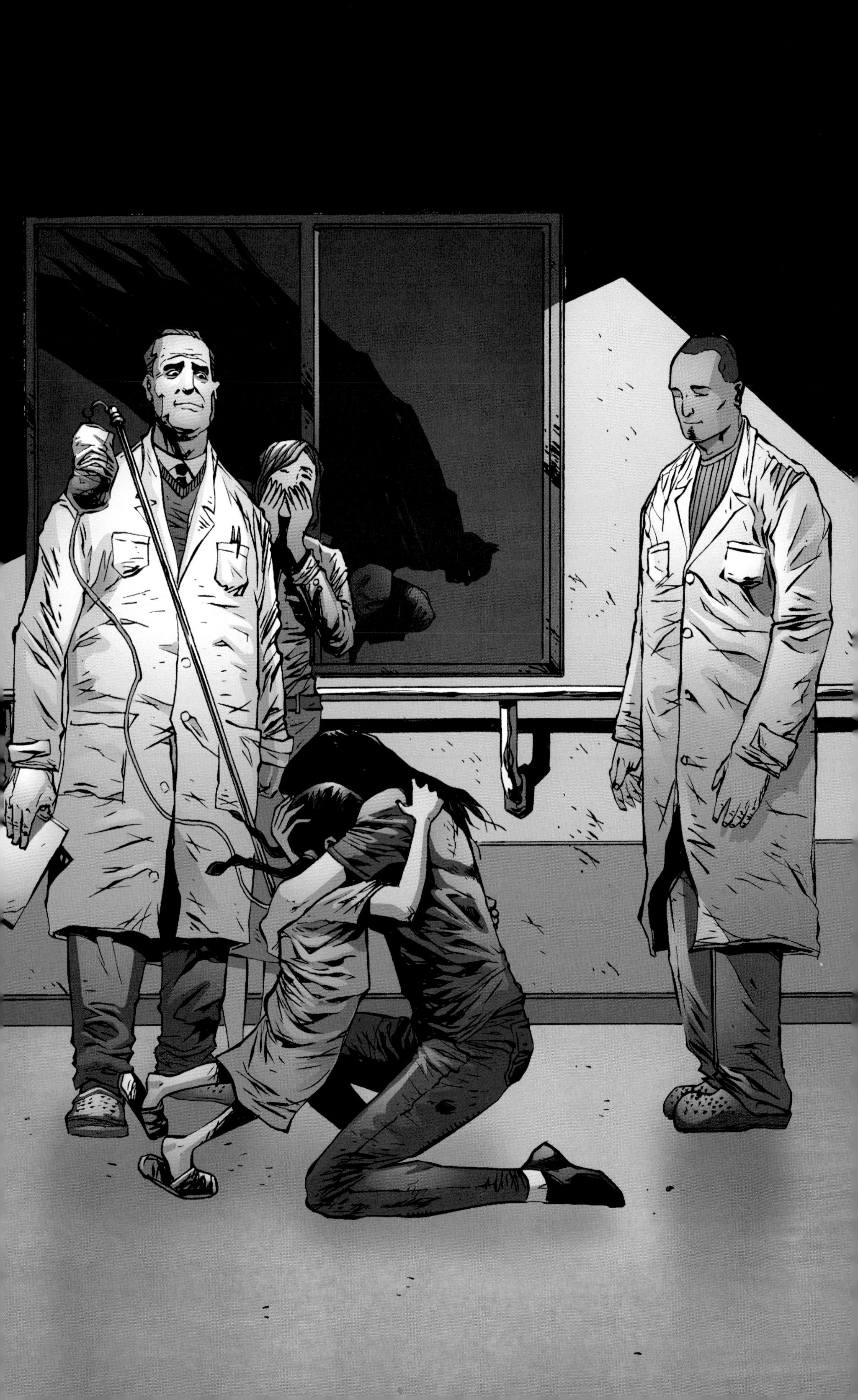

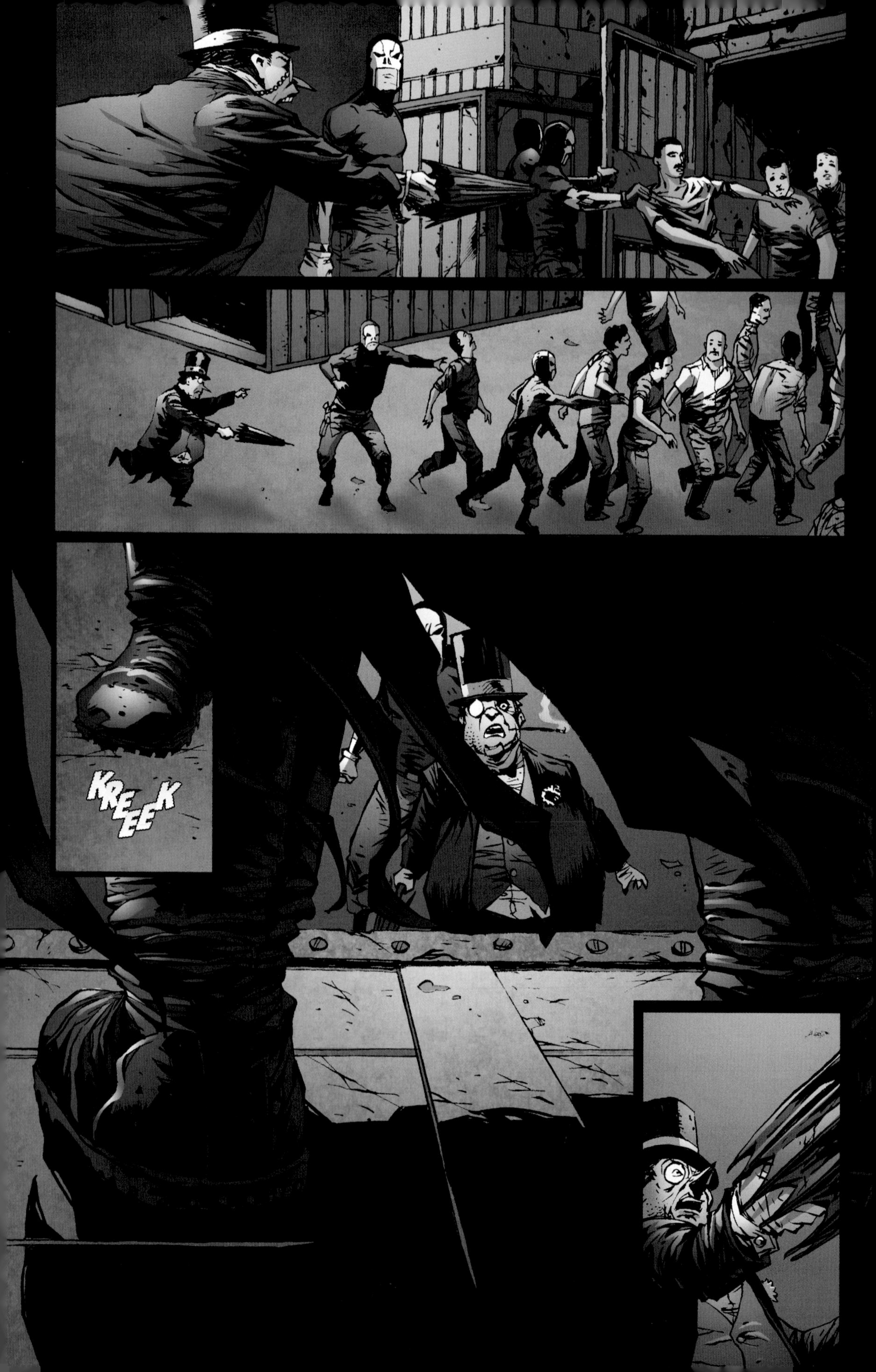
KREEEK

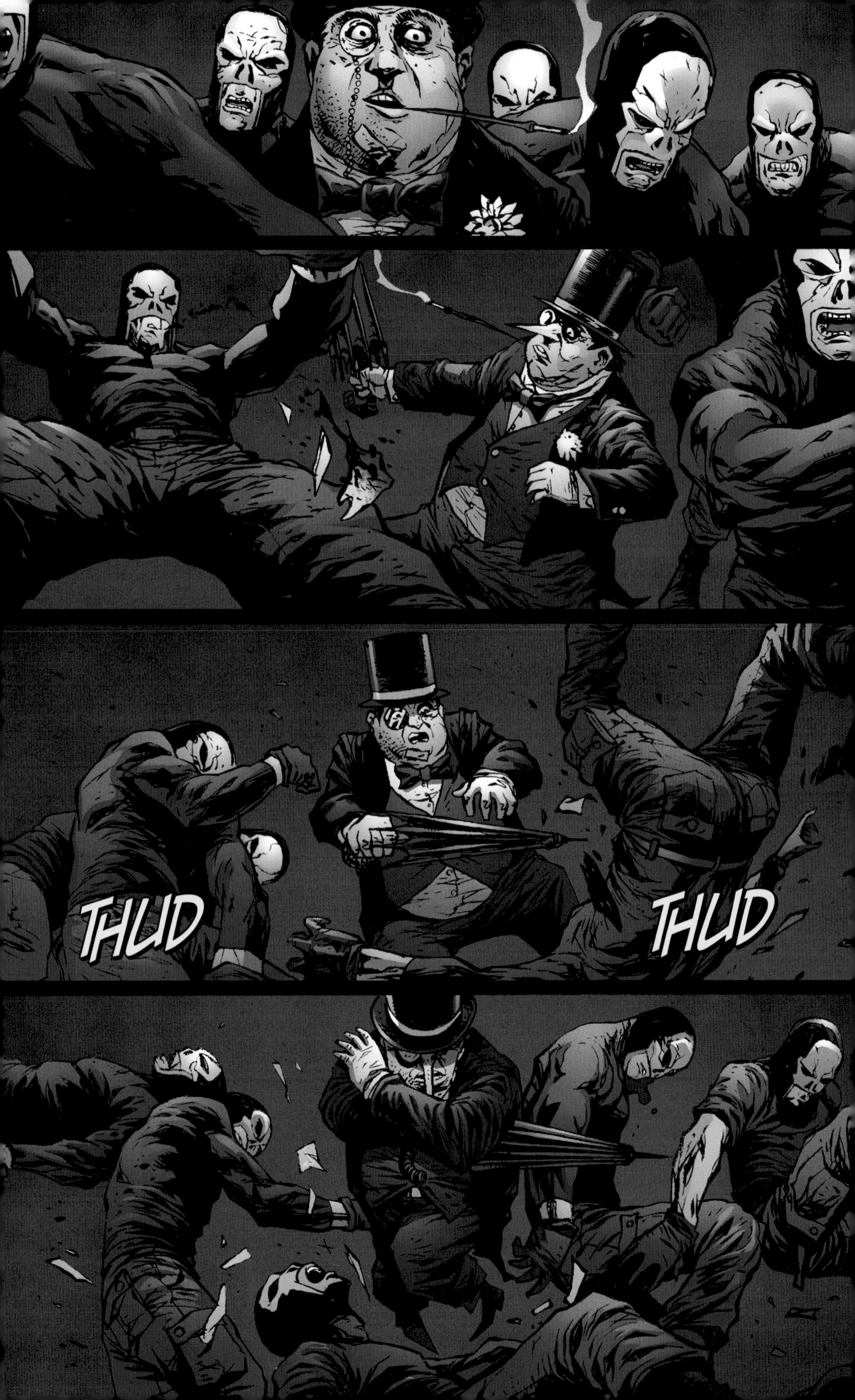
THUD
THUD

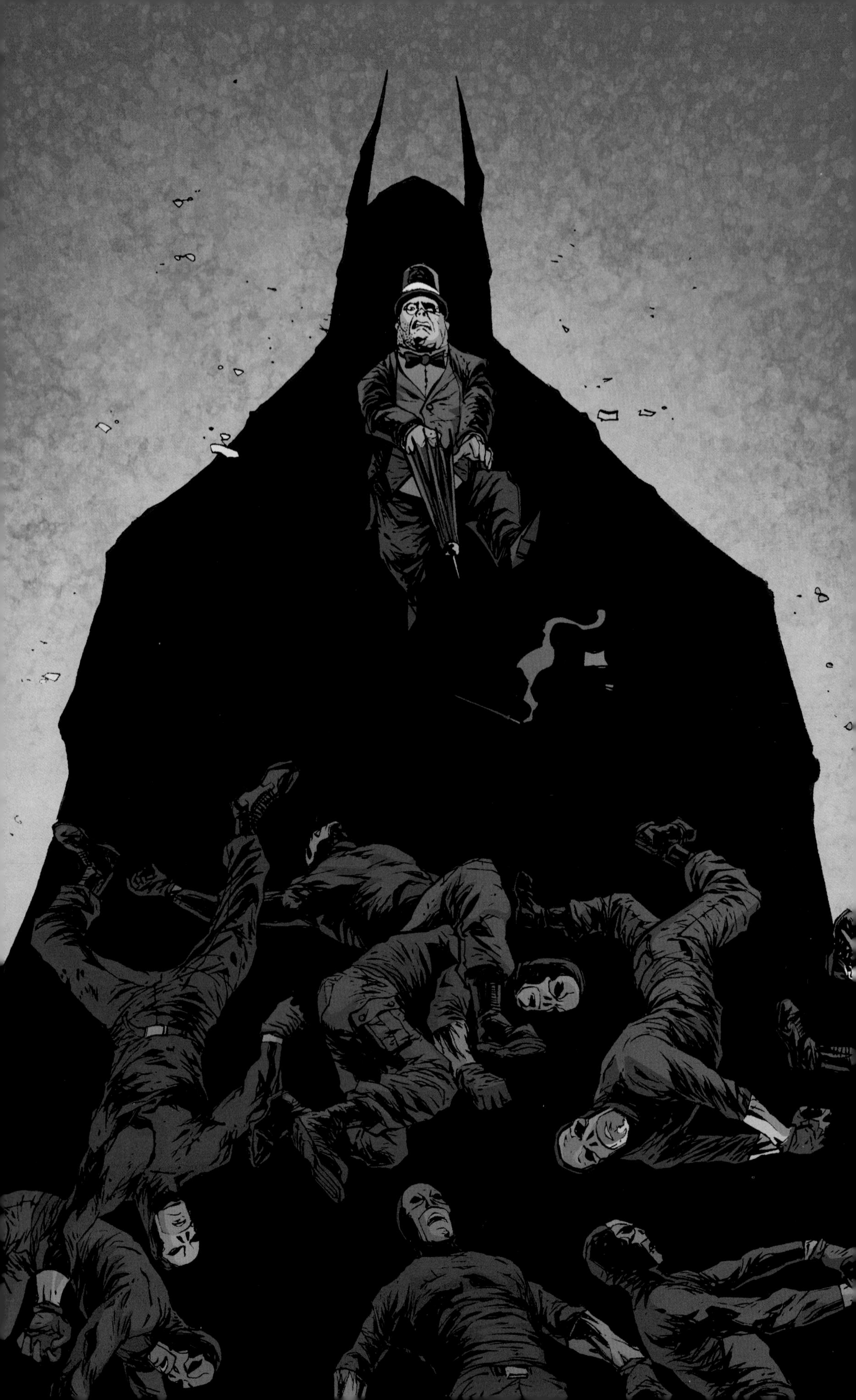

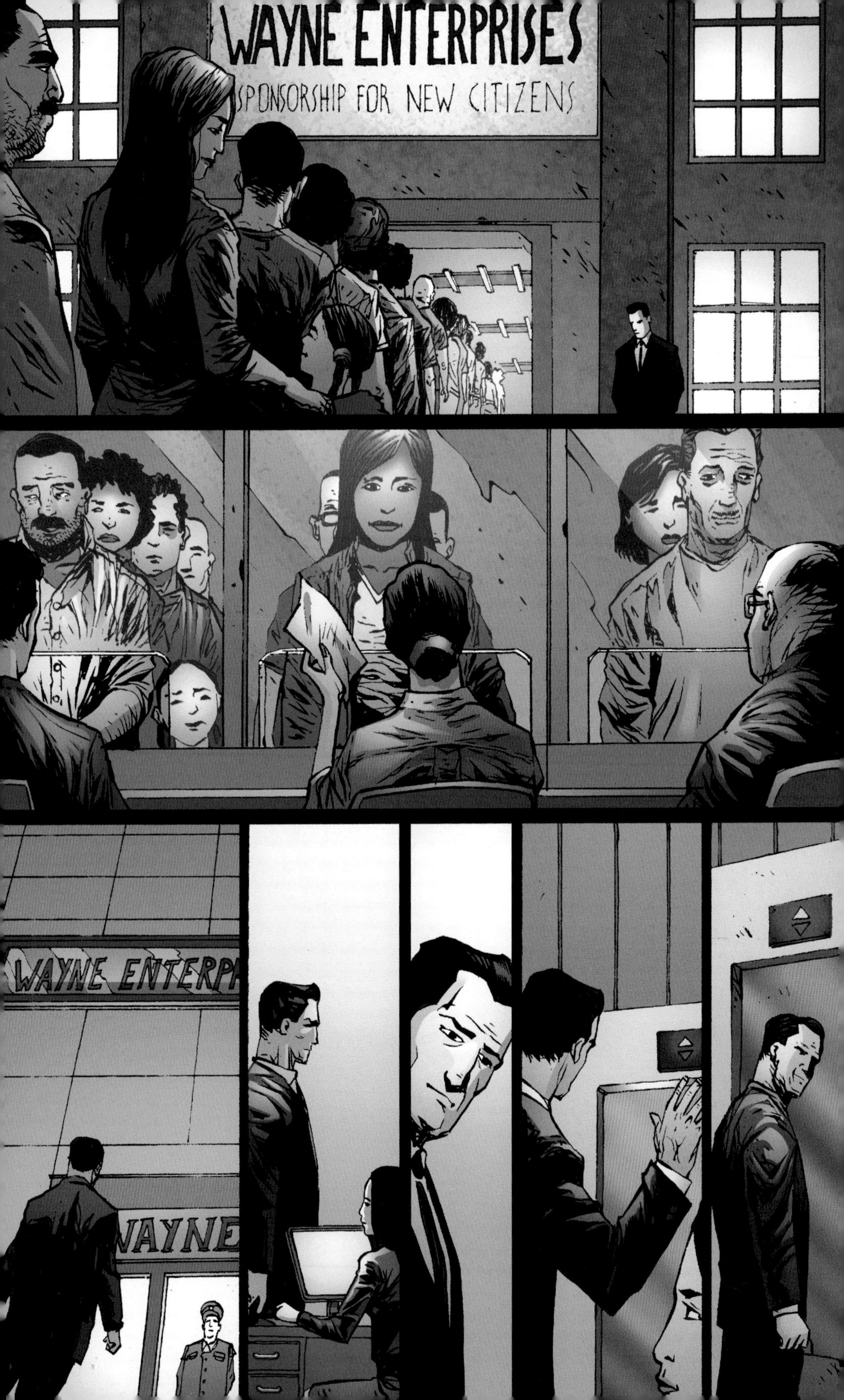

WAYNE ENTERPRISES
SPONSORSHIP FOR NEW CITIZENS
WAYNE ENTERP
WAYNE

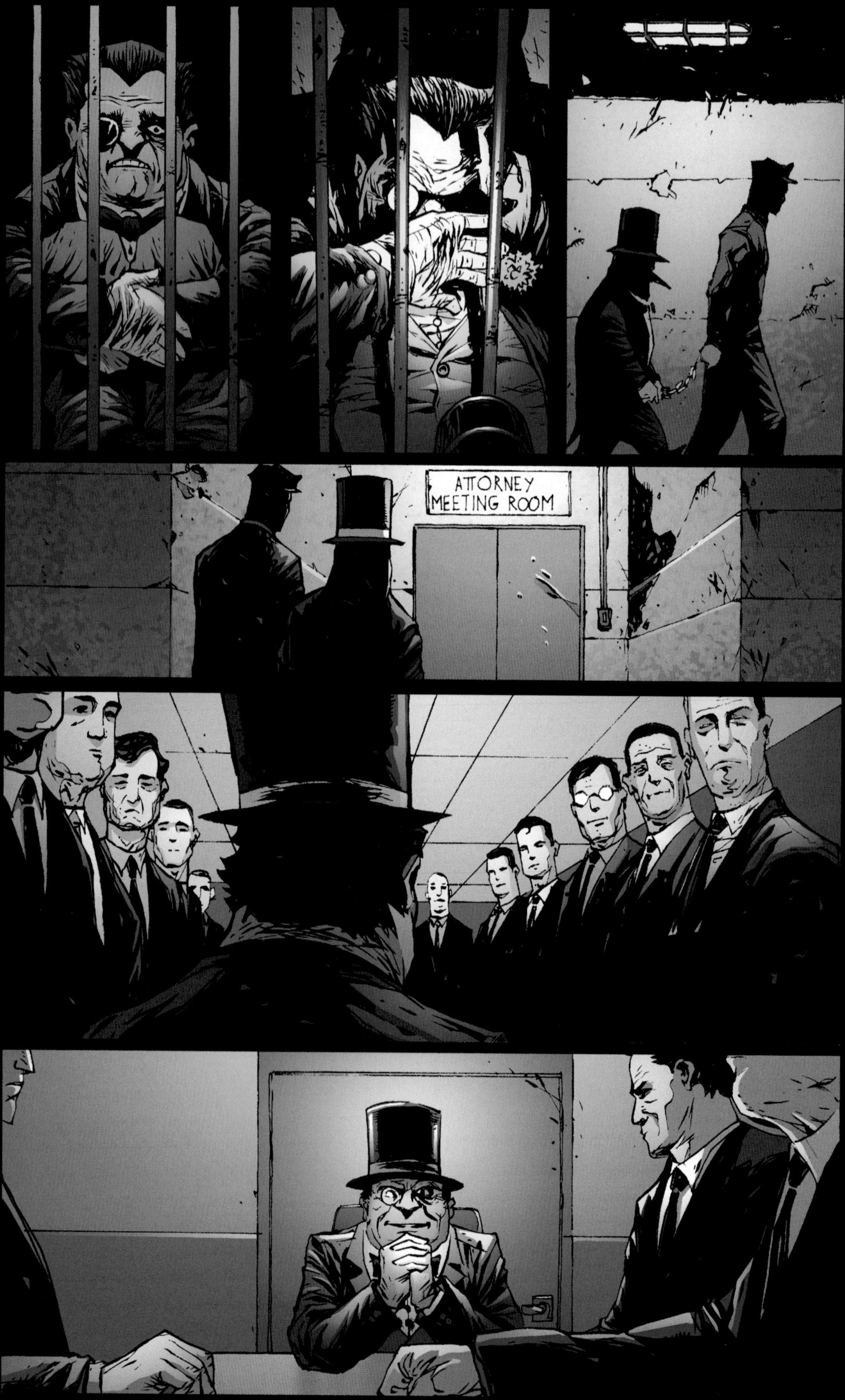
ATTORNEY
MEETING ROOM

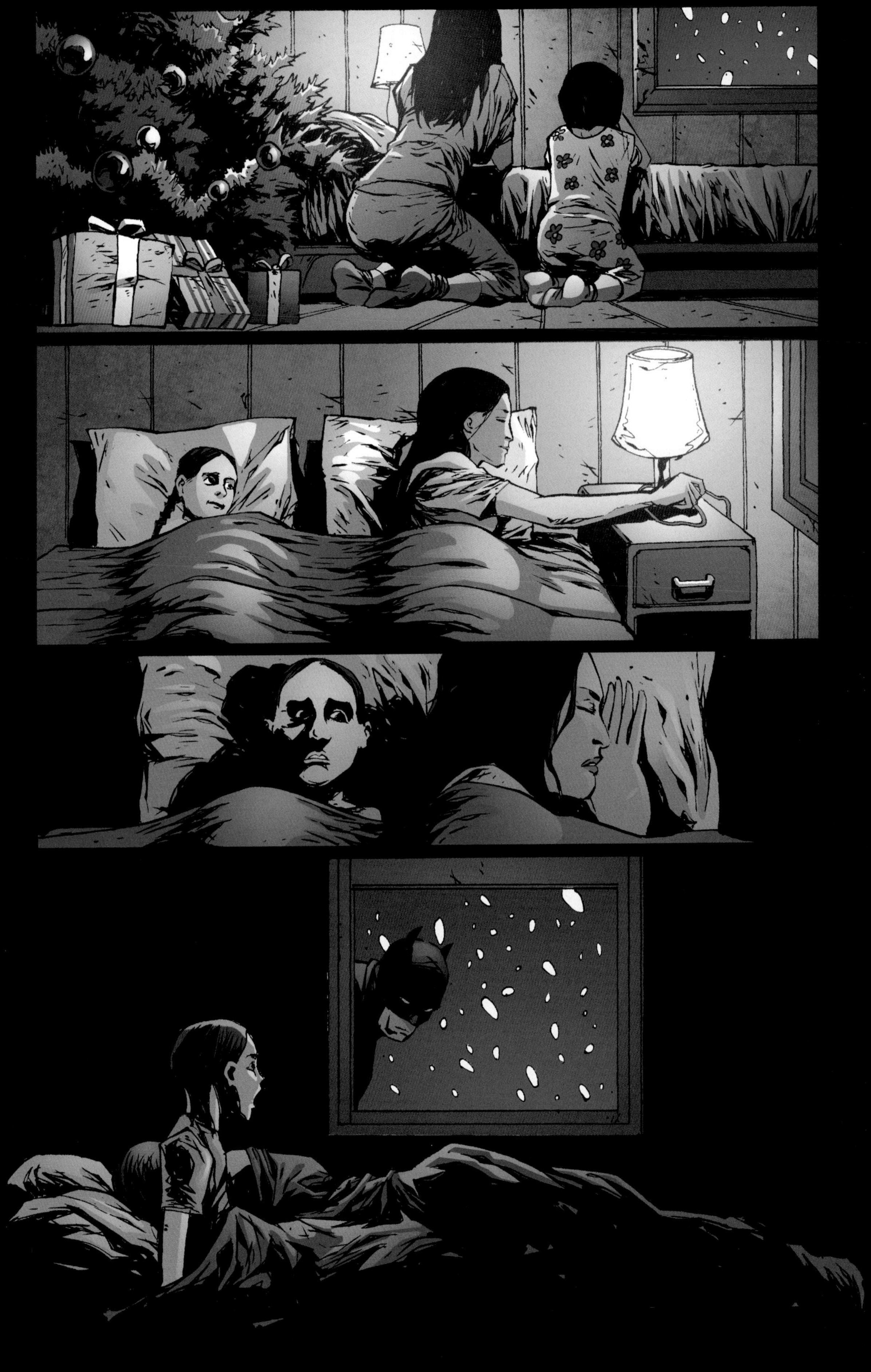

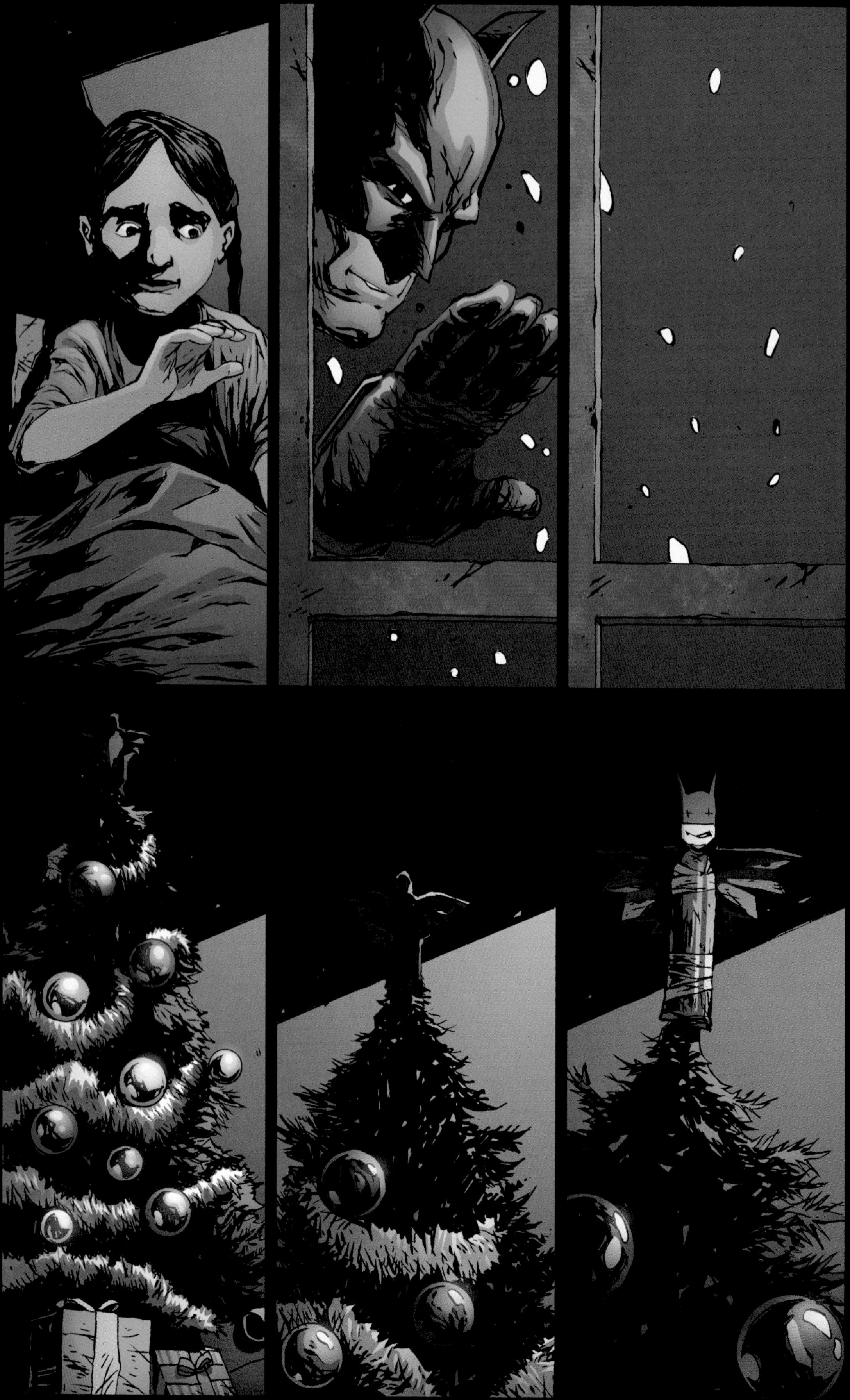

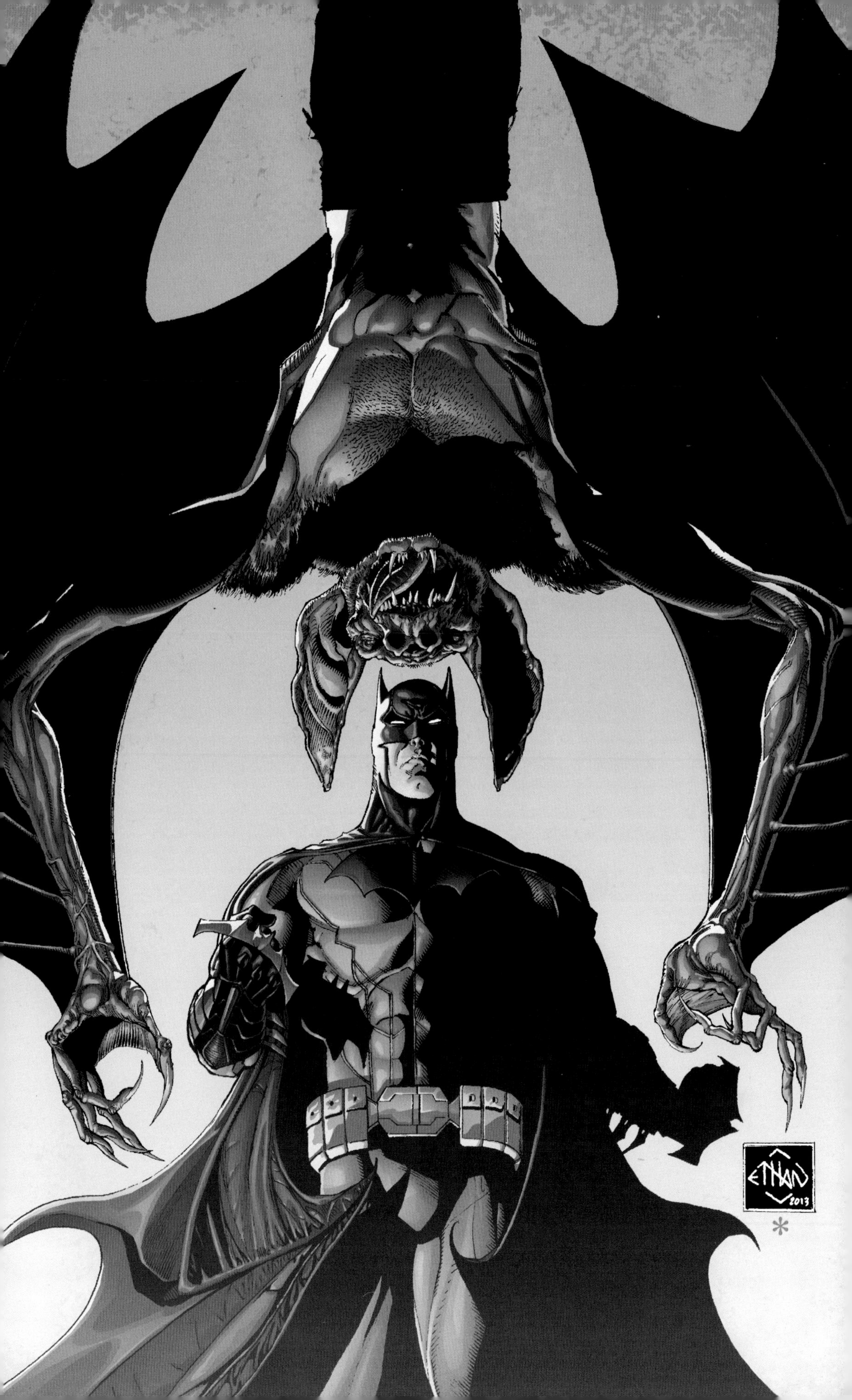
ETHAN
2013

CORPORATE RAIDER

ETHAN VAN SCIVER artist cover art by **ETHAN VAN SCIVER & HI FI**

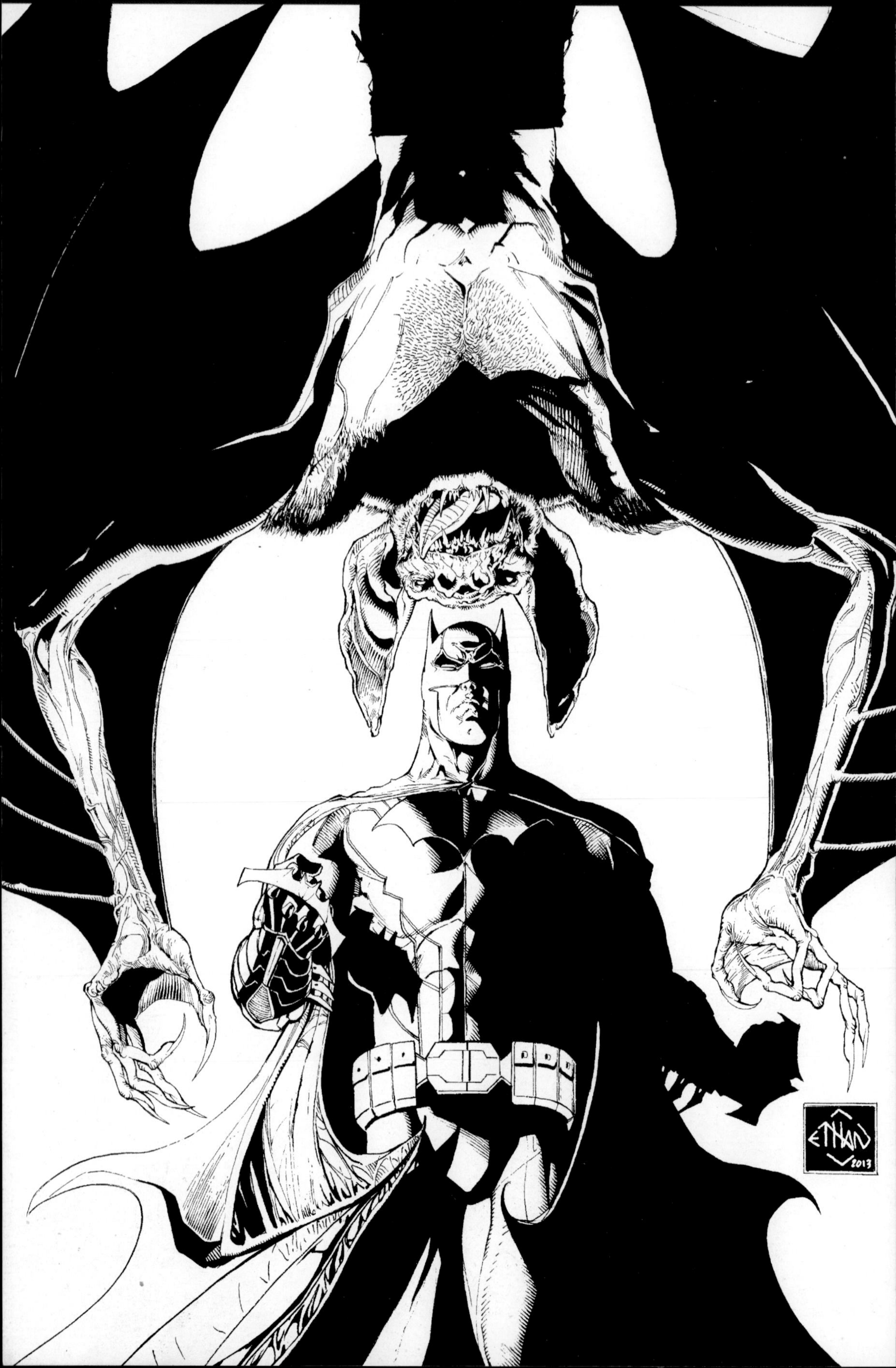
ETHAN 2013

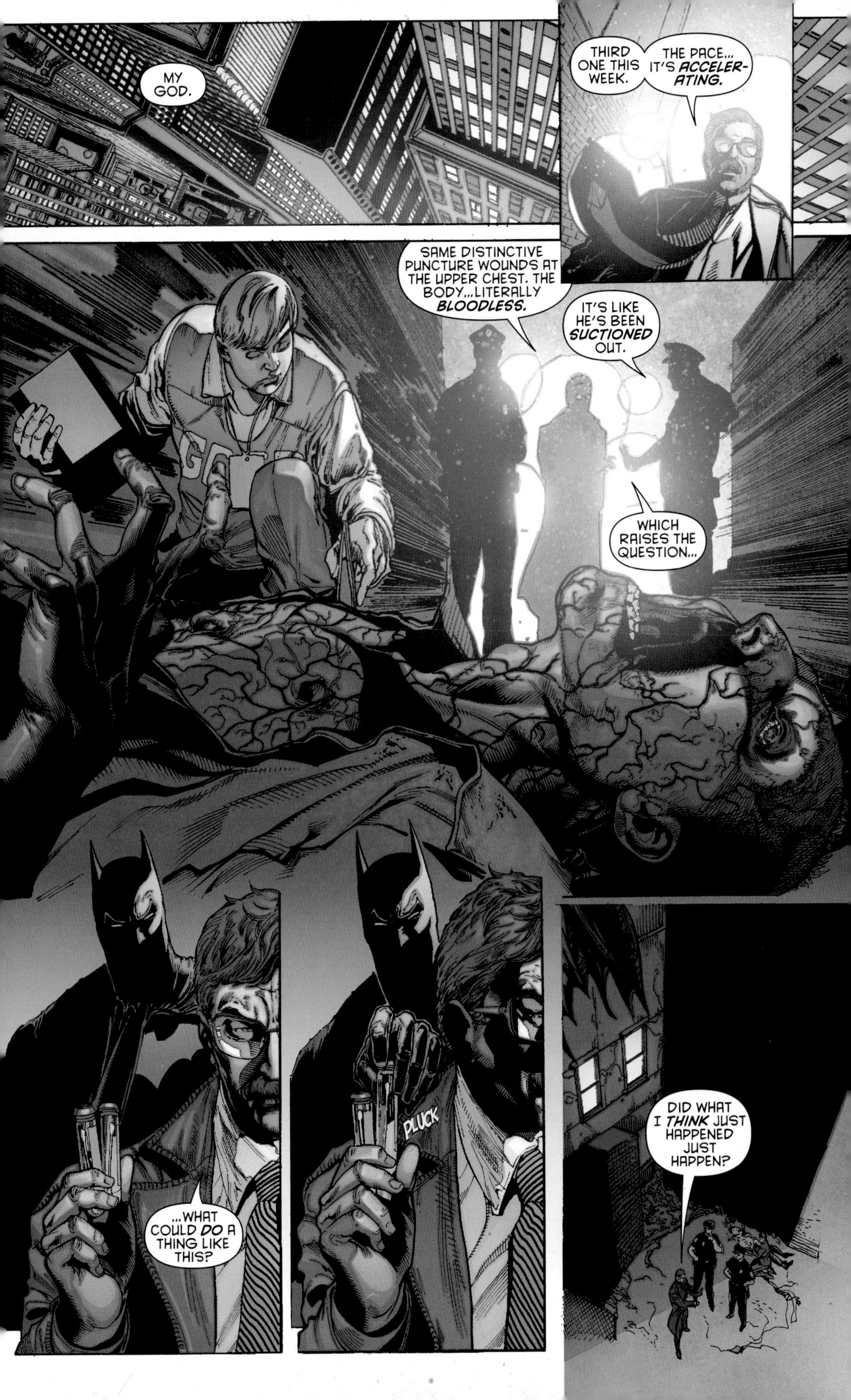
MY GOD.
THIRD ONE THIS WEEK.
THE PACE... IT'S ACCELERATING.
SAME DISTINCTIVE PUNCTURE WOUNDS AT THE UPPER CHEST. THE BODY...LITERALLY BLOODLESS.
IT'S LIKE HE'S BEEN SUCTIONED OUT.
WHICH RAISES THE QUESTION...
...WHAT COULD DO A THING LIKE THIS?
PLUCK
DID WHAT I THINK JUST HAPPENED JUST HAPPEN?

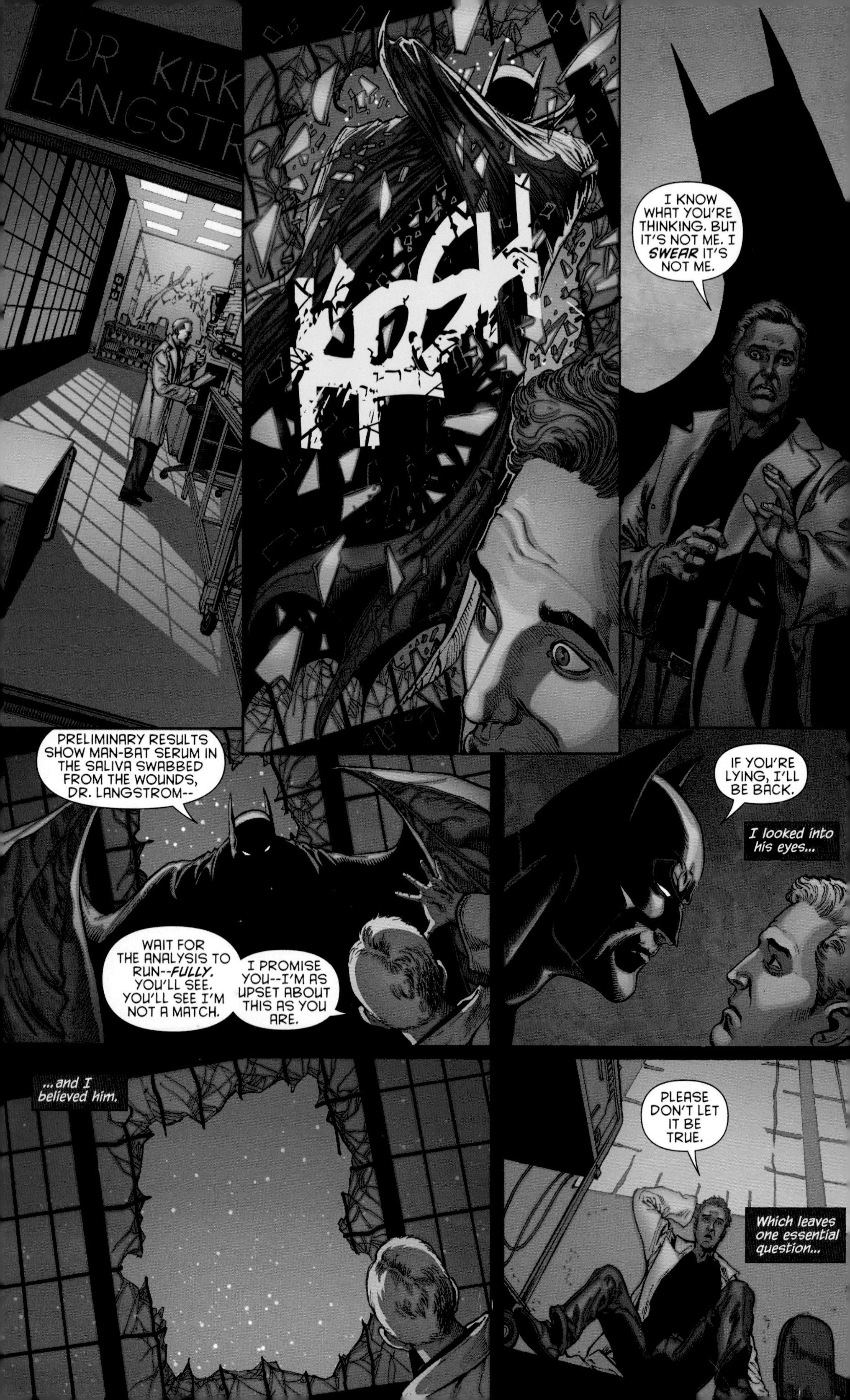
DR. KIRK LANGSTR
I KNOW WHAT YOU'RE THINKING. BUT IT'S NOT ME. I **SWEAR** IT'S NOT ME.
PRELIMINARY RESULTS SHOW MAN-BAT SERUM IN THE SALIVA SWABBED FROM THE WOUNDS, DR. LANGSTROM--
WAIT FOR THE ANALYSIS TO RUN--**FULLY.** YOU'LL SEE. YOU'LL SEE I'M NOT A MATCH.
I PROMISE YOU--I'M AS UPSET ABOUT THIS AS YOU ARE.
IF YOU'RE LYING, I'LL BE BACK.
I looked into his eyes...
...and I believed him.
PLEASE DON'T LET IT BE TRUE.
Which leaves one essential question...

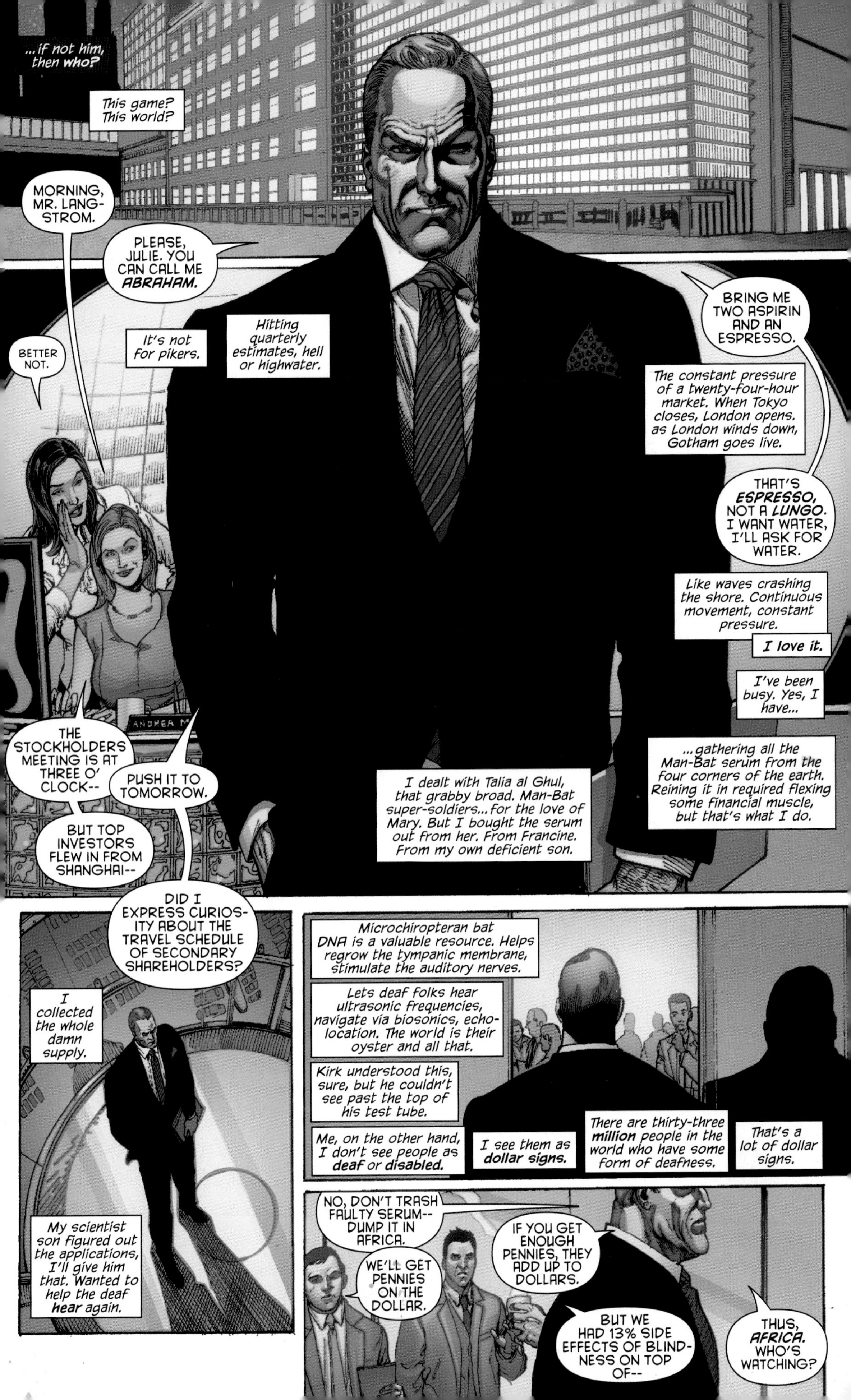
...if not him, then who?
This game? This world?
MORNING, MR. LANG-STROM.
PLEASE, JULIE. YOU CAN CALL ME ABRAHAM.
BETTER NOT.
It's not for pikers.
Hitting quarterly estimates, hell or highwater.
BRING ME TWO ASPIRIN AND AN ESPRESSO.
The constant pressure of a twenty-four-hour market. When Tokyo closes, London opens, as London winds down, Gotham goes live.
THAT'S ESPRESSO, NOT A LUNGO. I WANT WATER, I'LL ASK FOR WATER.
Like waves crashing the shore. Continuous movement, constant pressure.
I love it.
I've been busy. Yes, I have...
...gathering all the Man-Bat serum from the four corners of the earth. Reining it in required flexing some financial muscle, but that's what I do.
I dealt with Talia al Ghul, that grabby broad. Man-Bat super-soldiers...for the love of Mary. But I bought the serum out from her. From Francine. From my own deficient son.
ANDREA M
THE STOCKHOLDERS MEETING IS AT THREE O' CLOCK--
PUSH IT TO TOMORROW.
BUT TOP INVESTORS FLEW IN FROM SHANGHAI--
DID I EXPRESS CURIOS-ITY ABOUT THE TRAVEL SCHEDULE OF SECONDARY SHAREHOLDERS?
I collected the whole damn supply.
My scientist son figured out the applications, I'll give him that. Wanted to help the deaf hear again.
Microchiropteran bat DNA is a valuable resource. Helps regrow the tympanic membrane, stimulate the auditory nerves.
Lets deaf folks hear ultrasonic frequencies, navigate via biosonics, echo-location. The world is their oyster and all that.
Kirk understood this, sure, but he couldn't see past the top of his test tube.
Me, on the other hand, I don't see people as deaf or disabled.
I see them as dollar signs.
There are thirty-three million people in the world who have some form of deafness.
That's a lot of dollar signs.
NO, DON'T TRASH FAULTY SERUM-- DUMP IT IN AFRICA.
WE'LL GET PENNIES ON THE DOLLAR.
IF YOU GET ENOUGH PENNIES, THEY ADD UP TO DOLLARS.
BUT WE HAD 13% SIDE EFFECTS OF BLIND-NESS ON TOP OF--
THUS, AFRICA. WHO'S WATCHING?

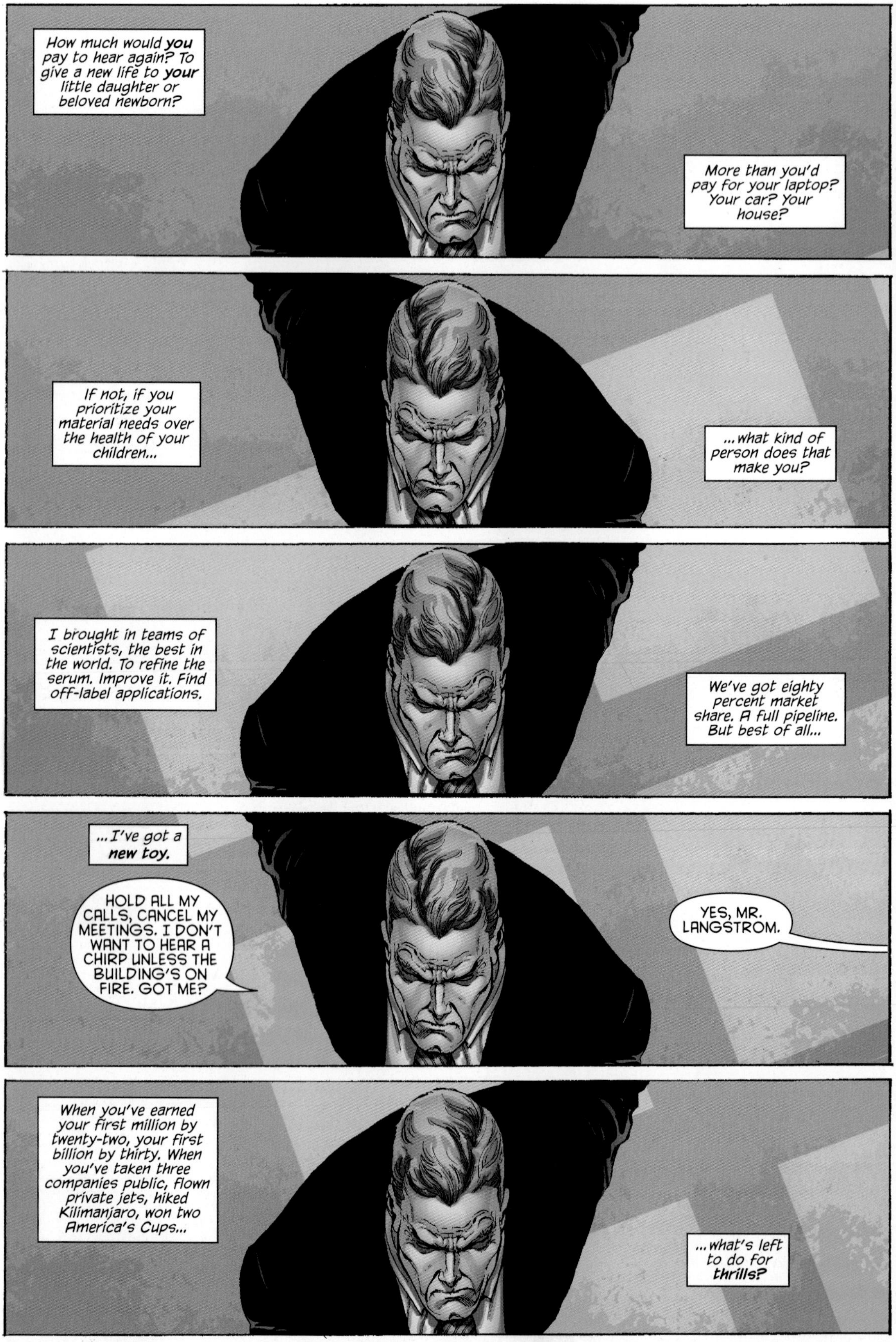
How much would you pay to hear again? To give a new life to your little daughter or beloved newborn?
More than you'd pay for your laptop? Your car? Your house?
If not, if you prioritize your material needs over the health of your children...
...what kind of person does that make you?
I brought in teams of scientists, the best in the world. To refine the serum. Improve it. Find off-label applications.
We've got eighty percent market share. A full pipeline. But best of all...
...I've got a new toy.
HOLD ALL MY CALLS, CANCEL MY MEETINGS. I DON'T WANT TO HEAR A CHIRP UNLESS THE BUILDING'S ON FIRE. GOT ME?
YES, MR. LANGSTROM.
When you've earned your first million by twenty-two, your first billion by thirty. When you've taken three companies public, flown private jets, hiked Kilimanjaro, won two America's Cups...
...what's left to do for thrills?

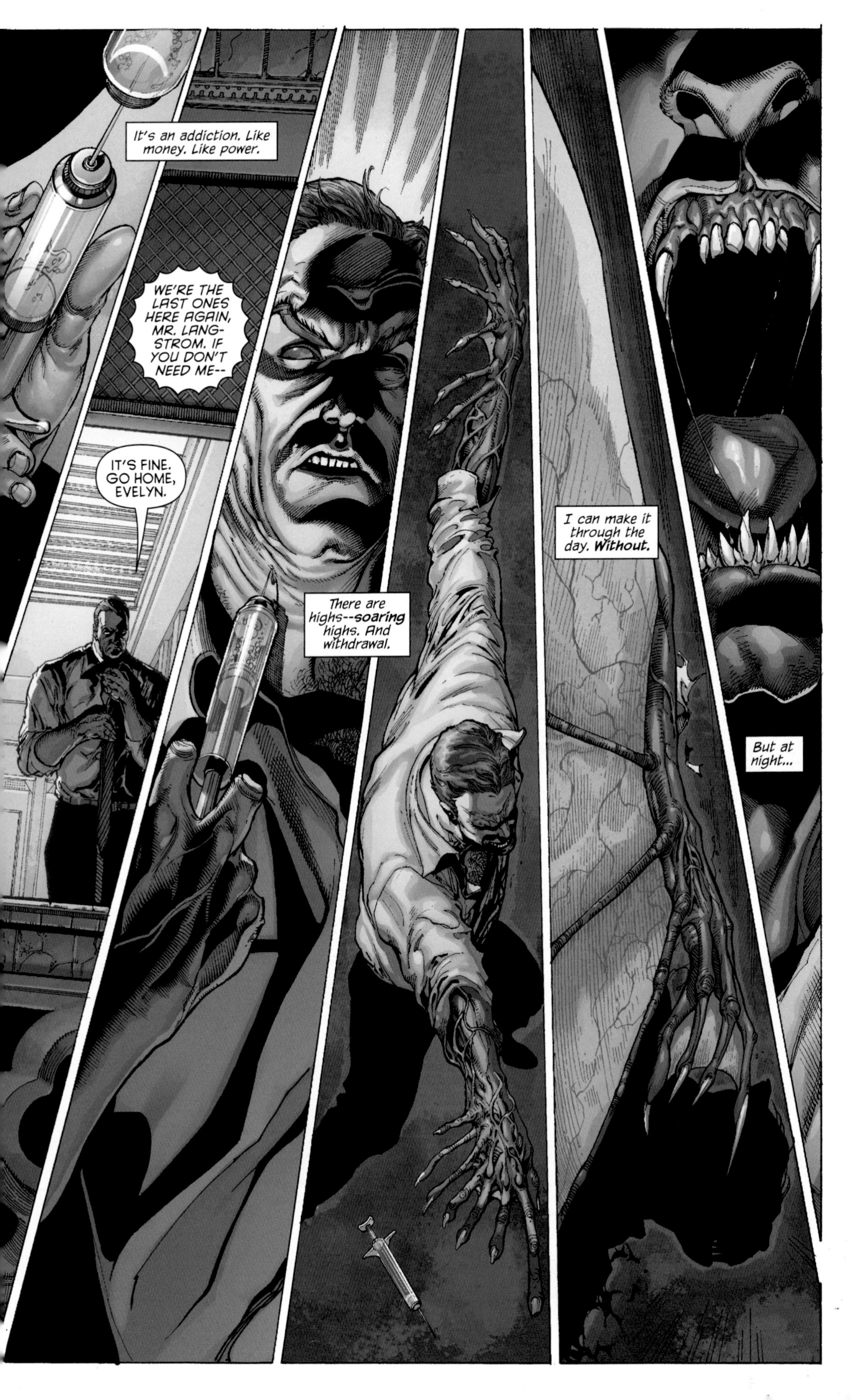
It's an addiction. Like money. Like power.
WE'RE THE LAST ONES HERE AGAIN, MR. LANGSTROM. IF YOU DON'T NEED ME--
IT'S FINE. GO HOME, EVELYN.
There are highs--**soaring** highs. And withdrawal.
I can make it through the day. **Without.**
But at night...

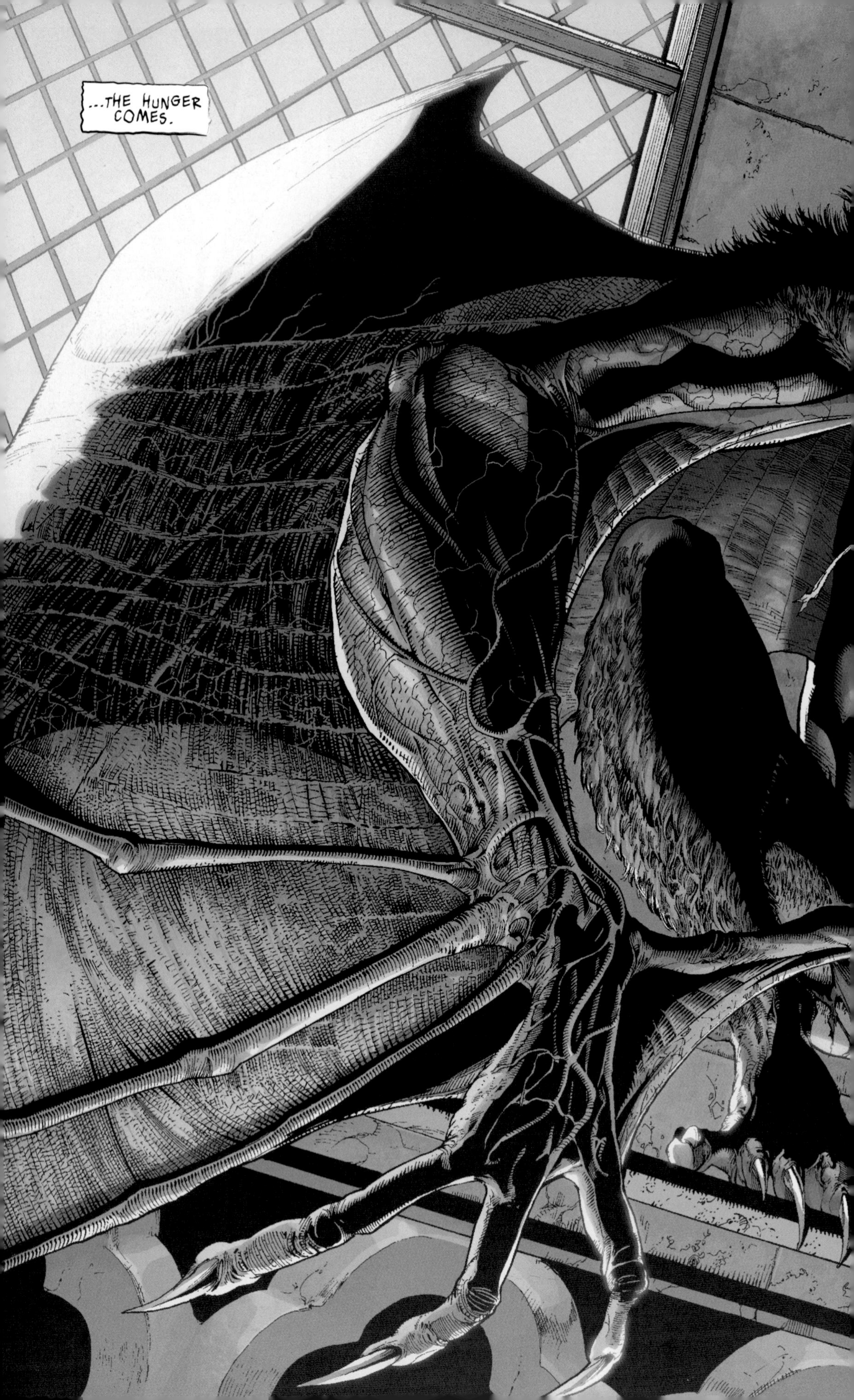
...THE HUNGER COMES.

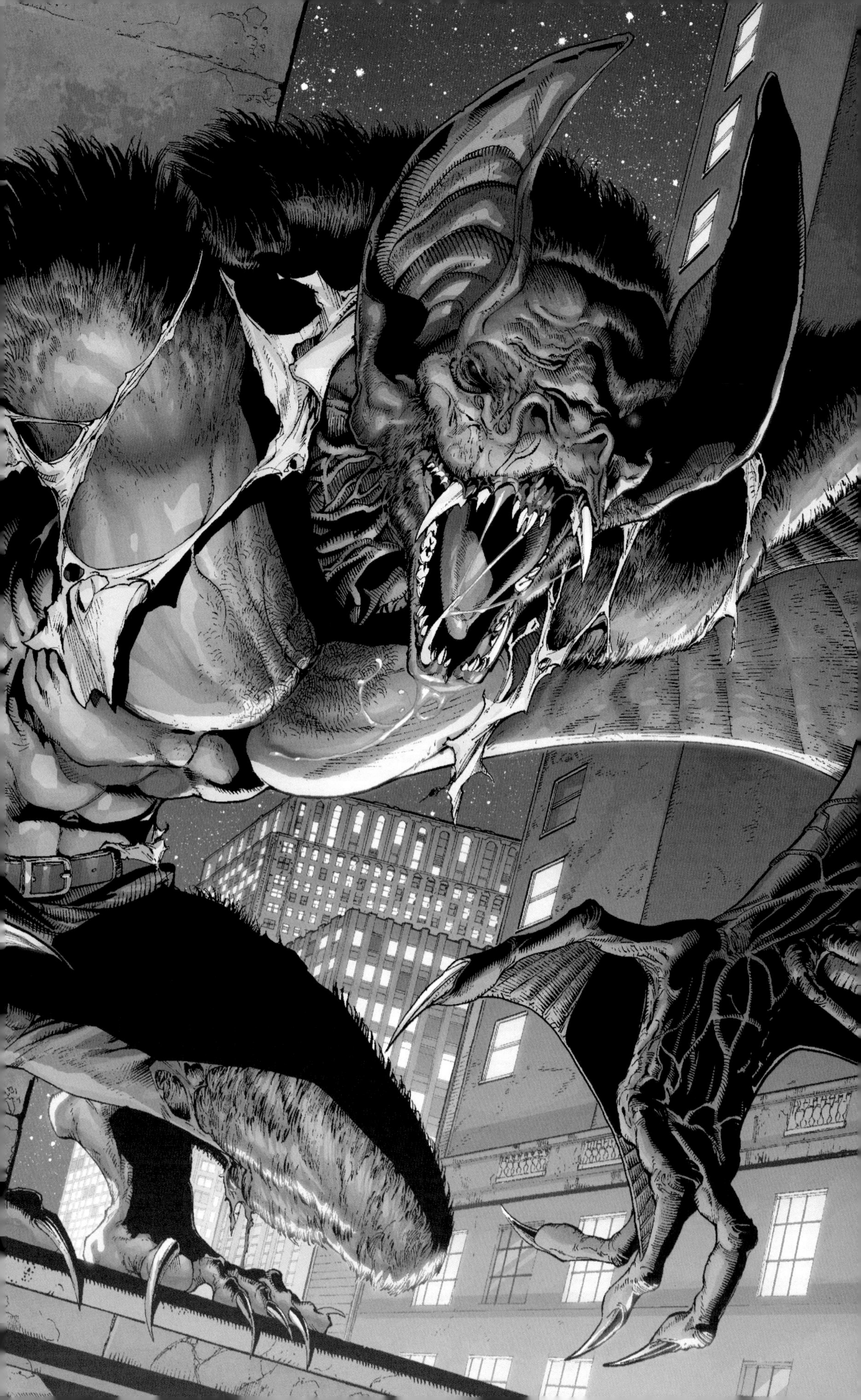

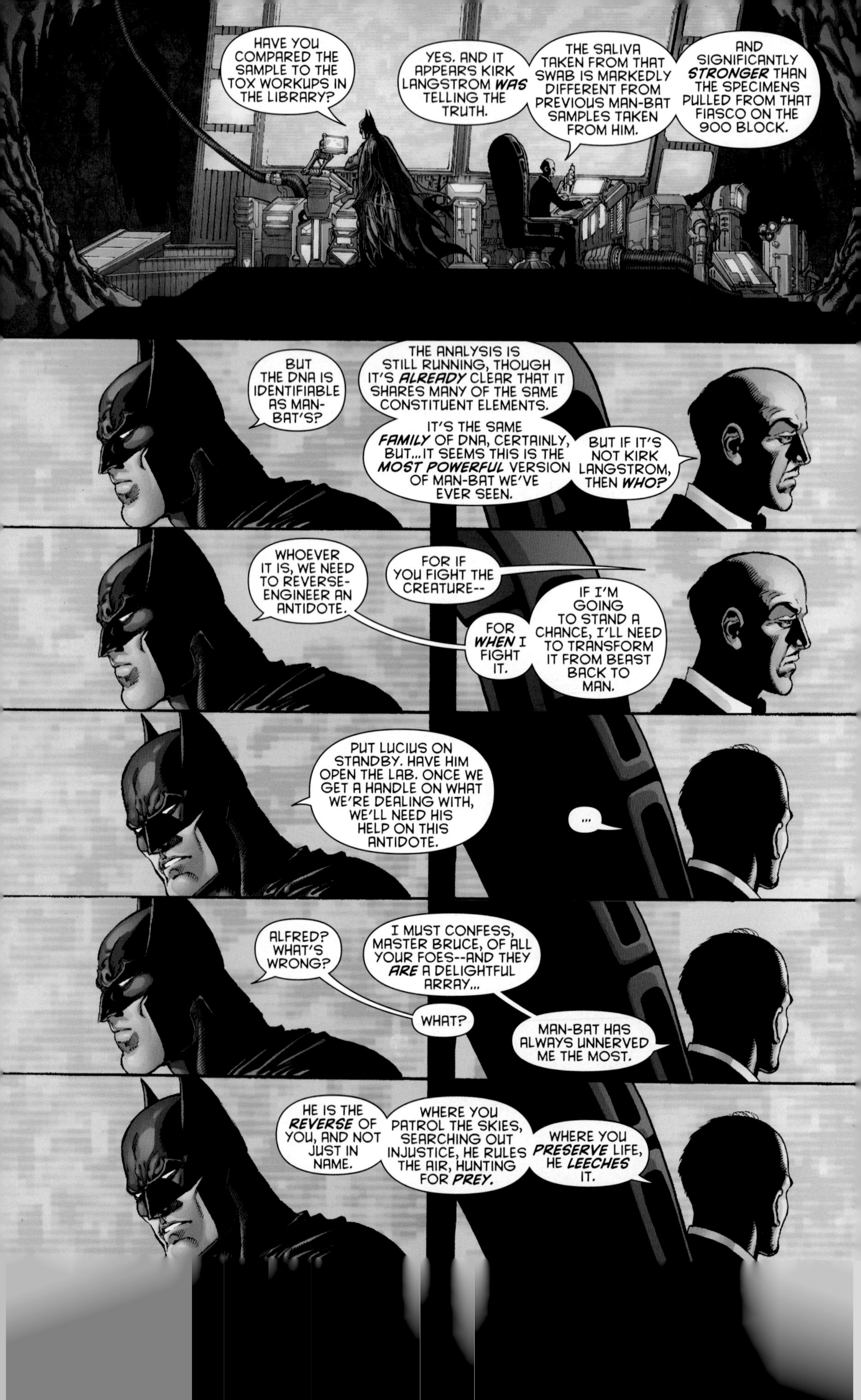
HAVE YOU COMPARED THE SAMPLE TO THE TOX WORKUPS IN THE LIBRARY?
YES. AND IT APPEARS KIRK LANGSTROM WAS TELLING THE TRUTH.
THE SALIVA TAKEN FROM THAT SWAB IS MARKEDLY DIFFERENT FROM PREVIOUS MAN-BAT SAMPLES TAKEN FROM HIM.
AND SIGNIFICANTLY STRONGER THAN THE SPECIMENS PULLED FROM THAT FIASCO ON THE 900 BLOCK.
BUT THE DNA IS IDENTIFIABLE AS MAN-BAT'S?
THE ANALYSIS IS STILL RUNNING, THOUGH IT'S ALREADY CLEAR THAT IT SHARES MANY OF THE SAME CONSTITUENT ELEMENTS.
IT'S THE SAME FAMILY OF DNA, CERTAINLY, BUT...IT SEEMS THIS IS THE MOST POWERFUL VERSION OF MAN-BAT WE'VE EVER SEEN.
BUT IF IT'S NOT KIRK LANGSTROM, THEN WHO?
WHOEVER IT IS, WE NEED TO REVERSE-ENGINEER AN ANTIDOTE.
FOR IF YOU FIGHT THE CREATURE--
FOR WHEN I FIGHT IT.
IF I'M GOING TO STAND A CHANCE, I'LL NEED TO TRANSFORM IT FROM BEAST BACK TO MAN.
PUT LUCIUS ON STANDBY. HAVE HIM OPEN THE LAB. ONCE WE GET A HANDLE ON WHAT WE'RE DEALING WITH, WE'LL NEED HIS HELP ON THIS ANTIDOTE.
...
ALFRED? WHAT'S WRONG?
I MUST CONFESS, MASTER BRUCE, OF ALL YOUR FOES--AND THEY ARE A DELIGHTFUL ARRAY...
WHAT?
MAN-BAT HAS ALWAYS UNNERVED ME THE MOST.
HE IS THE REVERSE OF YOU, AND NOT JUST IN NAME.
WHERE YOU PATROL THE SKIES, SEARCHING OUT INJUSTICE, HE RULES THE AIR, HUNTING FOR PREY.
WHERE YOU PRESERVE LIFE, HE LEECHES IT.

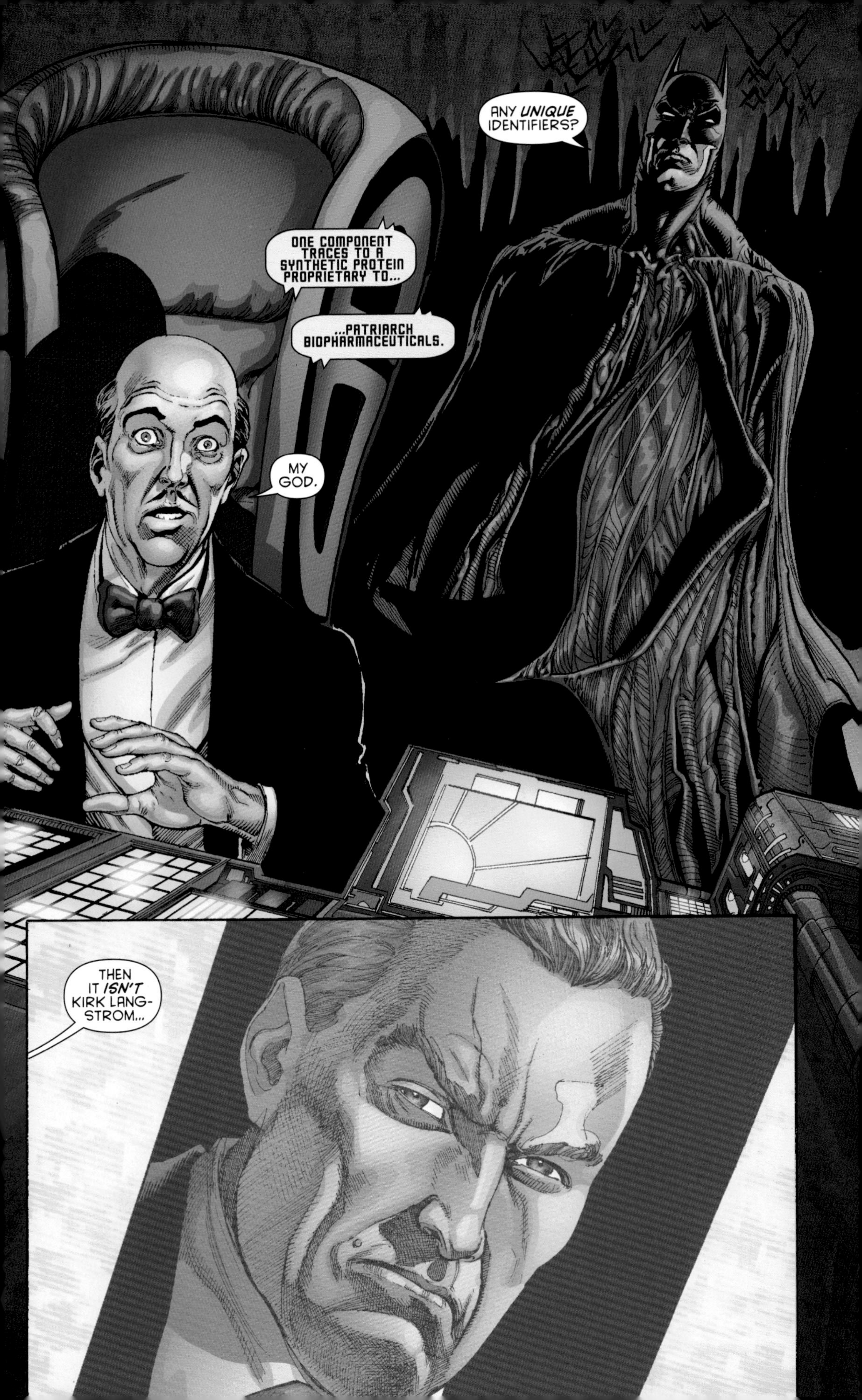
ANY UNIQUE IDENTIFIERS?
ONE COMPONENT TRACES TO A SYNTHETIC PROTEIN PROPRIETARY TO...
...PATRIARCH BIOPHARMACEUTICALS.
MY GOD.
THEN IT ISN'T KIRK LANGSTROM...

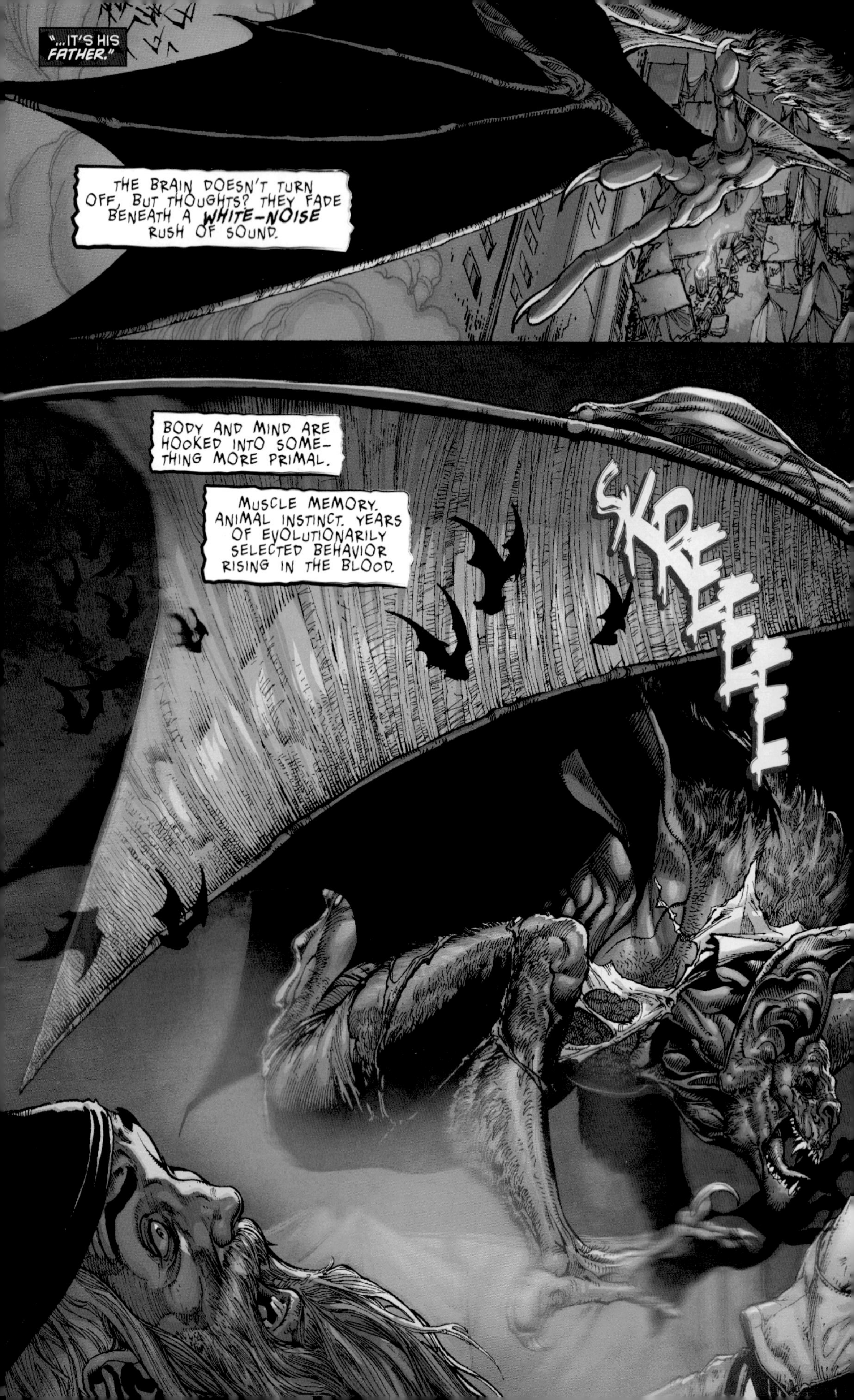
"...IT'S HIS *FATHER.*"
THE BRAIN DOESN'T TURN OFF, BUT THOUGHTS? THEY FADE BENEATH A *WHITE-NOISE* RUSH OF SOUND.
BODY AND MIND ARE HOOKED INTO SOMETHING MORE PRIMAL.
MUSCLE MEMORY. ANIMAL INSTINCT. YEARS OF EVOLUTIONARILY SELECTED BEHAVIOR RISING IN THE BLOOD.
SKREEEEEL

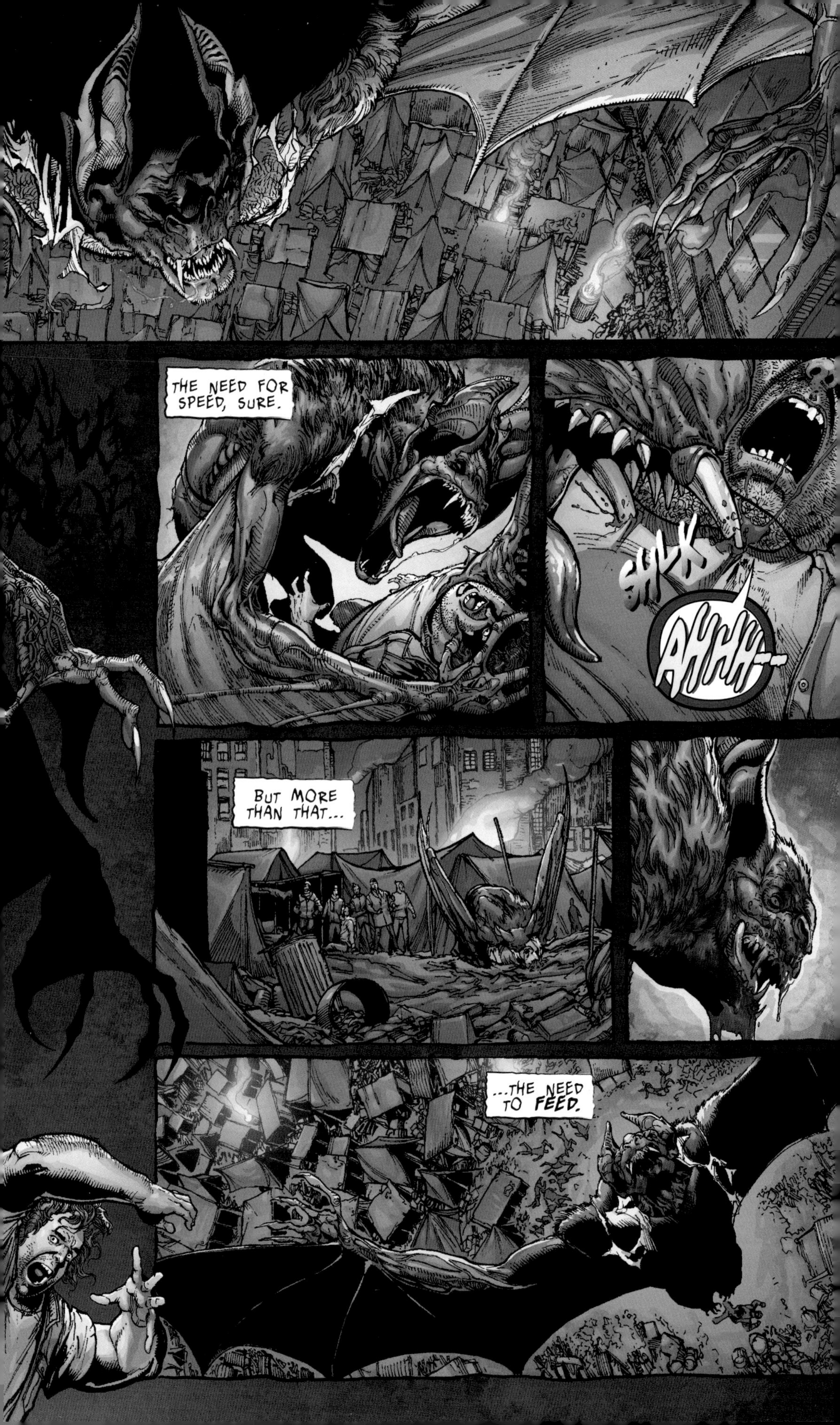
THE NEED FOR SPEED, SURE.
SHK!
AHHH--
BUT MORE THAN THAT...
...THE NEED TO FEED.

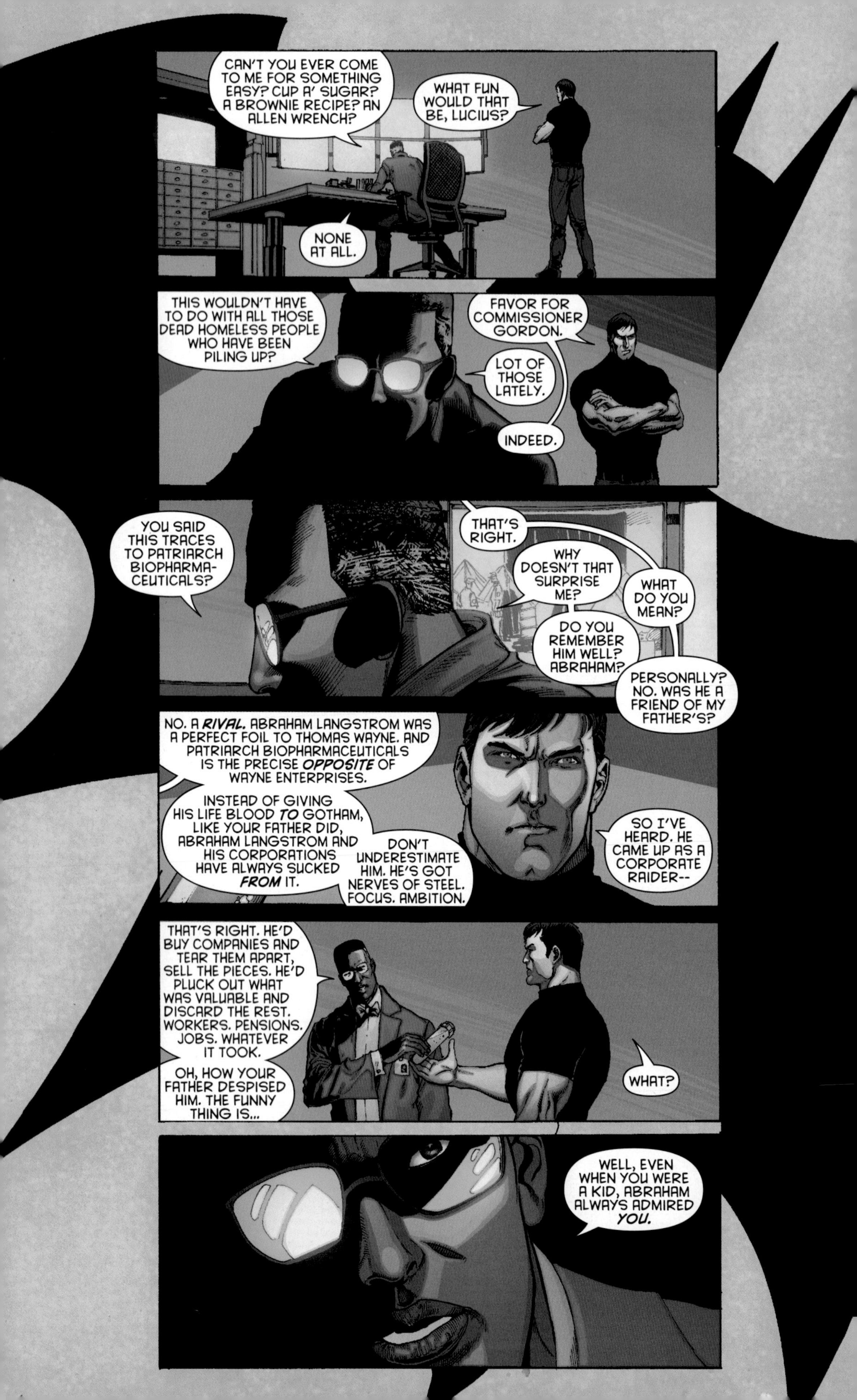
CAN'T YOU EVER COME TO ME FOR SOMETHING EASY? CUP A' SUGAR? A BROWNIE RECIPE? AN ALLEN WRENCH?
WHAT FUN WOULD THAT BE, LUCIUS?
NONE AT ALL.
THIS WOULDN'T HAVE TO DO WITH ALL THOSE DEAD HOMELESS PEOPLE WHO HAVE BEEN PILING UP?
FAVOR FOR COMMISSIONER GORDON.
LOT OF THOSE LATELY.
INDEED.
YOU SAID THIS TRACES TO PATRIARCH BIOPHARMA-CEUTICALS?
THAT'S RIGHT.
WHY DOESN'T THAT SURPRISE ME?
WHAT DO YOU MEAN?
DO YOU REMEMBER HIM WELL? ABRAHAM?
PERSONALLY? NO. WAS HE A FRIEND OF MY FATHER'S?
NO. A *RIVAL.* ABRAHAM LANGSTROM WAS A PERFECT FOIL TO THOMAS WAYNE. AND PATRIARCH BIOPHARMACEUTICALS IS THE PRECISE *OPPOSITE* OF WAYNE ENTERPRISES.
INSTEAD OF GIVING HIS LIFE BLOOD *TO* GOTHAM, LIKE YOUR FATHER DID, ABRAHAM LANGSTROM AND HIS CORPORATIONS HAVE ALWAYS SUCKED *FROM* IT.
SO I'VE HEARD. HE CAME UP AS A CORPORATE RAIDER--
DON'T UNDERESTIMATE HIM. HE'S GOT NERVES OF STEEL. FOCUS. AMBITION.
THAT'S RIGHT. HE'D BUY COMPANIES AND TEAR THEM APART, SELL THE PIECES. HE'D PLUCK OUT WHAT WAS VALUABLE AND DISCARD THE REST. WORKERS. PENSIONS. JOBS. WHATEVER IT TOOK.
OH, HOW YOUR FATHER DESPISED HIM. THE FUNNY THING IS...
WHAT?
WELL, EVEN WHEN YOU WERE A KID, ABRAHAM ALWAYS ADMIRED *YOU.*

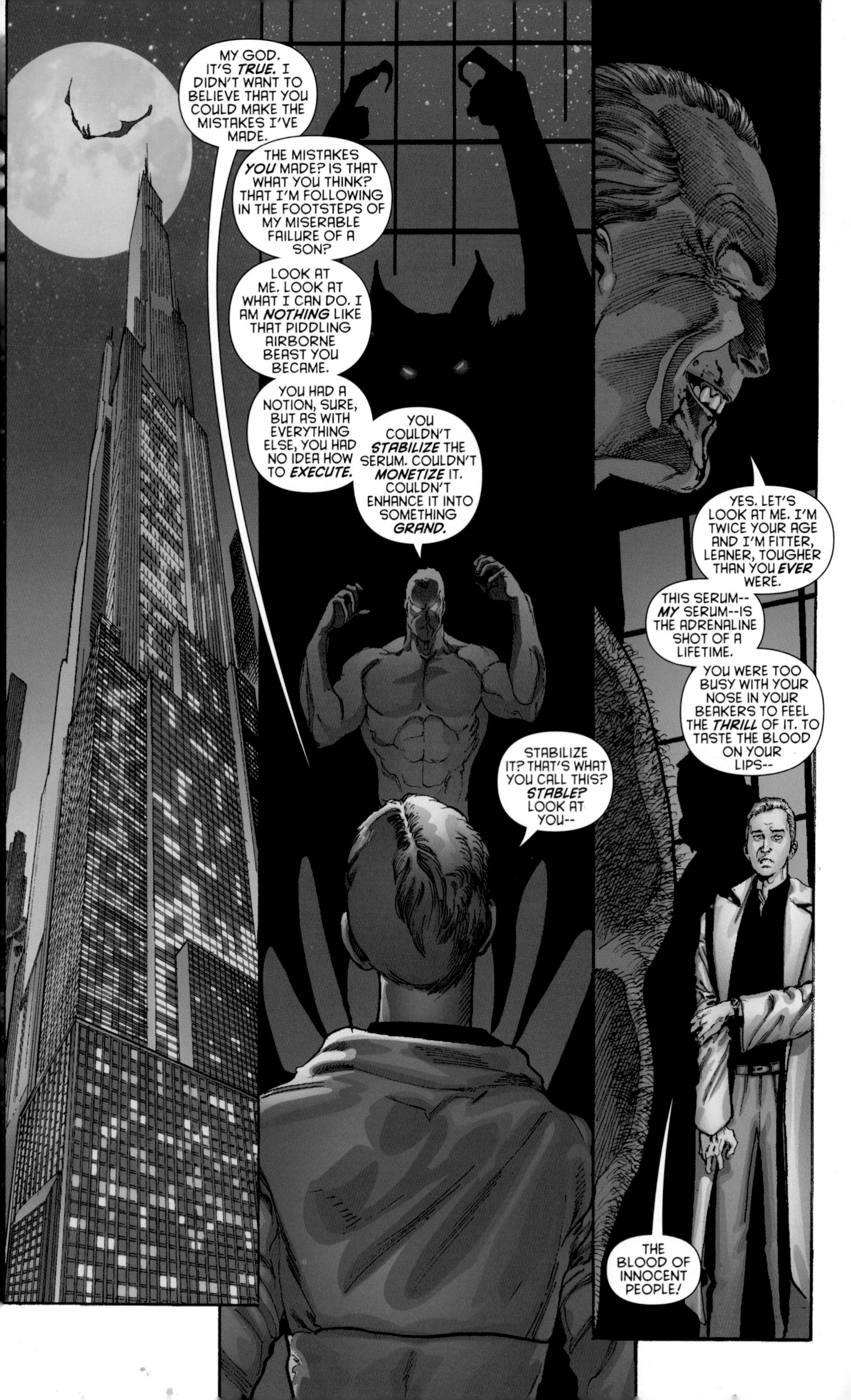
MY GOD. IT'S *TRUE.* I DIDN'T WANT TO BELIEVE THAT YOU COULD MAKE THE MISTAKES I'VE MADE.
THE MISTAKES *YOU* MADE? IS THAT WHAT YOU THINK? THAT I'M FOLLOWING IN THE FOOTSTEPS OF MY MISERABLE FAILURE OF A SON?
LOOK AT ME. LOOK AT WHAT I CAN DO. I AM *NOTHING* LIKE THAT PIDDLING AIRBORNE BEAST YOU BECAME.
YOU HAD A NOTION, SURE, BUT AS WITH EVERYTHING ELSE, YOU HAD NO IDEA HOW TO *EXECUTE.*
YOU COULDN'T *STABILIZE* THE SERUM. COULDN'T *MONETIZE* IT. COULDN'T ENHANCE IT INTO SOMETHING *GRAND.*
STABILIZE IT? THAT'S WHAT YOU CALL THIS? *STABLE?* LOOK AT YOU--
YES. LET'S LOOK AT ME. I'M TWICE YOUR AGE AND I'M FITTER, LEANER, TOUGHER THAN YOU *EVER* WERE.
THIS SERUM-- *MY* SERUM--IS THE ADRENALINE SHOT OF A LIFETIME.
YOU WERE TOO BUSY WITH YOUR NOSE IN YOUR BEAKERS TO FEEL THE *THRILL* OF IT. TO TASTE THE BLOOD ON YOUR LIPS--
THE BLOOD OF INNOCENT PEOPLE!

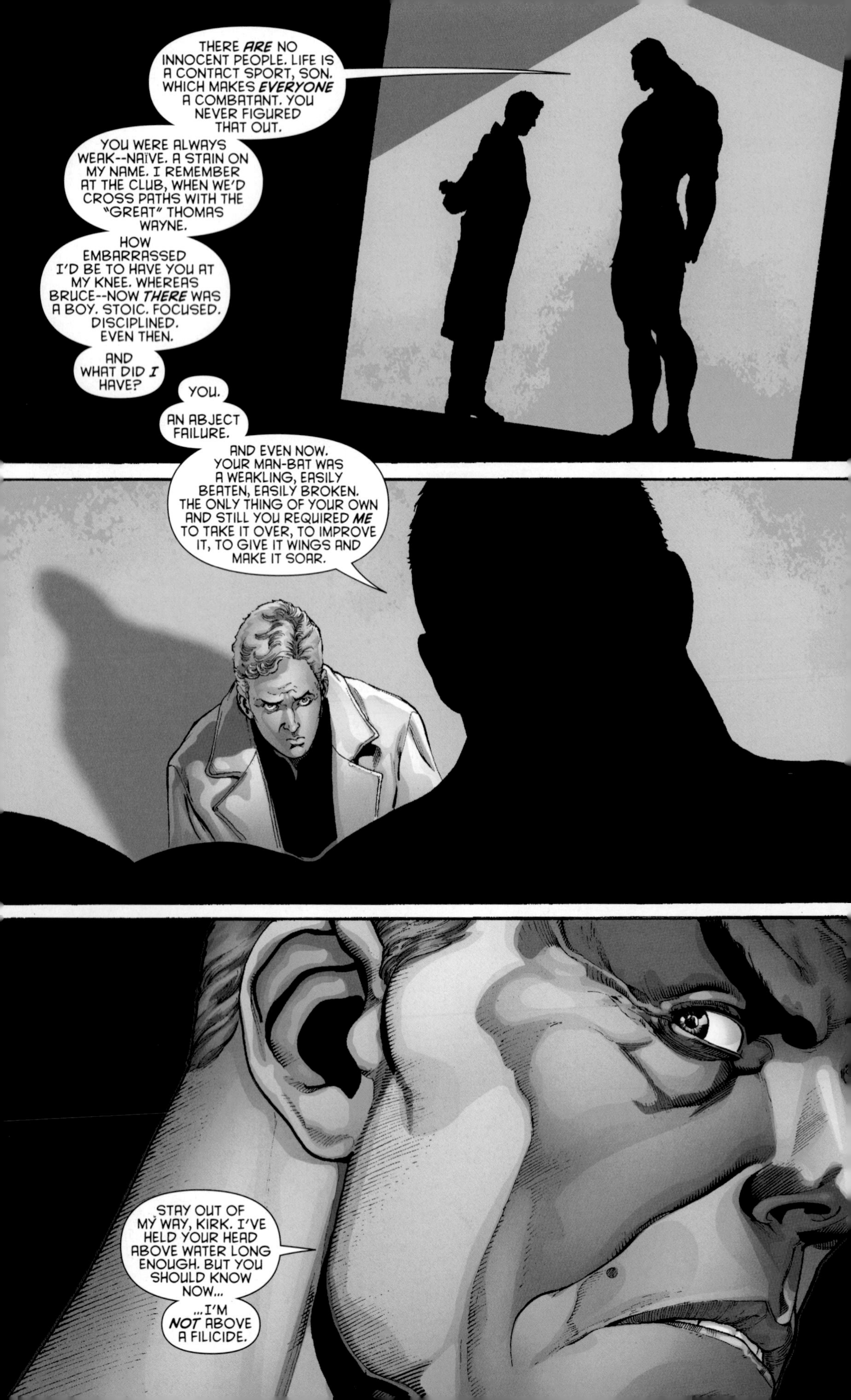
THERE ARE NO INNOCENT PEOPLE. LIFE IS A CONTACT SPORT, SON. WHICH MAKES EVERYONE A COMBATANT. YOU NEVER FIGURED THAT OUT.
YOU WERE ALWAYS WEAK--NAÏVE. A STAIN ON MY NAME. I REMEMBER AT THE CLUB, WHEN WE'D CROSS PATHS WITH THE "GREAT" THOMAS WAYNE.
HOW EMBARRASSED I'D BE TO HAVE YOU AT MY KNEE. WHEREAS BRUCE--NOW THERE WAS A BOY. STOIC. FOCUSED. DISCIPLINED. EVEN THEN.
AND WHAT DID I HAVE?
YOU.
AN ABJECT FAILURE.
AND EVEN NOW. YOUR MAN-BAT WAS A WEAKLING, EASILY BEATEN, EASILY BROKEN. THE ONLY THING OF YOUR OWN AND STILL YOU REQUIRED ME TO TAKE IT OVER, TO IMPROVE IT, TO GIVE IT WINGS AND MAKE IT SOAR.
STAY OUT OF MY WAY, KIRK. I'VE HELD YOUR HEAD ABOVE WATER LONG ENOUGH. BUT YOU SHOULD KNOW NOW...
...I'M NOT ABOVE A FILICIDE.

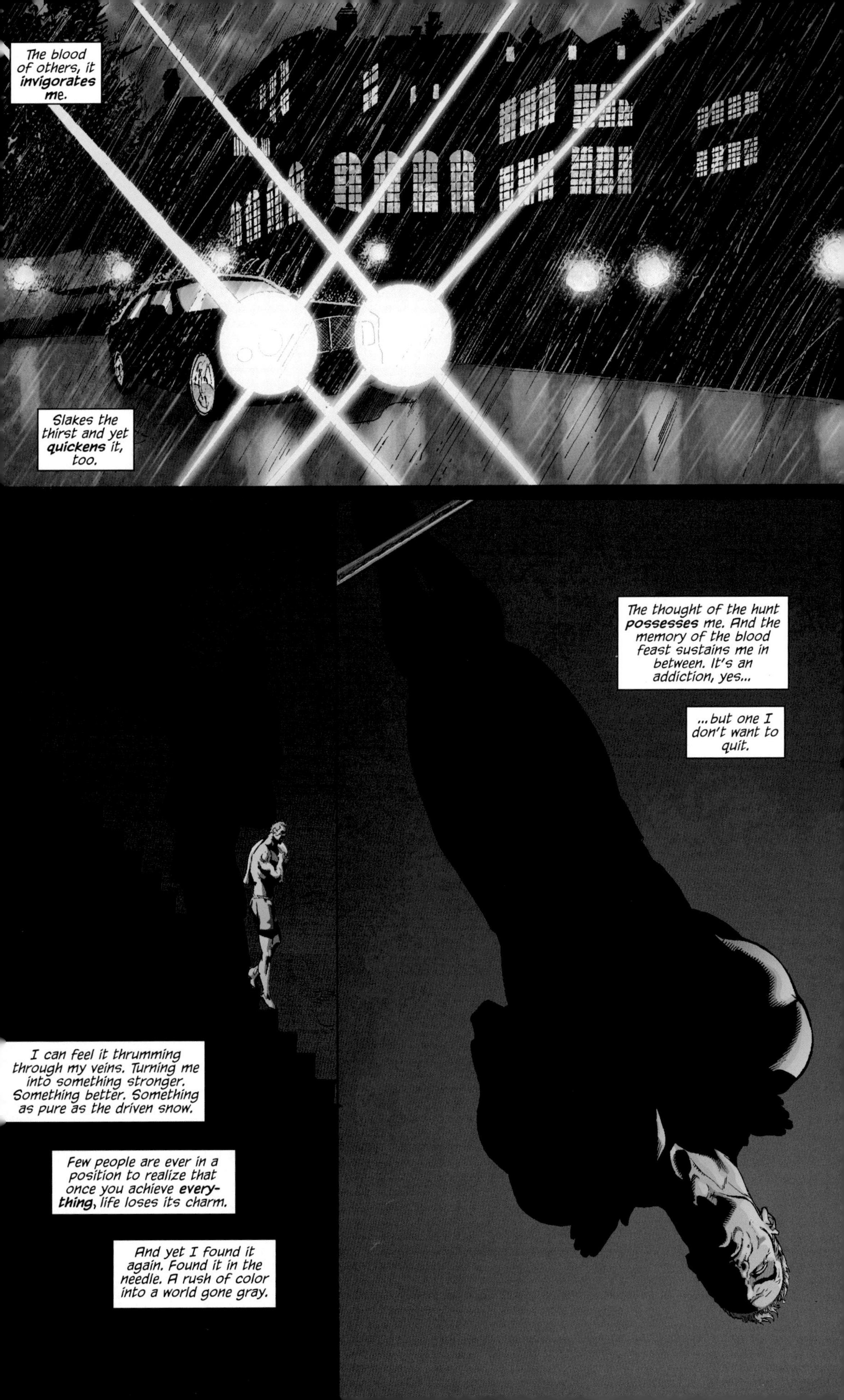

The blood of others, it **invigorates me**.
Slakes the thirst and yet **quickens** it, too.
The thought of the hunt **possesses me**. And the memory of the blood feast sustains me in between. It's an addiction, yes...
...but one I don't want to quit.
I can feel it thrumming through my veins. Turning me into something stronger. Something better. Something as pure as the driven snow.
Few people are ever in a position to realize that once you achieve **everything**, life loses its charm.
And yet I found it again. Found it in the needle. A rush of color into a world gone gray.

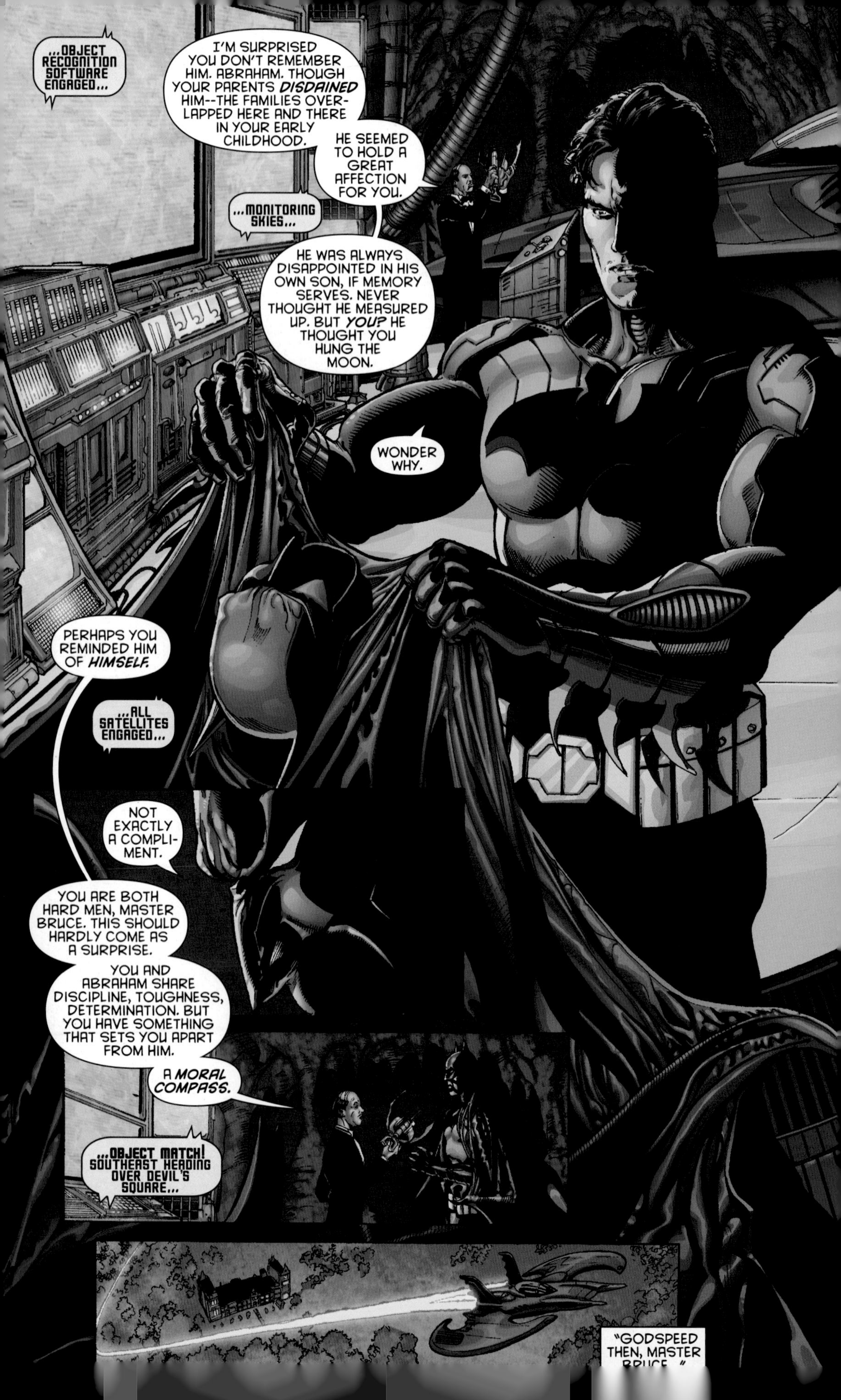
...OBJECT RECOGNITION SOFTWARE ENGAGED...
I'M SURPRISED YOU DON'T REMEMBER HIM. ABRAHAM. THOUGH YOUR PARENTS DISDAINED HIM--THE FAMILIES OVER-LAPPED HERE AND THERE IN YOUR EARLY CHILDHOOD.
HE SEEMED TO HOLD A GREAT AFFECTION FOR YOU.
...MONITORING SKIES...
HE WAS ALWAYS DISAPPOINTED IN HIS OWN SON, IF MEMORY SERVES. NEVER THOUGHT HE MEASURED UP. BUT YOU? HE THOUGHT YOU HUNG THE MOON.
WONDER WHY.
PERHAPS YOU REMINDED HIM OF HIMSELF.
...ALL SATELLITES ENGAGED...
NOT EXACTLY A COMPLI-MENT.
YOU ARE BOTH HARD MEN, MASTER BRUCE. THIS SHOULD HARDLY COME AS A SURPRISE.
YOU AND ABRAHAM SHARE DISCIPLINE, TOUGHNESS, DETERMINATION. BUT YOU HAVE SOMETHING THAT SETS YOU APART FROM HIM.
A MORAL COMPASS.
...OBJECT MATCH! SOUTHEAST HEADING OVER DEVIL'S SQUARE...
"GODSPEED THEN, MASTER BRUCE..."

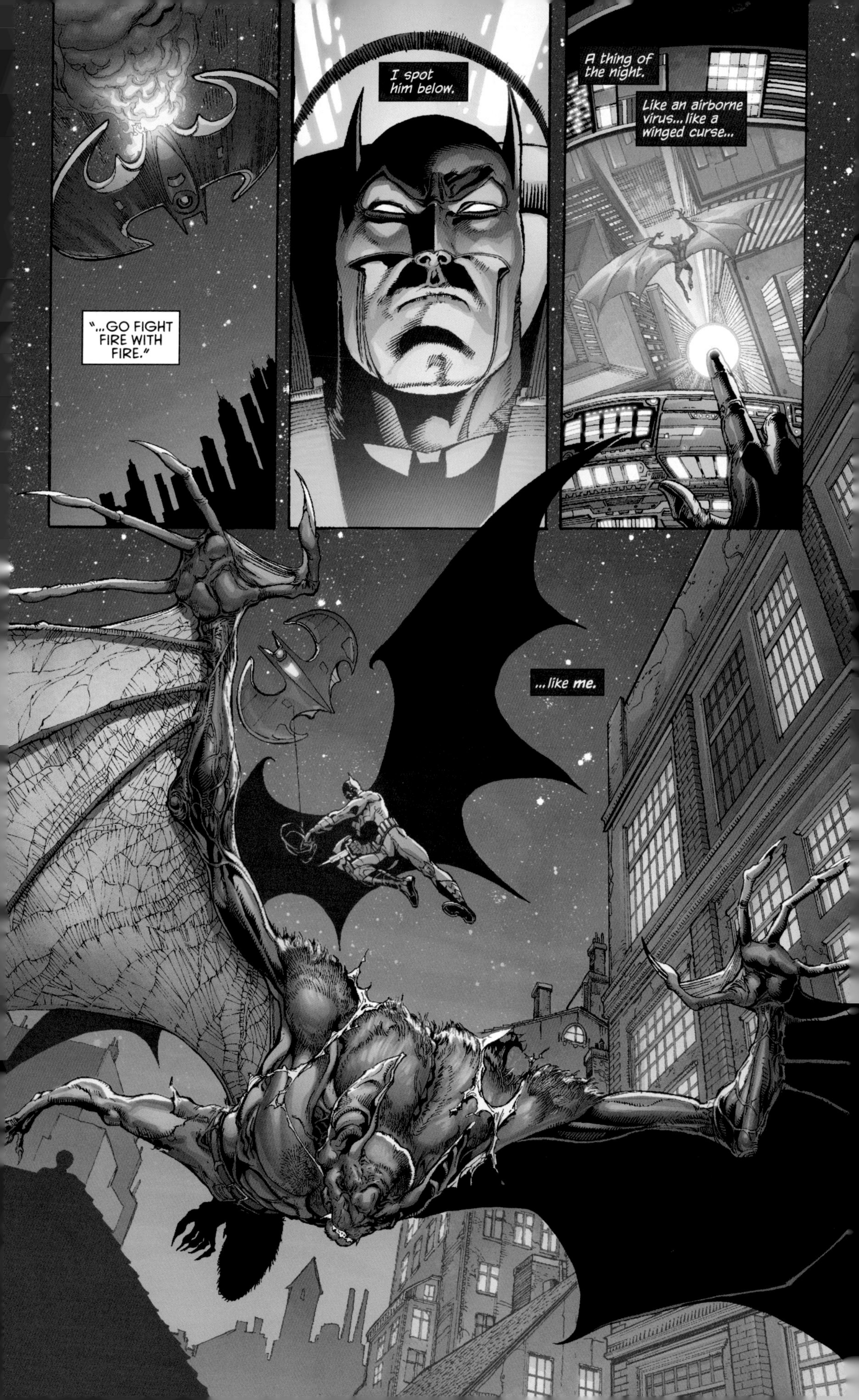
"...GO FIGHT FIRE WITH FIRE."
I spot him below.
A thing of the night.
Like an airborne virus... like a winged curse...
...like me.

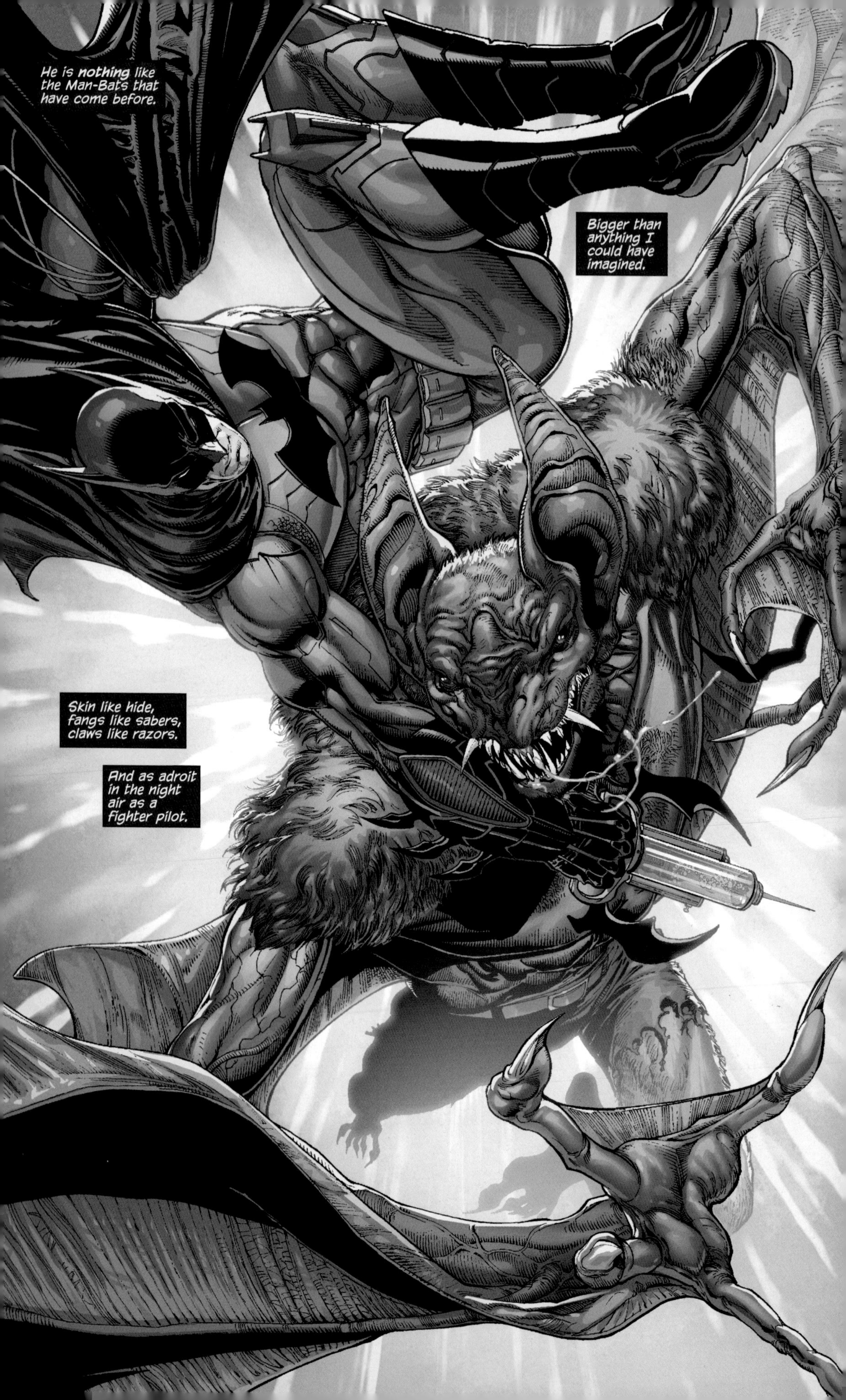
He is **nothing** like the Man-Bats that have come before.
Bigger than anything I could have imagined.
Skin like hide, fangs like sabers, claws like razors.
And as adroit in the night air as a fighter pilot.

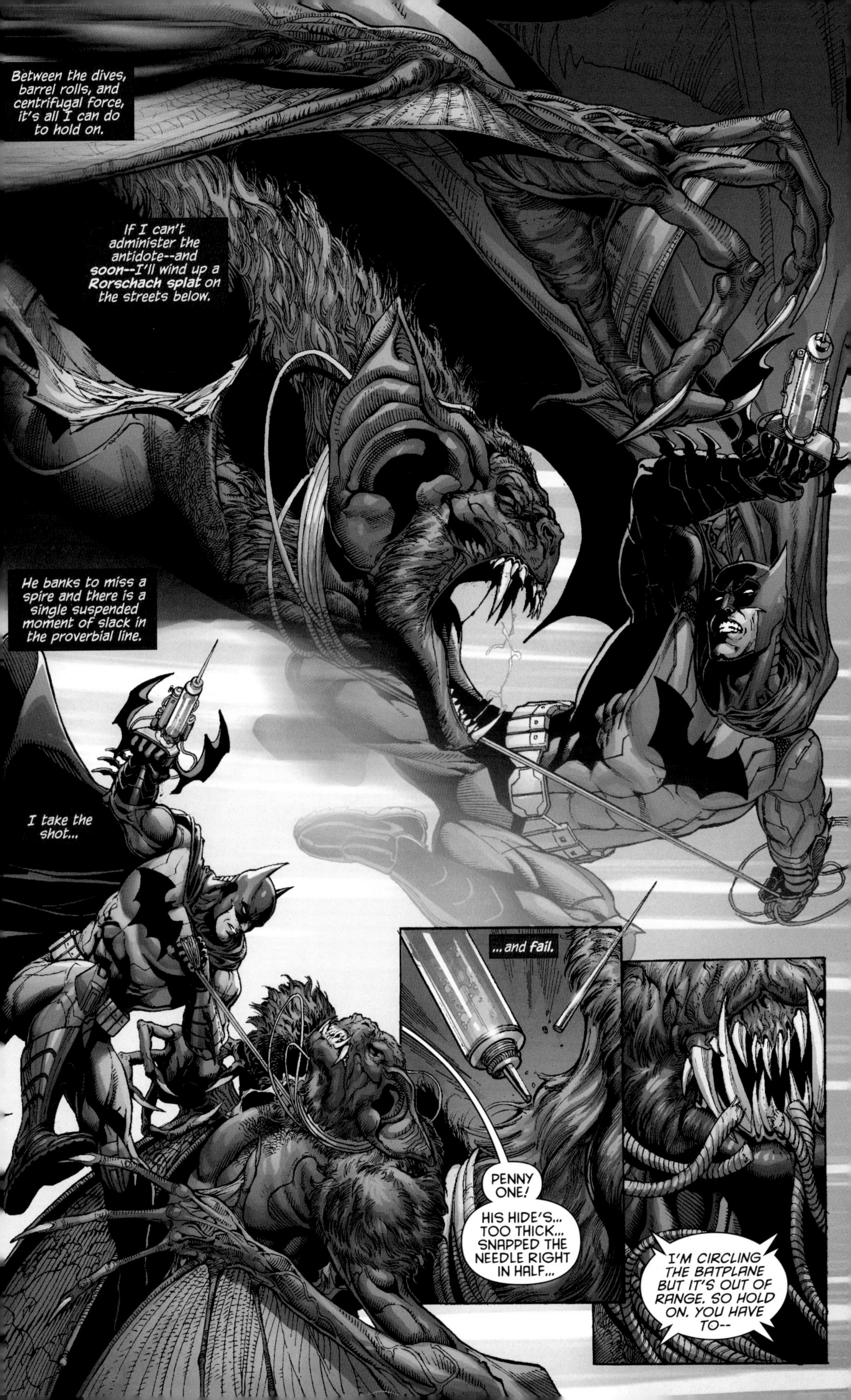

Between the dives, barrel rolls, and centrifugal force, it's all I can do to hold on.
If I can't administer the antidote--and soon--I'll wind up a Rorschach splat on the streets below.
He banks to miss a spire and there is a single suspended moment of slack in the proverbial line.
I take the shot...
...and fail.
PENNY ONE!
HIS HIDE'S... TOO THICK... SNAPPED THE NEEDLE RIGHT IN HALF...
I'M CIRCLING THE BATPLANE BUT IT'S OUT OF RANGE. SO HOLD ON. YOU HAVE TO--

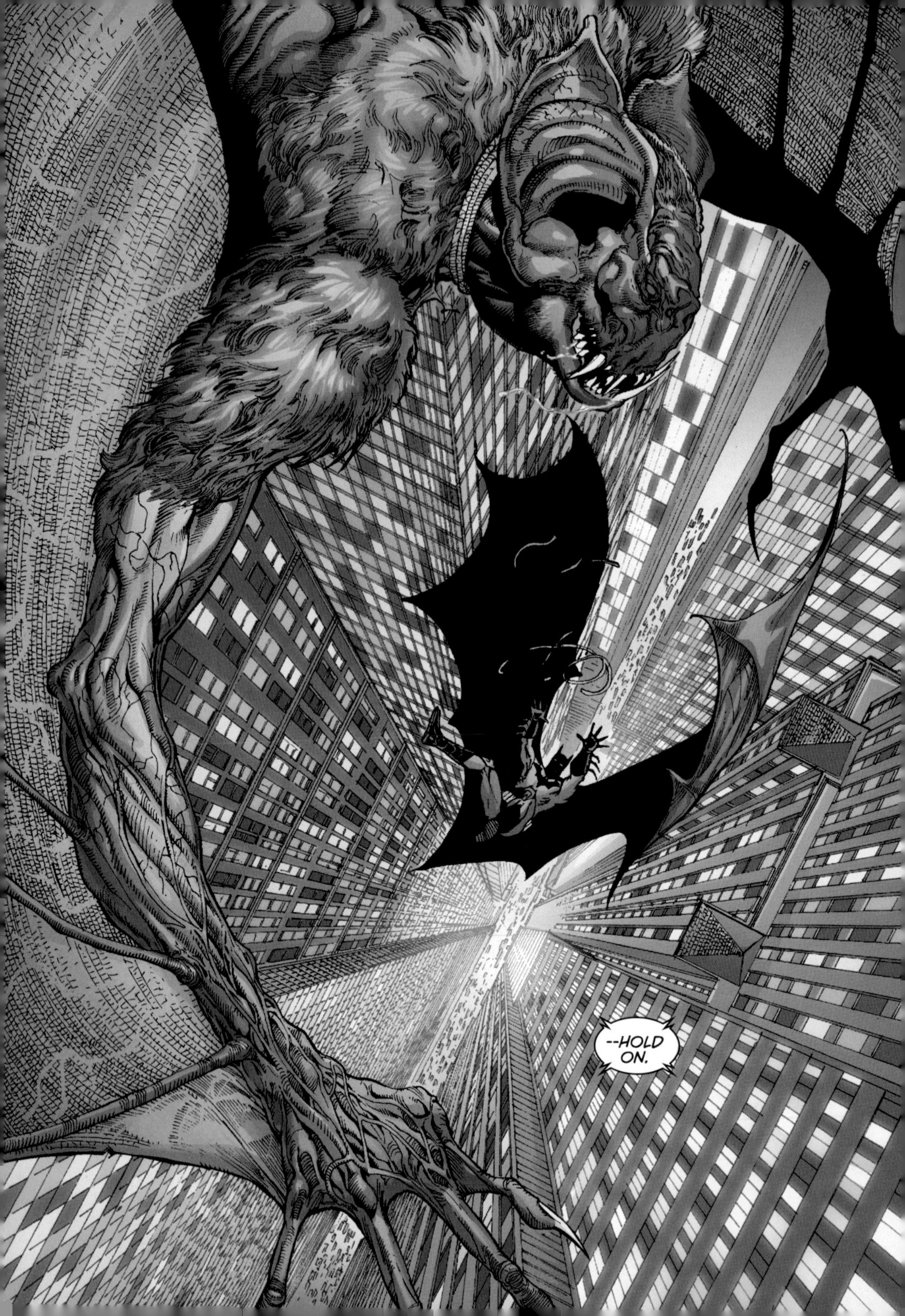
--HOLD ON.

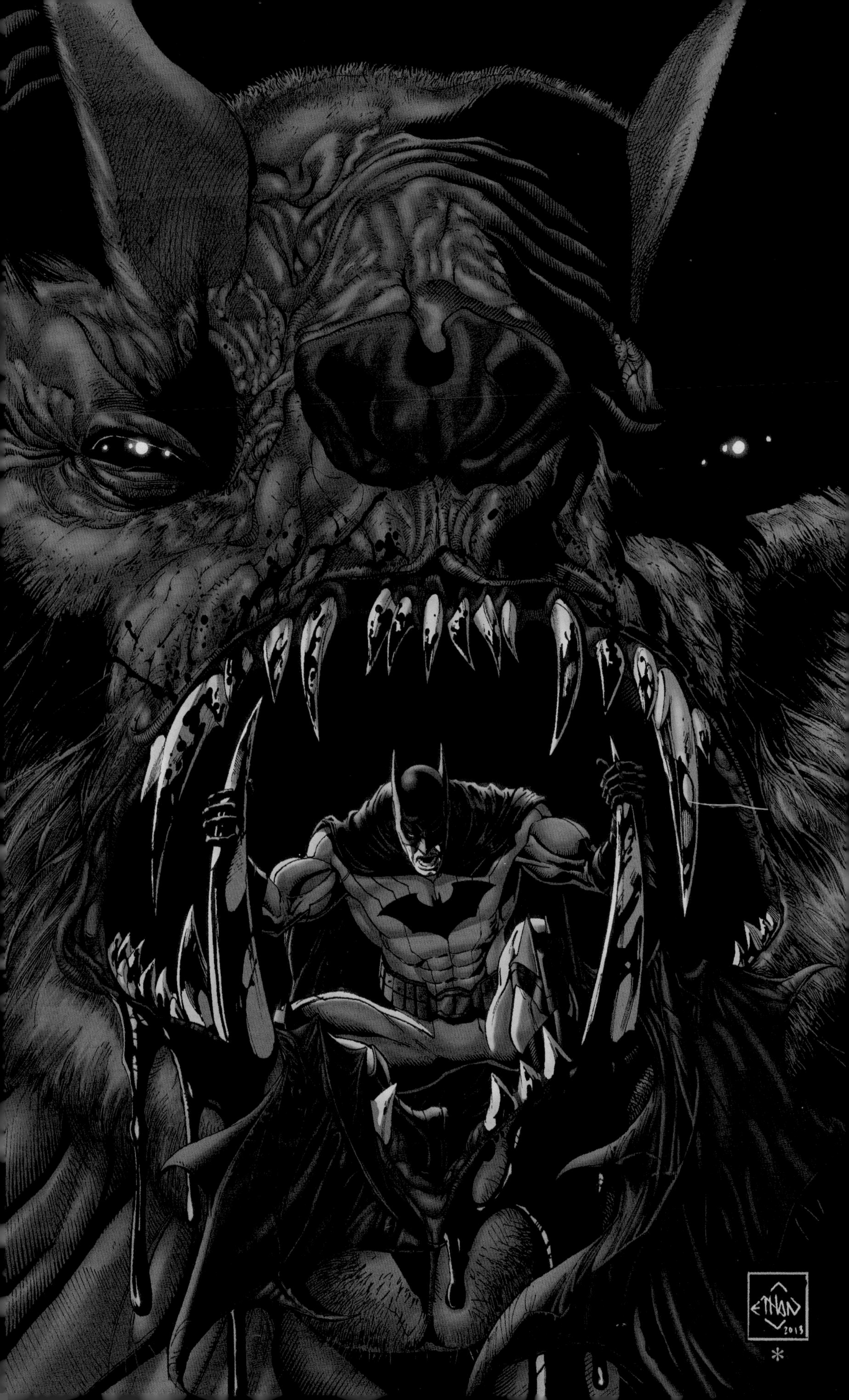

IN THE SHADOW

JORGE LUCAS & ETHAN VAN SCIVER artists cover art by **ETHAN VAN SCIVER & HI-FI**

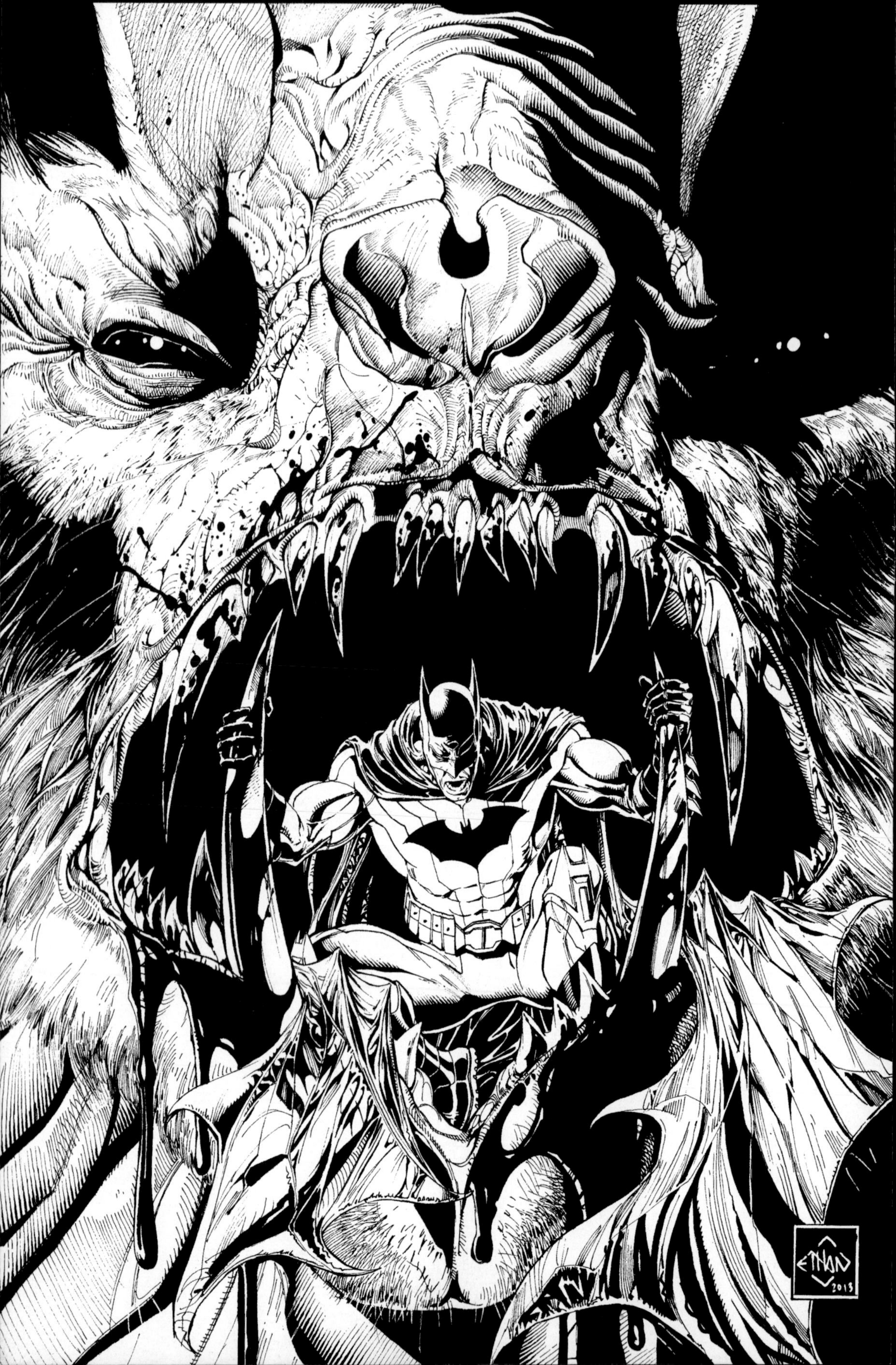
ETHAN 2013

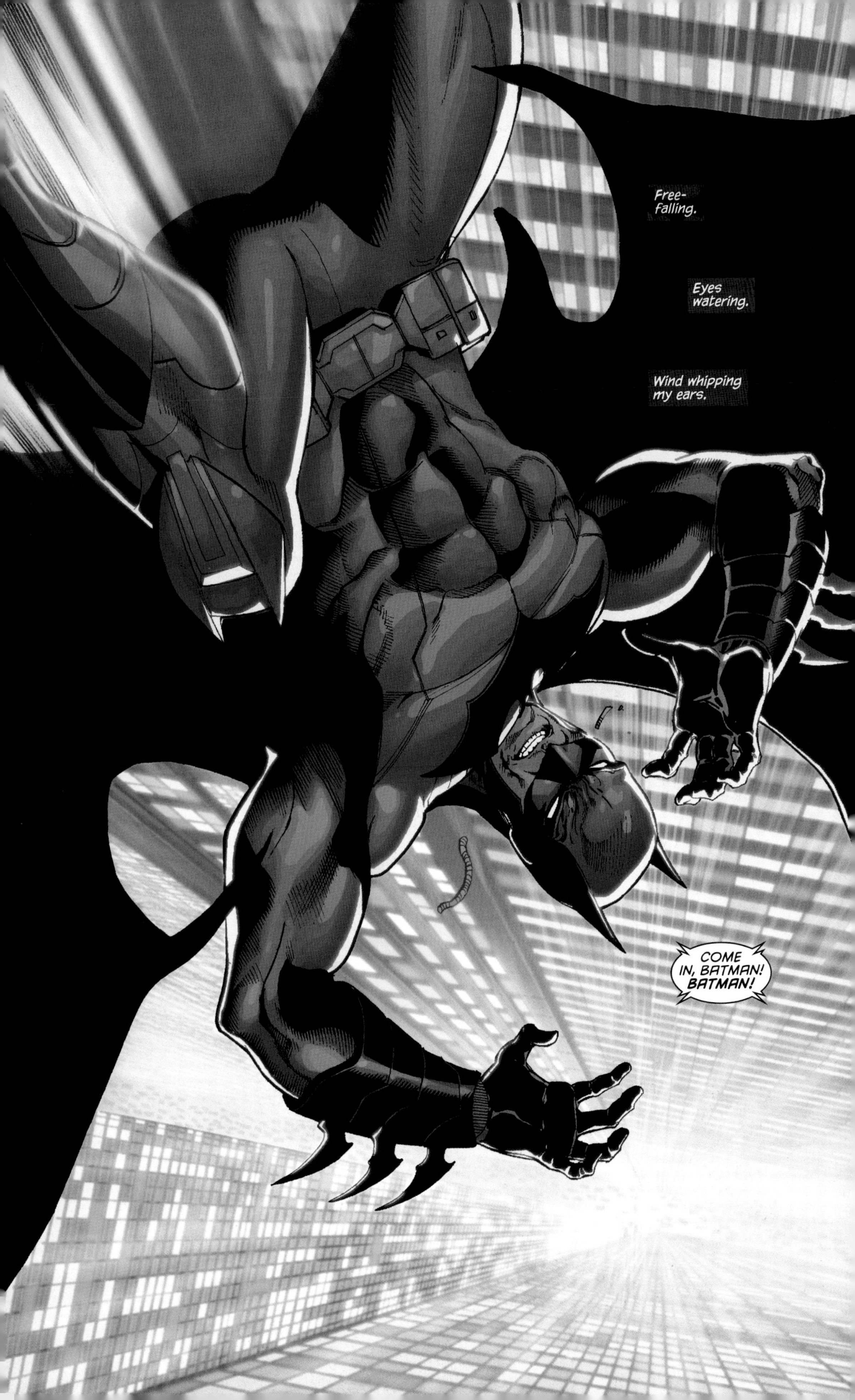
Free-falling.
Eyes watering.
Wind whipping my ears.
COME IN, BATMAN! BATMAN!

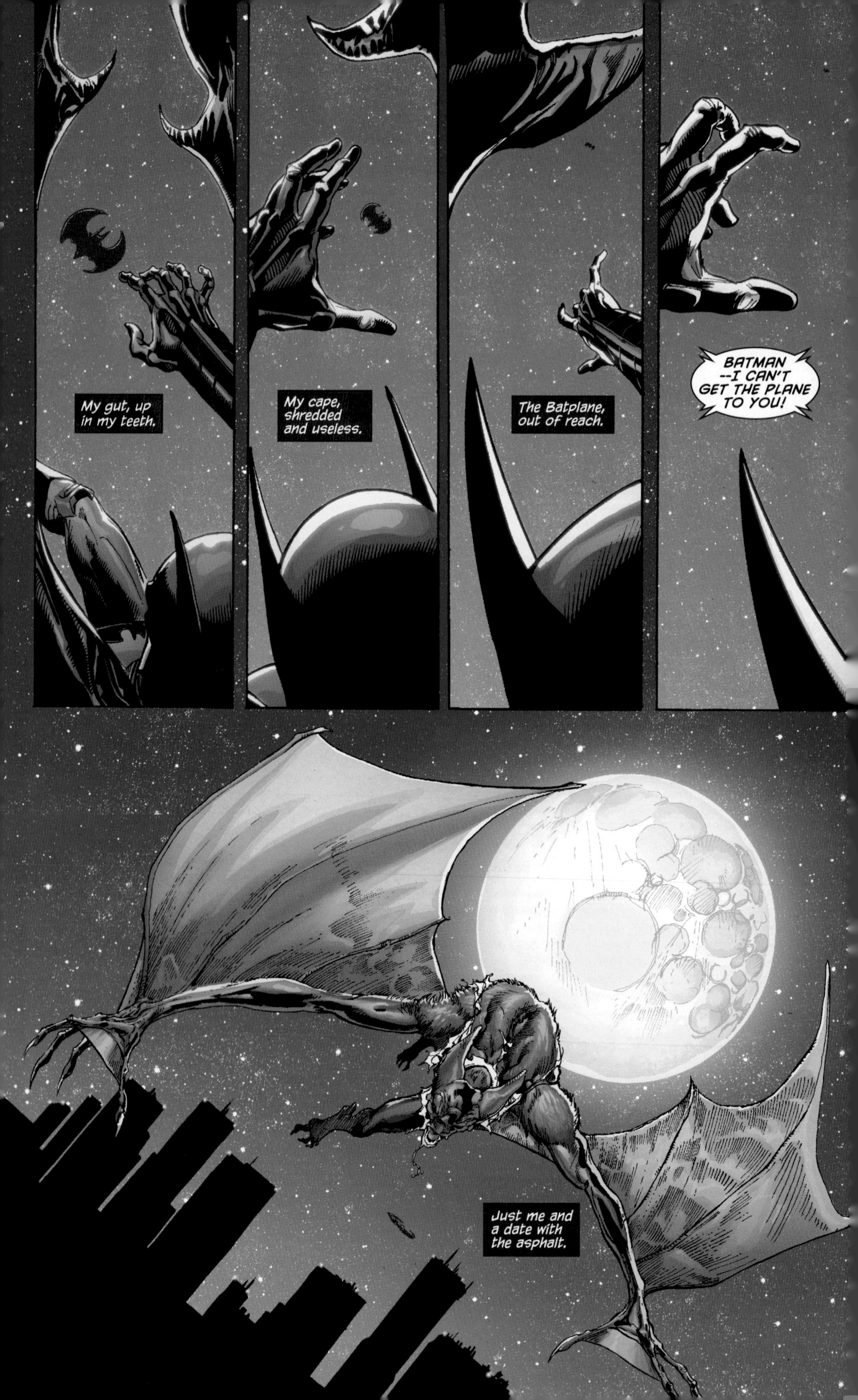
My gut, up in my teeth.
My cape, shredded and useless.
The Batplane, out of reach.
BATMAN --I CAN'T GET THE PLANE TO YOU!
Just me and a date with the asphalt.

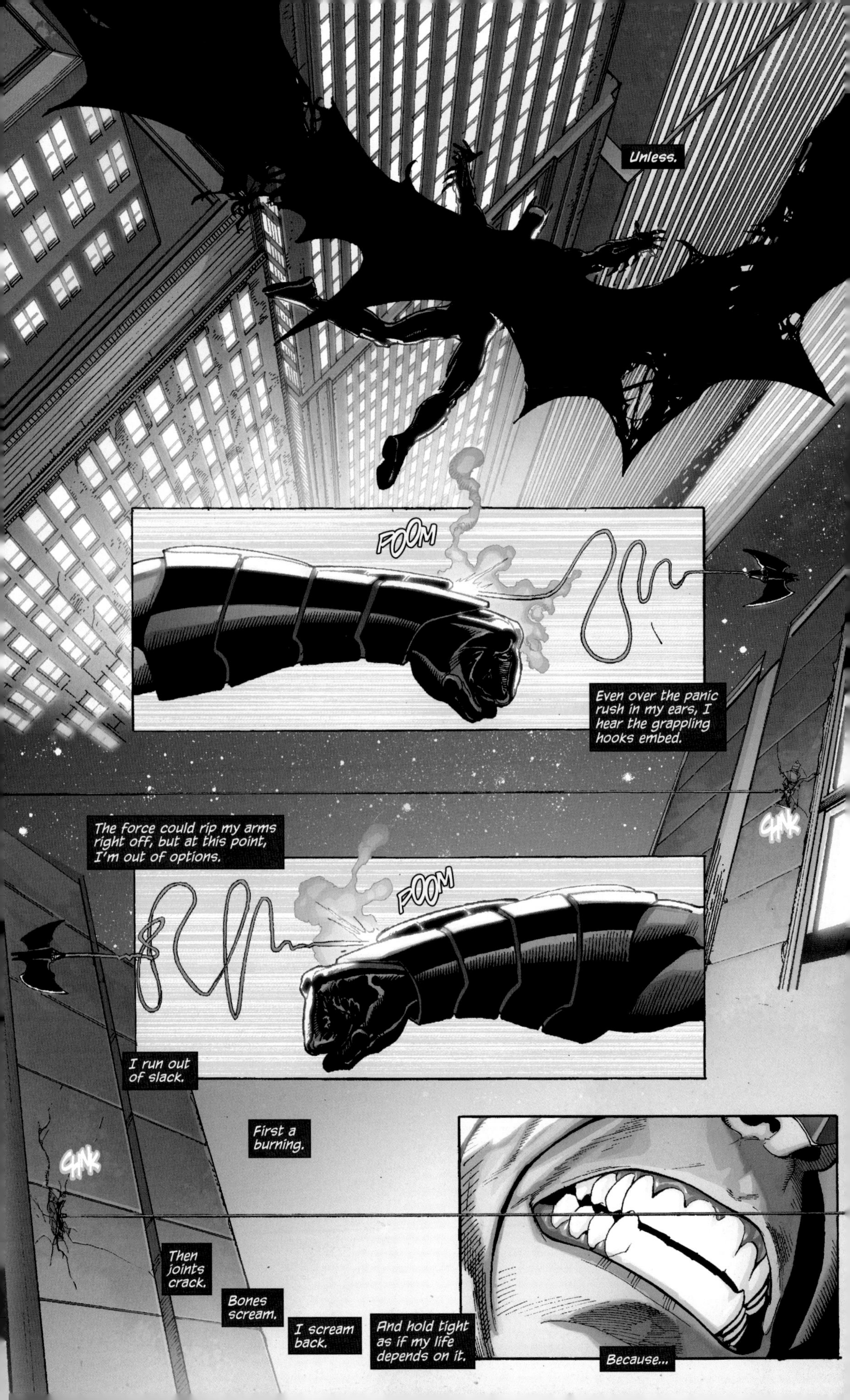
Unless.
FOOM
Even over the panic rush in my ears, I hear the grappling hooks embed.
CHINK
The force could rip my arms right off, but at this point, I'm out of options.
FOOM
I run out of slack.
CHINK
First a burning.
Then joints crack.
Bones scream.
I scream back.
And hold tight as if my life depends on it.
Because...

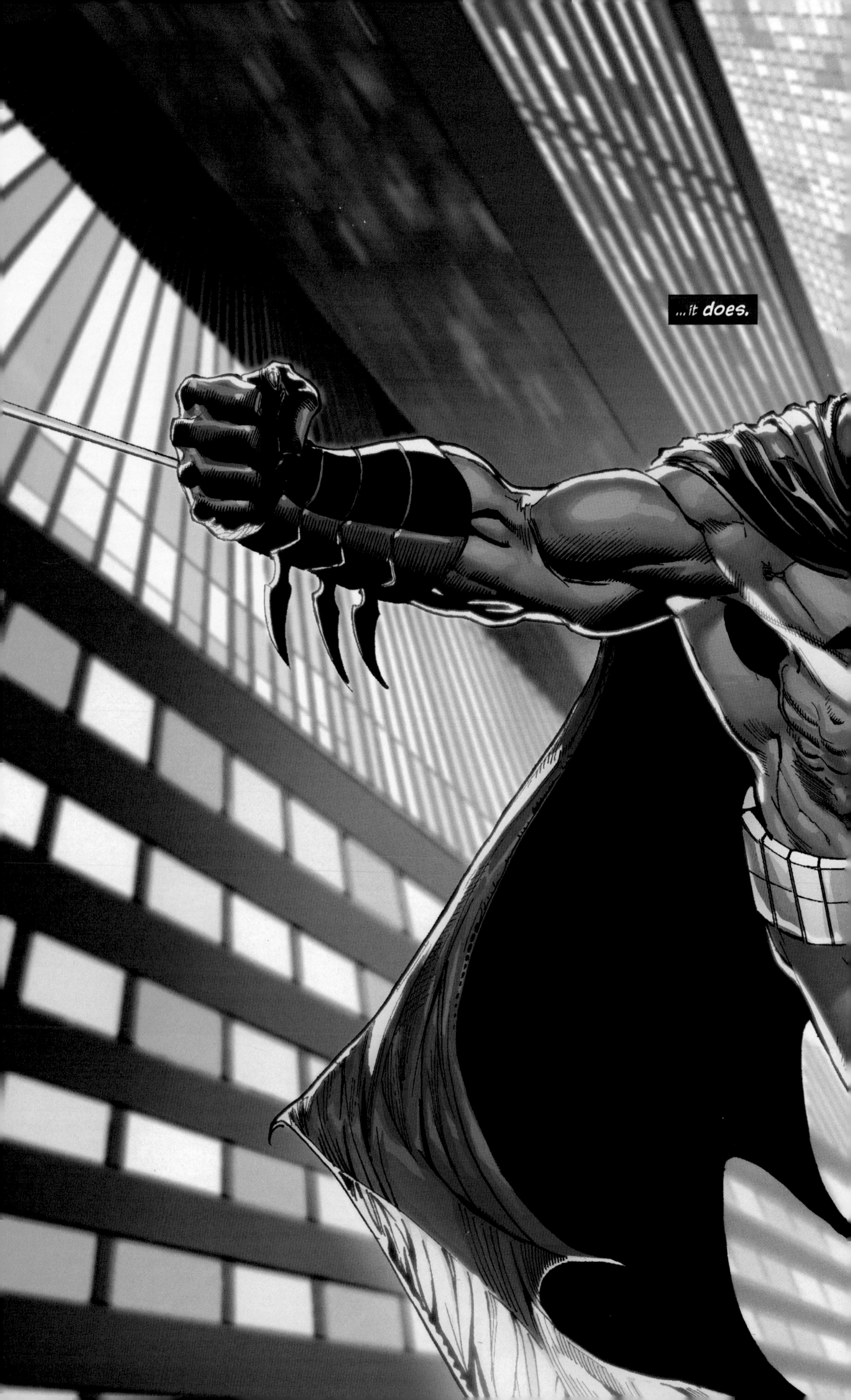
...it does.

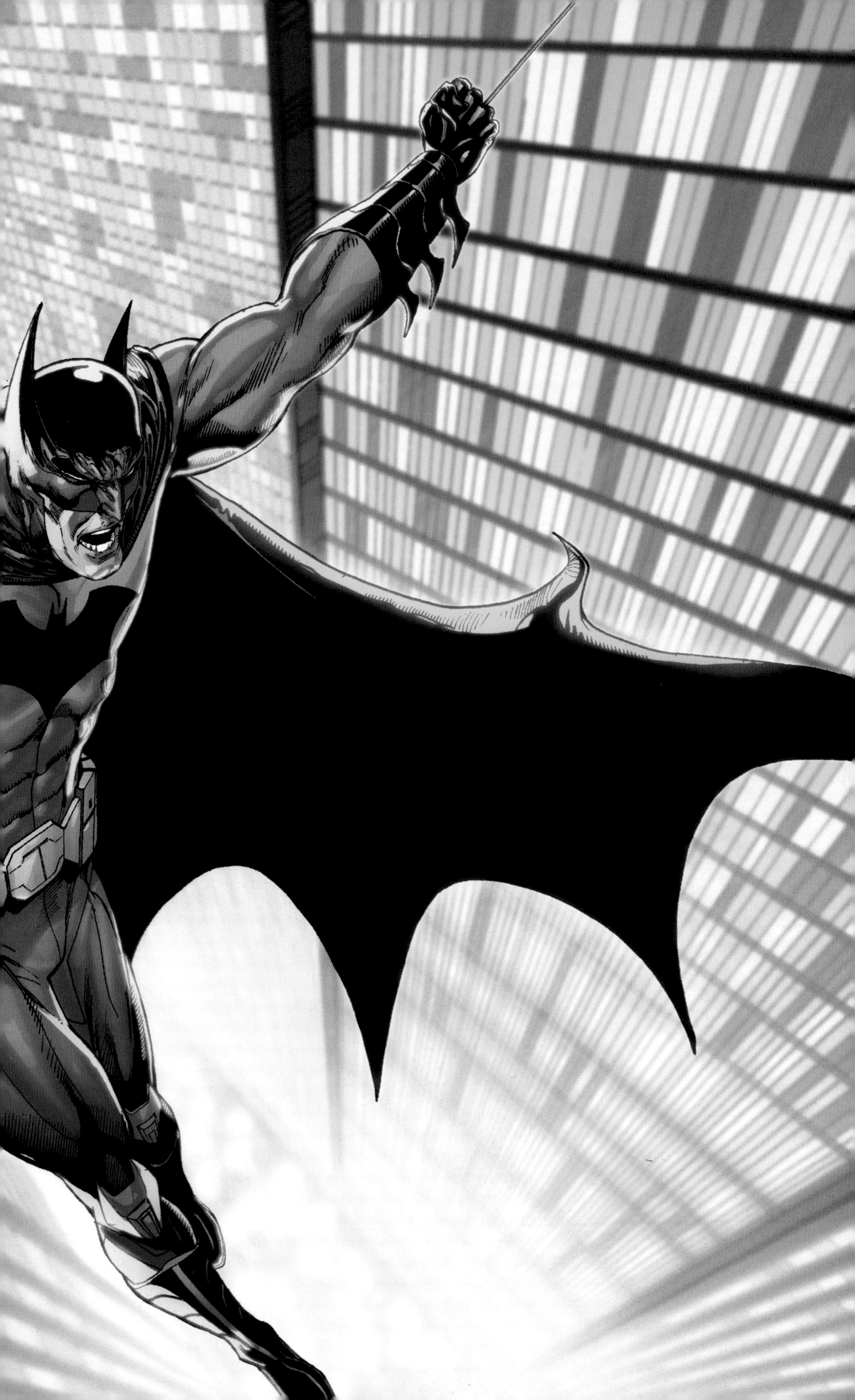

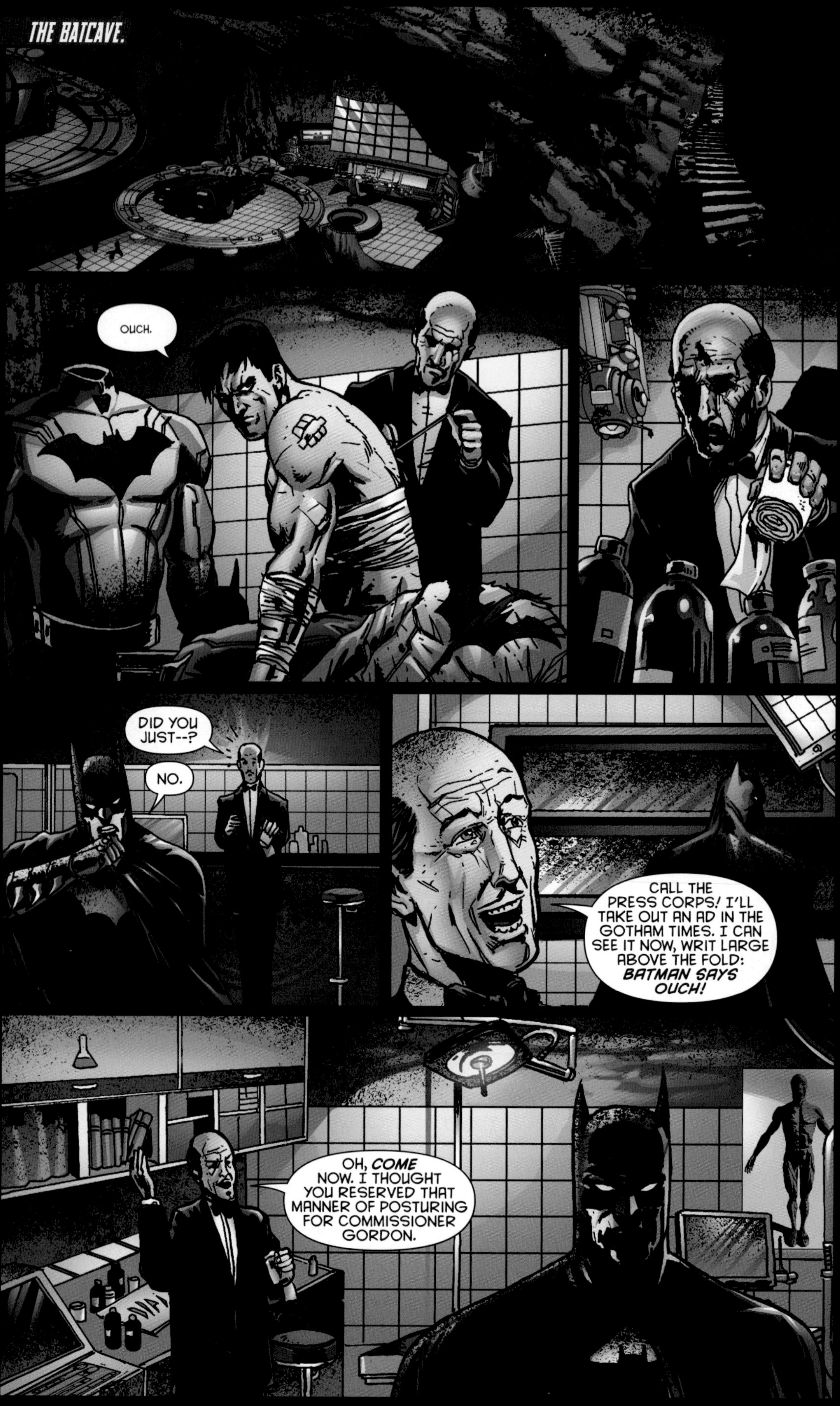
THE BATCAVE.
OUCH.
DID YOU JUST--?
NO.
CALL THE PRESS CORPS! I'LL TAKE OUT AN AD IN THE GOTHAM TIMES. I CAN SEE IT NOW, WRIT LARGE ABOVE THE FOLD: BATMAN SAYS OUCH!
OH, COME NOW. I THOUGHT YOU RESERVED THAT MANNER OF POSTURING FOR COMMISSIONER GORDON.

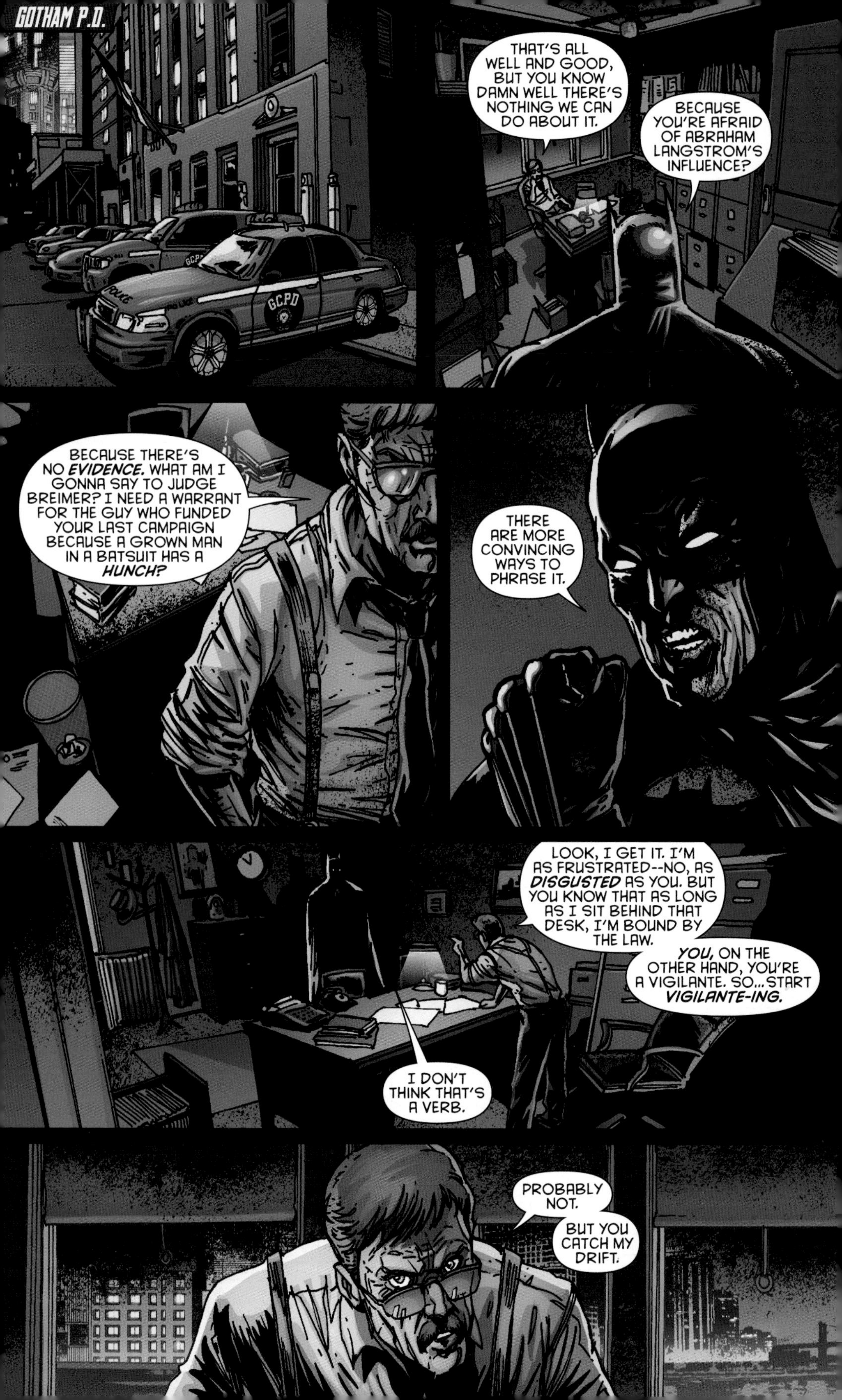
GOTHAM P.D.
THAT'S ALL WELL AND GOOD, BUT YOU KNOW DAMN WELL THERE'S NOTHING WE CAN DO ABOUT IT.
BECAUSE YOU'RE AFRAID OF ABRAHAM LANGSTROM'S INFLUENCE?
BECAUSE THERE'S NO EVIDENCE. WHAT AM I GONNA SAY TO JUDGE BREIMER? I NEED A WARRANT FOR THE GUY WHO FUNDED YOUR LAST CAMPAIGN BECAUSE A GROWN MAN IN A BATSUIT HAS A HUNCH?
THERE ARE MORE CONVINCING WAYS TO PHRASE IT.
LOOK, I GET IT. I'M AS FRUSTRATED--NO, AS DISGUSTED AS YOU. BUT YOU KNOW THAT AS LONG AS I SIT BEHIND THAT DESK, I'M BOUND BY THE LAW.
YOU, ON THE OTHER HAND, YOU'RE A VIGILANTE. SO...START VIGILANTE-ING.
I DON'T THINK THAT'S A VERB.
PROBABLY NOT.
BUT YOU CATCH MY DRIFT.

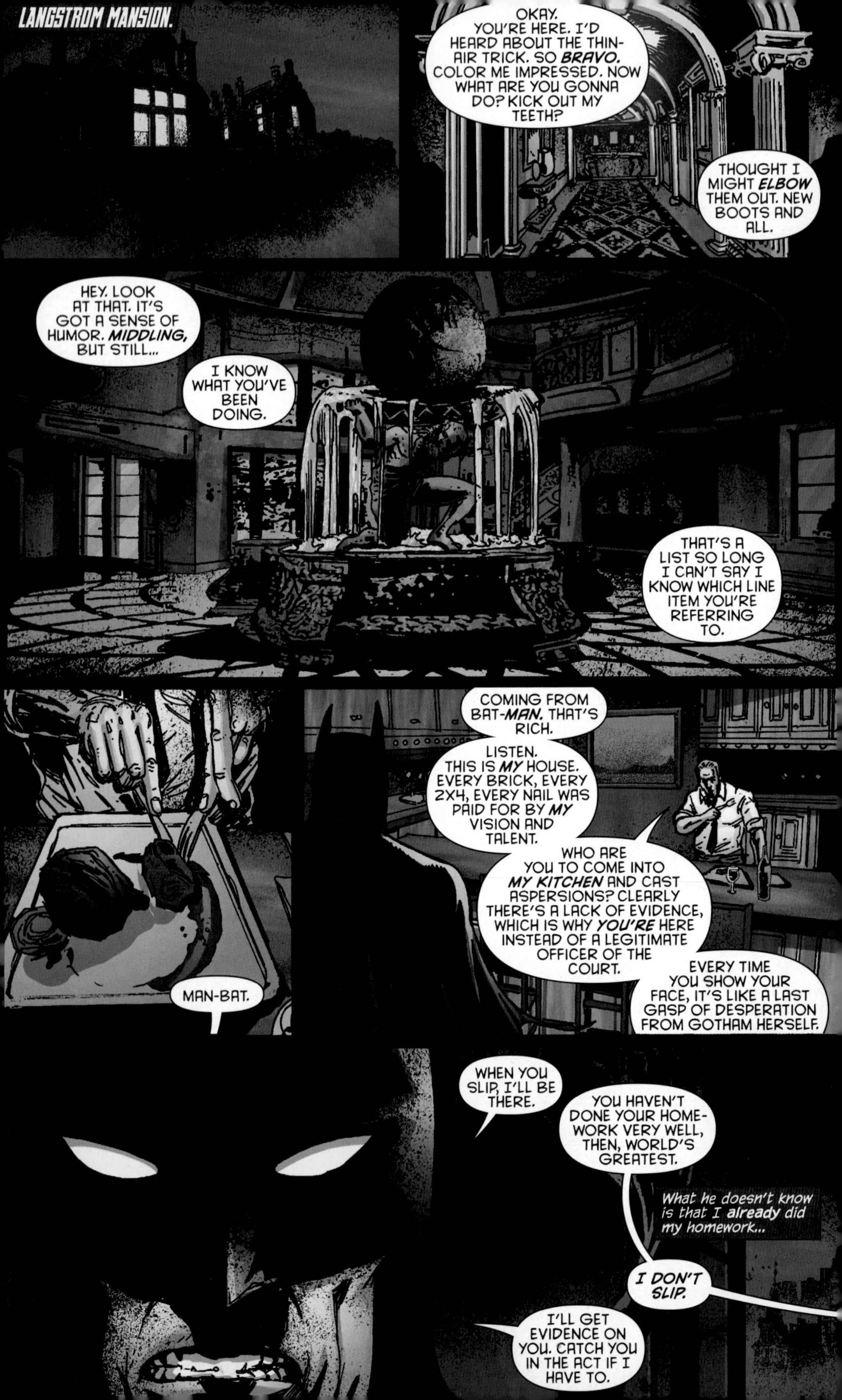
LANGSTROM MANSION.
OKAY. YOU'RE HERE. I'D HEARD ABOUT THE THIN-AIR TRICK. SO BRAVO. COLOR ME IMPRESSED. NOW WHAT ARE YOU GONNA DO? KICK OUT MY TEETH?
THOUGHT I MIGHT ELBOW THEM OUT. NEW BOOTS AND ALL.
HEY. LOOK AT THAT. IT'S GOT A SENSE OF HUMOR. MIDDLING, BUT STILL...
I KNOW WHAT YOU'VE BEEN DOING.
THAT'S A LIST SO LONG I CAN'T SAY I KNOW WHICH LINE ITEM YOU'RE REFERRING TO.
MAN-BAT.
COMING FROM BAT-MAN. THAT'S RICH.
LISTEN. THIS IS MY HOUSE. EVERY BRICK, EVERY 2X4, EVERY NAIL WAS PAID FOR BY MY VISION AND TALENT.
WHO ARE YOU TO COME INTO MY KITCHEN AND CAST ASPERSIONS? CLEARLY THERE'S A LACK OF EVIDENCE, WHICH IS WHY YOU'RE HERE INSTEAD OF A LEGITIMATE OFFICER OF THE COURT.
EVERY TIME YOU SHOW YOUR FACE, IT'S LIKE A LAST GASP OF DESPERATION FROM GOTHAM HERSELF.
WHEN YOU SLIP, I'LL BE THERE.
YOU HAVEN'T DONE YOUR HOME-WORK VERY WELL, THEN, WORLD'S GREATEST.
What he doesn't know is that I already did my homework...
I DON'T SLIP.
I'LL GET EVIDENCE ON YOU. CATCH YOU IN THE ACT IF I HAVE TO.

IF I **WAS** MAN-BAT--AND I'M NOT SAYING I AM--YOU'D NEVER CATCH ME. BECAUSE I'D BE SO MUCH MORE POWERFUL THAN YOU. POWERFUL ENOUGH TO, SAY, SNAP A NEEDLE RIGHT IN HALF BEFORE AN ANTIDOTE COULD BE ADMINISTERED.

...that fancy Bentley of his, his chauffeur recently made a few **upgrades**.

WHY THE HOMELESS?

THEORETICALLY, OF COURSE?

OF COURSE.

...new brake pads... ...new **G.P.S.**

WELL, I BELIEVE MAN-BAT'S CLEANING UP THOSE WHO TAKE A TOLL ON THE CITY. THOSE WHO DON'T CONTRIBUTE.

THOSE WHO WON'T BE **MISSED**, YOU MEAN.

NO RELATIVES TO STAY ON TOP OF THE POLICE, TO PRESS CHARGES, TO BRING INFLUENCE TO BEAR.

I pulled data off the unit, gave it a quick look. One trip in particular jumped out. Past a **homeless shelter** on the hill. Clearly, he's casing the place...

AND THERE'S THAT.

...and that means...

GUESS WHAT?

I MISS THEM.

...I will too.

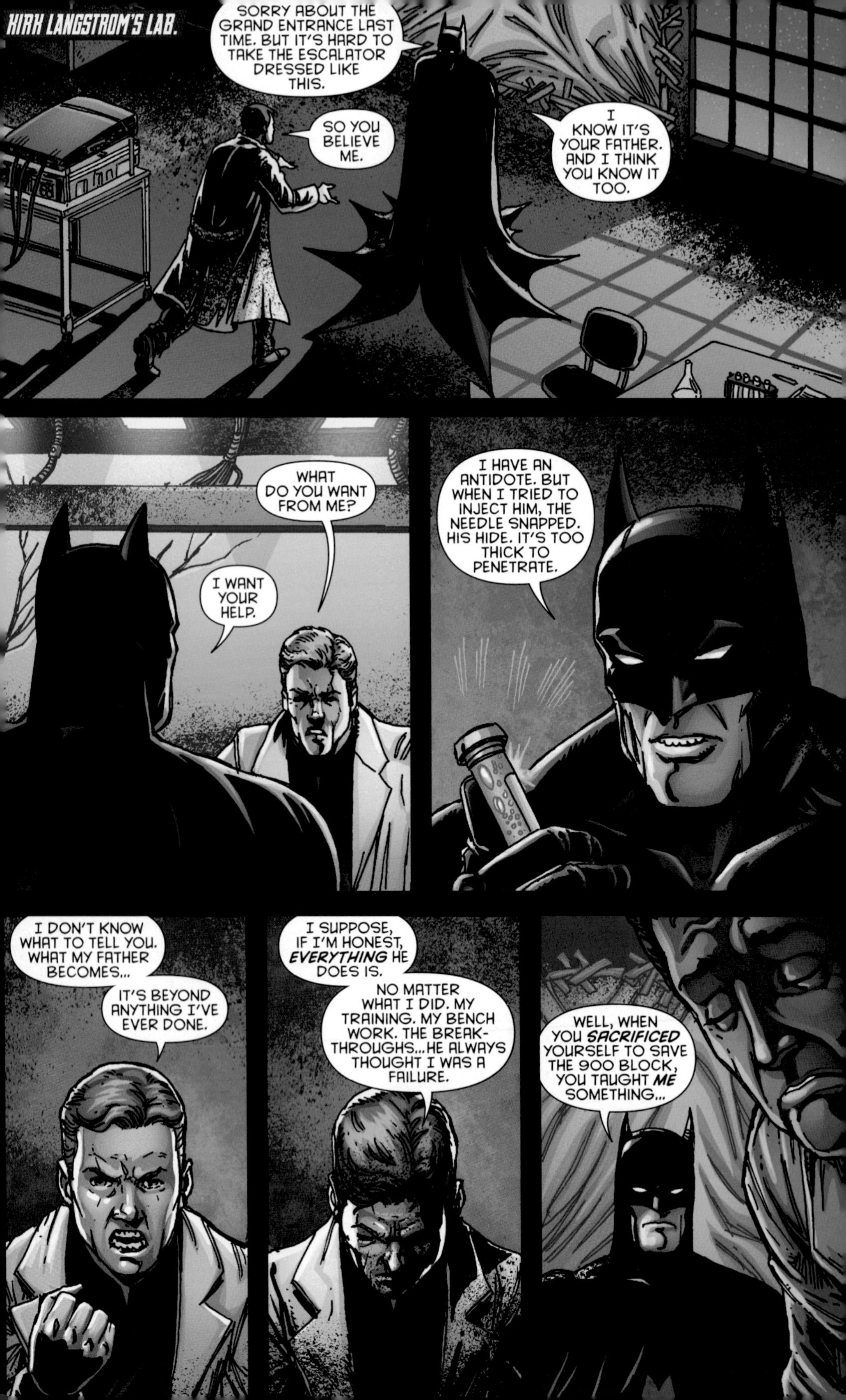
KIRK LANGSTROM'S LAB.
SORRY ABOUT THE GRAND ENTRANCE LAST TIME. BUT IT'S HARD TO TAKE THE ESCALATOR DRESSED LIKE THIS.
SO YOU BELIEVE ME.
I KNOW IT'S YOUR FATHER. AND I THINK YOU KNOW IT TOO.
WHAT DO YOU WANT FROM ME?
I WANT YOUR HELP.
I HAVE AN ANTIDOTE. BUT WHEN I TRIED TO INJECT HIM, THE NEEDLE SNAPPED. HIS HIDE. IT'S TOO THICK TO PENETRATE.
I DON'T KNOW WHAT TO TELL YOU. WHAT MY FATHER BECOMES...
IT'S BEYOND ANYTHING I'VE EVER DONE.
I SUPPOSE, IF I'M HONEST, EVERYTHING HE DOES IS.
NO MATTER WHAT I DID. MY TRAINING. MY BENCH WORK. THE BREAK-THROUGHS...HE ALWAYS THOUGHT I WAS A FAILURE.
WELL, WHEN YOU SACRIFICED YOURSELF TO SAVE THE 900 BLOCK, YOU TAUGHT ME SOMETHING...

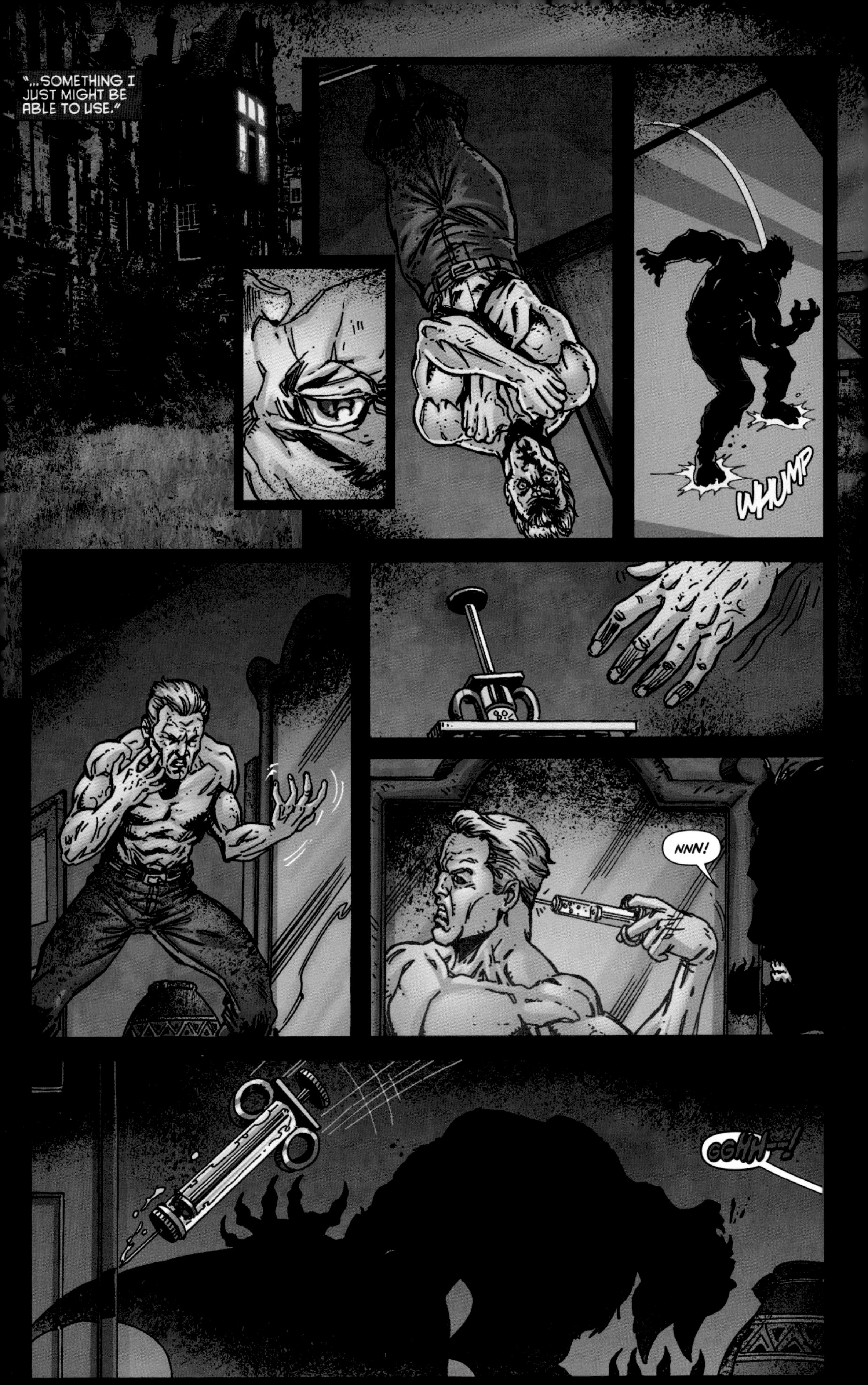
"...SOMETHING I JUST MIGHT BE ABLE TO USE."
WHUMP
NNN!
GGHAA--!

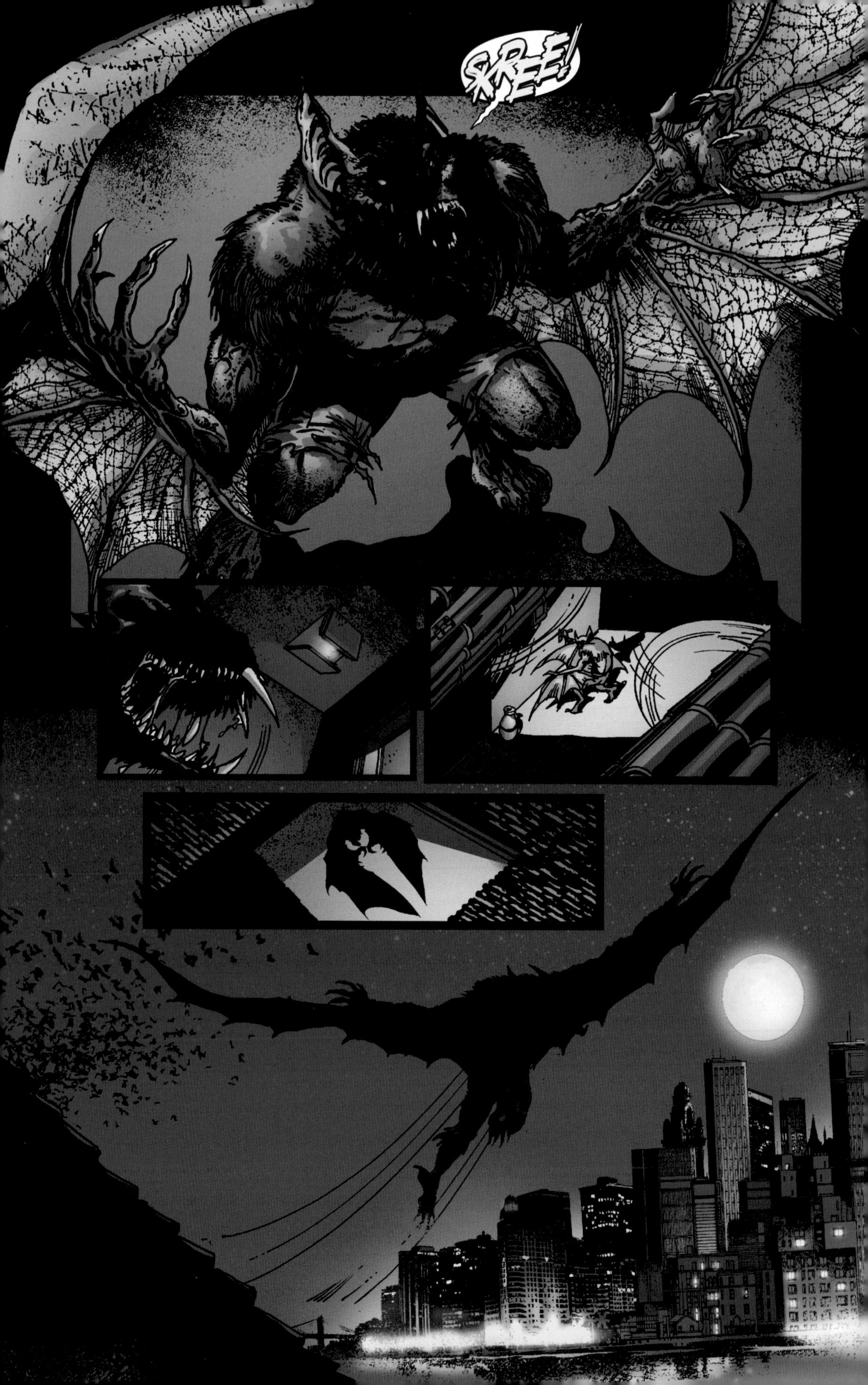
SKREE!

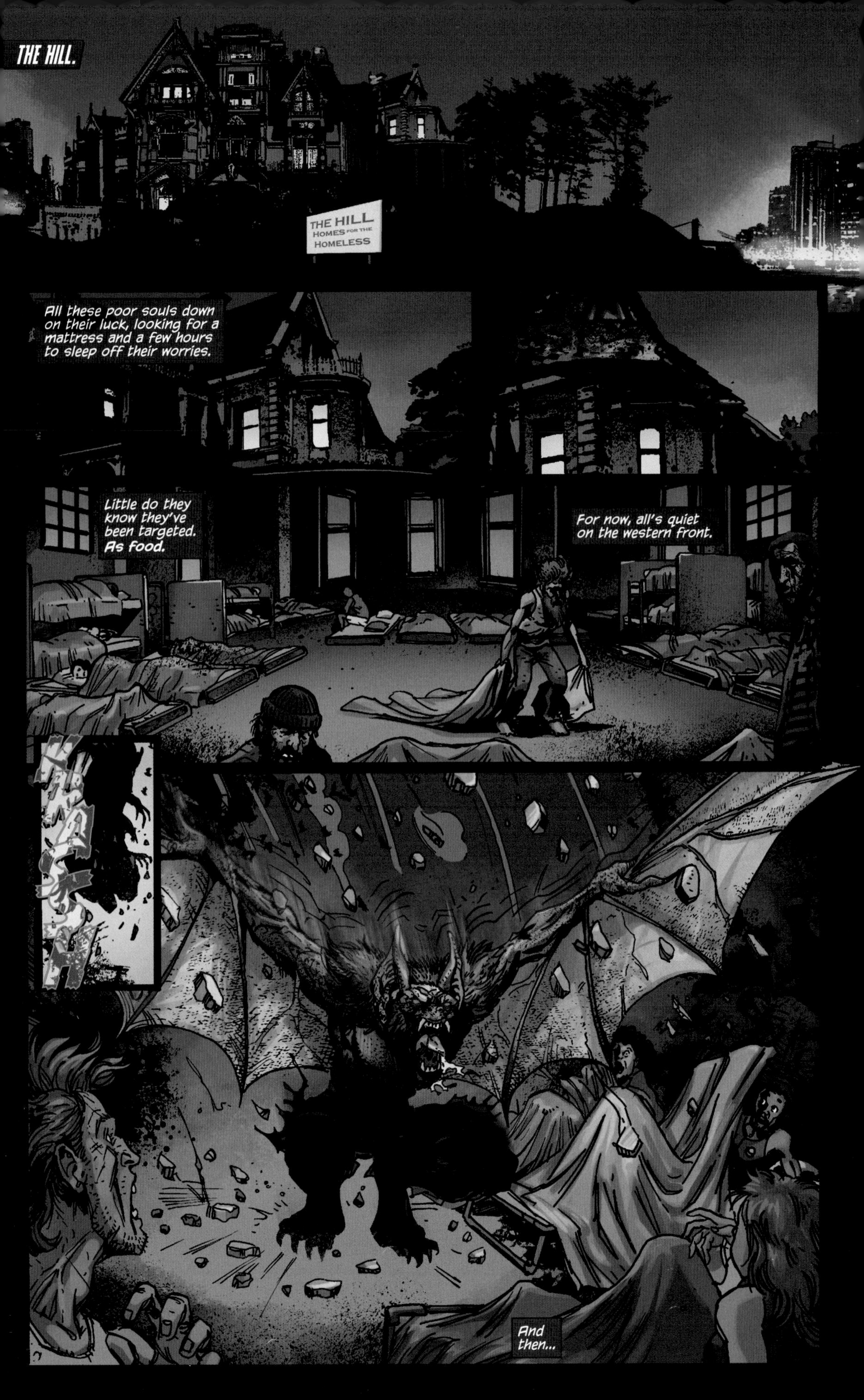
THE HILL.
THE HILL
HOMES FOR THE
HOMELESS
All these poor souls down on their luck, looking for a mattress and a few hours to sleep off their worries.
Little do they know they've been targeted. As food.
For now, all's quiet on the western front.
And then...

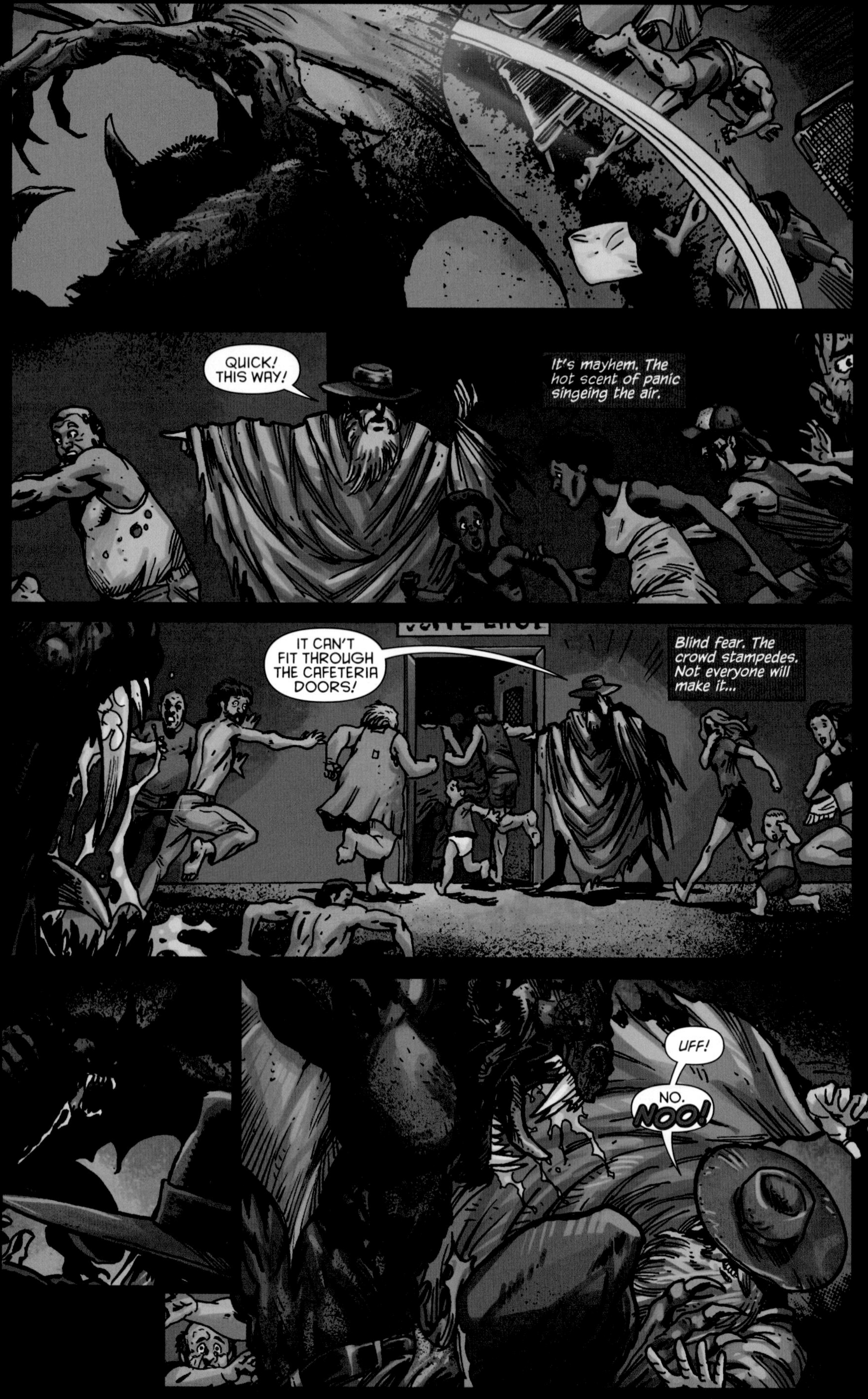
QUICK! THIS WAY!
It's mayhem. The hot scent of panic singeing the air.
IT CAN'T FIT THROUGH THE CAFETERIA DOORS!
Blind fear. The crowd stampedes. Not everyone will make it...
UFF!
NO. NOO!

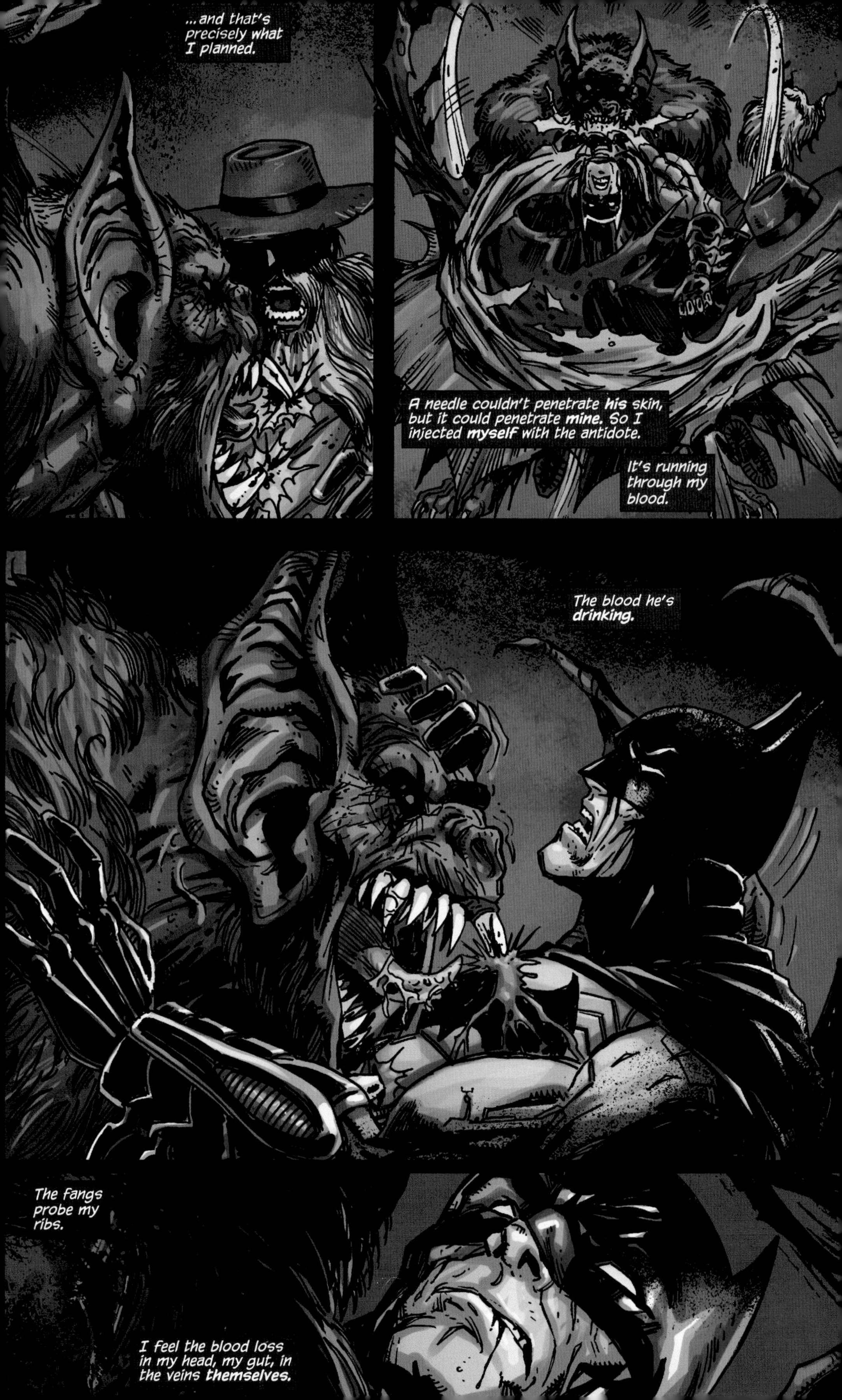
...and that's precisely what I planned.
A needle couldn't penetrate **his** skin, but it could penetrate **mine.** So I injected **myself** with the antidote.
It's running through my blood.
The blood he's **drinking.**
The fangs probe my ribs.
I feel the blood loss in my head, my gut, in the veins **themselves.**

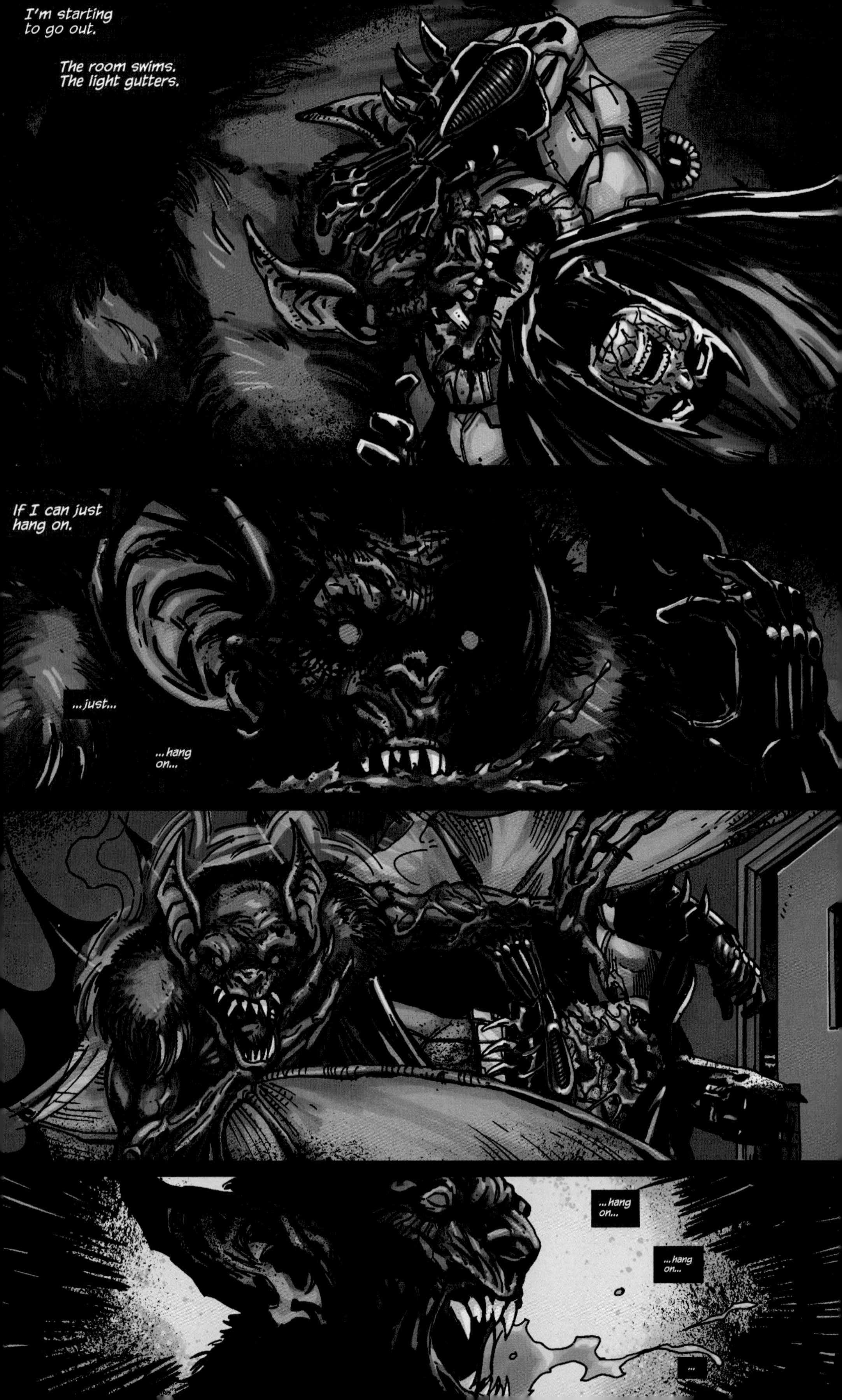

I'm starting to go out.
The room swims. The light gutters.
If I can just hang on.
...just...
...hang on...
...hang on...
...hang on...
...

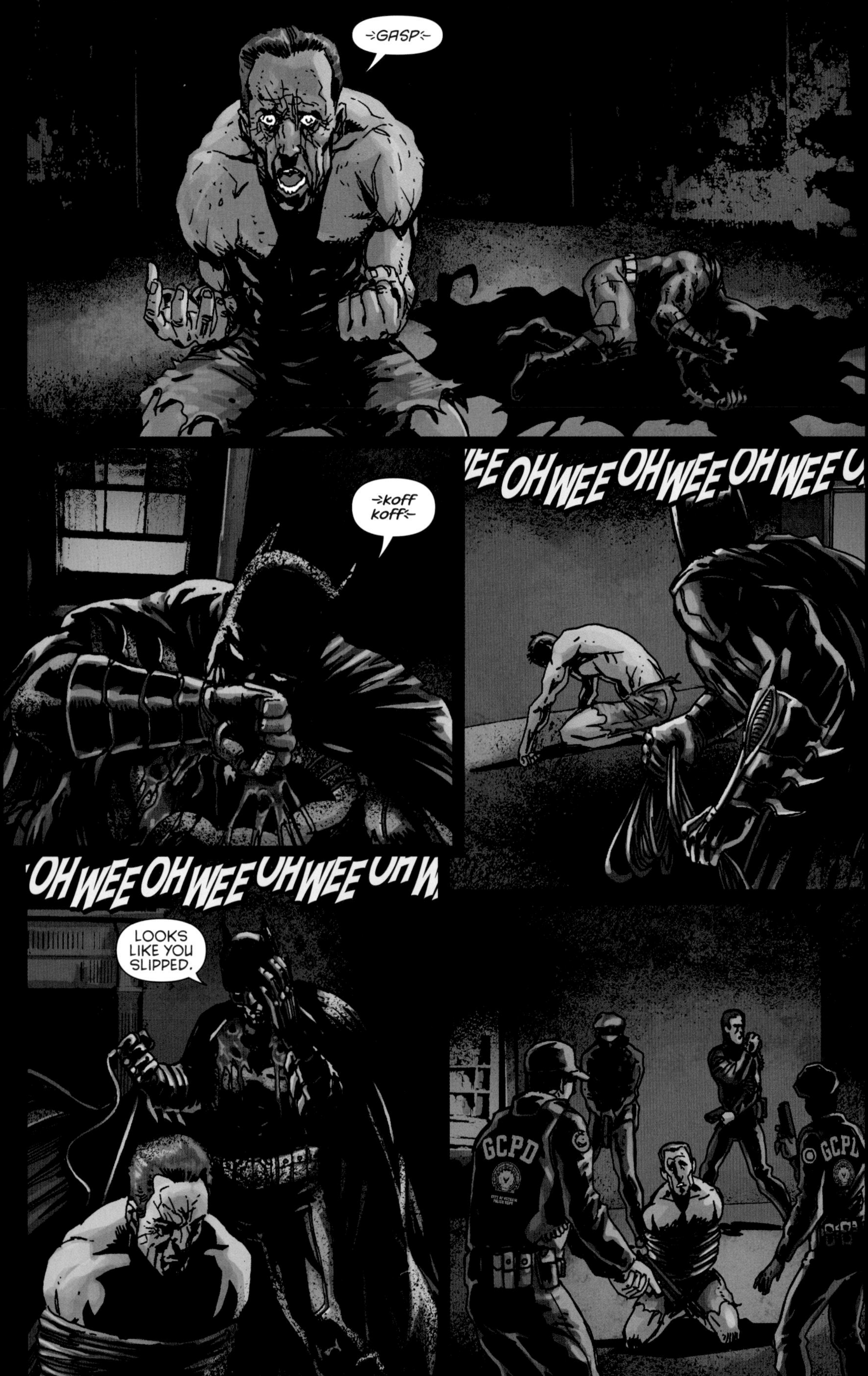

GASP
koff koff
OH WEE OH WEE OH WEE OH WEE
OH WEE OH WEE OH WEE
LOOKS LIKE YOU SLIPPED.
GCPD
GCPD

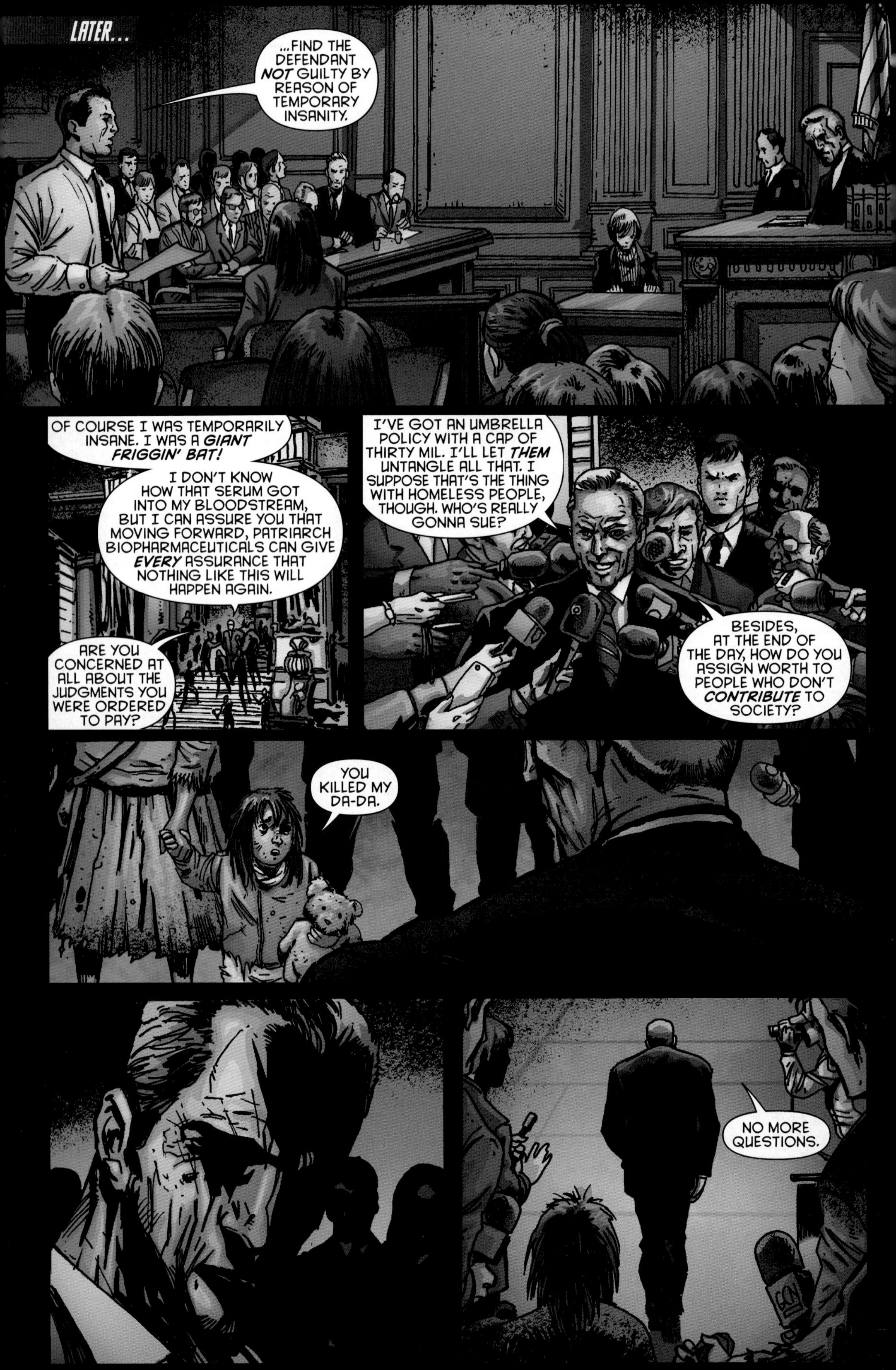
LATER...
...FIND THE DEFENDANT NOT GUILTY BY REASON OF TEMPORARY INSANITY.
OF COURSE I WAS TEMPORARILY INSANE. I WAS A GIANT FRIGGIN' BAT!
I DON'T KNOW HOW THAT SERUM GOT INTO MY BLOODSTREAM, BUT I CAN ASSURE YOU THAT MOVING FORWARD, PATRIARCH BIOPHARMACEUTICALS CAN GIVE EVERY ASSURANCE THAT NOTHING LIKE THIS WILL HAPPEN AGAIN.
ARE YOU CONCERNED AT ALL ABOUT THE JUDGMENTS YOU WERE ORDERED TO PAY?
I'VE GOT AN UMBRELLA POLICY WITH A CAP OF THIRTY MIL. I'LL LET THEM UNTANGLE ALL THAT. I SUPPOSE THAT'S THE THING WITH HOMELESS PEOPLE, THOUGH. WHO'S REALLY GONNA SUE?
BESIDES, AT THE END OF THE DAY, HOW DO YOU ASSIGN WORTH TO PEOPLE WHO DON'T CONTRIBUTE TO SOCIETY?
YOU KILLED MY DA-DA.
NO MORE QUESTIONS.

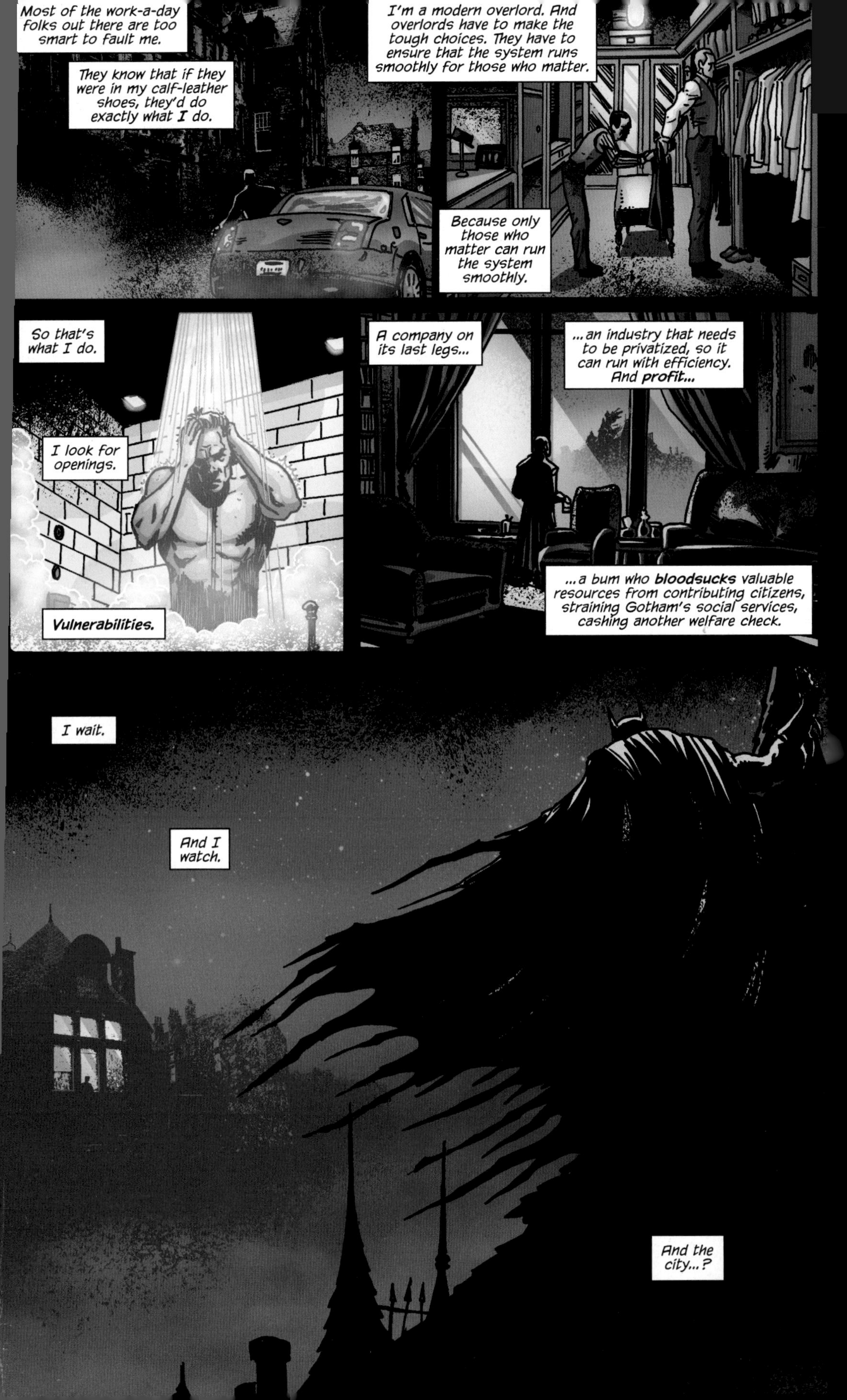
Most of the work-a-day folks out there are too smart to fault me.
They know that if they were in my calf-leather shoes, they'd do exactly what **I** do.
I'm a modern overlord. And overlords have to make the tough choices. They have to ensure that the system runs smoothly for those who matter.
Because only those who matter can run the system smoothly.
So that's what I do.
I look for openings.
Vulnerabilities.
A company on its last legs...
...an industry that needs to be privatized, so it can run with efficiency. And **profit...**
...a bum who **bloodsucks** valuable resources from contributing citizens, straining Gotham's social services, cashing another welfare check.
I wait.
And I watch.
And the city...?

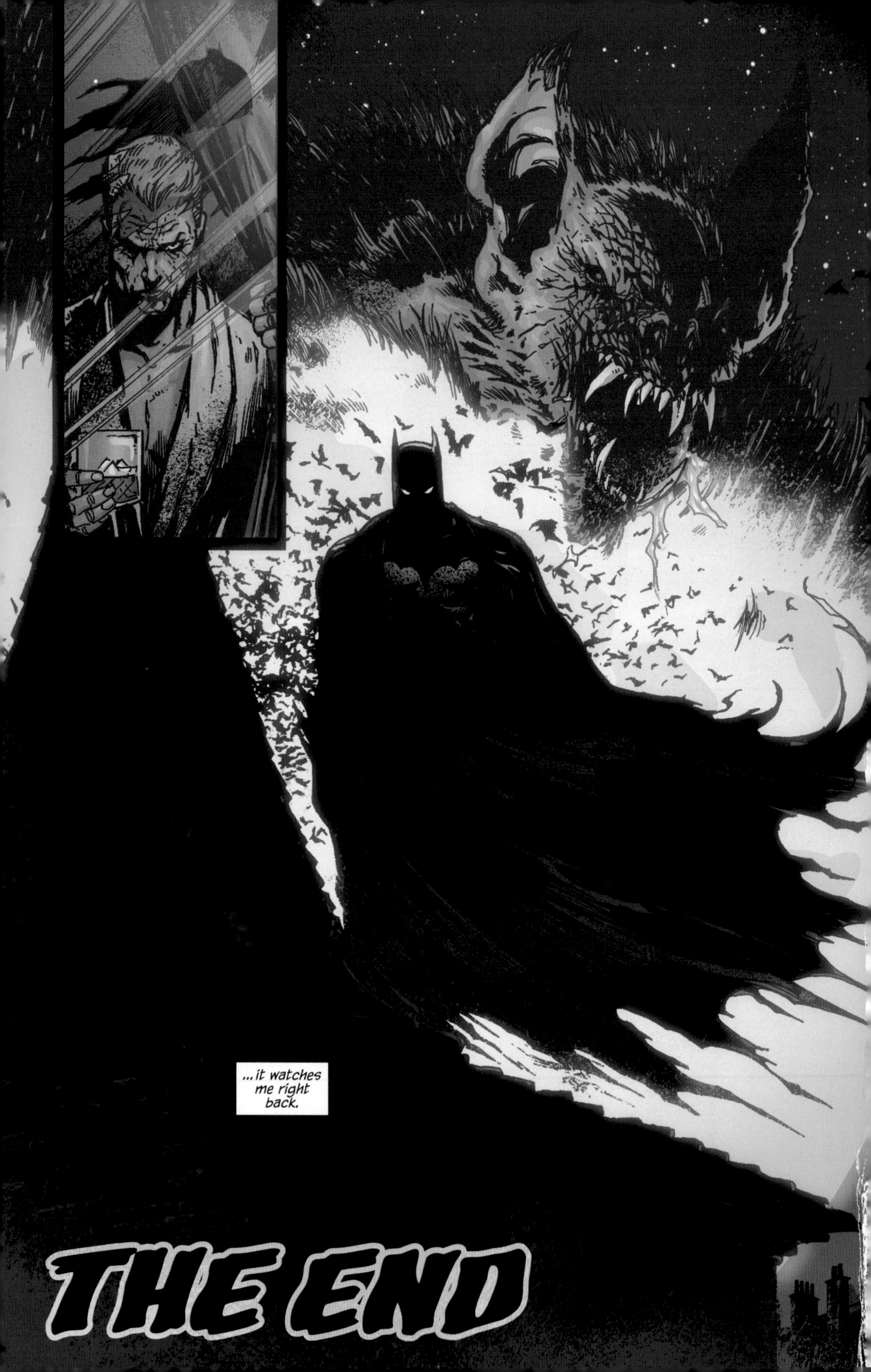
...it watches
me right
back.
THE END